DIS-
RUPT

Filipina Women: Daring to Lead

2.0

About the Filipina Leadership Global Summit

The Filipina Women's Network's (FWN) annual Filipina Leadership Global Summit brings together highly successful Filipina women global leaders, influencers, thought leaders and public figures for discussions, learning journeys, and kwentuhan sessions on how to succeed as multi-cultural professionals. At the summit, Filipina women discuss cooperative ventures and public and private partnerships. The high-powered gathering is a vital part of FWN's Pinay Power 2020 Mission: A Filipina leader in every sector of the economy. The Global Summit is the leading forum in the Filipina global community and contributes to an expanded understanding of the Filipino culture's influence.

www.filipinasummit.org

About the Global FWN100™ Awards

The global FWN100™ Awards is a strategy to execute FWN's Mission—a Filipina woman leader in every sector ot the global economy by 2020. The 100 Most Influential Filipina Women in the World Award™ recognizes women of Philippine ancestry who are influencing the face of leadership in the global workplace, having reached status for outstanding work in their respective professions, industries and communities. These distinguished women are recognized for their achievements and contributions to society, femtorship and legacy. What makes this award distinctive is the awardee's commitment to reinvent herself by paying forward to the future of the Filipina community by femtoring ONE young Filipina and thereby contributing to FWN's pipeline of qualified leaders and increasing the odds that some Filipina women will rise to the 'C-suite' position in all industry sectors.

www.filipinasummit.org/fwn100

About FEMtorMatch™

FEMtorMatch™ is the Filipina Women's Network's strategic tool for developing the next generation of Filipina leaders through local and global partnerships between female mentors, calle FEMtors™, and female mentees, called FEMtees™. FEMtorMarch™ provides structured one-on-one mentoring that harnesses the power of the internet to broaden and deepen the reach of traditional mentoring. Thus, both FEMtors™ and FEMtees™ can reside anywhere in the world.

www.femtormatch.org

DIS-RUPT

Filipina Women: Daring to Lead

2.0

The Second Book
on Leadership
by the Filipina
Women's Network

Edited by
MARIA AFRICA BEEBE

with
Associate Editors:
GLENDA TIBE BONIFACIO
VANGIE MENESES

Filipina Women's Network
San Francisco, California

Second Edition
Copyright © 2016
by Filipina Women's Network
Manufactured in the United States of America.
Edited by Maria Africa Beebe, Ph.D.

ISBN-10: 1-5441-0368-9
ISBN-13: 978-1-5441-0368-6

Library of Congress Control Number: 2017903015
CreateSpace Independent Publishing Platform, North Charleston, SC

Cover Design: Lucille Tenazas, Tenazas Design/NY
Interior Design: Edwin Lozada, Carayan Press

Published by
Filipina Women's Network
San Francisco, CA 94119 USA

http://filipinawomensnetwork.org
Email: filipina@ffwn.org

And many other women
Naming
Half the world together

Can   move their earth
Must   house their fire
Be   water to their song
Will   their dreams well.

[FROM *DREAMWEAVERS* BY MARJORIE EVASCO]

CONTENTS

Becoming Strategists

Foreword

Marily Mondejar
Founder and CEO
Filipina Women's Network

Filipina Disrupters

A quick search on the internet for literature on Filipina women leadership yielded zero results in 2014.

When you search today, our first book on leadership *DISRUPT. Filipina Women: Proud. Loud. Leading Without a Doubt.* dominates the results.

This is exactly why the Filipina Women's Network (FWN) launched the book series on leadership and Filipina women. The book series aims to fill the gap in the leadership literature that highlights the unique qualities of Filipina women whose culture, values, and faith make them effective leaders and managers. The book series on leadership chronicles Filipina women's leadership expertise and how we contribute in the global workplace.

The DISRUPT leadership series is a key component of our game plan to elevate the presence of Filipina women in the public and private sectors.

Warren Bennis, a pioneer in leadership studies, said, "good management is more an art than a science and that superior executives are made, not born, and, for the most part, self-made." The 35 authors of *DISRUPT 2.0. Filipina Women: Daring to Lead.* describe their actual experiences; hardships and successes from the bottom to the upper ranks in foreign and local workplaces.

These women were driven from contemplation to action. They took pleasure in the disruptions they initiated in their personal and professional lives that resulted in achievement. The stories the authors describe have two prevailing themes that make these women truly extraordinary; the opportunity to learn and the courage to face the uncertainties that came with the challenges.

Courage was required to leave the comfort of family and extended family to live in a country whose culture often clashed with their values. But they learned to accept a new way of life and embrace the opportunity.

Courage was required to start a business or embark on a career path that might take years to succeed and become corporate savvy.

Courage was required to seek economic, social, political, and personal opportunities to improve their lives. But they learned to become global citizens.

The stories in this book are impressive, refreshing, and practical. Many corporations and organizations can learn from the wealth of information in these stories and based on the stories of success, rethink their talent search efforts and development to include Filipina women.

This book reminds me of my Mom, the first feminist I ever knew and her advice: Do not ever depend on anyone else for your livelihood. Be the person who signs the paycheck, not the one waiting to see if you will get one. Make sure you always have extra cash, cash inside your bra, walking around money. But her most important advice was to share your gifts and your blessings. Pay them forward. Continue to build your resume not just with degrees but also with accomplishments you would like to make for your community.

These authors leave a legacy to remember.

Preface

Ambassador Delia Domingo Albert

Fourteen words of wisdom.

In 2014 I was offered an award from the Filipina Women's Network (FWN) in recognition of 43 years of dedicated service to the country in my profession as a diplomat. During these years of service, I broke the proverbial "glass ceiling" in Asian diplomatic history by becoming the first career woman diplomat to become the Secretary (Minister) of Foreign Affairs in the region.

Shortly before accepting the award on stage, we were advised we would be making brief remarks of not more than fourteen words, the limit set to give equal time to all awardees. The instruction reminded me of the speech we had to craft within minutes during the final oral examinations to pass the series of tests to become a Foreign Service Officer of the Philippines.

What words of wisdom could I share in a few seconds with such a group of accomplished women? My mind switched to "search" as I listened to the other awardees as they delivered their inspired messages. Indeed, I was moved by passionate words of devotion and commitment of the many Filipina women both to their work and family that they identified as serving as a stabilizing force as they faced social, economic, and political challenges.

There is a growing recognition and acknowledgment of the significant role that women play in almost every facet of society. This much I gathered from the individual remarks of the awardees. It was indeed heartwarming to listen to how each awardee overcame barriers and in the process achieved success in their chosen professions. Truly, every woman that gained control over her destiny changed generally held misperceptions about Asian woman, and especially about Filipina woman. In my work as a diplomat serving in various countries, I have met a great number of them who have done our country proud.

In Australia, I initiated the Filipino Achievers Award to recognize the outstanding Filipina women who contributed selflessly to Philippine-Australian relations and that raised the level of appreciation and respect for Filipinos in general.

I am heartened by the publication of *DISRUPT 2.0. Filipina Women: Daring to*

Lead, the second book on Filipina women leadership, a notable effort by the FWN to document the success stories of Filipina women at home and overseas. It underscores the vast reservoir of knowledge, skills, talent, and the pervading humanity of the Filipina woman.

The book highlights the role of Filipina women leaders who act as a beacon of hope, a catalyst for change, a mentor, and a role model to the many Filipinas around the world. The book further examines such experiences as life and work disruptions, leadership competencies, and legacy building aimed at preparing the next generation of Filipina women leaders.

Reading through the individual stories, one discovers the countless opportunities to move forward as well as the means which are available to the women of today. These opportunities are discussed by 35 women in their respective sectors whether it is in business, in gaining knowledge and skills through education, in using modern day technologies, or in political leadership.

I believe that any reader of this collection of narratives will gain valuable insights from the many eminent writers, each being a master in her own chosen field.

I congratulate all the authors who contributed to *Disrupt 2.0: Filipina Women: Daring to Lead*, who gave their valuable time in order to share their hard-earned knowledge and wisdom with the public. It is my hope that the personal stories will provide encouragement and inspiration in their quest for success of every Filipina woman.

And back to my message shared at the 2014 awarding ceremonies of the 100 Filipina Women achievers. I have to admit I thought hard about what brief message to share. I debated within myself what to share in the seconds prior to being called. As a diplomat I decided to shorten a famous quote from Madeleine Albright, the first woman to serve as Secretary of State of the United States when she addressed a group of women in the United Nations. Her message as edited to 14 words: "There is a place in hell for women who do not help other women."

For this book however, I have decided to sound more positive and to encourage successful Filipina women such as those whose life and professional stories are in DISRUPT 2.0 to re-visit their hometowns and share their successes with the women who need their help. After all, I believe that "there is a special place in heaven for Filipina women who help other women." Fourteen words to remind us all of our humanity as caring women of the Philippines.

Introduction

Maria Africa Beebe, Ph.D.
with
Glenda Bonifacio, Ph.D., Vangie Meneses, Ed.D.

DISRUPT. Filipina Women: Proud. Loud. Leading without a Doubt (2015) (subsequently referred to in this book as Disrupt 1) made a significant contribution to redefining how Filipina women in the diaspora are perceived. This book, *DISRUPT 2.0. Filipina Women: Daring to Lead* is designed to intensify this process by providing additional stories in their own words of successful global Filipina women. The Filipina Women Leaders (FWLs) who shared their leadership stories in both books have been awarded either an FWN100™ Global award (after 2013) or a FWN 100™ U.S. award or both. FWN established the award as part of its strategy to recognize Filipina woman leaders in every sector of society.

DISRUPT 2.0 celebrates, affirms, and acknowledges Filipina women whose vision and impact go beyond the boundaries of the Philippines. This book is a celebration of Filipina women who have achieved success in their professional careers and made a difference by their practice of leadership. The book is an affirmation of the leadership competencies of Filipina women with a global mindset. Each chapter author has acknowledged her willingness to expand her role as a model, coach, and mentor.

The purpose of the book is to inspire, motivate, and nurture other women world-wide, not just Filipina women, who:

- Have leadership responsibilities in cross-cultural and global situations;
- Seek leadership development opportunities in the diaspora environment; and
- Teach leadership not only to inform but also to transform.

The work of the Filipina Women's Network (FWN) is pivotal in the process of recognizing the leadership of Filipina women outside the Philippines through the annual FWN100™ Global and FWN100™ US awards. The FWN sponsored books make the stories of their lived experiences in providing leadership and appropriately applying theory accessible to next-generation leaders. Each author in Disrupt 1 ended with a list of leadership tips. In Disrupt 2.0 authors focused on the leadership competencies they have learned over time. FWN Founder and CEO, Marily Mondejar suggested the use of the Center for Creative Leadership's (CCL) (2015) "Benchmarks by Design" as a guide for the FWL authors as they reflected on the following:

1. What skills and competencies got you to where you are today?

2. What skills and competencies did you have to learn that got you to the next leadership level?

3. What skills and competencies do you need to acquire or learn to sustain your current leadership level?

A synthesis chapter examines the leadership themes that arise from the individual chapters and focuses on leadership competencies that were successfully used in various global settings. It is obvious that competencies which constitute the "how" of leadership are viewed by these Filipina women as significant, but, perhaps, of greater significance is the "why" of leadership. The "why" of leadership for most of these women made reference to finding purpose and meaning in life, achieving impact in their work, and giving back to their local communities. The authors have gone beyond what Petrie (2014) called a horizontal development of new skills, abilities, and behaviors to a vertical development of making sense of the world in more complex and inclusive ways. In their narratives, the authors examined their leadership qualities, their leadership actions given the leadership context they encountered, and their own leadership development process. Despite experiencing disruptions in their lives, the Filipina women who shared their stories demonstrated the will to keep taking additional steps forward. In their own unique ways, these women disrupted the status quo and became strategists. As global leaders, they possess a global mindset consistent with Cabrera's (2012) definition of what it really means to be global; "they are able to contribute to the improvement of the multiple contexts in which they operate" (p. 1).

Van Velsor, McCauley, and Ruderman (2010) asserted that context includes such "broad elements as national culture, age and gender mix of the population, economic conditions, organizational purpose and mission, and business strategy. It can also include role- and person- specific elements, such as the leader's level in the organization, social identity, and current challenges" (p. 5). Common contextual experiences include sharing divergent views of Filipina identity in the global context, key Philippine socio-historical heritage, and transnational reach or migration from the Philippines. Leadership themes, including definitions of leadership, global leadership and cross-cultural leadership studies, leadership for sustainability, and Filipina leadership that provide the framework for the women's narratives are summarized in the following page.

DIVERGENT VIEWS ON FILIPINA WOMEN

Filipina is the feminine form of Filipino, the term used for people who originate from the Philippines; or were descendants of people who originated from the Philippines. Mixed race Filipinos are sometimes labeled as *mestizo/mestiza*. Pinay is a colloquial term for Filipina that provides a more grounded view of their realities as active agents of change (Bonifacio, 2013). There are a variety of views of Filipina identity in the global environment. In some places in the diaspora, the prevailing narrative about Filipina women blurs the distinction between "Filipino" as the name of a national identity and "Filipino/a" as the generic term for designating a subservient class dependent on foreign economies (Rafael, 1997). Without first confirming the actual contents of the 1987 edition of the *Oxford Dictionary*, the Philippine Chamber of Commerce and Industry decried the dictionary for defining Filipina as domestic help (Tomeldan,1988, p.3). The entry, however, never existed. A similar furor happened in Greece when Professor Babiniotis included an entry in a modern Greek dictionary that defined *Filipineza* [Filipina] as "a domestic worker from the Philippines or a person who performs non-essential auxiliary tasks." Liebelt (2008) cited other authors who noted that being "Filipina" was equated with being a caring maid vulnerable to exploitation and abuse (Gonzales, 1998; Ignacio, 2005; Parreñas, 2001; San Juan, 1998; Tadiar, 2004). According to Ebron (2003) Filipinos and domestic work are synonymous in Italy.

Other writers have noted that the job of a domestic worker is a position that carries with it trust, respect, and responsibility; qualities which have been recognized as essential to leadership. Liebelt (2008) concluded that some Filipina domestics who work in the diaspora "conceive of themselves as cosmopolitans who reach out beyond their cultural, religious, and ethno-national origins; to feel at home in the world despite their working-class occupations and non-elite status. They are, in Werbner's (1999) words, 'working class cosmopolitans.'"

The negative view of Filipinas who work as domestics is not shared by the authors in this book. Many of them grew up with maids or *yayas* [nannies]; many entrusted the care of their children to *yayas*. They are now, together with other domestic tasks, called *kasambahay* [househelp]. They invariably are considered members of the family and the household, not mere paid employees as they are considered in the West and elsewhere. Many of them in the Philippines tend to come from poor family relatives in rural areas who provide domestic services in order to continue their studies in the city.

SOCIO-HISTORICAL HERITAGE

From the first millennium, small maritime states influenced by India, China, Islam from Arabia, and independent barangays (villages) comprised what is now known as the Philippines. In 1521, Spain colonized and named the islands after King Philip of Spain. Spanish colonialization established the Catholic church. After a hard fought revolution, the Filipinos declared independence from Spain in 1896. However, in 1898 Spain ceded the Philippines to the US for $20 million. The subsequent American rule was contested by the Philippine Republic resulting in thousands of deaths among Filipinos. Although the war ended in 1902, veterans of the *katipuneros* [revolutionaries] who fought against Spain continued to battle the American forces until 1913. The US occupation of the Philippines changed the cultural landscape in the Philippines in at least three ways: the disestablishment of the Catholic church, the introduction of English as an official language of government and education, and the establishment of public schools initially staffed by American teachers called Thomasites. The first wave of Filipino immigration to the U.S. started during this period.

As of 2015, according to the Global Gender Report, the Philippines ranked first in Asia and among the top 10 countries with the smallest gender gaps with gender gap understood as the discrepancy in opportunities, status, attitudes, etc., between men and women. The report noted an upturn in "Economic Participation and Opportunity" as the number of female legislators, senior officials, managers, and professional and technical workers increased; a rise in "Political Empowerment" as more women gained ministerial positions; and progress in the closing of the gender gaps in "Health and Survival" and "Educational Attainment."

MIGRATION AND DIASPORA EXPERIENCE:
FILIPINOS IN THE WORLD

Estimates are that as of the National Census in 2015, the Philippine population was 102.2 million people. Of these, approximately 11 million were Overseas Filipino Workers (OFWs), mostly women. OFWs can be found in 170 countries, with one million in Saudi Arabia alone, followed by the United Arab Emirates, Malaysia, and Canada. The U.S. remains as the top destination for both immigration and labor, something that can be explained by the historical ties between the U.S. and the Philippines. Overseas contract workers are sometimes referred to as "servants of globalization" (Parreñas, 2001) but hailed as the *bagong bayani* [new heroes] and saviors in the Philippines (Coloma, 2008).

Overseas Filipinos generally fit the definition of diaspora; referring "to emigrants and their descendants who live outside the country of their birth or ancestry, either on a temporary or permanent basis, yet still maintain affective and material ties to their countries of origin" (Agunias & Newland, 2012, p. 15). Mangahas (this edition) has shared that what is striking about the Philippine diaspora is "The breadth of foreign employment, in terms of destination and the range of occupations and skills. The Filipinos are perhaps the largest sized work force on foreign ships, as seafarers and also as performing artists." Mangahas added: "There are many Filipinos in the health industry in Europe and the Middle East. Filipinos are theater professionals in South East Asia, sales clerks in duty free stores in major Middle East airports, and domestic workers in many households all over the world." Filipinos in the diaspora have contributed up to 10 percent of the Philippines GDP with about $20 billion in official remittances in 2012 (Scalabrini Migration Center, 2013). An additional 5 percent or about $10 billion may have come from unofficial remittances (Remo, 2013).

FRAMING THE LEADERSHIP OF FILIPINA WOMEN IN A GLOBAL CONTEXT

A brief summary of definitions and theories of leadership, global and cross-cultural leadership, and leadership for sustainability is useful in understanding the leadership of Filipina women.

Definitions and Theories of Leadership

Rost (1999) collected 200 definitions of leadership. His analysis traced the evolution of leadership studies and is summarized by Northouse (2015) in the following definition: "Leadership is a process whereby an individual influences a group of individuals to achieve a common goal" (p. 6). This definition is consistent with the FWN100™ Global award that honors the 100 most influential women in the world.

According to Northouse (2015), the 21st century approaches to leadership can be summarized as: (a) Authentic leadership with its focus on four distinct but related components; self-awareness, internalized moral perspective, balanced processing, and relational transparency; (b) Spiritual leadership whereby leaders and followers seek to satisfy their spiritual need to make a meaningful contribution; (c) Servant leadership that puts the leader in the role of a servant who utilizes caring principles to focus on followers and their needs; and, (d) Adaptive whereby leaders encourage followers to adapt by solving problems, challenges, and changes and to develop their own leadership.

Hooijberg, Hunt, and Dodge (1997) introduced the concept of leadership "repertoires." Repertoires refer to the "portfolio of leadership roles a managerial leader can perform." This repertoire allows the leader to take an appropriate leadership role for a particular situation while also meeting the expectations of the different stakeholders. These authors cite further research that "managerial leaders with large behavioral repertoires are more effective than those with smaller behavioral repertoires" (p. 8) and that behavioral repertoire not only impacts managerial but also organizational effectiveness. Hooijberg et al. (1997) notion of repertoire is consistent with Beebe's (2016) articulation of a leadership repertoire that is discussed below.

The Center for Creative Leadership's (2015) "Benchmarks by Design" allows the choice of competencies most relevant to leadership. Ninety competencies are categorized into three sets: leading yourself, leading others, and leading the organization. In addition, five "derailment factors" are identified: problems with interpersonal relationships; difficulty with building and leading a team; failure to meet business objectives; difficulty changing or adapting; and too narrow a functional orientation. As indicated earlier, the CCL's Benchmarks were shared with the Filipina women who agreed to examine their leadership competencies for this book.

Global Leadership

The differences in how leadership has been defined "can lead to disparate approaches to conceptualizing, measuring, investigating, and critiquing leadership" (Hernandez, Eberly, Avolio, & Johnson, 2011). The problem is further complicated by the differences in mental models people from different parts of the world bring to the workplace (Gentry & Eckert, 2012).

Leadership research has been conducted predominantly from a Western viewpoint. Researchers have begun to engage in the systematic exploration of the cross-cultural aspects of leadership and the vast, diverse cultures and organizations from which leadership emanates (Hernandez et al., 2011). One such study is the Global Leadership and Organizational Behavior Effectiveness (GLOBE). GLOBE has sought to address the gap in cross-cultural leadership studies with their research on culture and leadership in 61 countries (House, Javidan, Hanges, &

Dorfman, 2002). The Philippines was considered part of the Southeast Asia cluster described as high in power distance and group and family collectivism practices (Gupta, Surei, Javidan & Chhokhar, 2002). Gupta et al. indicated that Filipinos have "the highest scores on four societal practices: groupism, collectivism, humanism, and gender egalitarianism" (p. 22).

The significance of culture is underscored by the Global Competence Aptitude Assessment Model (Hunter, 2004, p. 2) that defines global competence as "Having an open mind while actively seeking to understand cultural norms and expectations of others, and leveraging this gained knowledge to interact, communicate and work effectively in diverse environments." Another leadership assessment is the Global Competencies Inventory (GCI) proposed by Stevens, Bird, Mendenhall, and Oddou (2014) that measures "the degree to which individuals possess the intercultural competencies that are associated with global leader effectiveness" (p. 115).

LEADERSHIP FOR SUSTAINABILITY

The University of Cambridge Institute for Sustainability Leadership (CISL) developed a Sustainability Leadership Model that has three components: "the external and internal context for leadership; the traits, styles, skills and knowledge of the individual leader; and leadership actions" (Visser, 2011, p. 4). Visser acknowledged that "none of these elements is unique to sustainability leaders, but collectively they encapsulate a distinctive set of characteristics and actions in response to sustainability challenges."

FILIPINA LEADERSHIP

A summary of the key findings from two studies about Filipino leadership in the Philippines provides a link between the leadership stories of the FWN100™ Global Filipina women and the broader discourse of leadership. Cuyegkeng and Palma-Angeles (2011) defined Filipino leadership as visionary with the ability to engender meaningful change and transform individuals and their institutions through gradual reforms. According to Cuyegkeng and Palma-Angeles (2011), Filipino leadership depends on good judgment in choosing a team to formulate strategy and the ability to negotiate cooperation and build trust and relationships while showing humility. In one of the few studies examining the leadership of Filipina women, Roffey (1999) identified six competencies needed by Filipina women for effective leadership and management of businesses based in Metro Manila. These competencies are: (a) interpersonal; (b) leading by example; (c) initiating; (d) external public relations; (e) market and customer orientation; and (f) integrity and honesty. Roffey noted that in contrast to research on western-based business leadership, Filipina leaders view the organization as an "extended family." In the extended family model leaders have "personal responsibility for the social and psychological well-being of their employees" and employees expect to be "looked after by their managers" (p. 383). Roffey concluded that effective Filipina leaders in subsidiaries of multinational corporations demonstrated professional skills and transformed strategic vision into operational reality. In examining the role of family kinship, including fictive kinship, Roffey also concluded that effective leaders were able to navigate the "contradictions between contemporary professional and managerial expectations and cultural dynamics" (p. 388). Effective leaders used their networks with integrity and practiced ethical business with their kinship networks.

Beebe (2016) has suggested that themes articulated by Filipina women in their leadership stories in Disrupt 1 concern the how and why of leadership that make up their leadership repertoires. At the center of their leadership repertoires is the Philippine cultural norm, *kapwa* [broadly, shared humanity]. *Kapwa* is a prime Filipino value that demonstrates the Philippines' collectivist cultural orientation, where empathy, togetherness, cooperation, collaboration, and other derivatives come to play to achieve a goal or to help those in need in the community (Bonifacio, 2013). This cultural norm, arguably, impacts leadership.

Understanding how to lead better requires a process of self-awareness, self-transformations, and self-transcendence. Judging by the stories shared by the Filipina women in DISRUPT 1 and now in this book, they have shown attentiveness to experience, intelligence in understanding that experience, fairness in judging that experience, and responsibility in deciding how to use that experience in leadership.

Book Organization

Disrupt 2.0. Filipina Women: Daring to Lead is made up of 35 chapters organized into six sections:

Leading the Filipina Women's Network (FWN). The chapters in this section provide the context for the FWN100™ Global leadership awards, the leadership summits, the partnerships with other organizations that focus on women and leadership, and networking Filipina women leaders from around the world.

Disrupting Disruptions. The chapters in this section share a common theme of lives being disrupted through migration, illness, and sudden loss of a loved one and how the individual coped with the disruption and moved on with her life.

Disrupting the Status Quo. In these chapters, the women demonstrate how as agents of disruption, they disrupted the status quo by being among the first Filipinas to accomplish something of significance, or by exceeding expectations and being the pearl with the best luster.

Becoming Strategists. In these chapters, the women discuss the leadership competencies they have used to grow their companies, consulting firms, and their public sector departments; and the intersections between their corporate and pro-bono selves.

Leadership for Sustainability. The chapters in this section focus on leadership promoting a better environment through sustainability in housing and the transportation sector.

Across-Generations: Mothers and Daughters. Several chapters discuss how leadership values get passed across generations and how a shared experience could be interpreted differently. Daughters respond to their mother's narratives, a mother responds to a daughter's narrative, and a daughter writes her narrative as an expanded eulogy and thank you letter to her mother.

Leading the
Filipina Women's Network

MARILY MONDEJAR

FOUNDER AND CEO
FILIPINA WOMEN'S NETWORK

Owning Your Influential Power
as a Leader

I had a dream .

For the last 13 years the Filipina Women's Network has played a significant role in empowering Filipina women. I am very proud of the 35 authors of our second book on Filipina leadership. We have come a long way! The business of empowerment is an ever-changing process in our workplaces, in our businesses, in our communities, in our lives.

Early in my career, I sought women who looked like me and who also were facing career challenges on how to succeed as bicultural immigrants in the United States. I clearly remember the moment the Filipina Women's Network (FWN) became the seed of an idea. I was speaking to a group of Filipina women about life and career planning. The questions being asked were the questions I have asked myself many times. The desire to succeed and do better for ourselves and our communities was deep and apparent. I had been thinking and feeling that if we, Filipina women, could join forces, we could make a significant difference. Together, we could be a hell of a voice.

So I put out a call for board members. We gathered for a board retreat and laid out a plan. One of our first acts was to convene a Filipina Conference at the Moscone Convention Center in San Francisco in 2002. We have been gathering annually ever since. The annual meeting of Filipina women, we now call FWN Leadership Summit has become a tradition that we have kept alive. The Summit is a place to re-ignite passions and friendships and a time to expand our professional and personal networks. Our annual summit continues to empower hundreds of Filipina women along with the Filipina Women's Network to flourish and thrive. Many of our founding members continue to be actively involved with FWN, including Commissioner Helen Marte who wrote the first check in 2002 for member dues.

But we need to be more strategic for the Filipina Women's Network to be sustainable. Two key words that characterize our actions are power and influence. How do we create a powerful voice? How do we expand our sphere of influence? How do we focus on larger economic issues that significantly impact the Filipino world community? Change is difficult for many of us. I am actually one of those who believes in and enjoys change. I believe that it is time for us to widen our scope, to extend our reach, and to amplify our influence. It is in our own interest to expand our perspective to embrace new ideas and to intensify our economic influence as part of a world community. We have to look out for our sisters. We have to look out for our next generation of leaders. Too often we get caught up in our own self-interest, something that is not an entirely defective action because self-interest can be the spark that gets us a place at the table. Let us not forget that we are members of a larger world family.

I found what I believe is the best definition for empowerment: "measures designed to increase the degree of autonomy and self-determination in people and in communities in order to enable them to represent their interests in a responsible and self-determined way, acting on their own authority" (Wikipedia). Based on this definition, the measures that guide the power and influence of the Filipina Women's Network are:

1. The 100 **Most Influential Filipina Women in the World Award**™ recognizes women of Philippine ancestry who are influencing the face of leadership in the global workplace, having reached status for outstanding work in their respective professions, industries, and communities. These distinguished women use their leadership to contribute to society, femtorship, and legacy. Since 2007 hundreds have been selected from an outstanding field of nominees from around the world. (See Appendix D for a complete list of FWN100™ Global and U.S. awardees.) The Search Committee is comprised of a team of former FWN100 ™ Global and U.S. awardees who select and interview qualified nominees. Factors they consider include the size and scope of the nominees' positions, influence in their industries and communities, board affiliations, and leadership roles. What makes

this award distinctive is the awardee's commitment to pay forward by femtoring ONE young Filipina and thereby contributing to the pipeline of qualified leaders and increasing the odds that some Filipina women will rise to the 'C-suite' position in all sectors.

2. **FemtorMatch™** is part of the Filipina Women's Network's strategy for achieving its Mission 2020: to develop next generation of Filipina leaders through local and global partnerships between female mentors, FEMtors™, and female mentees, FEMtees™. FEMtorMatch™ provides structured one-on-one mentoring that harnesses the power of the Internet to broaden and deepen the reach of traditional mentoring. Thus, both FEMtors™ and FEMtees™ can reside anywhere in the world. FemtorMatch™ provides an opportunity to assess and improve the competencies and skill sets of Filipina women.

3. **Filipina Leadership Global Summit** brings together Filipina women global leaders, influencers, thought leaders, and public figures for discussions, learning journeys, and *kwentuhan* strategies on how to succeed as multi-cultural professionals. The Summit enables one-on-one private chats to ignite cooperation through public and private partnerships. The high-powered gathering is a vital part of FWN's Pinay Power 2020 Mission: A Filipina leader in every sector of the economy. The Global Summit is the leading forum of its kind for the Filipina global community and inspires a renewed understanding of the Filipino culture's influence on leadership. The Summit raises funds for FWN's programs that foster the Filipina women's socio-economic, political, and educational advancement in addition to raising awareness of FWN's pipeline development of qualified next generation leaders. More information about the Summit can be found at: http://www.filipinasummit.org

4. The **Filipina Women Leadership Book Series** aims to fill the gap in the leadership literature by highlighting the unique leadership qualities of Filipina women that combines culture, values, and faith. Awardees are invited to contribute their leadership lessons they have learned as they navigated their careers and businesses while competing in the global workplace. The series is a profound chronicle of Filipina women leadership in the diaspora sorely lacking in the archives outside of the Philippines. The first book

DISRUPT. Filipina Women: Proud. Loud. Leading Without a Doubt. represented the succes stories about life and career disruptions of 37 authors from the U.S., Philippines, Singapore, Brazil, Japan, U.A.E., Canada, Poland, on leader identity, cultural adjustments to achieve success and victories over domestic violence, incarceration, poverty, discrimination and harassment. *DISRUPT 2.0. Filipina Women: Daring to Lead.* are about the leadership competencies needed for leading oneself, leading others, leading organizations, and legacy building for next generation leaders.

5. **Training Filipina Women Who Could Be President** is a selective part-time leadership development program for future politicians, entrepreneurs, and senior and executive leaders in the U.S. Based on established leadership competencies that includes cohort training, coaching, and femtoring; the program gives Filipina women leaders the skillsets and networks they need to develop and manage highly effective campaigns and organizations in both the private and public sectors.

These programs have proven effective in positioning Filipina women as stakeholders in the economies of the world. Our energies are very much needed. I feel very strongly that we as business people and community leaders must be involved. Many of our institutions are failing us; government, education, health care, social services. Most of our political leaders have clearly failed us and are paralyzed by inaction and special interests. Having qualified Filipina leaders at the decision-making tables will generate policies that benefit our community. The word "community" is the key. We are in this together or we will go down together. We are becoming a dominant institution and will continue to be in the foreseeable future. Let's step up to the plate and help bring community stakeholders to the table together.

As my fellow book authors have demonstrated, we need to get involved in public service and civic engagement. Let us create a vision for our future and our children's future. My strong belief is that we can contribute to the solutions of the issues confronting us; caring for the less fortunate, educating our children, increasing economic vitality, expanding affordable housing, caring for the elderly, and increasing social services. I believe that until we sit down with business folks, labor, government, neighborhood people, community activists, the artists and educators; all the stakeholders in our communities; we will not be able to effectively deal with our challenges. We cannot keep on fighting amongst ourselves while the world and its great opportunities pass us by. No one is going to do it for us. We need strategies and implementable plans to get us where we choose to go.

Our community needs us. It needs our ideas, our expertise, our entrepreneurial energies, our ability to take risks, and our strong sense of getting things done. We know how to try new ideas. We know how to overcome failures. We know what it is like to succeed. We are creative. We are risk takers. We are not greedy. We are the last ones to take a paycheck. We know how to create opportunities. Filipinos are known to take two or three jobs at a time. It is infuriating when we know that government could do more to facilitate our growth and success and remove roadblocks. But when government does not, often we do not speak up. So let us get those seats at the table. Let us create change in our cities, in our communities, in our adopted countries, and in our home country. We are well beyond the tweaking stage. If you are up to it, get involved in your neighborhood, in your school, in the garden project, or any project that is important to you and your family. Call your mayor, your city council, your supervisor, your congressional representative, your senator, your president. They need your ideas and solutions. They need us. We have a social responsibility as a people to make our lives better and to make our communities better. There are no white knights. Just you and me. I am very proud and fortunate to have been part of the growth and the changes in the Filipina women communities in 20 countries worldwide.

Our time has come.

FRANCINE MAIGUE

DISTRICT DIRECTOR, CALIFORNIA STATE ASSEMBLY
INTERNATIONAL FRIENDSHIP COMMISSIONER, CITY OF CHULA VISTA
PRESIDENT | CEO, FILIPINO AMERICAN CHAMBER
OF COMMERCE OF SAN DIEGO COUNTY
FWN100™ GLOBAL 2015 – "THE GLOBAL FACE OF PINAY POWER"

Becoming A Global Pinay Powerhouse

RESPECT THE KIND

You don't have to like me
Let's make that very clear
If firm-but-friendly's not your style
You will not want me here

Some drill sergeant, I am not
I don't lead with shame nor fear
But fine details, I was taught
Are good friends one treats so dear

I was raised to make my mark
To be better than the last
To raise my voice and raise my fist
To be bolder than the past

If my light outshines you
Please know I mean no harm
Cause my success is ours, my friend
You need not be alarmed

Try and keep me where I am
And you'll stay just where you are
We're meant to rise up hand-in-hand
We've already come so far

Cut me loose if you crave glory
I give credit where credit's due
I'm not led by my hero's story
Ego blocks the pure and true

One meeting a month...just one
Is one too many, you see
Those "one" meetings add up, up, up
And there's just one of me

I want to help, I want to serve
But you'll excuse me, please
To eat, sleep, breathe, see my family
You know, basic human needs

You just can't guilt me, I won't believe
That I'm the reason why
This or that just won't come through
When I'm the ride or die

I work hard, I smile through pain
My kindness is no lie
I'll give you more than you expect
If you say jump, I'll fly

I'm in demand not on demand
You can't just turn me on
Call, post, text me all you want
Sometimes, I can't/won't respond

Help me help you help them all out
We can't just cry and whine
If you want change, you must pitch in
Together, let's strategize.

It was a rough day at work, one of the roughest in a long time. It also happened to be the same day that a high school student, a bright, young woman with promising leadership skills, came in to shadow me for her big senior project.

Out of all the powerful women leaders in our community, she picked me. She said she picked me because she wanted to be just like me in the future...wanted to do what I did, lead the way I did, serve our community the way I did. This remarkable young woman with all the potential in the world aspired to be me, someone whom she viewed as fearless, influential, the embodiment of what it meant to be truly "empowered"...and I was having a baaaaaaaaad day.

It was as if a mirror was held in front of my life. Sadly, I didn't recognize the woman, the leader reflected back at me...and my mentee saw it all. Would she see what I saw on my bad day?

Here's what I saw...

Physically, this woman was 50-60 pounds overweight--the biggest she'd ever been. Doctors, family and friends each expressed their concerns...some more kindly than others. Her health was strained by neglect. She'd go too many hours without eating, then binge eat to fill the hole. She would plan to workout then choose sleep instead and, even then, was still too tired to function at 100%. Unused exercise DVDs, equipment and workout clothes took up space in a room that started to resemble the turmoil inside her. All the good intentions and investments piled on her body and piled up in her space. Without time to do laundry, she found herself abusing her bank account to keep up her professional wardrobe. With every purchase, the size of each item grew. A former beauty queen and professional dancer and choreographer once known for her athleticism, she now grew more immobile each day. High blood pressure and migraine headaches became standard.

Mentally, this woman was overcommitted and overdrawn. Her mind was never at rest. She gave and gave, propelled by the urgency to meet deadlines, make good on promises and empower, assist and satisfy others. Her cell phone followed her to the bathroom. Her eyes locked only with computer screens. If she didn't immediately reply to an email, she knew someone was judging her. She twitched to grab her cell phone and jumped at texts--programmed like a dog with a shock obedience collar. The accessible, confident, highly charismatic leader...was now retreating, doubting her abilities, disappointed in knowing but not doing better...feeling altogether disenfranchised.

Emotionally, she struggled to find joy...JOY—the very thing she loved most and worked so hard to deliver to others. She felt terrorized by the demands and expectations of others and began to feel apathetic towards the use of technology and social media, tired of the connectivity, tired of the need for constant monitoring and updating and tired of the invasion of her life. Wounds of the trauma of daily stress were starting to show all over her. She felt guilty in taking time to do anything else but work...She felt most guilty, though, in sacrificing time, attention and dedication to her family. Those missed memories were experiences she could never get back. (A niece only graduates from kindergarten once. One's aging parent shouldn't have to feel scared and alone at a telling doctor's appointment.) When she let her guard down, even for a moment, to enjoy and take a break or to attend to someone she loved...she was criticized and made to feel irresponsible.

Despite all her schooling and degrees...Despite all her strongly held values...Despite all her best efforts and better intentions, she was spiraling and fading.

Was this the life she wanted? Not only was this <u>not</u> what she wanted...It wasn't what she earned. This wasn't what she deserved. It didn't look (or feel) like Global Pinay Power.

She worked hard to graduate from some of the most prestigious universities in the world and had just paid off her student loan...Where was the return on investment?

She was a knowledgeable, compassionate leader...understanding when others dealt with illness and stress, willing to work before the sun rose, go without so much as a quick lunch break and slave late into the night to compensate when others couldn't complete their tasks, offering support and humble guidance. Why was she struggling to get others to deliver quality work?

She was mentoring other women leaders, especially youth...She spoke of fighting against injustice...She spoke of empowerment and heightened representation...She spoke of knowing one's value and not compromising... Was she practicing what she preached?

This wasn't me...until it was.

Thank God there are lessons in failures, hurdles and bad days (baaaaaaaaad days).

You don't have to like me
Let's make that very clear
If firm-but-friendly's not your style
You will not want me here

I'm an extrovert, as confirmed by an exhaustive personality exam conducted by one of my professors at Harvard, my inability to feel embarrassed (most days) and the life long assertion of my parents who were/are comforted (and sometimes concerned) by the fact that their kid lives by the motto: "I am who I am wherever I am." As such, I'm bubbly, upbeat and friendly. I can't help it. I like being happy, and I like when others are happy.

And I reallllllllly like being nice to people—turning strangers into fast friends, playing hostess, putting folks at ease...I enjoy laughs on the regular with people whom I share a single elevator ride. My interns are never asked to fetch coffee. Instead, I'm likely to run out and bring back lunch for the whole office. I can't attend an event without making sure I procure extra giveaways as *pasalubongs* for whomever I may see next. Surely, this is a strong nod to the Filipino Spirit of Bayanihan [being your neighbor's hero...not for glory but because it's only right to do so... because you hope they'd do the same for you in a time of need...because it's for the greater good when we take care of one another.]

I call teams "families" and buy into the whole idea that colleagues (heck, even competition) can be friends.

I had a friend once describe me as a Disney Princess. I interpreted her comment to mean "kind and patient." ...and, ok, I have a sing-song voice and cheery mannerisms. My nephew described me as "unicorns and rainbows." My takeaway from that was "positive and eternally optimistic." Plus, I love believing and witnessing beautiful miracles. Some of my mentees have deemed me "Hufflepuff" (a house in the Harry Potter series whose members possess traits like dedication, hard work, fair play, patience, kindness, tolerance, loyalty, welcoming of toil, etc.) I took it as a compliment.

Some people know me as a former Miss Philippines, one who won Best in Talent, Best in Evening Gown and an academic scholarship...I was also voted Miss Congeniality. I was even UCLA's Homecoming Queen.

But here's the thing folks must know: I'm not nice to be popular. My smile is not a front. I don't feel the need to fulfill a stereotypical checklist of what is expected of me as a woman or as a Filipina to ensure that I am liked as a leader. I truly believe leaders can and should be genuinely kind and still run tight ships that deliver quality results and bottom lines.

To know me is to know I care about people...as in, everyone. I care enough to utilize positive reinforcement, but I coach folks to be their very best and reach whatever goals towards which they strive. Caring doesn't make me a doormat leader nor one that's too positive to have healthy perspective, though. I am equal parts optimist and realist. When we've got a job to do, we gotta work...and why shouldn't it be our best work possible? I remind folks that God is in the details, and I push hard... but it's always out of love.

I have high standards, but I am compassionate enough to also know to how and when to choose my battles. I can be both the rallying coach and the most low-key person in the room. I can be very hands on but prefer to let people blossom in their skills and confidence. I have a high tolerance for people and team members who are still finding themselves and testing different limits ('cause aren't we all?). But I'm the kind of friend and mentor who cares enough to tell you when you have "spinach in your teeth." I'll tell you nicely, but I will tell you.I figure that it's better for you to hear it from me with love than for you to go out into the world being less than your best.

We can, in fact, work towards our greatest, our infinite potential—finding the best within ourselves, our world and each other and still smile along the way. I'll demand the best out of you (like I do myself), but I promise to love you through it.

Some drill sergeant, I am not
I don't lead with shame nor fear
But fine details, I was taught
Are good friends one treats so dear

As a female and Filipina leader, I don't want to be respected simply for doing my best impression of a male drill sergeant. I don't believe in breaking people down only to bring them back up in discipline. I can lead what have historically been "boys' clubs" while unabashedly still being a lady. I don't need to be dismissive and punitive to remind people of my authority. I don't need to wear muted color pantsuits all the time. I don't need to use obscenities to ensure directives aren't mistaken for suggestions. That's just not me, and pretending would be a lie--that's not being an empowered woman leader.

I embrace the fact that I'm familial in my leadership style...that I don't have to raise my voice to make a point...that I can hold people accountable with a smile. I don't believe being brash makes you brave. There is value in tact. I've witnessed far too many women overcompensate in order to find respect in male-dominated fields. We shouldn't have to work twice as hard or be twice as loud to get the same results as our male counterparts.

I question any member of any team that doesn't buy into these values because it shows that they hold themselves above others; they don't think others deserve the same courtesy or respect they demand for themselves. It also shows that they don't really support true female empowerment or leadership, if they still expect females in leadership to act like men. I've never changed who I am in order to fit in. Why would I start now?

I was raised to make my mark
To be better than the last
To raise my voice and raise my fist
To be bolder than the past

I'm a strong advocate of collaboration, but I don't sacrifice true progress and innovation by playing it safe, sticking to what's been done before or settling for old standards...nor do I pretend everyone's ideas at the table are always good ones just to stroke egos. I think there is evil in groupthink.

When I do raise my voice, it's to address injustice. I have a hard time not speaking up in the face of adversity, rudeness, condescension and unfair people and situations.

I'm also bold in taking on the new. "Impossible" and "challenging" are not the same, and I'm not frightened by (in fact, I take greater pleasure in) chartering new territory. After all, if you only do what you've always done, you'll only go where you've always gone.

Growing up, I was a "Why?" kid, always wanting to know how things, systems and people work. Now I'm a "Why not?" adult, wanting to know how things, systems and people can be/do/feel better.

My parents raised me saying, "Be the best of what you are, and always leave a place better than you found it." I'm so grateful to Mom and Dad for instilling those principles and habits in me. I'm also grateful that they still remind me of those words and their meaning when necessary. I love how those words can apply to <u>any</u> situation or environment I am in, whether it's tidying up a restaurant table we've dined at, excelling in school or helping a whole community rise.

> *If my light outshines you*
> *Please know I mean no harm*
> *Cause my success is ours, my friend*
> *You need not be alarmed*

If you have to dim your shine to make someone feel better about him or her self, you do an injustice to your work and anyone who has ever invested in you. You shouldn't feel guilty for your achievements and talents. Humility and self-degradation are not the same...anyone who can't see the difference, has never really pursued a dream. Don't bully yourself or allow others to bully you for being great. Don't swallow the poison.

You earned your success. Why shouldn't you enjoy it? Winners shouldn't be smug, but losers shouldn't be babied. #realtalk #toughlove

I'm not driven by the promise of glory, but I don't feel guilty for my success.

Surely you had to overcome your own challenging circumstances and insecurities to get to where you are. Allow others, especially the bullies (they come in all ages, shapes and sizes) to do the same. *dusts off trophies guilt-free*

> *Try and keep me where I am*
> *And you'll stay just where you are*
> *We're meant to rise up hand-in-hand*
> *We've already come so far*

Some men dare to put their hands in my face, in conversations in which they disagree with me and at boardroom tables at which they have trouble seeing me sit at the head. Since Sheryl Sandberg's famous TED Talk and book, *Lean In*, it's become a standard talking point for people to say how important it is for everyone, including women, to "have a seat at the table." I want more of our women, especially our Filipinas, to not only have a seat at the table, but to be comfortable and respected at the head of it.

Some of my male colleagues wanted me at the head of boardroom tables...until I was.

Chauvinism has a funny way of rearing its ugly head. It's a bad seed that grows silently inside someone and bursts out in condescending words and hands in our faces. I make it a point to high-five the men who put their hands in my face saying, "If anyone raises their hand to me, surely they want a high-five, not to stifle, silence nor shun me...'cause that would be, well, rude." They tend to laugh nervously and shrug it off, saying something like, "Oh, you're so funny," which is received with silence and stares from the rest of the table. Not only does this show these men that what they've done is not okay (I mean, I don't see them raising hands to interrupt their male colleagues), but it also shows everyone else at the table that raising hands to women to try and "shut them up" is not okay. A simple high-five can have a heavy impact on calling someone out on a disrespectful action they may or may not realize they've done. It also manages to hold everyone at the table accountable, so it doesn't happen again, and still move a meeting along.

I'm understanding of the fact that even some of our strongest male supporters may trip on their machismo from time to time, but I don't want our women, especially Filipinas, to be ok with making themselves small and submissive EVER. Let's not run from conflict or confrontation. *Huwag tayong maging mahinhin.*

> *Cut me loose if you crave glory*
> *I give credit where credit's due*
> *I'm not led by my hero's story*
> *Ego blocks the pure and true*

When people say they want to help, you have dig a little deeper and figure out if they really want to help or if they want to be a hero. It's not the same.

Some people want to align their personal and/or professional brand with yours without breaking a sweat. They live to be noticed and want to appear as if they did something, but they spend more time posting and tagging you in pics online than actually helping you with any real cause. *Kunwari lang sila.* *removes tag*

Some people believe in pay-to-play awards. I politely decline any award I didn't actually earn. (Thanks, but no thanks. My family, friends and I aren't interested in buying a table just so I can add a plaque to the mantle.)

Glory and praise can suck the humanness right out of people. Influence and power should be used for the greater good not personal evil. Superheroes we may be in our own way...but we all have an Achilles heel.

A couple of decades ago, my fellow cast and crew mates of a local theater production presented me with their Rose Award. The award was for "the most Christ-like individual." The significance of such an honor from my peers has never been lost on me. I remind myself to be the person my peers believed me to be—Christ-like in my relationships, demeanor and countenance. It's a big responsibility and honor of which I will spend the rest of my life trying to make myself worthy.

One meeting a month...just one
Is one too many, you see
Those "one" meetings add up, up, up
And there's just one of me

I've found that, in trying to be the most effective female and Filipina (and a young one at that) leader, I am often faced with the challenge of having to decide how much of myself I am willing to sacrifice in order to advance different issues, local to global. I'm tested all the time...and, while I am always up for growth and positive change, there are simply some things that I just can't/won't compromise.

High energy I may be, but I'm still human, not a machine.

Just one meeting...plus countless emails, texts, posts, messages, phone calls, committee and subcommittee meetings...It all adds up. Limits. We have them. Yup, you have them.

I'm all for pushing limits, envelopes and expectations...but, sometimes...you don't have to kill yourself to prove that you tried.

I once had an intern call me to ask, "Um, Francine, I'll be in at my usual time today, and I know you're busy, but do you think, um, I could maybe have, um, a little bit of your time to, please, um, speak to you?" She was nervous, very nervous. I got nervous. I answered, "Sure, of course. Are you okay? Is there something you wanted to specifically speak with me about?" She didn't want to give details over the phone and said it was best if she came in to tell me in person. Alright...

It turns out she was offered an assistant manager position at a company for which she worked part time. In addition to the new position, she was guaranteed training to set her on a managerial track with more hours...which would make it difficult, too difficult for her to really commit to our office in the way she wanted. "I don't want to be one of those interns that only comes in sporadically. I care about this team too much."

This was the same young woman that, during her initial interview for our internship, was brave enough to share with me that she was currently learning to deal with anxiety. I was so proud of her. I was proud of her during her initial interview and now. Proud certainly of her hard work which brought her the offer of an assistant manager position but, most importantly, for knowing her limits and recognizing the implications of pushing herself too far beyond them.

I thank my former intern for displaying an important professional and real life management skill. I thank God for bringing her into my life even for a brief time. Clearly, it was a lesson He had been trying to teach me for decades, a lesson I had been too busy to appreciate. Lord, I get it now.

I want to help, I want to serve
But you'll excuse me, please
To eat, sleep, breathe, see my family
You know, basic human needs

I don't gamble. I don't smoke. I drink one cocktail max.

Service is my vice...serVICE.

Like any recovering "addict," I'm doing my best to take the steps necessary to free myself from my dangerous habit of over committing myself in the name of helping others.

Here's my serVICE take on the 12 Steps to Recovery:

1. I admit I have been powerless over the desire to help others—that my life, for a time, had become unmanageable.

2. I trust in the Power greater than me, who can help restore me to sanity.

3. I always give my will and life over to the care of God, knowing that He wants joy and fulfillment for my life as much as He calls on me to serve others.

4. I've made a searching and fearless moral inventory of myself.

5. I admit to God, to myself and to others the exact nature of my harmful serVICE habits, which have impacted me physically, mentally and emotionally.

6. I am entirely ready to better myself, removing the defects of character that have inhibited my growth and quality of life.

7. I humbly ask God to help me on this journey to fully recognize, understand and resolve my shortcomings, so I may do and be better, more effective, happy and satisfied.

8. I've made a list of all persons I may have disappointed or neglected due to a full schedule of serVICE and am willing and determined to make amends with them all.

9. I am committing quality time to show these people just how much they are a priority in my life, reciprocating the love, time, attention and support they have graciously given and continue to give me.

10. I continue to take personal inventory, and when I am wrong and fall back into hurtful habits, I promptly admit it.

11. Through prayer and meditation, I continue to stay in conscious contact with God, praying for knowledge of His will for me and the power to carry it out.

12. Having had a spiritual awakening as the result of these steps, I try to carry this message to others (Hi! That's you. ☺) who may also be working to find balance in their will to serve their community, and I practice these principles in all my affairs to create and sustain harmony, joy, efficiency and satisfaction in all aspects of my life.

You just can't guilt me, I won't believe
That I'm the reason why
This or that just won't come through
When I'm the ride or die

Don't apologize just to appease someone who is angry. If you did nothing wrong, you must absolutely defend yourself, your choices, efforts, words, actions, work. As women and Filipinas, saying sorry can be a knee jerk reaction. Resist, my sisters.

We may not be perfect, but that doesn't mean we're not great. Don't let anyone tear down what you worked so hard to build, whether it be a project, relationship, event, team, company or reputation. It's one thing to be humble enough to take healthy criticism. It's another to be Jedi mind tricked into believing you're a failure when you've invested so much into creating something special. See and speak the truth, my sisters.

> *I work hard, I smile through pain*
> *My kindness is no lie*
> *I'll give you more than you expect*
> *If you say jump, I'll fly*

Chins up, Overachievers. Ya done good. You are excellent.

You work hard. You surprise people with your innovation, your unparalleled dedication, your phenomenal achievement. You earn any esteem and accolade that comes your way. But don't let things happen faster than you can appreciate them nor faster than you can accept a compliment.

Also, excel in saying thank you and giving compliments. Pay the positivity forward. Don't let blessings happen faster than you can write thank you cards. #workhardthankhard

> *I'm in demand not on demand*
> *You can't just turn me on*
> *Call, post, text me all you want*
> *Sometimes, I can't/won't respond*

I've been simultaneously in demand yet inhibited, popular yet searching for peace, successful yet unsatisfied, totally in control and totally overwhelmed.

When people start to treat text messaging like emails or a direct conduit to your soul, know that you don't have to respond right away...or at all. You're only as accessible as you allow yourself to be. You can be open and helpful without losing ownership of your life.

If someone demands to be the center of your universe, they ought to earn their way there...and that pathway won't be paved with incessant, immature, guilt-laden (often middle of the night) messages.

Also, daggers don't deserve or warrant responses. But here's a good test if you want to resolve a situation in which someone has initiated conflict with rude texts, posts or emails. Call them back. Cowards don't pick up the phone. If someone really wants to resolve something (s)he'll pick up. Some people just want to complain on a level of crazy. And you don't need to deal with crazy. We ain't got time for that!

Help me help you help them all out
We can't just cry and whine
If you want change, you must pitch in
Together, let's strategize.

When people say you should lead, you have to dig a little deeper and figure out if they want you to lead or if they want you to do all the work. It's not the same.

Be wary of the people who love to have meetings because it makes them feel important.

Hold as a pet peeve meetings which wax poetic but end with no timeline, action plan or delegated duties. If all you leave a meeting with is a sense of inspiration, you've wasted your time and an opportunity to make any real change.

Make it clear to folks that emailing reply-to-alls does not constitute actual leadership nor substantial participation...that they actually have to show up for your team to have productive meetings and programs...that being a leader is more than having a title to add to one's resume, bio or LinkedIn profile. There are types who crave attention. Those aren't leaders. There are types who have trouble taking criticism and direction but have no problem taking credit. Those aren't leaders. There are types who pretend to be present just long enough to have a say, assume some sort of authority and convey control. Those aren't leaders. For some, it's all about power and glory instead of the bigger picture, the greater good...real and sustainable change and service. Anyone can hide behind a computer screen or cell phone and click "Send." Anyone can take an oath. Anyone can wear a nametag. Real leaders show up to #dowork.

Sometimes folks go through personal crises. Sometimes folks aren't the right fit for a role. Some folks are simply in a space in which they don't like who they are or what they do...What results is toxic for individuals, teams and organizations. Help folks find their way. When people are in the right role at the right time and want to be where they are, they find satisfaction in hard work, do their best work, act their best and feel their best. Best begets best. Everyone deserves to get to that role, place and time.

Finally, don't fall for the folks who want you to do something "because you do it better." It's like teaching a child to do chores. At first, parents will be better at making beds. Real empowerment is teaching someone to make their own. Imagine the ways you could help save the universe if you allowed others to use their superpowers, too.

✦ ✦ ✦

Often, as leaders (especially as women...especially as <u>Filipina</u> leaders), we dedicate and sacrifice so much of ourselves for the good of others. We'll do anything to ensure that our organizations and communities rise, thrive and progress. In those quiet moments with ourselves, though, we have to be able to answer to our own physical, mental and emotional limits.

How do we find harmony (even when balance is not possible) amongst all the demands being a leader places on us? How do we satisfy the needs of those we lead and serve and still satisfy our needs as well? In empowering others, we can't allow ourselves to be disenfranchised.

Understanding these things about the world and my place in it hasn't always come easily nor has it come without a lot of self-evaluation...constant self-evaluation. I make a conscious effort to see the lesson in all people and experiences that enter my life.

Accepting the dare to grow, lead and succeed is a choice I've made and continue to make in (tough) loving company. I credit my parents, sister, brother-in-law and incredible family members, friends and mentors who made (and still make) exploring the depths of my potential a most wonderful journey. I credit my young, ambitious, talented, brilliant nieces, nephew, interns and students for teaching me some of my most important life lessons. I thank God, Mama Mary and all my angels for sending these blessings, people, lessons and opportunities to me.

God bless you on your journey. When bad days (especially baaaaaaaaad days) come across your path, know that you have a sister in your corner who, not only understands what you're going through, but believes without a doubt that you can, will and must rise.

It's important to stay true to who you are and what you value in order to be both an effective and satisfied leader. No martyrdom here. Say it with me: Effective leaders can be satisfied. To me, that's what being truly empowered looks like, and I hope to help other Filipina leaders channel their power, too. #globalpinaypower

I'm still becoming the Global Pinay Powerhouse I know I can be, that I was created to be—the Global Pinay Powerhouse of whom you can be proud.
Come, my sister. Let's be great together.

Love,
Francine

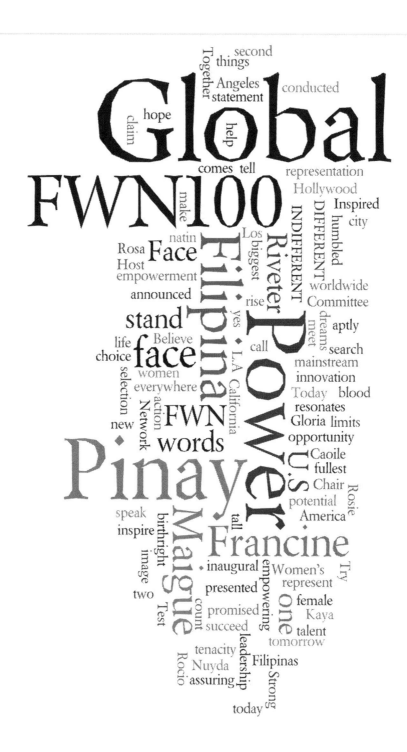

Disrupting Disruptions

JUANITA NIMFA YAMSUAN GAMEZ

President and CEO, Mission-Hope Development Services, Inc.
FWN100™ GLOBAL 2015 & U.S. 2007

From Travails to Success:
Caring Leadership

Why do Filipinos care so much? Anthony Bourdain attempted to answer this question in the April 22, 2016 episode called Unfinished Business in the Philippines. Based on Bourdain's own experience of entrusting the care of his daughter to a Filipina nanny, he wanted to know "why so many Filipinos are so damn caring. Why they care so much—for each other—for strangers. Because my experience is far from unusual." Bourdain marveled at perhaps thousands, maybe millions of children who were raised by Filipino nannies. He added that these nannies were "usually mothers of their own children who they were forced to leave behind in the Philippines."

My name is Juanita Nimfa Yamsuan Gamez. I am one of those mothers. I went to the United States leaving behind my husband and seven of my eight children in the Philippines to seek a better life for my family. Like many Filipinos, I did not have an easy life when I first migrated to the U.S. I was 42 years old when I moved here in 1995. I started out as a caregiver, working three jobs, and seven days a week, because I was a full time housewife and basically had no real employment experience and the easiest and most available job one can find in the States or most elsewhere in the world is in the healthcare industry, notwithstanding what one's educational attainment is. All over the world, Filipinas have migrated and most of them worked as nannies for young children and caregivers for the elderly. As mentioned by Anthony Bourdain, providing loving care is inherent among us, Filipinos.

This characteristic trait together with our hospitality and being highly-educated (we are mostly college graduates, we can speak English and are easily adaptable and can learn new things easy) are probably the main reasons why our services are most sought after all over the world. Giving care is inherent and comes to us naturally because it has been ingrained in us and passed on from generation to generation as we see our parents care for their parents and our grandparents did the same for their parents. In the same token, the parents and grandparents take turns taking care of the children in our closely knit and usually extended family. It is also worth noting that the success of the Overseas Filipino Workers goes hand in hand with their success in raising their children while they are thousands away from home. Filipinas are guided by Proverbs 22:6, "Train up a child in the way he should go, and even when he is old, he will not depart from it" in raising our children. By sending them in the right path from the time they are born, they will never leave this path.

In 2001, I opened my first day program for the disabled. I now operate six day programs and two care homes that serve over 500 vulnerable individuals in Alameda and Contra Costa counties in the state of California.

Caring and Leadership

In reflecting on my life experience, I have come to realize the connection between caring and leadership. As a caregiver, I took care of persons who could be young, old, sick, or disabled. As a successful businesswoman in the health care industry, I take care of many more persons. As President Ronald Reagan said: "The greatest person is not necessarily the one who does the greatest things. He/She is the one who gets the people to do the greatest things."

Readiness for Caregiving

When I immigrated to the U.S. I had no work experience except being a full-time housewife. In the Philippines I raised my eight children, with the help of *yayas* [nannies]. While I was growing up, I learned to take care of, provide the needs of, and look after my grandparents, my parents, and any old people in the extended family. This is not unusual in the Philippines where we do not have care homes or care facilities. The family takes care of their own. Given that I had a lot of experience in caring, the easiest job to land in the U.S. was in caregiving.

Being the youngest in a family of two boys and two girls, I observed and absorbed a lot. From my father and uncles, I received praises for being smart and intelligent. My oldest sister was a formidable force. So was my mother. And my grandmother. They were all of strong characters. From them, I learned to differentiate good from bad. I learned to follow the good and to discard the bad. Although, in life, you learn lessons, the hard way, through experience. Not always successfully.

One leadership lesson I learned early on happened when I was class president in third grade. One of my assignments was to make sure my classmates were quiet and ready for flag ceremony but one classmate kept on chattering. Without thinking about it, I slapped her face which I immediately regretted. From that day on, I have learned that leadership should not be forced. Leadership involves a lot of patience to come up with a result that will make you proud for the rest of your life. I hope I have instilled this in my children who patiently waited in the Philippines while I, the maverick, restarted our life in the U.S. I had to reinvent myself from a simple housewife, to a woman in charge of her children's future.

Meeting the Health Care Industry Requirements

The owners of the health care facilities I worked for noticed that I was very hard working. They started sending me to seminars. That is how I got my education about the health care industry. I did have a solid educational background in the Philippines. I was a scholar at the Philippine Science High School and then went to the University of the Philippines although I did not finish my degree because I got married young and started having children.

As I started learning the ropes of the industry, I began to think: "There's only 24 hours in a day and seven days a week. If I want to work as a nurse, I can only work a maximum number of hours. Whereas, if I opened my own care home, my own residential care facility, I can definitely do much better." I must admit that initially the process of discernment was tied to the best way to have enough money and time to raise my children.

Having thought about the possibility, I set about reinventing myself. There is that seed of leadership that God had sown in all of us. However, it takes a lot of learning to nurture that seed to make it grow in a mutually beneficial way. Not only good for myself and my family but also to touch and make a difference in many people's lives.

There were health care industry requirements to be met. One of which is a facility. As a first time home buyer in the U.S., I was able to take advantage of a government program that did not require a down payment. Before that happened, my eight children came and the apartment we were renting was cramped and one of the closets became my bedroom and my friends teased me as the closet woman.

Other licensing requirements are set by the state of California where I reside and where I opened my business. Among these requirements are: a high school education or equivalent (Check), and shall have had at least two years of experience or training in one of the following: (a) Care and supervision of clients in a licensed day care facility. (Check.) (b) Care and supervision of one or more of the categories of persons to be served by the facility. (Check.) You can read about these requirements at http://www.dds.ca.gov/LivingArrang/CCF.cfm and http://www.dss.cahwnet.gov/getinfo/pdf/adcfman.PDF.

I had to be a maverick to pull through from the travails in life to succeed in a foreign country and without the right degree nor corporate experience to start a business. It also required incredible sacrifice, perseverance, and lots of hard work to start the first day program for the disabled in 2001. I called it "Mission Hope." I know God gave me this opportunity. Money cannot buy the happiness that I get when I serve my clients. It is just overwhelming. My heart swells up when I see a client happy. As Margaret Thatcher once said "I do not know anyone who has gotten to the top without hard work. That is the recipe. It will not always get you to the top, but it will get you pretty near."

As I have said earlier, I now operate six day programs and two care homes that serve over 500 vulnerable individuals in Alameda and Contra Costa counties in the state of California. I employ over 200 people who need jobs in today's tough economy. It's time for me to help with jobs, help anybody who needs my help to help themselves.

Serving the Community

I have become a leader in the community. I served as the founding president of the United Association of California Care Providers, a group that has been lobbying for more government funding for the disabled.

In 2008, I was also recognized as a notable citizen through a California State Assembly resolution. From 2011-2013, I served as a Commissioner for the Contra Costa Women's Commission, which advises the board of supervisors and other entities on issues relating to the changing social and economic conditions of women in Contra Costa County.

I set up the Caring Hearts Foundation in 2009 (see http://www.caringheartssfoundation.net/). Its mission is to create lasting solutions to alleviate poverty, hunger, educational and economic inequality and social injustice among marginalized families in the poorest, especially the constantly typhoon-ravaged communities in the Philippines. The hope is to be able to provide assistance in times of dire need, health crisis, to cover educational, burial and other emergency needs, and to provide micro-financing to help them become self-sufficient. For example, we helped Jenielyn Canlapan open up a little store in front of her house so she can make money and still be able to look after her 2 young children, plus we sent her money to buy a tricycle for her husband to drive to make a living for their family.

Being Self-Aware of my Leadership Qualities

As the President and Chief Executive Officer, I am good at hiring the right people, delegating responsibilities, and empowering my staff. I try to lead by example, by showing people around me how to work with belief and passion in one's heart so that what one does is beneficial and meaningful. I show humility when I mingle and work alongside anyone in whatever duty they are assigned in my company. I show respect and care for every individual I work with or provide service for. I do not carry the leader and founder of the company's hat over her head, but that of a humble servant's heart. Keeping this balance between wanting to exude a sense of humility while at the same time showing great sense of leadership is an art a good leader has to master.

To get to where I am, I had to overcome being shy, being reserved, and not being forward, another common Filipino trait. That is how our elders taught us; not to talk back, especially to one's elders. Upon coming to the U.S., I also had to overcome speaking English as just my second language on top of being an Asian woman and a single parent with eight children. Now, as a business woman, I have learned to speak up my mind. I have learned to speak when I know I am right. I have learned to speak the truth. Speaking my mind out, is the only way I can use my ideas, and my experience to affect innovation and change in my own family, my business, my community, and influence and encourage others to follow the example I had set in opening and running my businesses.

CARING AND LEADERSHIP: KEY TAKEAWAYS

As I struggle to find words to explain the connection between caring and leadership, an article about "A Caring Leadership Model for Nursing's Future" by Williams, McDowell, and Kautz (2011) was sent to me. It fully captures my life experience of working in the health care industry and the core values that have motivated me and kept me going. These are:

1. "Always lead with kindness, compassion, and equality." It was my caring ways which led to my inspiration to set up residential care facilities for the developmentally disabled. I believe that the people we work with can sense this kindness and concern.

2. "Generate hope and faith through co-creation." My guide here is President Ronald Reagan who said "Surround yourself with the best people you can find, delegate authority, and don't interfere as long as the policy you've decided upon is being carried out." My children are grown and have become partners and co-owners of the company. I have delegated day to day responsibilities with them. I am semi-retired and enjoying being a grandmother to nine grandchildren and more on the way. While my children are known as COOs (children of owner), I have given them the opportunity for decision-making and to be the owners of the business themselves.

3. "Actively innovate with insight, reflection, and wisdom." Trying to balance innovation with insight is not always easy. It is like baking a cake. A good cake requires many ingredients. How the ingredients are mixed together, setting the temperature for baking, and length of time for baking depends on who is baking and for what reason. The same is true for mixing caring with leadership. There is concern. Discipline. Passion.

4. "Purposely create protected space founded upon mutual respect and caring." I try to assist the company staff by being intentional in caring for their needs even as they care for those we serve.

5. "Embody an environment of caring-helping-trusting for self and others." While the business is about caring for others who are unable to care for themselves, it is important to take care of yourself.

These five core values may help answer Bourdain's question about "why Filipinos care so much." But the most important reason why Filipinos are caring is because it is ingrained in our culture, carried in our genes from generation to generation, as we are born into families that share the same values. We take pride in being kind and caring especially when we are able to provide care for our own children, our own parents when they get old and feeble, and we are so willing to extend this same kindness and caring for others who need our help. This culture of kindness and caring can also be traced to our Catholic upbringing, the Philippines being a majority Catholic country. It has been inculcated in our minds from a very young age that to sacrifice one's life for the service of others will be rewarded immensely with God's blessings and will assure us a path to heaven.

Lastly, I, Nimfa Yamsuan Gamez may someday be gone from this earth, and my name may never be remembered because success like any material thing could just be a fleeting moment, but no one can take the thought that I have in me. I know I worked hard and did my best to make my family and others' lives and easier. "What is significant in being an entrepreneur is living a few years of your life like most people won't, so that you can spend the rest of your life, like most people can't!" As President Reagan indicated, "There is no limit to the amount of good you can do if you don't care who gets the credit." Accolades are not paramount in my work, but I want my story to inspire and to Share His Glory.

TRISH QUEMA LA CHICA

Policy and Advocacy Director
for the Hawaii Public Health Institute (HIPHI)
FWN100™ Global 2015

Surviving San Francisco:
How I Landed My Dream Job at 28

I was twenty-two years old, working for ABS-CBN, the largest broadcasting company in the Philippines. But I was desperate to leave Manila. Desperate to leave my job, life, and family behind. I never expected to start a new life in San Francisco, one of the largest cities I had ever visited, but I did. In the last seven years, I have gone from being a lost and unemployed immigrant to a happily married soon-to-be mom, living in Hawaii (paradise!) and working at my dream job. It was not easy; I stumbled and I struggled and I took risks. In college, I was a hopeless romantic concerning my future career. I wanted to do something meaningful, although I did not have concrete plans for what that meant. In fact, there were countless times over the years when I doubted that I would ever get my dream job. Throughout this chapter, I will be sharing experiences that have had a tremendous impact on my life. There are quite a few insights that I have learned, but the common thread across all of them is that people are motivated by doing work that is meaningful. And I define meaning in knowing that your work contributes to something larger than yourself. In this chapter you will get to know my story, and hopefully the insights that I have culled over the years will help you to find meaning and purpose in your life too.

IF YOU DO NOT LIKE SOMETHING, CHANGE IT.

I was raised by my father single handedly since I was three years old. As an only child, I felt that I was catapulted into adulthood at a very young age. I could cook, clean, do the groceries. My mom was always the hard worker in the family, while my dad dabbled in different gigs that would allow him to be self-employed. My mom left for the United States when I was three, to better provide for us, as I was told. But she never returned. She never came back. And so it was just my dad and I. He opted to stay at home and focus on my upbringing. However, as the years went by, my dad never quite found the motivation to return to work. I never questioned this though, I just thought that my dad was different from other dads. In the earlier years, he occasionally hung out with friends who experimented with drugs. In fact, I still have vivid memories of entering my dad's room to find him passed out on his bed. He also dated a lot and I would get introduced to a new 'girlfriend' every six months or so. Do not get me wrong, I love my dad. Despite some of his shortcomings, he managed to bring me a lot of happiness while I was growing up. He was at every school program and performance. He bought my first bike (a gift from 'Santa'), danced with me in the rain, and made me laugh until my stomach hurt. He checked all my homework, he ironed my school uniforms, and he would take me on fun trips, when we could afford it. With my unemployed dad, we had to rely on willing family and friends who could support us. We were lucky that my grandmother and eventually, my mom, after we had reconciled, could provide us with enough money to help meet our daily needs. What my dad lacked in financial capacity, he made up for with his unconditional love. "My heart is your heart," he would always say. Out of our struggles grew an unbreakable bond.

Changing the World: Initial Steps

I went to the Ateneo de Manila University. THE Ateneo. I majored in Communications and minored in English Literature, initially because I thought I wanted to become a lawyer. That was the common narrative for becoming successful, right? Go to school, get good grades, get a good job, find a good partner, get married, have kids and *yayas* [nannys] who could help take care of them, and live a life happily ever after. Good school and good grades, check. A good job was next, and I was fortunate to have been offered an entry-level journalist job, to do research for *The Correspondents*, ABS-CBN's investigative documentary show. My job was to produce documentaries, using storytelling to inspire and compel social change. Wow, I could change the world, I thought. For three years, I covered all sorts of stories; from exposing corrupt government practices to providing a firsthand look into the harsh realities of poverty. I was immersed in different environments; entering violent riots, watching children forage through trash, interviewing battered wives, criminals, and terminally ill patients. I missed holidays and important family time, traveling for days and weeks. But I became a journalist because I was able to make a difference, albeit small. Being able to help mattered to me. They were just temporary solutions really, but these became the highlights of my journalism career. I was once able to bring an entire team of mental health specialists to Oriental Mindoro, a province in Southern Luzon of about 700,000. Many residents who were mentally ill were shunned by society. A handful were even placed in cages, kept away from the rest of the family, because their families did not know what to do with them. The story aired, and those residents were eventually given proper medical attention. Despite these attempts to affect change however, I soon realized that my actions were limited in the media industry. "We're in the media. Certainly we can do more?" I asked one of my senior producers. "No," she said. "Your role is to deliver the news, not to intervene."

Swimming with Sharks

That was not the first time I felt helpless. In one of my stories, I met this new mayor who told me that people like us are just "small fish, in an ocean of sharks." He shared that to survive in politics, "we had to play by the rules of the game." He told me about the time when he received a call from the governor, inviting him to his home. He had been trying to get hold of the governor for months, because the chairs in the local elementary school were in disrepair. The mayor brought with him a robust, wooden chair that he had specially made. It was the perfect solution for his school. At the house, the governor took him outside, and asked for a plastic chair to be brought to him. He placed the chairs side by side. The governor asked his staff to throw both chairs, with all their might into the wall. The plastic chair quickly broke apart, while the wooden one remained sturdy and intact. "Which of these chairs do you think you'll need?" The governor asked. "The wooden one, of course," the mayor said. "It'll last longer." "Yes, the wooden one will last years, but plastic chairs break within a year. Only broken things get funded. If we pay for something that works, the money will stop coming. If we give people what they need, then they will stop asking for help. People need to have problems to complain about, so you can become their hero. Only heroes get elected."

Breaking Point

I got mad. It was frustrating to realize that there was so little I could do. Story after story, I grew more dispirited and I hated that feeling. One day, my dad suffered a heart attack. He spent several days at Philippine General Hospital, where my dad's friend knew the head cardiologist. His medical bills were ballooning, and so was my anxiety. Since graduating from college, I had assumed full financial responsibility for our family. I was only earning about Php 20,000 [US$431] a month, not much, but enough to live paycheck-to-paycheck. My dad had to go through a non-surgical procedure that would open his blocked arteries. It was a relief to have avoided surgery, and we were lucky to have had an abundance of family and friends who pitched in to help settle our hospital bills. At first, my dad did not even want to get the treatment, because we did not have the money to pay for it. It broke my heart. "You want to die instead?" I asked him. When the donations poured in, I broke down and cried. People are more willing to help than you might expect.

It was my dad's condition that ignited my desire to leave the Philippines. I no longer wanted to be dependent on other people should another dire financial event come up. Remaining in my job was not going to be enough to support my family. Then an opportunity came; I received my green card. My mom, who had earned her citizenship after living in the U.S. for so long, offered to petition for my visa before I turned 18. I went through some major introspection. I had the opportunity to live in the U.S., get a master's degree, and some work experience; then return to Manila and bring back what I had learned. Maybe even start my own company or nonprofit and finally make a difference. But it meant having to leave my dad behind. I shared my doubts with him, and he told me to go. "Go for your dreams," he said. "Don't let me be the anchor that weighs you down. Opportunities to change your life don't come often, and I don't want you to end up like me. You're my greatest achievement, and I know you can do it."

And so, I left.

It Takes a Thousand Times More Effort Than You Realize.

There is nothing more daunting than being on your own for the first time. Thankfully, Cricket, my boyfriend of five years moved to San Francisco with me. He was going to start his master's program at the Academy of Art University, while working freelance as a web developer. We managed to find a place to rent; a small room in a shared five-bedroom apartment in the Tendernob neighborhood, close to downtown San Francisco. My boyfriend's family accompanied us from Manila to help us move. I remember hauling our stuff into our cramped space: our entire life, packed into six *balikbayan* boxes. When his family left, I cried. "This is it," I told Cricket, "we're really on our own."

Adjusting Expectations

Our monthly rent was $850. Our combined life's savings was about $4000. Although Cricket had some income from his online work, it was not going to be enough. I had to find a job soon. I started the process while I was still in Manila; submitting applications to various job postings. I even landed one phone interview which I had to do at 2:00 in the morning, given the time difference. It was with Full Court Press Communications and I was interviewed by one of the founders. But I did not get the job. He loved my energy, but I did not have any experience working in the Bay Area. Being an Ateneo alumna and a journalist would have opened doors in Manila. But in San Francisco, I was pretty much a nobody. I put tremendous pressure on myself to find the perfect job. Initially, I tried to apply for manager level positions at tech companies and nonprofit organizations. When my applications went unnoticed, I had to adjust my expectations. "Fine, I'll start at entry level," I told myself, "but definitely no retail or barista positions." I frantically applied everywhere and hoped for the best. Each day, I would scour Craigslist, Idealist, and every other job portal I could find. I must have sent 10 to 15 applications each day. My heart would jump whenever I received a new email. Yet, the response was always disheartening: "After reviewing your application, we regret to inform you that you have not been selected for the next step in the hiring process."

Self-Awareness

Three months had passed. We were so broke. One day we even walked for an hour from our apartment on Sutter street to Fisherman's Wharf to claim a coupon for free iHop pancakes. We could not afford to take the bus. When I absolutely had no choice, I tried to pass myself off as a minor so I could pay the youth fare of $0.75, compared to the regular rate, $2.25. Despite our penny-pinching ways, we still managed to make new friends and explore our beautiful city. My favorite place to hangout was the old Borders bookstore (now DSW) by Union Square. I would haul a stack of self-help career development books to the cafe on the second floor and do my research. How to write a good cover letter. What questions to ask during an interview. How to find your dream job. What color was my parachute? I was so worried. What if I never found a job? Am I letting everyone down?

Getting Creative

My application had to stand out. It was 2010 and San Francisco, like the rest of the nation, was still experiencing high unemployment following the financial crisis. One employer told me they received 400 applications for one position. 400! How could I even compete? I had to get creative. I sketched and designed a little ad that I would attach to every email. Titled, "How Can I Benefit You?," it was a fun and colorful infographic that listed the top four qualities that I felt made me a unique candidate for any position: (1) I am creative, (2) I am goal-driven, (3) I am passionate about service, and (4) I spread sunshine. The image ends with a mini-Trish caricature in a green shirt, waving 'Hi!' This strategy worked. Hiring officers began to notice my application and I received a few interview requests. In July, I was offered a contract position as a Campaign Fellow, along with 10 others for the United Way of the Bay Area (UWBA). Finally! Someone decided to take a chance on me! They even contacted my supervisors in Manila to check my references. I started in August, five months after moving to San Francisco. UWBA was located on Main Street in the Financial District and the offices had a beautiful view of the bay bridge. I was so excited and took a lot of photos. The job though was only for three and a half months, so I maximized every opportunity to network and learn new skills. I scheduled informational interviews with various directors and top leadership during my spare time. I was a sponge. I was absorbing everything I could about nonprofit management, corporate giving, and grant writing. I befriended everyone. Every. Single. Staff. Member. I had friends in accounting, human resources, marketing. The Human Resources Director, Natalie Cedeno, was particularly fond of me. She liked hearing about my work in Manila and offered generous tips on how to improve my resume and reach out to potential employers. When the three and a half months were up, UWBA decided to extend my contract, while the rest of the nine fellows left. I eventually ended up filling various temporary positions. My favorite was launching Holiday-in-a-Box, a program that fostered partnerships between 40 community-based organizations and SF Bay Area corporations in order for underserved children and families to be able to celebrate and open gifts during the holidays. I was also given the opportunity to fill in as the temporary assistant to the CEO, which gave me a lot of insight into her role and how she managed key relationships. I ended up staying for four additional months. Unfortunately, there was no funding to hire me full time, so before long, I was back on the job boards, applying for new opportunities.

Landing a Full-Time Position

Two months later, in May 2011, I landed my first full-time position as the Program Assistant for the Chronic Diseases Program at the Asian & Pacific Islander American Health Forum (APIAHF). Whew, what a mouthful. APIAHF is the oldest and largest national health advocacy organization working with Asian

American (AA), Native Hawaiian, and Pacific Islander (NHPI) communities across the nation and in U.S. Territories. At APIAHF, I got to work on different initiatives —cancer survivorship, racial equity, health care reform, and data advocacy. I had an amazing supervisor and mentor, Roxanna Bautista, who taught me the value of putting community first and how to lead with love. Through her mentorship, I was promoted a couple of times, eventually leading different projects and programs, conducting trainings across the nation, and speaking publicly to raise awareness on different health disparities. I was at APIAHF for almost four years.

Lessons Learned: A Few Survival Tips

Job hunting in San Francisco was a daunting and humbling experience. Like other immigrants, the idea of working and living in America appealed to me. Many jump through hoops just to get a U.S. visa, but what my first year in SF taught me was that moving to a new country was just the first step. Learning how to survive took a thousand times more effort than I expected. Like many, I was shocked by how challenging it was to find a job. What I also thought was an impressive resume, initially did not impress anyone at all. Achieving big dreams will never be easy. If I had never left the Philippines then I would not have advanced in my career. I would not have the opportunity to work for a large national organization doing policy and advocacy. I would not have earned valuable mentors who wanted me to grow and be successful. Surviving San Francisco helped me realize that I was capable of so much more than I expected and that achieving my goals were possible. And all the setbacks I experienced taught me valuable lessons that I continue to apply to this day. So before I forget, a few survival tips:

1. Step outside of your comfort zone. It is hard to break out of your comfort zone. But if you are comfortable you are less likely to make new goals. Start with a plan. You will expect to deal with new and unexpected changes but do not be afraid to challenge yourself and I guarantee that you will be surprised by what you are capable of.

2. Be prepared to adjust your expectations, but keep dreaming. Achieving your goals will not happen overnight. Accept fear and uncertainty when something is not working out, but do not give up. Your dreams or goals may change, but so will you. Change brings new knowledge and experiences that will allow you to discover new insights about yourself. Keep going and keep dreaming.

3. Do not overanalyze – the best things in life are unexpected. I was obsessed with the expectation that everything in my life must go according to plan. But I had

to stop trying to create a plan for every goal that I had. The path to your most important goals will not always be linear. While it is good to have an idea of what we want our future to be like, we should not overthink or over-anticipate every single detail.

4. Have courageous conversations. You will be expected to deal with difficult colleagues and unbearable bosses. I will be honest and say that there is really no easy way to deal with it. Difficult conversations call for courage and are driven by a sincere desire to achieve better outcomes. To this day, it is still a struggle for me but I find these conversations necessary to preserving relationships and peace in the workplace. Conversations are powerful. They address situations that make us feel overworked, undermined, misunderstood, underutilized, and overlooked. Your ability to speak up about issues that weigh you down is crucial to your success, growth, and development.

When an Opportunity Comes, Take It. And If It Changes Your Life, Let It.

I now live and work in Honolulu, Hawaii. It is seriously one of the most beautiful places on earth. In February 2015 one of my mentors, Hawaii State Senator Josh Green shared with me an opportunity to join newly-elected Governor David Ige's Healthcare Transformation Office as a Policy Analyst. After speaking with him about it, I decided to apply for the position. I was interviewed by the team over several weeks, and I was offered the position in late February. During that time, I was also preparing for one of my biggest life events—my wedding, which was set for March of that year. I also had another outstanding job offer with the University of California San Francisco (UCSF). Everything seemed to be happening all at once and I was voicing my dilemma to Cricket, who was then my fiancé. I was vacillating. I told him that between the UCSF and Hawaii offer, that I was more inclined to accept the former. I reasoned that we already had an established life in SF, renting a 2-bedroom apartment right next to the ocean. We had a dog and we were surrounded by a wonderful group of friends. Accepting the Hawaii offer meant having to leave everything behind, again. "So, why not?" he asked. "How often will you get a chance to live and work in Hawaii? Besides, isn't that your dream job?"

Readiness for Policy Leadership

I have always wanted a career in public policy. While working full time in SF,

I also studied full time for my Masters in Public Administration at the University of San Francisco. I worked during the day, studied for tests and wrote papers in the evening, and attended classes from 8am to 5pm, every Saturday. For two and a half years. It was pretty intense. But it was worth it. Gaining further insight into the policy process validated my desire to be in public service. Some of my favorite courses included: public policy analysis, quantitative methods (statistics!), program evaluation, human resource and planning management, public sector budgeting, and economics. Prior to graduation in 2014, we were asked the classic question: "Where do you see yourself in three to five years?" I said I was going to be a Policy Analyst. And here I was, being offered the opportunity to work as a Policy Analyst for the Governor's Office, just six months after completing my MPA. And I was about to turn it down. Thanks to my fiancé, I jumped on the opportunity. I landed my dream job, and we were on our way to Hawaii.

A New Beginning

The next two months was a flurry of activity. I accepted the offer in early March, and negotiated a start date of mid-April. We were set to leave for Manila within a week, to prepare for our wedding. But because we were moving to Hawaii after the wedding, we had to readjust all of our plans. It was too expensive to ship furniture to Hawaii, so Cricket and I had to sell almost everything that we owned. On the day prior to our departure for Manila, we were frantically advertising items on Craigslist as 'Free!' Everything that we could not sell or part with, we stored at my mom's garage in Hollister, a two-hour drive south from San Francisco. My mom has been pretty supportive of all the career and life changes that I have had over the years. I owe it to her for making it possible for me to move to California. It was not easy, but my mom and I managed to rebuild our fractured relationship. The physical proximity gave us an opportunity to create new memories, especially with her family. My mom had remarried a few years after moving to the U.S. in the 90s. She also has a daughter, who is ten years my junior. I love my sister and stepdad dearly. Although my mom had her own family when I reentered her life, I never felt like an outsider. Both Cricket and I were welcomed into their family wholeheartedly, and they continue to be such a big part of our life. Despite being estranged from my mom for many years, I let go of my resentments and focused on improving our relationship. She was still my mother after all. "*Mahal na mahal kita anak, kung alam mo lang.* [You don't know how much I love you.]" she would say.

On March 21, 2015, I got married to the love of my life. Our ceremony was on a cliff, overlooking the sea, in Nasugbu, Batangas. While stating his vows, Cricket recalled our early life in San Francisco when "we would split a single hotdog for lunch" because it was all we could afford. He continued, "Do you remember the time when we broke up?" Yes I did. I was in tears and so were our guests. People were surprised to hear that there was a point when we were not happily living together in SF. We were both struggling to make ends meet and it was affecting our relationship. But we had faith that we would make it, and we made a choice to at least try. "I was broke, but not broken, because you believed in me," he ended.

LIVING MY DREAM

It has been a little over a year since we moved to Hawaii; dog and ten *balik-bayan* boxes in tow. After renting in Waikiki for a few months, we purchased a small starter home in Mililani. Every weekend, we are basking on the beach or hiking a new trail. My husband has his own web and mobile app development company now. As a Policy Analyst in the Governor's Office, I facilitated the development of the State Health Care Innovation Plan designed to help improve health systems performance, increase quality of care, and decrease costs for the residents of Hawaii. Nine months later, in January 2016, I started a new job as the Policy and Advocacy Director for the Hawaii Public Health Institute (HIPHI). In this role, I work closely with state legislators and community advocates to advance policy initiatives on building healthier communities. I spend a lot of my time advocating at the State Capitol, working to influence statewide and county legislation that aim to protect and improve population health. In addition, I track, analyze, and research data and national issues relevant to our policy priorities. I love my job. I am surrounded by staff and community partners that truly want to make Hawaii a better and healthier place to live in.

I can say that I am now on a clear path to achieving my goals, but I also know that there is still a lot to learn. I am fortunate to have found meaning in my work, attaining successes along the way, both big and small. I do not know whether I will be successful or not in making a difference, but it does not make me any less committed. Malcolm Gladwell (2008), in Outliers, talks about how those who do and achieve extraordinary things are not successful based on personal merit and effort alone, but due to a combination of different factors. All the struggles, financial constraints, and job rejections I experienced were only temporary setbacks. I bounced back, I never gave up. And I would never have been able to do so without my dad, my mom, my mentors, and my husband—all of whom inspired me to keep going. When I was in doubt, they reminded me that I was capable of doing extraordinary things.

I look forward to seeing other young and early career professionals create their own conditions for meaning and success. Hopefully, I can also play a role in propelling them towards their dreams. For now, I will be embarking on a new journey when my husband and I welcome our first child into our life in a few months.

Son, this is mommy's story, and this chapter is for you.

ROCIO NUYDA

Former Chairman FilAm Arts
Owner, Grace Events
FWN100™ Global 2016 & U.S. 2012

Rocio, a Morning Dew

I wore a blue and white jumper uniform with black flat shoes and white socks to match. As soon as I entered the portals of St. Agnes' Academy, I, and other high school students had to speak English or face a demerit that led to disciplinary measures. The school was run by the Benedictine nuns of St. Scholastica College in Manila, and was the counterpart school of St. Scholastica in Legazpi City of the Bicol region.

During the early years, I tried on many occasions to sneak out from oratorical or declamation practice usually at the end of class taught by a German nun who was also the school directress. I thought of these oratorical practices as disruptions because they prevented me from playing on the school ground with my schoolmates. I was the school's perennial bet in regional competitions. This went on through all four years of high school when every year I brought home the gold medal, defeating every school who tried to dethrone me. I started competing in mid elementary school at age eight, and continued competing until I graduated from high school at the young age of 14. I was always the youngest in the class, having jumped ahead by one class year after I was accelerated mid-year from Grade 1 to Grade 2. I was told I was achieving beyond my years. I did not understand what this meant then but I remember that it sparked a confidence in me, and this was when my leadership skills started. Super achiever. Confident. Disruptor. I built on these qualities to demonstrate leadership by inspiration and by empowerment. My story chronicles the paths that I continue to tread to survive, to provide, to fulfill, and to succeed. It is leadership by a woman in a male dominated norm of business, a legacy that I hope to bequeath to my children and their children.

My Beloved Father and His Death

My first memory of a disruption in my life, was the untimely death of my father. He had been a popular judge in the second district of the region. I recall a daily line of callers coming to our home, bringing with them humble offerings of live chicken, local delicacies like *puto* [steamed Filipino rice cake shaped like an American muffin] and *suman* [glutinous rice cake cooked in coconut milk]. Visitors in their tattered shirts and buri hats, and with smiles often marred by missing teeth; would look at me as the judge's daughter. My father was revered and loved. This was my first insight on how people can demonstrate love if treated kindly. It was a mental note that I carried all through my life.

I remember the hushed visits of the doctor taking care of my father. As a child I could only look in wonderment, and not question. I was 5 years old then. I remember one day in the dark of the night, my mother, my brother and I were transported in a private car from the hospital where my father was confined to our home many miles away. My mother was quietly sobbing as she hugged me and I did not know why. I remember seeing my father laid in a coffin a few days after, and the honor guards standing beside him. I remember the long lines of mourners, and other unfamiliar faces. I remember being told that my father went to heaven and it would just be my mother, brother, and I. I wondered what this disruption meant and what would become of us.

My mother moved us from our small town big home to the small home of my grandparents in the big city. I remember being enrolled in the school of the nuns who wore starched white habits. I felt a disruption. The disruption was intense, it motivated me to become a gold medalist, land all the lead roles in the school's annual plays, and many noteworthy extracurricular activities where I played a prominent lead role, a leadership role. I developed a passion to prove myself because I felt different from others; unlike them, I did not have a father. I had to shield myself. I had to prove that I was not unique and would not be denied a normal life. Because I did not have a father. I had to excel. I had to lead because I thought that in leading, I could be normal. I could make a mark! Through the indirect expression of art, I started to hone my leadership.

At age 14, I was off to college at the Philippine Women's University in Manila. I gained maturity by being part of the university's core leadership group of women. I was the President of the Liberal Arts Department, run for the position of Vice President of the Student Council albeit losing to a student in the Business

Department, because my department had fewer students than the Business Department. I was on the editorial staff of the school newspaper. I took on lead roles in the annual plays and presentation. I was tapped as spokesperson in speaking assignments and handpicked by my professor in the Radio and Television Workshop to co-host a very popular television weekly show, Jam Session.

I was a communication arts major, and did not wait to be assigned plum roles. I initiated. I took them. I remember the hurdles to get a face to face interview with the newly crowned and first Ms. International, Gemma Cruz Araneta. I managed to get into the airport arrival area where she was mobbed by media, and I, in my maroon and white school uniform with microphone in hand and a media tag on my chest, squeezed through the throng and somehow managed to get an appointment to interview her at her home. Being pitted against the professional was not a deterrent. It was an unprecedented coup, and I got a perfect top grade. How I did this, I cannot even begin to recreate.

I remember being recruited to co-host a highly rated television show with the popular Eddie Mercado and Boots Taylor. I found out later on, that I was recommended based on a "take-charge personality," grit, confidence, and glib.

By now, I knew that I could lead and that disruptions were (and are) not obstacles. I discovered that I had an innate ability to use genuine and sincere communication in engaging others and have them buy in to an idea. I discovered that I could motivate. The orphan child could not be stopped.

Motherhood, Career, How Do They Blend?

As soon as I graduated from college, my future husband was in a hurry to marry. It was a whirlwind romance. We only began a serious relationship a year before marriage. We shared similar roots because our families were from the Bicol region; I, from Spanish Filipino grandparents, and he, from a Filipino Congressman of the region. Our interactions were few and far between, but he swept me off my feet. He was an eloquent man who knew what he wanted and went for it, decisively. He too, was a leader.

This was a major disruption because it meant breaking away from a first love, another man who I committed to love, other than my soon-to-be husband. A first love that lingered in my mind, then and many years to come. I was torn and confused. How I decided would dictate the course of my life and a fate that was bitter sweet in more ways than one. Bitter because first loves are etched with a permanence that is hard to overcome, and sweet because my marriage although short was a friendship formed with a partner who showered me with the kindest gestures of love and affection.

My marriage bore five children, year after year. I had to choose between the high calling of motherhood and building a career. I chose to stay home. Noble as motherhood was, it was still a disruption to my dream of making a name in the media industry, whether as a face on screen, working in the background in production, or in journalism where my love for writing could be utilized.

Staying home did not diminish my passion for engagement. One night, I sat watching my oldest son and daughter in a school play. I thought that such presentations, especially if they were held annually could be more artistic with a professional stage and improved design. The children had talents that needed to be honed. I thought that they could be exposed to the legitimate stage. I thought that greater artistic experience would lend towards a more rounded education, after all life imitates art or depending on one's outlook, art imitates life.

After the play was over, I spoke to the teacher, asked some questions and then I took the next step.

The next day, I volunteered to run for the Parents Board, comprised of notable business persons, highly renowned, and well connected. After all, this was De La Salle Zobel, an ivy league school in the Philippines. That year, I was elected a member of the Parents Board. It was a working board, in close connection with the school.

By design, I did better. I got the plum and desired position of Chairman of Cultural Affairs. I initiated a collaborative partnership between the Parents Board and the school officers to consider and look into a more artistically robust school play. I developed a production plan to stage the school play at the Cultural Center of the Philippines (CCP). The plan included soliciting the help of CCP'S Artistic Director, the late Tony Espejo as Director with the school's drama teacher as an understudy, the film Director Joel Lamangan, the late Tony Fabella and Eddie Elejar to direct the choreography, a voice coach, and a soprano Aurelia Jimenez. Oh yes, and hire the full orchestra of CCP for music.

It was considered an ambitious undertaking and when presented to the Parents Board, I was met with a disapproving uproar. I was told, "It is an ambitious project, the board cannot finance it." My reply was, "I only need the board's approval, I will find financing elsewhere". And financing I found elsewhere. Financing was at a high estimate of thousands of pesos to cover the expense. It was a disruption that did not derail me. It was a disruption I initiated.

I went to work. I carefully assessed the roster of parents and their inclinations and capacities to be involved. I considered that these are parents who can well afford to give time and resources, that perhaps all it took was to rally them behind a worthy cause; the development of their children. I mapped a working and organizational committee to spearhead the project. I chose and picked the parents, sent the invitation, and called for a first meeting. The key was to sell the idea convincingly, invoke their interest by highlighting the all-important factor that there was more to gain than lose, and convince them that the benefit would be indelible in the lives of their own children who would experience and learn theater arts in its full context from learned and professional artists. Surprisingly, I had a one hundred percent positive response.

The Cultural Center of the Philippines was viewed as an impossible dream. My next step was to reach out to the desired artists, and with clear communication of the desired benefits and goals, they were all on board. They offered their services for an honorarium and not for their full professional fees. They understood the goal, bought in on the idea, did not consider monetary compensation, and said, "We have an Operetta to present. Let's get to work". Again, this was leadership by effective communication and the innate gift to inspire.

Meanwhile, my committee and I began the laborious process of finance. We undertook the infamous cultural week on the school ground. We had visual and performing art competitions, games, vendors' stalls that paid a percentage of sales, art donated by famous artists sold and auctioned, sponsorships, etc. We invited judges who were recognized in film, and visual and performing arts. These renowned personalities were a crowd drawer that boosted ticket sales.

I stood firm on leading and remained committed to the goal. Delightfully, parents who were once distant and uninterested came in droves; they wanted to participate and offered their rich resources towards reaching the financial goal. Financing the operetta was no longer a disruption, it was a reality. A reality that was standing room only. All tickets were sold. We landed good reviews. Our operetta yielded a considerable profit that was later donated to the school to establish it's very first Performing Arts department, where students could participate in theater arts. I was pleased to be informed that in subsequent years a fully equipped theater and auditorium was built for the school's Performing Arts Department. I was even more pleased to be informed that a school play about the evolution of the department was presented paying tribute to me as the lead character who in real life had inspired the department's formation.

AN ASSASSINATION, ANOTHER DISRUPTION

1983 was a disruptive year. The assassination of Benigno Aquino, the opposition leader to then President Marcos of the Philippines was a turning point. My husband, born to an American mother and Filipino father and himself a Filipino

American chose to immigrate the family in 1984 to the United States. For the next year, many cultural adjustments took place. The children's education took a dive from a private Catholic school to the American public school system; not so much because of academic quality or deficiencies but because of the cultural and religious adjustments that it entailed. They experienced a more liberal permissiveness that warranted a great deal of family dialogue. They were used to regimented study habits but they had to adjust to a more progressive method. Logistics in travel to school and work became a challenge. We had no driver to take us where we wanted to go so we had to to take public transportation a great deal of the time. House chores were assigned to the children since we no longer had housemaids.

I applied for my first employment in a diamond retail store, behind the desk as an office associate. I sensed some reservation on the part of the interviewer since I was a new immigrant with no local experience, so when asked why I should be hired having zero experience in retail, I responded, "because I am a woman who loves diamonds and that is going to reflect positively in my interactions with your clients". I got the entry level job, rose to become Office Manager, and later became Regional Trainer for all stores nationwide, despite an accent that was not bad but differed from my trainees. The dual roles of full time mother and a career woman was a disruption to the norm.

My Beloved Husband and His Death

My husband of 22 years died suddenly from cardiac arrest in 1988. Left with 5 children, with the oldest who was 18 and the youngest who was 7, I was afraid of the future and the unknown. By then, I was no longer doing retail work, but was working for a bankcard processor. Quite serendipitously, I was promoted to Customer Service Manager, a month before my husband's passing, with a significant increase in pay. Interviewing for the position of customer service representative was a riddle to the interviewer at the time of my application. Asked why I was interviewing for the job, given that I was in management with my retail employment, I responded, "I am interested to provide an exemplary telephone service that pleases the clients because they will feel the smile in my voice. Consequently, I see a professional growth in this."

I remember the owner and Chief Executive Office came to me one day and asked if I could take the transfer of one employee to my department. I was told that his Manager thought that he was not a match to telephone interface, clients could not understand him, and that he was of Indian descent and had a thick accent. This did not sit well with me and I agreed to take him and put him in charge of credit card fraud, if only to prove a point about discrimination. In this position, he thrived. That year, he was the company's first Employee of the Year. A day later, the owner of the company told me, "I wish I can clone ten of you."

The challenge of single handedly putting five children through school and college, feeding them, clothing them, and caring for them while I conscientiously carried a full time job required yeoman's capacities to cope. Keeping track of five, ensuring their physical safety, attending to all school requirements and activities, providing counsel when needed, and maintaining a family unit that was conducive to thriving healthily and happily were challenges that kept me on my toes 24x7 and beyond. I was also running a full division of 120 employees at work.

Such was the full impact of the 1988 disruption. Meanwhile, I was steadily climbing the professional ladder and slowly breaking the glass ceiling having moved and landed a plum position as Director of Merchant Services, for the largest credit card processing center in the United States. It was here that I overcame the myth of "only boys can land the top positions" and "women do not belong to the boys' club." I was the lone minority and the only woman in a male dominated board room during executive operational meetings. These meetings called for each department head to report on their respective areas as well as respond to questions and provide clarifications. I took extra care to ensure that my reports were supported by pertinent and accurate documentation inclusive of financial data that was critical and imperative from my post of overseeing a multi-million credit card transactional portfolio. I was the company's link to the major credit card associations of the country, the mouthpiece, and author for the company's industry compliances and regulatory issues that arose. I had to save the company from expulsion on many occasions by accurate and convincing counter responses to what were deemed to be violations, citing rules and laws by the book. The company's survival depended on my expertise and regulatory knowledge to present a defense. The pressure to gain a favorable decision and free from stiff fines in the thousands was a test of skills and will to disrupt. I was the company's designated disruptor with Visa, MasterCard, and American Express and all the other major credit card associations of the country.

I was, almost always the only department head who distributed reports and in some instances provided visual supplements. I realized that such approach gained respect from peers and confidence from my direct report. I anticipated the questions, and was ready with answers. I offered new information, innovations and qualified them to gain approval. I spoke with an accent but nobody seemed to notice. Everyone noticed, however, that I always dressed the part.

During my tenure, the company experienced a slow pace in business and needed to align with its network processor, First Data Resources, the largest in the world, in order to pioneer a change in the network's processing methods. To bypass the bureaucracy of waiting for our turn was almost impossible. Many tried but failed, many resigned to wait their turn, but I did not sit and wait. I researched the network's organizational structure known to be complex for its vast departments comprised of hundreds of employees headquartered in Omaha, Nebraska on an expansive property that looked like a campus. It would be looking for a needle in a haystack to determine who can make a decision in favor of my company. After all, this was the world's largest network processor in the world. Determined to disrupt, I found a connection. I took the next step and asked to attend the big conference of the American Banking Association where I was certain that all of the industry's players would be attending. I researched the profile of my connection, her strengths and inclinations, her family, and her interests. I sought her out, found her, and opened a conversation about my company's need. She visited, consulted, dialogued, and within short months of interaction, my company's desired system change was addressed and resolved. She became our champion within her network and we became good, personal friends. As a result, the company became the pilot for processing excellence and rocketed to become the largest and number one card processor in the United States.

I joined this company a few months after I was widowed. I applied for a none management position in Customer Service because I was not ready to take on the responsibilities in management under the circumstance of grief. It did not take long for me to observe the deficiencies and with an earnest intent for improvements; I asked to speak to the owner. I put on the table my recommendations. On the spot, I was offered the position of Customer Service Manager. During this time, the owner asked that I initiate ways to generate income within the department. A customer service fee was introduced, but implementation meant marketing the fee to the client base and initiating service methods that justified the fee. It was a laborious implementation to ensure acceptance and avoiding complaints. On the day of the kick off, the lines were normal in volume and complaints were nil, and the department began earning its keep, to the satisfaction of the owner.

In this position I employed qualified Filipino Americans. In addition, I realized that I had the authority to request that qualified Filipino immigrants were sponsored for work visas and ultimately sponsored for permanent residency. As of my final count, there were 100 Filipino Americans and Filipino immigrants who benefited from employment and sponsorship. I still get phone calls from some who say, "Yesterday I had a situation at work and I remembered what I learned from you, and I applied it. It worked! Thank you for making me a permanent resident."

Leading 120 employees who worked in four key departments with four Managers directly reporting to me was a high pressure responsibility.

Leadership by inspiration and empowerment works best for me. Putting the right combination of employees to implement a project is one of my favorite practices. Clear and consistent communication of roles, responsibilities, objectives, desired end results, accountability, periodic progress reports and reviews, and team work were elements of success. More important, is the buy-in to the concept by a cooperative team who took ownership of the task. The desired result can be attained when the leader inspires, motivates, empowers, and rewards. Recognition of a job well done provides inspiration to do better and for others to perform as well. A leader does not always have the right opinion. Listening and giving credence to meritorious opinions encourages creativity and innovation. A leader with enough humility to admit mistakes and quick enough to recognize that others are correct. Commendations from clients carry weight and deserve recognition. Continued education, staff development of staff, performance reviews delivered factually with careful thought and preparation, and well-deserved promotions are also key to successful management and leadership.

I view myself foremost as a leader with a mother's heart. Compassion without compromise of values, discipline, and policies are factors that define my leadership style.

REFLECTIONS

Most Filipina women, including myself have the gift of gab. Our English literacy and fluency sets us apart from other minorities. We understand the value of education and higher learning so we pursue it. We understand the importance of power dressing in being able to influence others to follow our lead. We are socially adept and can be thrown into the deepest conflicts based on racism and are able to counteract vitriol with grace and grit. We are a people of cultural inclinations to loyalty and service, without deprecating oneself. We are able to adapt to cultural swings. Our faith is deeply rooted giving us the moral compass to be decent in all things, and such can never be compromised. We are naturally respectable in our demeanor and decorum, manner of speech, and compassion to others. While some retain the Filipino tendencies of humility and service, this behavior is calibrated and balanced by those with stronger personality to express, dissent, and disagree while not losing the polite countenance that comes natural to us. We lead with compassion and we inspire rather than demand.

Filipina women exert influence in more ways than one. The Philippine cultural values of *bayanihan* [spirit of cooperation to achieve a goal], *pakikisama* [fellowship], and *palabra de honor* [word of honor] are inherent in Filipinas. Such values are formed through our socialization in the Philippine culture. As Filipina immigrants we continue to be able to apply these values in the workplace and in our general day to day interaction with others here in the U.S. and wherever our assignations take us in the world. These values enhance our leadership. Values that caused bewilderment in instances when my children would call and ask to speak to Mrs. Nuyda, I was asked, "Why can't your children simply say your name. Mrs. Nuyda is too formal between children and their mother." Cultural but correct.

Retirement and Morning Dew

Upon retirement, I was at the peak of my career as Executive Vice President of Client Services Division; a position next in rank to the two owners. It was also at the peak of my financial stability. This slice of my life took me to the uncharted territory of politics and community service. A sense of gratitude took me over and I felt a desire to pay forward.

When the strongest typhoon to hit land devastated the Philippines in 2013, I sympathized with the death, disruption of lives, and destruction of property. I rallied many Filipino Americans to mobilize and help those severely affected. I chaired a fundraiser that broke the myth of the limits to donations. Being an alumna of the Benedictine order of St. Scholastica's and St. Agnes, I became aware that the school in Tacloban was razed to the ground. A call to alumnae and benefactors was the order of the day. I set a high goal that we surpassed by leaps and bounds. This took a village, including the presence of an influential global Filipina, Cris Comerford, who was the crowd drawer. Many other elements were in place; an appeal to the humanity of the community, a team of committee members committed to succeed, and a community of Filipino Americans who responded positively to the call. Leadership by inspiration, with attention to detail and organization was the driving force. This advocacy earned the distinction as one that broke the myth of the limits of fundraisers, a disruption to the norm. After the dust settled, the gross yield tripled the goal for an amount that was far beyond all expectations.

Yet, I faced many distractions. I was legally bound to partner with a non-profit organization. My first choice was to partner with the highly accredited Gawad Kalinga; but we needed to iron out details. At the time, I was Chairman of the Association for the Advancement of Filipino American Arts and Culture in Los Angeles, a non-profit whose focus was the Arts. At the onset of the project, the organizational objectives did not seem to align. But upon further deliberation, it became clear that part of the FilAm Art's mission was *KAPWA* or community service. Although this delayed project mobilization, the partnership did get formed and was able to forge ahead.

During my Chairmanship at FilAm Arts, I disrupted the norm of doing business as usual by introducing a more assertive approach to fill the financial void. I dared to step out of the comfort zone to think progressively. I disrupted the status quo by challenging the board to look within its structure of competencies for improved measures. There was a renewed awakening that led to many positive changes.

Politics by definition is not my favorite preoccupation. After all, it was dirty politics that disenchanted me when the Philippines was under martial law; while we lived in the Philippines my oldest son knew of only one President, a dictator for 18 years. A revered opposition leader was gunned down brazenly. Cronyism was rampant; corruption was a way of life.

The leader in every one of us reaches a saturating point of "enough is enough". In 2010, I got involved in the tandem campaign of Benigno Aquino Jr. and Mar Roxas, candidates who were deemed honorable and incorruptible. Similarly, I have been involved in the 2016 Presidential campaign in the U.S. because I believe that voting for the right candidates is a moral responsibility.

A slice of life it is indeed. There are many more to tell but I end with a philosophy of faith and the obstinate belief that you are what you make of yourself. Your fate is dictated by you and you alone. When a door closes, a window opens. There is a rainbow at the end of a storm, a gold pot at the end of a tunnel, and one experiences the reward only when armed with tenacity not to fail, but to succeed. A leader is only as good as its followers; a follower's success is a reflection on good leadership.

As I end this chapter I reflect that morning dew is the literal meaning of my Spanish name. The Blessed Virgin appeared in the marshes of a Spanish town called Rocio in the cool early morning when dewdrops enveloped the setting. Rocio is Morning Dew. Quite remarkably, my career followed a similar path of cool and collected leadership, strong in faith that if God leads you to it, He will take you through it. I am a Filipina and I am a gift to my world.

JOHANNA MELISSA DISINI ORQUIZA

MUSICIAN & COMPOSER, WALT DISNEY STUDIOS
FWN100™ GLOBAL 2015

The Big Bang

CLANG!! THUD!!
I collapsed on the floor, landing on my right side, numb, with pain throbbing in my head. A metallic ache kept ringing in my ears. My head throbbed. I was dazed and confused.

"What just happened?" I thought to myself. The ringing did not stop. My vision seemed out of focus.

Moments earlier, I was going about my routine, chastising myself about getting my chores done as quickly as possible. I numbly raced around while listing my "to do" list in my head. I grabbed the laundry basket, marched upstairs to the master bedroom, opened and leaned over a middle drawer to tuck away clean shirts, and then, THUD.

I moved my right arm to prop myself.

"What hit me? Was it metallic? What was on the bureau?" I thought my husband had casually tossed his dirty clothes there.

"Get up." I thought to myself. I tried to move my right leg. Nothing happened.

"Get up! Get up!" I willed myself to get up again. I waited ... nothing.

"Let's try the left leg," I thought to myself. No movement with the left leg. My right leg remained unresponsive.

I started talking to myself. Calmly, unemotional, at first; then impatiently, then confused.

"Get up! Get up!" I chanted. My body would not cooperate, but I willed it to, yet nothing happened.

I lay there, helpless, and tried using my right arm to prop myself up. I lay there on my right side, with legs that could not feel, could not move, and would not co-operate. I touched my head, and I could feel a hot bump, swelling to the size of a small golf ball, and was aware of the warm temptation to fall asleep.

"No!" I thought to myself, referencing the victims of head injuries who unintentionally fell asleep and hemorrhaged to death. I forced my right hand to search for my cell phone.

"Where is it?" I started to panic, as sleep started to engulf me, and tears began to form.

"Honey! I took the dog out. Where are you?"

My husband was home.

I was rushed to the emergency room, ushered in within 15 minutes because of head trauma and lack of sensation and feeling in my legs. Seven rounds of MRI's later, they concluded I had a spinal contusion, severe spinal stenosis, meaning a back thirty years older than my actual age, and a severe concussion. That metal clang I heard? It was caused by a fire extinguisher that fell 5 feet and hit the side of my head.

I was lucky. The doctors said I could have been paralyzed.

THE SLOW STEPS: SELF-TRANSCENDENCE

Recuperating at home with my new friends, Mr. Cane and Mr. ADD (Attention Deficit Disorder), the steady hum of silence sat strangely with me while I lay in bed for weeks.

I had always worked relentlessly since my early twenties and at one point, held down two jobs while going to graduate school. Bed rest was a difficult requirement, but I surrendered to it completely. I was constrained from doing anything physical, but my greatest frustration was the restriction of not doing anything that could be mentally stimulating. My husband would leave for work, and I would sit in bed, frustrated that I could not read anything on my iPad or watch TV because they were too stimulating. Lying in bed, with nothing to do, I had the concentration of a gnat.

I spent the time staring at the swaying leaves on the trees, back and forth, back and forth, like the grass skirt of a hula dancer. Sometimes the leaves would move fast, sometimes slow; sometimes not at all. Fast, slow, not at all. Fast, slow, not at all.

Maybe that's what life is all about? Fast, slow, not at all. What is success? Fast, slow, not at all. What is a loving family? Fast, slow, not at all. What is a good relationship? When will I stop using Mr. Cane? Will my brain ever be back to normal?

Fast, slow, not at all. Will I ever walk without pain again? Fast, slow, not at all. What am I doing with my life? How did I get here?

I concluded I was just a statistic, a random probability. A majority of injuries occur at home, but I could not shake the feeling that things needed to change; things that I took for granted like the ability to write music, or working at Disney for 14 years on blockbuster movies. I had opportunities that my relatives in the Philippines would never experience, and being female in the U.S. were not being fully realized.

Inheriting Lola Nene's Determination

My grandmother, Lola Nene was a rice farm landowner from Cabiao, Nueva Ecija with barely a fifth grade education. My grandfather, the first radiologist in the Philippines thanks to a University of the Philippines scholarship at the turn of the century, died at the age of 40. He chose not to practice his specialty but returned to the province where he believed he could be the most help as a family physician.

When he passed away, he left my grandmother, who had no formal higher education, with four children to feed. My father said that at the time, education for women was not a necessity and was thought to be a wasted investment. Why educate women when they would just marry and have children? Men had a higher chance of success, so it made sense to invest in what would have the higher return.

Regardless, my Lola Nene managed to receive a good return on her four "investments." Through sheer determination, cigars, and through an apparently unorthodox means for a woman, she managed to encourage and support my dad and three uncles to become doctors and my aunt to be a nurse. All of her children immigrated to America during the U.S. health care shortage in the 1970's.

My Lola Nene was a tough nut, a smart businesswoman, and strict mother. My father would always talk about how Lola Nene would dote on me, how I was the favorite, and that as I grew older, I became the spitting image of her both physically and mentally. Ironically, she was a pianist. I knew that my generation needed to honor the sacrifices she made for my father's family.

My Vision Quest

So, as I adhered to the doctor's orders for bed rest, I started thinking, what could I do to help my family, my community, and my world? Was it even ok to have these thoughts? Are these imperialistic tendencies? That is bad. What right do I have to think I could make a difference? Am I stepping out of social bounds? Why was I not fully participating in life? Was I morally guilty because it felt like I was squandering the opportunities before me, though in reality, I was just struggling with the question of "What is enough?"

Explaining the Context of My Chosen Career

It was time to assess the situation, as I realized, I sure am lucky.

As a musician and composer working in the entertainment industry, I can tell you from 14 years of experience, Hollywood does not deal well with sexism, ageism, and racism for fear of economic or socioeconomic reprisal. Hollywood's biggest stars, including Jennifer Lawrence, Sandra Bullock, Julia Roberts, and Angelina Jolie have criticized the entertainment industry for its gender-based economic inequity. The Screen Actors Guild (SAG) has addressed this issue of female ageism by giving its members "transitioning classes" for actresses hitting the ripe age of 30; and it's not only sexism and ageism that plague Hollywood.

In 2014, of the top grossing films, only 1.9% were directed by women, 18.9% had female producers, 21% had a female lead, and 11.2% had female writers. For women film composers, it is a more sobering tale. Dr. Martha Lauzen, Executive Director of Center for the Study of Women in Television and Film published the 2015 Celluloid Ceiling report, the annual study that tracks the employment of women working on the top 250 domestic grossing films. Lauzen reported that, "Women comprised 2% of all composers working on the top 250 domestic grossing films in 2015." In 2014, it was 1 percent according to the Women's Media Center Women in Film Los Angeles

The industry's struggles for ethnic diversity, unfortunately, still include Asian caricatures of the "dragon lady," "the submissive doll," or the "nerdy friend." The sexist, ageist, and racist status quo permeate every sector of the entertainment industry. Affecting change as an Asian American female composer thus is an intensely personal quest.

The Filipina Women's Network (FWN) has helped me solidify this advocacy. I knew I was different, but before FWN, I thought it was a racial problem to be eradicated. I know my parameters are different, but my "differences" should not be viewed as a weakness, but a strength.

Balancing Expectations and My Artistic Voice

In the early stages of my career, I grappled with what was expected of me from multiple external factors; my family, my Filipino upbringing, my American workplace, Hollywood, which is its own unique beast, and my diverse group of friends. How do I resolve to balance these expectations, this advocacy, and preserve my own artistic voice?

After the accident, I tried to understand what made me happy. Happiness was such a fresh concept to think about to me that I felt like a toddler learning to walk. So, if I was thinking like a toddler, I figured, let's go for it.

What did I like to do as a child? I liked to eat bread, bacon, eggs and rice, play the piano, and play with my brother and sister. I was a fat and happy kid.

Why did that give me joy? Well, carbs produce more serotonin in the brain, bacon and eggs taste good, my brother and sister are awesome, and playing the piano allowed me to process my emotions and my world. Can I combine my wasted opportunities and happiness? Why did I feel like I was wasting time when I was working around the clock? Does my work help people? Does my work in film affect people? Should I have become a health care worker and work directly with people instead of working in entertainment?

Months passed, and my frustration grew. I returned to work, but even that had its challenges. I could not immediately execute my ideas due to the residual effects of the concussion.

Judging my Self-Worth

One night, I was scouring the web for do-it-yourself decorating tips when I came across a picture that helped change my thinking. It was a white canvas, with cursive handwriting and lyrics scrawled across the board. Desperate to stay focused on the positive, I reworked this project for myself. I was brutally honest about my insecurities. Others call them weaknesses. I see them as what makes us human and interesting.

This exercise made me more determined to understand these beautiful cracks in everybody. Then I realized, strengths and weaknesses are essentially the same, so philosophically, why do we label them as good or bad? At its core, is it the label of strength or the label of weakness, a perception based on a preconceived set of circumstances? What is considered "strength" in one environment could be a hindrance in another. The physique of a bodybuilder would be a barrier in the sport of track and field. A tall, lean, volleyball player's build, with extremely long arms would work against her as a gymnast. Good or bad. Aren't they both?

Over the course of two weeks, I compiled my favorite quotes. I bought a white canvas, a brush, acrylic paints in three shades of blue. Blue is supposed to be calming. I started to handwrite quotes that would motivate me out of my well of self-pity.

Propped against the wall in the kitchen, the board was visible and forced me to face my fears each day. I tried to handwrite the quotes evenly, but it got scrunched towards the end when I ran out of space. I am a perfectionist, so I was in a dilemma. Do I throw it out because it is imperfect? I decided not to, and that was the first lesson the board imparted.

As a child, I loved playing the piano but hated practicing so I would push my natural talent so I could be as lazy the rest of the time. I am lucky I went as far as I did in life, considering that becoming a musician was a last minute decision; an act of defiance towards my family. Luckily, I have learned the virtues of an extreme work ethic and have made up for lost time. "Do what you love. Life is too short to waste your time."

In the past, my family countered my decisions on what school I should have accepted, what profession I should have pursued, and which suitors were the most appropriate to entertain. Next lesson learned. "The past should be left in the past, or it can steal your future. Just because someone doesn't love you the way you want, doesn't mean they don't love you."

I had been working on my weaknesses and/or strengths but I still had not figured out how I could directly ease some of the frustrations I felt towards the inequity in the world.

What is exactly my place?

Physical rehabilitation forced me to accept small victories. Walking with pain or without a crutch now felt like a luxury. I learned to appreciate the little things and with the clarity of someone who had something taken away from her, I understood and embraced "Every day is a gift."

My failure in past relationships forced me to rethink how I wanted to frame exchanges in my marriage and my personal life. I became grateful, learned to accept why things did not work in the past, and how they only made my personal relationships stronger. "Live life for what tomorrow can bring and not what yesterday has taken away. Every day is a new opportunity to make new happy endings."

As the weeks went by, I was feeling more and more optimistic about the situations in front of me, even if a lot had not changed from years before. "Your life is the greatest creation you will make."

The message board helped me reframe how to interact with daily, stressful situations. It forced me to look at my failures every day. When a project would come up, I would accept it. "Opportunity is nowhere."

I knew that statistically, women do not volunteer for a project if they felt they did not have the necessary skills. I learned to embrace the challenge each project presented and worked as hard as I could, knowing I could fail; spectacularly. I embraced the possibility of failure, because what else did I have to lose? "If I want to succeed at _, I must first be bad at __."

My spectacular failures have led to spectacular victories. On my first job, I was so shy and nervous, I made stupid typing mistakes. I did not interact with the office staff as much as I should have because the Asian way is to work silently and be rewarded for your hard work. Boy, was I naive. The entertainment industry's cache is all about what is interesting about you, good or bad. I am grateful for those moments because I have learned more from failing than I have from watching.

As I practiced what I learned, I noticed an immediate change. Ultimately, the vulnerability that came with trying to be better attracted a sense of community, awe, humor, horror, distaste, and negative feedback from the people around me.

Some of them thought my refusal to gossip was because I held them in low regard, which was far from the truth. I did not want to speak ill of anyone for my own mental sanity. I tried and failed visibly, instead of doing it discretely, causing mixed reactions.

The people around me were used to never seeing any vulnerability from me; never seeing me questioning myself made me more human. I tried to be a nicer person. My actions were not predicated on their expectations so some people supported me while others who did not understand me or my stance not to engage took it as an affront to their own decisions.

As time passed, they realized it was not about them, but ultimately it was about me. Some people will congregate with others with whom they have things in common. I like to mingle with a diverse crowd and include those whose opinions do not agree with mine and thereby I could develop an understanding of how other people see the world. Next lesson. "Dream big, work hard, surround yourself with good people."

COMPOSING MUSIC

Let me tell you about my musical composer self. I have a solid grasp of the fundamentals of music, maybe in part because of the genes I inherited from my Lola Nene and in part because I do love playing the piano. I know how to combine the parts or elements of music to create a piece of music. And I have gotten very good in persuading others to my musical point of view. What else should I pursue as a musical composer leader?

Lack of Female and Filipina Composers

Do you know any female composers? We are definitely not mainstream. Here are some classical music statistics. During the 2014-2015 season, there were 21 orchestras. These 21 symphony orchestras performed more than 1,000 different pieces, in part or full, by 286 different composers for a total of almost 4,600 times.

- The average composition date of a piece performed is 1886.
- Only 9.5% of pieces performed were written since the year 2000.
- A little more than 11% of the work performed are from composers who are still living.
- Female composers account for only 1.8% of the total works performed. When looking at the 11% of the works from living composers, female composers account for only 14.8%.

During the 2014-2015 season, females accounted for only 1.8% of the works performed by symphonic orchestras.

Do you know any Filipina women classical composers, dead or alive? Of the 1.8% being played, none are Filipino, much less females. We have songwriters but Filipino classical composers are a rare breed. Germans account for more than 23% of the total pieces performed, followed by Russians at 19% and Austrians at 14%; in large part due to Mozart. American composers made up less than 11% of the pieces performed.

As a Filipina American composer working in the entertainment field, my biggest musical frustration is the lack of a popularly recognized Filipino classical concert composer. The closest we have is Nicanor Abelardo, known for his native arts songs. He lived from 1893 to 1934. Let me repeat that. He lived from 1893 to 1934.

It has been almost one hundred years since a strong, iconic, classical, Filipino composer was recognized in the concert world. By comparison, almost every Asian country has multiple LIVING classical composers who have written symphonic works played by orchestras around the world. Tan Dun, from China, Ryuichi Sakamoto from Japan, Narong Prangcharoen from Thailand are among the few. Currently, one strong Filipino contender has emerged, Nilo Alcala, choral composer from University of the Philippines.

I thought more seriously about this when I realized the recent growth in popularity of Filipina American writers in literature such as Mia Alvar (2015) and Jessica Hagedorn (2011). The literary world has wholly embraced the immigrant narrative from the Philippines. Why has the classical music community failed to do the same? Was the lack of Filipino composers never addressed within the Filipino community? The more I dug, the more I realized the answers of what constitutes Filipino music or native Filipino music led to more questions. The question was not just about the anthropological study of Filipino ethnomusicology, but encompassed bigger queries concerning immigration, colonization, assimilation, racism, and social stratification.

Lorenz (1925) in The 'Round the World Traveller: a Complete Summary of Practical Information insightfully described how Filipinos were perceived at the time Nicanor Abelardo was composing.

> Many of the characteristics of the Filipino people are very admirable, such as boundless hospitality, natural kindliness, personal cleanliness, with high degree of patriotism and desire for education. Woman is man's full social equal. The Filipino teachable and precocious, although apt to be super-ficial. He is quite artistic and very musical, every village having its own band. In Manila, grand opera is the fashion, given by Filipino artists (although many of these are predominantly Spanish), and Filipino composers have actually produced creditable operas. The Manila Constabulary Band took the second prize (the first going to Sousa) at the St. Louis World's Fair, competing with contestants from all over the United States and from other nations. The Filipinos are so passionately fond of music that one hears the sound of it from every direction—pianos, violins, mandolins, guitars, all being skillfully played, and pianolas and victrolas are everywhere in evidence. (pp. 264-265)

Please keep this all in mind while I continue.

Understanding the Challenge of Musical Art Complexities

As a Filipina grappling with cultural identity in the arts, my biggest strength is my insatiable curiosity. I feel that problem-solving skills used in mathematics, neuroscience, and science apply to the complexities of the musical arts.

Two years ago, while accompanying my mother to attend my uncle's funeral in Quezon City, I arranged to visit the music library at the University of the Philippines, Diliman. "Life is a gift. Never take it for granted."

My late uncle was a professor and secretary at the university's law school. One of the last things he did was photocopy hundreds of pages of Filipino songs to play through. As I studied these hundreds of pages, I became increasingly frustrated to see all the songs sounded like Spanish cancions or Western songs. "Not getting what you want can be a wonderful stroke of LUCK."

Basically, Filipino music, according to the collection of the U.P. library, constituted of sound-like parodies of Spanish love ballads, tangos, American ragtime, or jazz. Why had the library overlooked indigenous native songs, when Beethoven, Mozart, Brahms, Bartok, Liszt, and Chopin celebrated their folk songs and incorporated them in the classical music canon. Why did the Filipino classical composers not do the same thing?

Should I have gone to a fiesta instead to truly understand Filipino music? Would that have given me a more inclusive representation of the music from a country fraught with cultural disparities? How did a nation that is a haven to so many religions, tribes, and languages have an entire written musical identity distilled into something so elementary? It is as if you heard a song on the radio, then someone wrote it out for a piano and singer; and those songs were the exemplification of a nation's musical identity. It is not only grossly unfair and oversimplified; the questions within the framework of Western classical music were not even asked.

I then realized the musical infrastructure itself had not supported or encouraged young talented musicians to travel this classical Western symphonic path, even though the country had been ruled by Spain for more than three hundred years. Even Latin American countries, once colonized by Spain, have classical, orchestral composers today. You do not have to look far; Gustavo Dudamel, a native of Venezuela and conductor of the Los Angeles Philharmonic Orchestra, is a product of this Spanish classical infrastructure.

The valuation of music in Filipino society was not the primary problem. Almost every Filipino I know can do something musical; it's the primary way of interacting besides food. Even in the smallest villages, people sing and play the guitar and the piano. Many untrained singers have perfect pitch and do not even realize it. When cruise ships in the mid-twentieth century needed Western music players, they did not go to China and Japan. They sought performers from the Philippines because they could feel and play Western music. And that was when I immediately realized the nature of the issue.

The problem was lack of opportunity and resources in the Philippines. Talented musicians were getting exported out of the country the same way Filipino workers in healthcare, engineering, service, and labor are today. With additional research in conjunction with one of the lead scholars in Filipino and U.S. 20th century history, René Alexander Orquiza, Jr., a Harvard professor who happens to be my little brother, I realized that these questions needed to be asked. Dare we say, they had never been asked critically before.

SYMPHONIC TRANSCRIPTIONS OF FILIPINO MUSIC:
MY LEADERSHIP PATH

I am currently working on symphonic transcriptions of native Filipino music, composed, arranged, and translated for symphonic orchestra. Most metropolitan orchestras feature either an Asian composer on their programming or an Asian cultural celebration. In Los Angeles, the Hollywood Bowl programmed a Filipino Musical Night that consisted of choir, vocalists, and pop groups. The Hollywood Bowl houses two orchestras: the Los Angeles Philharmonic and the Hollywood Bowl Orchestra. The question here did not concern resources with the venue. There were simply no iconic classical Filipino composers whose music they could play.

Oh dear. What did I get myself into? My push for data could incapacitate me if I think about the probability for success.

How do I push change through when I know that I can be my worst enemy?

How do you push change through when most people don't know what to make of you?

How do you change the dialogue?

How do you change the parameters?

I am not here to tell you the way you can affect change. Every one of these FWN awardees in this book brings their own talents, personalities, and strengths to the Filipina narrative. I am here to help you question how you personally can affect change. What is it about YOU that is unique? What has happened to you that has made you stronger? What has happened to your mother, your sister, your grandmother, your aunt, your best friend that has helped form the decisions you have made? As an artist, I grapple with these questions every day. Emotions are universal and integral to good storytelling in movies and television.

What is it about you that can ignite happiness, insight, love, and optimism in others? You need to protect that spark with everything you have. Do not let others tell you that you need to change. Only you know what is unique to you. Often-times, it may be a seemingly insurmountable event that made you the person you are. Celebrate it. Do not let that fire burn out. That experience, that hurt, that scar is what will give you the strength to affect change. You can affect change every day by being the best person you can be.

You do not need to be rich, intelligent, famous, or well connected. You can be a service worker and affect change. You can be a CEO and affect change. You can be a nurse and affect change. You can be a high school student and affect change. But, the only way you will have the strength to stand up to the status quo is to know and celebrate what is unique about you.

You can be quiet; you can be loud. You can be aggressive or you can be easy going. There is only one you, and you owe it to yourself, to your family, to your community, and to others to be the best, kindest, strongest, fairest, person you can be.

When others see that you have the strength to question and follow through, whether you are a CEO or a domestic worker, others around you will question the status quo. You will affect change because YOU ARE CHANGE.

An unexpected event led me to create my message board, which led me to question the lack of Filipina composers, which led me to my advocacy, which now leads me to chase my dreams.

The big bang does not have to be literal. Go figure!

MARIA SANTOS-GREAVES

President, Surrey Hearing Care Inc.
FWN100™ Global 2015

Learning Management from the Most Unlikely

I am neither an academician nor a corporate communicator. I am an entrepreneur at heart and a manager by practice. Hence, as a leader ipso facto, I would like to share a few vignettes in my life which played a key role to where I am now. I conclude my vignettes with lessons in life which in many ways have given me the competencies to sustain and grow my business. In my case, my personal life has and will always be integral to my professional life. As a business owner, it has to be, for the boundary between the two is blurred.

The Embarrassing "D": A Stepping Stone

Up to now, I have only mentioned this to close friends. It was a chapter in my life that surprisingly led to where I am now. I was suffering from depression – which in the Philippines was never really called that. Call it what you may, but my family decided to tell my friends and relatives I had "mood swings". I was confined in the hospital several times and with some complications, too. My depression was triggered by my direct selling business. A lot of people owed me money and never paid me back. I was bankrupt, worrying non-stop, and had anxiety attacks because I was trying to solve my problem by myself. I felt so horrible at that time.

I remember waking up one morning and feeling so dizzy thinking my left ear was clogged. I could not hear as usual on that side. It turned out I had a high frequency loss. Fortunately, I can still get by because my right ear stayed normal. It was quite ironic that here I was, working in a hearing clinic, and now, I had become part of the world of patients I was dealing with. We never really found out the cause. Was it a medication or a virus?

I stopped working for a year and then I came and worked for another year and asked for a leave for absence for two months to visit my sister in Canada. I never came back. But that is another story.

This bout with depression taught me that life presents itself with situations you never wished; but without those moments of quietness, you would not have time to think of how you want your life to be. Take the time to be by yourself accepting the rollercoaster of life. This is a lesson I would apply again and again in the rollercoaster of business. In Facebook, somebody shared this quote, "God will often use Discomfort to move you into your Destiny."

Depression can be debilitating. Accept it and let it flow albeit gradually. Share your concerns with a trusted one; the mere act of unraveling your soul is cathartic and helps in the healing process.

I have closed this chapter of my life and moved on.

A NEWBIE IN CANADA: FACING MY SELF-WORTH

You can say it was a fluke, a God-orchestrated fluke. Although I had my passport with me, I really was just accompanying my parents to the Canadian embassy in Manila. My parents were applying for a visa to visit my sister in Vancouver. Right there and then on the spot, without any other documentation I told my parents after they got their visas I would try to get one. This was before 9/11. And to my amazement, I got my stamp, flew to Canada, and found a new destiny.

With liberal immigration policies, I was able to become an immigrant in the land of maple syrup, freezing weather, and with a preference for British English spelling. Armed with a Pharmacy degree from Centro Escolar University in Manila, and as an Audiometrist in the Philippines, I was eager to work and use my skills and abilities. Little did I realize, just as many other immigrants would surprisingly find out, that in Canada, a degree obtained outside Canada is viewed as under par compared to their degrees. It is really perplexing considering their own school graduates make as many serious mistakes as graduates of schools elsewhere. And in my observation non-Canadian school degree holders are very qualified if not superior to those who finished their education in Canada.

But earn I must, so I started working at a Dollar Store, then sold Registered Education Savings Plans of Canada, and then worked at a Call Center for three years, way before most Call Centers migrated to the Philippines and India. It was at this time I met my ex-husband. But this is another story.

Later I became an audiometric technician at Fraser Health and eventually landed as a receptionist in various hearing clinics. Hearing clinics prefer to hire front-desk personnel who can do multiple tasks. That was when I thought of starting my own clinic not only for financial security but also because of my personal desire to provide compassionate and complete quality care to those longing to hear better. I saw how profit-driven some clinics were and I resolved that if I had my own, the humanity would be just as relevant as profit.

More than a decade later, I have grown my company from one to four clinics. My business success was recognized when I was honored as one of Canada's Top 25 Immigrants in 2015. This is a peoples' choice award that recognizes inspirational immigrants to Canada, who have achieved success and made a positive difference in Canada. The award is an acknowledgement by the Canadian public of the need for positive role models who will inspire and motivate other immigrants, as well as other Canadians.

What did I learn from those days when I was a store clerk and reporting to others? It does not matter what kind of work you do as long as it is respectable. You have to able to learn to adjust to the situation. You need to be flexible. I did not mind starting from the bottom. And though there were times when I pitied myself, doing my best prepared me for bigger things to come.

Occasionally I fill in as a receptionist in my clinics. One's position should not be used as an excuse for refusing any tasks necessary to keep the business running. Pride isolates and deafens you to the real needs of the business.

STARTING SURREY HEARING CARE: WHAT DID IT TAKE?

I never dreamt of opening my own clinic., much less expected it to become a reality.

I had been working for another hearing clinic for four years when it dawned on me to open my own clinic. I always wanted the best for the client but if your boss does not feel the same it becomes difficult to provide the best kind of service. It was all about making money to them.

I started with nothing as I did not have much savings in the bank. I did not have an MBA nor did I have a business plan. All I had to start my own clinic were my courage, determination, and passion. *And I had my networks of people.*

Vikki Mackay, a Registered Hearing Instrument Specialist, agreed to be a partner and share in the capitalization. Jim Renshaw, owner of AIM Instrumentation helped us to get started by loaning us the equipment and booths. AIM Instrumentation was our biggest supporter. I made arrangements to pay them monthly. To this day, Vikki and Jim continue to be supportive of me.

In August 2009, we opened the doors of Surrey Hearing Care's first clinic. You can check us out at http://www.surreyhearingcare.com/.

I did not borrow in the beginning. Later, the bank approved a CAD$20,000 limit for my Visa card and a CAD$10,000 line of credit which we still have. My only investments were my skills and confidence to succeed.

After five months, I bought out Vikki for CAD$50,000 to become sole owner of Surrey Hearing Care. I only paid Vikki CAD$20,000 upfront and then CAD$500.00 every 15th of the month for the balance of the CAD$30,000. Vikki still works for Surrey Hearing Care.

My parents always supported me in this endeavor. My father was always near tears every time he saw patients streaming into the clinic. In 2016, we opened a fourth branch. My goal is to have six, but who knows?

People asked me, "how did you do it?" My answer: "I was not afraid to take the risk. You cannot be an entrepreneur if you want to play it safe."

I know I sound spiritual but I believe because of my faith in God and my true desire to be of service, God has opened "doors and windows". In books on entrepreneurship, God is often out of the picture. But I could never have done it without my faith. It has not been smooth sailing, but I am above water, and for that I am grateful.

A MOTHER'S COMMUNICATION STRATEGY: SUBDUING THE OTHER

On March 5th, 2015, I was scheduled to fly that evening with my son, my sister, her husband, and their kids to the Philippines. It was a Spring Break trip long in the planning. Every day had a set schedule. The second night would be a dinner buffet with my nephews and nieces in Manila. And there would be the trip to the fabled island of Boracay. My eighth-grade son was growing up fast, and I wanted to have as much family time with him before he left the nest.

But that morning, I got a call informing me my mother had collapsed in the bathroom. She was rushed to the hospital in an ambulance. As I walked towards the lobby desk, I calmly asked where I can see my mom. "Emergency Unit." There she was lying in bed, gasping for breath in her oxygen mask, eyes closed, head bobbing non-stop. She looked like she was going soon, if not in a few days.

"Ma, I'm here" I whispered close to her ear. "I am not leaving you. I am not flying anymore."

We waited all day and night for my mom to be tested and monitored. Earlier, my dad was asked to wait back in their home. My mom was moved up to the

Intensive Care Unit with her own room. Nurses and doctors were hovering around her. Half an hour later a young man approached me and said it's a matter of waiting to see how my mom would respond to the medication over the next four to five hours. At close to midnight, it was only her and me. Nothing but the whir of medical equipment could be heard. My mom was very still with her oxygen mask and vials of liquids dripping into her veins; I sat in a corner and gazed upon her face. I began recalling those years of growing up, going home from school, seeing my mom prepare a meal for the family with my Dad waiting at the head of the table to be served! Well, I married a Canadian man who fortunately did not expect such royal treatment.

My mother is alive and kicking to this day.

One of the things I observed about my mom was her patience; a virtue that we all know is hard to practice but necessary in facing the vicissitudes of life. My dad was a driven man and that is a trait I got from him. He was a direct, no-nonsense General Manager for country-wide operations in the Philippines and this behavior and attitude carried over to his home life. But my mom was the opposite; calm and often responding with that very potent silence which would severely irk my dad.

In management, silence and patience can be powerful tools for dealing with human resources issues. We all make mistakes and different people have different paces of learning and adjusting, but once they get it, it is worth the wait. My mother, in her quiet steady manner always succeeded in calming my highly excitable and verbal father. Yes, there are many times when you need to talk and clarify matters, but often timing is the key. And when you are willing to wait, you get better results. Think again, and again before acting.

MARRIAGE AND HR: DO THEY RELATE?

Years before I founded Surrey Hearing Care, I was a married woman. I was on my way to my lawyer with my sister when her husband phoned me that my son Sebastian (Seb), age four at that time, had hit his head on the corner of the wall while playing with his cousin Abigail. We rushed home and emergency paramedics were already there. My child's head was wrapped with strips of gauze wet with very dark red blood.

We were advised to bring Seb to a general practitioner (GP). The doctor was unable to stitch the cut in Seb's head, and to my shock, he referred us to a hospital emergency ward. I thought what level of medical care do we have? And this is a province of Canada that makes it extremely difficult for graduates of non-

Canadian medical schools to get a license and practice.

My son's Dad, Phil (not real name) , my ex-husband arrived and declared that I did not know how to take care of our child. Phil threatened to acquire sole custody of our son, and that he would take Seb to his home on the spot. The thought of losing my son purged the air from my lungs. In tears, I saw a police car at the parking lot of the hospital. The officers mediated and advised my ex that it would be best for me, as Seb's mother, to bring him home.

I was worried. I did not want to be separated from my son. Many thoughts ran through my mind, including returning to the Philippines with Seb and starting life there again. But I realized it would not be fair to Seb to take him away from his home country. And of course, taking him would cause even more problems as it will be perceived as kidnapping my own son.

I did not work for a year and filed a leave of absence due to stress. It was a good time to bond with my son but every Thursday my ex-husband would take Seb to his house until Sunday. It did not matter that my son resisted and was in tears. I could not do anything because that was part of our custody agreement. So I had to abide and be strong.

Because of my divorce, I considered myself a failure. Despite the hard work of trying to save my four-year marriage, there were moments of great anger and anguish. I ran away numerous times but kept returning with the hope that I could make it work. The sixth time was the last time. I left. I never came back.

You will really never know a person until you live together. And the same principle applies to work. You will only see the capability and character of an employee or a colleague when you both share the water cooler. That is why, in hiring, I make it a point to have several interviews and conversations. Knowing the technical complexities of the job is not enough. Values and shared world views do matter. A bit tricky to delve into with legal human resources restrictions, but nonetheless there is still room to investigate.

Also, there are cases when it is best to terminate employment; but I believe this should be handled with compassion and care in order for both parties to transition positively. Just like I experienced with my transition from being married to being single again.

STRESS MANAGEMENT: MY SON TRAINED ME

As a single mom, I had to deal with "boy" issues that I had not personally experienced growing up as a girl. Something new to me was when my now 15-year-old son Sebastian recently shared that he has not had his first kiss. I find it so cute.

His father wanted to name him "Ric" but I did not like it. We finally agreed on "Sebastian" after the red crab character in Disney's *The Little Mermaid* film.

I realized that my son is becoming a man. He loves to talk. He openly appreciates all my cooking. And occasionally he would surprise me with his own version of cooking Filipino cuisine, like *Sinigang*. Although he does not speak Filipino, unlike many migrant kids, my son loves being called a Filipino. And he does try to learn and speak the language. However, like any other teen and like a crab, a teenager can pinch with their logic. I think the best way to handle a teen is to go with the flow. Any kid will have some issues and concerns just like when Seb almost failed seventh-grade math. It would take numerous paragraphs for my parenting advice. Suffice to say, I have been able to develop a good relationship with my son. He is so proud of my achievements. He always praises me. He always says he loves me. What more can I ask as a mother?

He says he does not feel like going to his dad anymore but I always encourage him to see his dad even once a while.

Sebastian said that he is interested to pursue in college my field of audiology. What did I do right?

Is there anything I can relate in being a parent to being a manager? Just go with the flow. Stress can only be as stressful as you allow it to be. It is your choice, a daily choice, a difficult but possible shift in perspective.

Not Quite "Finally"

It may sound as a business strategy—our clinics giving back to the community through free hearing testing via our company's mobile hearing clinic van. We drive our hearing clinic vans all over the Lower Mainland, and provide information lectures at a number of community activities. It is a business strategy. But I do not lose sight of the fact that with marketing we must blend humanity, imparting warmth as we genuinely care for others and their hearing needs.

Owning and managing a business is a composite of vignettes – a dynamic osmosis of learning, gaining competencies, and finding inspiration from the most unlikely and informal sources. Yet when you think of it, it does make sense that a mom, a dad, a friend, a husband or an ex, and a child can train us to be better leaders. Actually, I think everyone can be a leader. The world teaches us the paragon of leadership is someone who commands, who stands six feet tall literally or figuratively. Yet, I am only 4 four feet and 10 inches. But paragons are paradigms waiting to be challenged and subject to change. My advice to you: *Go for it!*

✳

BENEL SE-LIBAN, CPA
with
CRIS B. LIBAN

PARTNER, VASQUEZ AND COMPANY, LLP
FWN100™ 2011

A Life That Matters

My leadership is centered in faith, powered by my will and determination to follow God's plan for me. Although I have been a reluctant leader, I became the first Filipino-American partner of Vasquez and Company LLP. I am also the Founder and first President of the International Society of Filipinos in Finance and Accounting (ISFFA). My activism is the result of realizing that the Filipino-American needs to be empowered and emboldened to succeed in their adopted land. Going against the perceived norms, I have challenged everyone I make contact with through my workplace, ISFFA, and my local and global community to make a difference in society by effecting change in oneself through their discovery of spirituality and purpose.

This chapter will provide insight into family and school influences on my upbringing, my college and career choices, and my brave move to America to seek independence, identity, and career. I married the man of my dreams, Cris, and am raising with him a loving and smart son, JP. Cris and JP are significant in my life. I will share how I discovered my purpose and passion to choose a life that matters.

AN EPIPHANY: CHOOSING A LIFE THAT MATTERS

My husband, Cris, and I had always wanted to have two children. After getting married in 1998 and enjoying almost two years of honeymoon as husband and wife, we were ready to be parents. We were ecstatic when Jean Paul (JP) was born in 2000. Everything went well with JP and we planned for our second child. The exciting news came for us in 2003 that I was again pregnant. We were looking forward to have another beautiful baby. Two months later we lost our baby through a miscarriage. We were very devastated but we learned to accept our misfortune and moved on.

A burning desire to have another child made us try again around 2006. Not too long afterwards, we found out that I was pregnant again. Because of the painful memories, this part of the story is best told by Cris:

> I was awakened by a howling cry one chilly morning two months later. Benel was bleeding. This brought back horrific memories of our first loss. I remember my heart trying to come out of my chest while methodically bringing my wife, our unborn, and I to the hospital. I remember praying to God to save my baby. I had no expectations, though. We have been through this before. However painful, I needed to take control of the situation.
>
> His will be done!
>
> The doctor came back with a diagnosis after a few hours of tests and procedures. Instead of a baby, Benel had cancerous cells in her uterus. We were shocked and confused. While Benel was showing symptoms of pregnancy, she was actually not pregnant. There was no baby to begin with but instead there was an abnormal tissue growth or mole in the uterus, a consequence of a genetic error during the fertilization process. Our dream of having a second child was demolished. I felt so helpless and sad while Benel dealt bravely with her emotional and physical agony. After the medical procedure to remove and monitor the growth in her uterus, she went to a weekly follow up procedure of monitoring her Human Chorionic Gonadotropin (hCG) hormone levels to ensure no recurrence of the growth. Absence of hCG hormone levels is good. Two more months through this process, the doctor gave us another shocking news that they detected new growth in her uterus. This was a highly risky growth that presented a cancerous-type threat to other parts of the body. The diagnosis involved chemotherapy treatment to aggressively retard the new growth. Benel was emotionally devastated, confused, and scared. I had to be strong for her; but candidly, I left it to Divine intervention to give us strength in overcoming our life's biggest challenge. I looked up and prayed that JP will grow-up with a healthy mom.
>
> There is a God.

At the conclusion of our trip to the Cedar Sinai Hospital oncologist a few days later, my uncle, Quintin Garcia recommended that we attend a healing service conducted by Father Fernando Suarez, a traveling Filipino healing priest who happened to be in Los Angeles around that time. We had no expectations when we went to Fr. Suarez's healing service at the Our Lady of the Miraculous Medal Catholic Church in Montebello, CA. We cannot recall much of the details of that evening except for an image of a few hundred people packed inside the church; and many more outside waiting to get in. It was an outpouring of support for an unknown healing priest at that time in Los Angeles.

As the priest began his healing service, we saw people who had entered the church in wheelchairs or crutches, stand up straight after being touched by Fr. Suarez and walk immediately without aid. We also saw people who claimed to have a hard time hearing suddenly hear. People were also able to suddenly raise their previously immobile arms. I asked Cris to pick up on the story:

> I remember seeing Fr. Suarez approach us as soon as we got to the front of the line, placing his hand on our foreheads, asking what we were there for, and suddenly all three of us; JP, Benel, and I falling into a trancelike state. Benel woke up from that trance wailing. JP and I fell to the floor as well, "slain", but woke up feeling renewed.

A week after the healing service, we went back to Cedar Sinai Hospital for a number of tests. While waiting for the chemotherapy prep, the oncologist excitedly surprised us with news that my hCG levels had gone down to almost negative. She canceled the chemotherapy order that day. Stunned but ecstatic over this news, we started ambling to the door to go home, crying. We knew in our hearts that we, as a family had experienced God's miracle through Fr. Suarez. My weekly follow-up tests continued.

After over a year of testing, the oncologist felt certain that there was nothing more to monitor. I had been healed of my cancer. No words can describe our joy that day; manifest of God's mercy and love for us.

The preceding events were the tipping point in my spiritual and leadership journey. These and the following reflections have been my eureka moments; and contributed to my life's reawakening; we are all here on earth for a reason. For that, I am grateful for being enlightened to how I should lead my life. My husband Cris tells me:

> Benel, you are an inspiration to your family and the Filipino-American community, you continually aspire to be a devout Catholic, a leader of substance, a loving daughter, a faithful wife, a wonderful mother, a loyal friend, and a proud Filipino. These are what matter most.

Learning Leadership Lessons from Family

I was born in Legazpi City, Albay, Philippines, under the shadow of the majestic, almost perfect cone of Mayon Volcano. The Bicol Region consists of six provinces that is part of Luzon Island, the largest island in the Philippines.

My parents had illustrious careers as hard-working lawyers representing others who could not otherwise defend themselves. Benel, my name is the contraction of my parents' names, Benito and Nellie Se. Dad ran for political office often, becoming Vice-Mayor of Legazpi at one time, but concentrated on his legal practice most of his life. Later in his career, he became a Regional Trial Judge in Manila where he tried drug cases.

Be Positive

Mom followed a different career path. Always on the go, she was determined to be the penultimate career government employee and be at the top of her game. While serving as a judge, she would bring me to different places within the Bicol Region; and while a Commissioner of Settlement of Land Problems, she took me to many parts of the Philippines. She took me on trips within the Bicol Region and throughout the Philippines. Upon reflection, my leadership evolved along with the opportunities to join my mom in these expeditions; allowing me to explore the country in depth, understand the cultural and regional differences among the Filipino people, and of course taste the delicious food served to us. Seeing and hearing other people's problems from my mom's point of view, I was being shaped to be a most tolerant and patient person. What I learned from these trips was that to fight for your rights is to fight for justice.

Value Education

As the Se children we heard an often used but never a cliché statement typical of a Filipino household, "*Anak, wala kaming kayamanan. Mag-aral kayong mabuti. Yan lang ang maipamamana namin sa inyo.* [Children, we are not rich. Study really hard. That is the only inheritance we can give you]." As a child I did not quite understand why my parents kept on saying this. It eventually became an annoying mantra. Years later, I sat down with my maternal *Lola* [grandmother] and she told me the backstory about these statements. My maternal *Lolo* [grandfather] was once a *Fiscal* [Prosecutor] and used to have the material wealth to live and raise his family comfortably. Unfortunately, when my Lolo became blind, unscrupulous relatives tricked him into signing agreements that transferred all his assets to them.

He lost everything. He and his family became destitute. However, my Lolo had a vast network of friends who helped him support the family, specifically in the area of education and career. He was able to have all of his children (including Mom finish law school and become successful professionals. From then on, I never questioned my parents on the value of education and building network.

There were only six children in the Se household: Marilou, Cielo, Ben, Joy, Victor, and myself. The Se household was often hyperextended with at least a dozen more children (the closest of which are Caroline and Susan who are orphaned cousins on my maternal side) who had become part of the family, earning our abode the endearing nickname of *Hospicio de San Benito* (a play on the name of a local Philippine Orphanage Hospicio de San Lorenzo). The house on Guevara St. in Legazpi City was the meeting place of all the Se children, cousins, and those who aspired to be cousins. In addition, my parents also provided financial assistance to all of our *yaya*s [all purpose nannies] who had aspiration to go to school and finish college.

I enjoyed my family's love for music, dance, games, and family reunions. My mother made sure that we were enrolled either in a piano or dance class. During family gatherings and reunion, the entire clan enjoyed the festivities through singing, dancing, playing musical instruments, and games.

Build Character

Our family had a very unique and amusing problem. When there were these many people vying for food during dinner, you had to be quick; otherwise you would not get the best part of the dish served. For example, most of the family wanted the *bangus* [milkfish] belly. When the fried milkfish was served, one needed to run, and run fast to get their share. Being late at the dinner table meant not only missing out on the choicest portion, the belly, but sometimes missing out on the fish altogether. Being a middle child with modest athletic abilities, I remember I always got there midway and never really experienced losing out. Family meals at the Se household were always served like a feast and were filled with laughter and storytelling. Like travelling around the Philippines with Mom, I never saw these experiences as formal training that were shaping my leadership skills. Looking back, these friendly competitions to get the choicest parts of the *bangus* were lessons on character building: compete well, justify what is right, but still be caring of others. Thus, love of life, family, and travel; and traits of team work, patience, compassion, and generosity started early within family life.

ST. AGNES ACADEMY AND LIFELONG FRIENDSHIPS

St. Agnes Academy, the oldest Catholic school in Legazpi, Albay provided primary, elementary, and high school education for all of us, Se children. In those days, many of the students from the other parts of the Bicol Region would begin their elementary education in their neighborhoods and later would either commute or move to Legazpi to attend high school at St. Agnes Academy.

Build Long-Lasting Relationships

As a lifelong Agnesian, I was exposed from the beginning to the Benedictine principle of *Ora et Labora* [prayer and work]. But unlike others who took life more seriously, my approach was different. I always got along with everyone. Maybe that's why my classmates voted for me as their class Mayor.

The glamorous or powerful title of the Class Mayor did not mean much. As Mayor of the class, I would be the eyes and ears of the teachers, class representative in activities and events planning, and figurehead class "leader". I remember sharing this with Cris: Titles did not go to my head, nor change my outlook with my classmates. If at all, I became more close to them. I was perceived as different in many ways at school. However, I always made things look easy and cool. I always created pizazz for what I did; including excitement on something that might otherwise be boring. I continue to think that because I made things look fun all the time, I was able to attract others to follow. I was not conscious about this. I just did this as part of my day. I was as carefree as you can get in high school. I did care a lot about everyone though.

Persevere and Be Resilient

I was often told, "Intellectual superiority connotes leadership potential." Before I had finished Kindergarten, I was promoted to the first grade at St. Agnes Academy where I was one of the youngest students. My experience skipping a grade was humbling, however, for rather than being at the top of my class during the first quarter of the following school year, I received failing grades in many of my classes. Mom had a "head scratcher" because I was supposed to have superior intellect. But compared to the people who were one to two years older than me, and one year ahead in education, I was no match. I could have just given up. I did not. My panicked mom immediately helped me make adjustments to my study habits and after a few more tests, I was able to catch up with all of my classmates. Mom and I both persevered. We were resilient and the effort completely paid off over the long-term. It was such a proud and rewarding moment for Mom and Dad when I graduated with honors both in elementary and high school.

Sustain Relationships

I continue to enjoy my special friendships with my high school classmates and friends. I have had memorable reunions and traveled with them over the years. It was a pleasure to be nominated by my classmates to be their representative as one of the 100 Most Outstanding Agnesians, of which I was selected, during the 100 Year Anniversary celebration of St. Agnes Academy in 2012.

EARLY CAREER

Although I grew up in a family of lawyers, my mom wanted me to become a doctor. But the sight of blood continues to gross me out immediately. If not lawyer or medical doctor, the next best thing to study was accounting. I became a reluctant accountant. Being the first batch to experience De La Salle University's trimester program, our cohort was subjected to a fast paced curriculum. It was a tough three years. Accounting, was a hard degree program and stressed me out. I reminded myself to simply survive the subjects. Focus, focus, focus.

Do Not Give Up

Graduating from one of the top university's in the Philippines was no easy feat. But getting hired by the accounting firm SGV was an almost impossibility for many accounting graduates. While I did not consider myself the best in my class, nor the brightest, my grades were more than decent. Somehow SGV recruiters saw the promise that coming from De La Salle would produce a great accountant or auditor one day.

I loved SGV and the reputation that came with it, but, candidly, I did not really connect with my first assignment. As a young CPA in the Philippines, my stereotype of a college graduate was to be able to dress well, and honestly, be in a really comfortable working environment. My first job as a manufacturing sector auditor was none of that. We were sent to an industrial location, in not so glamorous jeans, and performed inventory counts. Ok. I lived through a sheltered life in Bicol and Manila, enjoyed the life of a middle class family, and here I was counting parts. Hello. All of this education and accolades, and here I was shabby but not chic. I almost gave up. I did not. Maybe because I did not know any better or I was simply afraid to do something else.

Then again, why stir the pot.

Everything was going for me, right? What else could I ask for? I had great strong, loving and giving parents. They were able to provide for whatever I wanted. I get shuttled around with a driver. We had our yaya who helped us all the time. I had loving friends and family; and a life that is set and defined by a degree from one of the finest Philippine universities, and of course a Certified Public Accounting license.

GOING TO AMERICA

The unexpected call for America came one day from my sister Marilou. "Be, bakit hindi mo i-try dito sa US? Wala naming mawawala sa iyo kung i-try mo. Kahit two years lang." [Be, why don't you try it out here in the United States? It will be to your benefit if you do it. Two years would be a good start.]

I hesitatingly booked my flight and went ahead to try it in the U.S. for two years. Nothing can be more exciting for a 21-year old carefree spirit than to have an opportunity to have a good time and simply try it out in a foreign land.

Path to Independence

It was a rocky start from the beginning. I lived with my sister and brother-in-law who were raising two young sons. My 21-year old self did not know how to do laundry nor cook my own meals. It was tempting to go back to my comfortable life in the Philippines. Going around town, forget it. I did not have anyone to talk to outside of my circle of family and friends. I was very shy and was afraid to talk to strangers.

My sister and her family lived in the Mid-Wilshire, a densely populated residential neighborhood in the central region of Los Angeles, California. Mid-Wilshire is notable as one of the most diverse neighborhoods in Los Angeles. Not much has changed since I moved there in 1998. It is still a largely minority community, gateway for many immigrants seeking a new future in the United States. My lifestyle there was far different from the lifestyle I was used to in the Philippines. It was also dramatically different than my perceptions of America. This made me seriously reconsider a future in my adopted country. I had a choice. Adapt or else go back home to the Philippines as a "failure."

Weighing My Options

Please do not get me wrong. The word failure is a very relative term. As Filipinos, we are known to have a sense of *kapwa* [togetherness], a distinction from the western concept of self-reliance and independence. Kapwa in its most fundamental sense is a Tagalog word that covers the concepts of both "self" and "others," which describes the Filipino's sense of being a person in relation to the other. We actually help one another. Your issue is my issue.

In this context, visiting America and moving to America are two different things. Living in America required dramatic changes. This experience gave me insight into the best and worst of both worlds. Contrasting Western and Eastern lifestyles helped me realize that a fuller life was available outside the Philippine bubble. I came to realize that there are people outside the Philippines whose lives were enriched because of their struggles in life. Going back to the Philippines would have been a personal failure. I did not want to go back not having been able to accomplish something for myself.

Making Adjustments

While studying for my California CPA license, I decided to accept a job in a small accounting firm in Mid-Wilshire. It required a big adjustment moving from a huge accounting firm in the Philippines to a small firm with only six to eight employees. While it was a humbling experience; hard work, sacrifice, and perseverance were values that motivated me. At that time, I did not have a work life balance. I worked long hours during the week and studied long hours during weekends.

After passing my California CPA license, I found a job as Senior Auditor at Miller and Company, a CPA firm in Santa Monica; and later on was promoted to manager. I enjoyed my new job because of the additional compensation, but also for being able to work in one of the "coolest" places in Los Angeles. Since the office is located near the Third St. Promenade and the Santa Monica beach, it was an easy access to various places to eat, shop, and play. I fondly remember admiring the sunsets at the beach, enjoying either rollerblading at the beach strand or working out at the gym on weekdays, and then hanging out with friends on weekends. I also made sure that I took vacations and planned travel trips with families or friends within the U.S. or abroad. I planted permanent roots in Los Angeles as a first time homeowner in Century City. Finally, I learned to balance work and home life.

The most impactful career shift was being hired by Vasquez and Company's

Managing Partner, Gilbert Vasquez. Initially, I started as an Audit Manager, was promoted to Principal, and finally to Partner. Currently, I am also the Non-profit Practice Leader of the firm. I am proud to have contributed to the consistent growth of the firm's revenues and establishing a culture of family and work/life balance. I think that the firm understood the value of my marketing skills and ability to build long-term relationships. I attend various networking events, including being a member of City Club LA, a premier Business Club. Through the mentorship of my managing partner and exposure to non-profit organizations, I have understood the value of making a difference through personal change and empowerment. Inspirational mentoring moments with Carmelita and Pat O'Neill further enhanced my community involvement.

The Birth of ISFFA: A Vision

It started out as a balmy Lake Arrowhead, CA Sunday morning in the Spring of 2006. Gathered were a group of young but successful Filipino-American finance and accounting professionals. We decided to come together to begin a journey of hope. No one before us had thought this day was possible.

Build on our Heritage

Filipinos have distinguished ourselves by being humble and hard-working. But successful as we were, there was something missing. We shared a commitment to do what is right, not just for us, but for our community. It was time to become more explicit about having a life that matters.

Break Barriers

Still fresh in my mind was a sense of frustration from an experience many months earlier. That frustration was rooted in my inability to convince others at another setting, of the need to get out of our stereotype as simply hard working service professionals. Among the things of concern were (a) the need to be able to speak on an issue and come up with consensus; (b) the ability to speak publicly in any setting; (c) the creation of a pipeline of future leaders in the accounting and finance field; (d) ensuring access to mentors; (e) building a solid network; and (f) articulating a vision for the Filipino-American in the United States. The need to organize was not an obvious shortcoming. The Filipino-American community despite its reputation as one of the most economically successful people in this country was struggling for representation, to find our voice, and speak out our aspirations. We are a people who integrate well and become invisible even as we see other cultures become politically strong. We were not perceived to be politically significant because no one clearly and loudly heard our issues. We generally do not advocate for ourselves. While the group recognized that a few Filipino-Americans had overcome this issue, at Lake Arrowhead, we were determined to break this last barrier of success.

Reinvent. Learn from Others

Over the traditional Filipino breakfast of *tuyo* [dried salted herring], *champorado* [sweet rice with chocolate], garlic fried rice, *tocino* [sweet pork] and *longaniza* [sweet chorizo], we thought about a strategy to empower the Filipino-American finance and accounting leaders of tomorrow. This was not a simple task. My mentor Gilbert Vasquez provided a template of where we could start. As one of the founders of the Association of Latino Professionals for America (formerly Association of Latino Professionals in Finance and Accounting), he told me about how they were able to rally the Latino finance and accounting community to find their own voice.

Our Filipino-American heritage is not very different from theirs. The 17 of us at Lake Arrowhead were from many parts of the Philippines, or had grown up in Filipino families elsewhere in the world. We had grown up according to the traditions of our Philippine roots. All 17 of these young Filipino and Filipino-American professionals from varying backgrounds actually came to a consensus on what to do and how to go about developing a unified concept of empowerment.

The International Society of Filipinos in Finance and Accounting (ISFFA) was born, originally called the International Society of Young Filipino Accountants (ISYFA). It is a California non-profit public benefit corporation whose primary goal is to assist, educate, train and mentor emerging professionals, both domestically as well as globally. Since we started the meeting with a traditional Filipino breakfast, another important lesson might very well be: First, we eat. Then, we talk.

Embrace Change

It is a known fact that many immigrants who arrive in the United States have an extremely difficult time assimilating into the American way of life; both professionally and socially. Common difficulties experienced include speech, knowledge of business development, access to medical and dental care, the U.S. banking system, lifestyle, personal practices, and cultural differences. These obstacles oftentimes prove overwhelming to an individual with no help or mentor to assist them. Personal experiences from many such individuals; including many of the founding group members demonstrated how such initial barriers left deep scars of insecurity and uncertainty that became roadblocks to professional development and integration into their new home.

Most newly arrived individuals find themselves stretched financially due to the big gap in the currency exchange rates and the comparatively very high cost of living in the United States. Such individuals often have extreme difficulty in finding jobs; not only in their chosen field of study or experience, but in virtually any profession. This creates additional difficulties in providing immediate support for their families.

Beginning with a single chapter in Los Angeles, ISFFA has now grown to chapters in Los Angeles, New York, Chicago, and San Francisco. The organization has contemplated expansion to other parts of the United States and the Philippines. In 10 years, ISFFA has become the premier organization where successful professionals in finance and accounting meet, partner, and grow.

LOVES OF MY LIFE

Several years of looking for Mr. Right in the United States had not prepared me for what was coming in the Fall of 1997. After almost three weeks of touring Europe with my parents and my cousin Caroline, my mom asked about my plans of getting married someday. I just turned 30, heartbroken from a recent relationship and suffering from *OMS, Old Maid Syndrome*[1].

"*Be, anong plano mo?*" [Be, what is your plan?]" Mom nervously asked. I told my mom that if Mr. Right will come and sweep me off my feet, I will definitely get married. If not, I am happy being single. I would rather be single than be pressured and be married to the wrong guy.

Faith, Family, and Education were the three criteria that would take my heart away. A belief in one God and all the things that come with that. Having a relationship with his parents and ability to accept and develop a relationship with my family. Having the background and education that he is proud of and that I can be proud of as well. Faith, Family, and Education. In that order.

In life as well as in business, decisiveness is key when it comes to issues that

---

[1] "I was never really sick nor am I implying here that staying single is negative. In fact the opposite was true. I was comfortable with my life, I have a successful career, but just never had the luck to meet the man of my dreams. It is not for lack of trying. At my age at that time, I have a set criteria on who I want to spend the rest of my intimate life with. The people I was meeting did not come close to those criteria."

would involve other people's lives. I have persevered long. I would not settle for someone less than what I actually wanted.

I remember Cris coming into that reception room during Nella Zipagang's wedding reception. I was swept away. There he was, a doctoral student at UCLA, very handsome, with an uncanny ability to be able to talk about anything. I wondered how such a brilliant mind could also be most knowledgeable about mundane things.

The short three-month courtship led to a civil marriage that was followed by a big wedding in the Philippines. We are celebrating our 18th wedding anniversary in 2016.

Cris eventually finished his doctorate degree in environmental science and engineering while I pursued a professional career eventually breaking the glass ceiling as a Partner at Vasquez and Company, LLP. Once again, I asked Cris to pick up on the story.

> Benel has been a very supportive wife to my professional life. Throughout my career, I have held many prestigious and influential positons of authority, both in private and public office; the most significant of which was a recent appointment as an Advisor for the US Environmental Protection Agency (USEPA) Administrator. I am blessed to have Benel in my life. She has been my inspiration: **Influence does not matter if one does not effect a difference in other people's lives**. It's an interesting situation to be in when you live and breathe with someone who has seamlessly and silently accomplished much.

> Children do not come with instructions when they are born. In many ways, one just needs to wing it. We tried to read through those baby books while Benel was pregnant, but as soon as JP was born, all of those ideas and solutions went out the window with the bath water. Parenthood brings with it certain character building experiences.

> Benel has been a wonderful, loving and caring mother to JP. She believes in showering JP with love and experiences than material things. If his time permits, she enrolled JP in music, arts and sports classes. She loves planning all of JP's birthday parties and our family outings and travels. Despite her hectic career, she makes sure that she is present in all his important school activities such Awards and Sports events, Halloween, Christmas and other school events. She is also involved with the Mother's Guild Club at Loyola High School, the oldest (and probably the best darn) high school in Southern California.

> We are typical American parents to JP. We juggle family life with professional life and we also recognize the value for having to make time for a child. There is no such thing as a perfect parent, and one does not know either how their children would turn out to be when they grow up. Benel praises her parents: "As I take inspiration from my parent's success, it is my hope that we

would also turn out to be great parents."

JP has always been a quick study. He spoke his first "mama" and "papa" words when he was four months old. He first stood up in a hotel in Cancun when he was 10 months old. He was very astute in figuring out solutions to puzzles in nursery school. He discovered in elementary school that an "A" beside the name of a certain school subject is very good. JP passes by the dozens of Cris's elementary, high school, and college medals hung in front of his bedroom door every day. He discovered the value of receiving trophy's and medals throughout middle school, eventually graduating as the most decorated student and athlete when he finished middle school at St. Jerome School. In Loyola High School, he continues to excel in academics while still looking for his place in the football and shotput athletic teams. He has been selected to participate in the Los Angeles Mayoral Youth Council and is on his way to one day becoming an Eagle Scout in the Boy Scouts of America Troop 915.

We have never imposed on our son to be great. We simply advise him to compete against himself all the time. Greatness will come not for oneself, but with one's activities for the service of others. He is growing to be a Man for Others.

What Matters Most?

Soon after I was cured of cancer, I received a random e-mail from a friend who shared Michael Josephson's "What Will Matter?" poem. This poem provided inspiration and helped transform my outlook on life. I choose to live a life with meaning; a life that matters.

Michael Josephson's poem catalyzed my paradigm shift. I began to think very hard on what my role should be for the rest of my life. How can I make a difference? How will I wield influence and share resources to change the course of someone's life? My husband Cris offers this summary assessment:

> It has been remarkable and inspiring for me to witness Benel's transformation as a reluctant leader; and in fact, she often says that she never imagined she would be a founder of something much less an organization that would grow to be one of the premier Filipino-American organizations of its kind. But her life's journey has not always been like this. While growing up, there were instances of leadership at school and within her circle of friends; but again, never a conscious effort to actually learn leadership skills. She just made things fun and evolved as a leader, organically. I am glad that Benel has written this story about her leadership inspirations. Doing this with her made us look back from where we came from, what we have done, and what we as a family have accomplished. We have accomplished a lot but there is more to be done.

Unlike many of her colleagues, Benel lived a relatively normal uneventful life until approximately ten years ago when personal tragedies and professional frustrations in our personal lives and our civic engagements started turning our life around.

I do not think I have changed from who I was, the little girl from Legazpi, Albay. I am still the happy person, carefree, and always making things look fun. People get attracted to fun people; and I exemplify that. What is different now though is my ability to put things in perspective and the realization that when one is slighted and humiliated wrongly; one needs to fight back. My aspiration for those who read this story is not to impress them with the number of acronyms after my name nor the number of zeros in my financial statement; but in how others who follow these simple leadership lessons in turn could make transformative change in themselves and their communities. This multiplier effect is unique; stemming from an ability to provide hope, inspiration, and a template for those who seek success guided by a strong faith and belief. Choosing that life is what matters to me; and hopefully to you.

Leadership 101: Building Legacy

My husband and I have been blessed with God given talents and resources to do more for our community. As immigrants, Cris and I had an opportunity to reflect on the lifestyle we developed as independent Filipino-Americans in Los Angeles in contrast to the life we lived in the Philippines. Below is a summary of leadership competencies based on my life experience that I want so share with my son JP and with other chidren.

1. **Faith.** The cornerstone of my life is a belief that I was born for a reason and the belief that my God does not bring me life's challenges that I cannot solve.

2. **Vision.** Show others what you want to accomplish. Without clear vision others will get confused.

3. **Positive Attitude All The Time.** Frustration is one of the biggest enemies of success. I need to look beyond the present and move on no matter what.

4. **Passion.** As boring to some people as accounting maybe, and as boring some people think accountants are, I bring passion to my work and use it as a means to make a difference in other's lives.

5. **Communication.** Nothing can be more damaging to an individual or an activity than not being able to fully communicate what one wants or does not want.

6. **Be an Example for Others.** Integrity is key in any endeavor. Integrity creates credibility as well as an ability to multiply the common good I am preaching.

7. **Listen to Other People's Ideas.** Forming an opinion does not necessarily have to rely on your wisdom or experience. Valuing other opinions and ideas should be looked at and considered, no matter how absurd their views may appear at the moment.

8. **Reinvent from Others' Examples. Have A Mentor.** I learned fast that I had to reinvent myself contemporaneous with my move to the United States, and along the way found people whose life experiences I can learn from.

9. **Humble.** I listen well and understand what others' say in relation to what I believe in. I practice this sense of humility by admitting my faults.

10. **Strategic.** I form alliances with others to help me reinforce my weaknesses. I recognize the weak links and reduce the negativity and influences of such weak links.

11. **Innovative.** There is not one solution to a problem. If what you anticipate does not work, there is probably another better, more rational way to address the problem or issue.

12. **Fearless.** Life is short. We cannot have a perfect solution to an imperfect problem. You have to make a decision and stick with it.

13. **Not afraid of change.** Heraclitus once said "The only thing that is constant is change." Be bold in facing the unknown.

14. **Tenacity. Perseverance.** I never gave up on anyone or anything. I stay the course until I get what I need to get.

15. **Building relationships.** Not one individual is less important than the other. Everyone you meet is God's creation.

16. **Balance Everything.** Cris and I have lived a balanced life throughout our careers, and have shared with JP great cultural experiences through our travels. Exercise, eat well, get educated, interact, work for a living, and enjoy good simple food and wine. Not necessarily in that order.

May you all live a life that matters!

LETTER TO MY SON JP AND TO OTHER CHILDREN

First to JP.

Son, your dad and I have been privileged to be your parents and we hope you are grateful to God for being born in this family. There are billions of other opportunities out there but by some stroke of fate, you ended up being a Liban. We have worked hard to give you a good life and a great life foundation. We hope that you will make use of these skills in the years to come. You are at an age where you will soon make big decisions. Where to go to college, what course to take, what career to go into, who to marry, how many kids to have, and many other things that we can only hope to share with you during our twilight years. We hope we have prepared you well and for you to independently discover how to become a leader of your community and of your nation. We did our best, and now you are ready to fly on your own.

Finally, to other children.

I hope that my life story has given you inspiration. The future of our land is in your hands. You need to know how to experience being a child. Be adventurous. There is more to life than academics and computer games. Take in all the possibilities. Believe in yourself. Believe in God, respect your parents, the pursuit of education should be your life priority. Believe in yourself. Always tell the truth.

DOLLY PANGAN SPECHT

Owner, Perfect Plus Professional Support
FWN100™ U.S. 2009

Servant Leader

While thinking of what to write, what to discuss, what to share, my husband, Mike, tried to help me with ideas. In a sea of suggestions, one struck out. He said, "First, you break all the rules." It was from a book he was reading *First, Break All The Rules: What The World's Greatest Managers Do Differently* by Buckingham and Coffman (1999).

From this title he reminded me of all the times I have broken rules, and as a consequence made a difference.

First, Break All The Rules

When my daughter Michaela, our first born, started Kindergarten in 1992, the Catholic school she enrolled in did not wear uniforms. In fact, in the entire Archdiocese of Portland, it was the only Catholic school not in uniforms. Immediately volunteering into the parent association organization, I found myself very involved, offering my professional administrative services for share hours, a parochial requirement. When I proposed uniforms, the entire administration and school board laughed and said that my idea was preposterous, and that the school was not interested. Of course I challenged that rule and offered to take it to the entire school body for a vote. What I thought was a simple procedure turned out to be a very trying one, one that involved more research than I expected, and generated antagonism with hate mail that I had never encountered before. I stood my ground, used my own children as models for the sample uniform, and ran the entire uniform campaign. To make the challenge even more difficult, the school board wanted sixty percent approval, not even a simple majority rule. Of course I did not accomplish this on my own, but my perseverance won over some parent leaders and I can say that the uniform worn by the children of St. Anthony School in Tigard, Oregon is of my doing.

SAVING THE OUTDOOR SCHOOL
AND ALL THINGS EDUCATIONAL

Several years ago, I walked into the Oregon State Capitol as a volunteer for the Asian Pacific American Network of Oregon (APANO). Although I did not do very much for this organization except represent our Filipino community, I participated during a Legislative Advocacy Day at the State Capitol. It was on this day that we encountered Senator Ginny Burdick. Much to my surprise, she greeted me with "I remember you, you almost single-handedly saved the Outdoor School program from being cut out of Tigard school district's curriculum." And then she proceeded to talk about how I rallied parents and sponsors to keep the program alive and taking the issue as far as I could. Senator Burdick referred to the time when I was the vice president of Fowler Middle School Parent Support Organization. The outdoor school program was such an important issue for me personally that I was willing to fight for it and by our meeting I had already forgotten all about it. We even recalled that the humor and irony to this was that I fought for the program because I hated camping. Outdoor school in the curriculum was the only way my children were going to experience the exploration of nature.

While working as a parent volunteer throughout my kids academic life, I have encountered many experiences that have pushed me to do more, and mostly stemmed out for solving my own issue. Another example is the student supplies program I created. When I was a young student, I found school supplies shopping to be very exciting. When I became a parent, I learned that there had to be more thought put into the exercise so as to save money and find the best deals for my three children. Because I found good discounts in bulk-buying, I offered to buy supplies for other parents in my children's classes. This effort grew to become an entire school supplies program providing complete pre-packaged needs for every grade level, at a very discounted price. It became such a successful fundraiser and service program that a company decided to commercialize the system.

As a volunteer, I always felt the gratitude of others for what I do. As a volunteer, I have experienced over and over again the pleasure of giving instead of receiving. As a volunteer I discovered that many are inspired when time, talent and treasure are shared generously and freely.

It was during this time of school volunteer work that I discovered my knack for fundraising. Our parochial school had an annual auction held at our school gym, and was quite small and basic. During the early 1990s, school auctions were fellowship activities which raised funds. Equipped with my administrative expertise, I found much to contribute and do. I was so successful in raising the level of production and presentation, and also funds, I began to get hired by other schools. I have been credited with the development of auction programs that are widely used today. Our efforts allowed us to build a middle school, a library, and a social hall. Hands-on meant that I literally assembled, with my own hands, and power tools of course, close to 100 student desks! I instigated work parties among parents so we could all make a contribution to our school while developing life-long friendships among us. Many of these friends, and the elementary school principal were present our daughter's wedding, 22 years later in 2014.

Volunteer work has opened many doors for me. Aside from giving me the opportunity to meet and mingle with people from all walks of life, it has always been very gratifying to be among individuals with passion and dedication. As a volunteer, I was most complimented when the principal of our kids school made room for me in the building, giving me my own office and workspace when she recognized the value of having me at school fulltime. When it was time for her to move to a different school, she even offered me a paid position, as she knew I would not have any motivation to volunteer at her new organization.

My Income-Generating Endeavors

One of the greatest blessings of my life, so far, is that I have not had to work. Life has always been easy for me. Yet, I was first among my friends to do so. During a time when the prevailing cultural stereotype was that only students who needed to work actually worked, I started earning money by assisting a friend in her new job putting together catalogs for conventions. Then McDonald's, new to the Philippines at that time did something I consider revolutionary. They actively recruited young lads and ladies from exclusive schools to work their stores in affluent areas. I was hired to help in the opening of Store #4 in Makati, and not to flip burgers, but to be on the activities and marketing team, in charge mainly of socializing with customers and hosting parties. What a gig! I only worked there for a year, but a significant year in that I was on duty when the news of the assassination of Benigno Aquino, Jr. broke, and there was chaos in the restaurant. But I digress...

While at McDonalds, an executive from San Miguel Corporation offered me a job in their public relations department. At first I rejected the offer since I already had two sisters and three brothers working for the conglomerate from which our father had retired. I knew for a fact that I there would be comparisons as my father had set high standards. However, the offer was too good to pass. It was there that I met my husband and my life was suddenly changed.

Married and relocated to Southern California I had an opportunity for reinvention. A job was offered to me there, too. It was only when we moved to Oregon that I looked for a job for the first time in my life. I was only 25, and now a mother of two. I still really did not need to work, but having no social circle in our new city, I decided working would be the best networking opportunity. My mother lived with us anyway, so childcare was not a concern.

In 1988 I found Portland, Oregon to be unfamiliar with Filipinos and our skill set. I kept running into almost prejudicial inquiries during job interviews, as there was no such thing as political incorrectness at that time. Not too keen on my choices, I decided to try a temp service and because my organizational, communication, and typing skills were exemplary, yes, I typed, not keyboarded, 130 words accurately per minute, opportunities for work were abundant. During every temp job I was offered a permanent position. I finally took one at a secretarial service company. They offered me the opportunity to learn in one setting about varied businesses. When I left the secretarial service company, pregnant with our last child, some of my favorite clients put together a package that set me up in my own business, Perfect Plus Professional Support. The name was a play on a criticism made by my previous employer, who once told me "the problem with you is that you don't recognize things when they're good enough. For you, things always need to be perfect plus!"

Perfect Plus Professional Support kept me busy for more than 20 years. My clients all told me that I was great because I always came across as happy and loving the service that I provided. I was joyful in what I did because I had the freedom to choose which jobs I would do. In all of those jobs I had the flexibility of time, since they were all project based. In the beginning, one client even gave me the use of an executive suite for a year, rent-free. Another client gave me a computer, another a printer, and most importantly, they allowed me to bring my baby to everything.

For over 20 years, I received income from things I truly enjoyed doing. That was my measure of success.

BECAUSE I LOVE, I SERVE.

In 2004, my Assumption High School batch 1979 celebrated our jubilee year. In Assumption, tradition dictates that silver jubilarians host the homecoming activities in the month of October. By then I was the president of the Fowler Middle School Parents Association in Tigard. This year involved extensive bi-coastal, trans-Pacific volunteer work via emails and teleconferences.

Activities in both Assumption, Manila and Fowler, Tigard provided such enlightening lessons in volunteerism. Volunteer activity here in the U.S. is such an everyday natural thing to do. It was not true where I came from.

One of my best friends, Vicky Salvador, wrote a song that says "I've been loved, and I've loved in return, and it's this that I want you to learn: to respond to that call and say, because I love, I serve." This has become an anthem of sorts for Assumption girls, myself included. Another saying is "to whom much is given, much is expected." I live by that religiously, no pun intended.

In 2006, after a Catholic Mass where I was serving, a St. Clare parishioner approached me and asked. "Are you Filipina?" When I said yes the next question was "Are you from Assumption?" Surprised and excited by her question I replied, "Yes, are you?" She said no, but invited me to coffee later. Right off the bat we clicked, and she interrogated me about my non-involvement in the Filipino community. I told her I was very busy as it was with all my other volunteer work. She tried to talk me into stepping into a leadership within the Filipino community, which I firmly declined. At the end of our visit, she gave up saying, "Assumptionista ka nga!" ["You're an Assumption girl, alright!"] That statement challenged my very core, and I was determined to represent the very best of my alma mater!

I requested a task and was asked to chair a fundraiser for Gawad-Kalinga (GK) [to give care] Oregon, then just newly organized. We produced a well-attended fundraising concert which successfully financed the building of thirty GK-Oregon homes in Tarlac and Camarines Sur provinces in the Philippines. The overwhelming feeling of grace enraptured me during and after that experience. I even made it back to the Philippines to actively participate in a GK Build in 2007, and since then I have sponsored a volunteer team to work and participate in GK challenges.

In 2007, after the GK homes were built, another challenge was offered. I was tasked with fundraising for The Dambana, the Filipino Shrine at The Grotto, which is the National Sanctuary of Our Lady of Sorrows in Portland, Oregon. It is a legacy for all Filipinos that will remain long after I am gone. It brings me joy knowing I had something to do with that. There is no plaque, but I know that it is there because I helped.

There were more and more opportunities for involvement in the Filipino community, I asked myself why had I avoided engagement with my *kababayan* for more than 20 years? I think part of the answer was that I enjoyed doing things, accomplishing tasks by my very own merit, and not because of who I was by affinity. For all of my growing up years, I rebelled against the labels I had been assigned.

I was the granddaughter of national hero Epifanio de los Santos, the daughter of Manuel Pangan of San Miguel Corporation, and the sister of popular comedian Chiquito. I come from an accomplished family. For as long as I can remember I wanted to break out and be on my own, and this led me to my life in America. That said, I want to put it on record that I did not marry to come to America. I chose my husband because, above all else, he was the only one who offered me love without all the attached labels, and without even understanding what the labels were.

In 2010 I served as the president of the Filipino American National Historical Society of Oregon, the Chapter One of FANHS. During my tenure I co-wrote the book *Filipinos in the Willamette Valley*. This is a pictorial account of the migration and development of the Filipino community in Oregon. It is the 11th volume in a series of *Filipinos in...* titles all over the United States printed by Arcadia Publishing.

I recognize my accomplishments as projects that sometimes involved significant heartache, intrigue, and disappointments; and were always born out of sacrifice and lots of love; but that in the end produced long lasting results.

"LOVE NEVER SAYS: I HAVE DONE ENOUGH!"
– SAINT MARIE EUGENIE OF JESUS

Since I moved to the United States, my only connection to my previous life has been my association with my alma mater, Assumption College. Assumption is a Catholic institution founded in France by St. Marie Eugenie of Jesus. The campus I attended was established in 1958 at the exclusive enclave of San Lorenzo Village in Makati. Many critics have said we were just a finishing school, but our education stressed critical intelligence, thoughtful citizenship and compassionate service.

As the youngest child, and the only Assumption girl in my family, I did not share with my elder sisters any school affinities. Given that my closest sister is eight years my senior, it is understandable that we had very little in common, except our dress and shoe sizes. I instead developed a lot of other sisterly relationships in school. One of the best things about going to Catholic convent schools is that we were forced upon each other since we were together pretty much from Kindergarten through the rest of our academic life, and in my case, all through college. I spent a significant amount of my life with my friends from school, much more than with my family. It is therefore an understatement to say that Assumption has influenced my life.

In Assumption I was not an exceptional student. I belonged to an honors class, but was not counted among them. My saving grace, I believe, was my sense of humor. I like to believe that I get along with others based on shared laughter.

I have been told on more than one occasion that I am one of those with infectious joy.

In 2011, at the 10th Assumption Alumnae Association Abroad's (AAAA) Triennial, I volunteered to host the next gathering in Portland, even though there was not a local alumnae chapter. I was motivated by my drive to serve. Beginning January 2014, eight months prior to the event I began to overcome often very high hurdles. Many doubted my capability of putting this together and so reservations did not come in on schedule. I had minimal funding so I made a personal financial commitment to make all the bookings and vendor arrangements. That was understandable because there is no bulk of alumnae in the state of Oregon, therefore attendees would all have to travel in.

Through it all I was steadfast in my faith and conviction that I was doing this as a service to all. It was my conviction that I would be guided by the spirit of our Mother Foundress, St. Marie Eugenie of Jesus. I had very little encouragement, but those who supported me were strong and steadfast in pushing me forward. I was extremely grateful for a handful of elder alumnae who provided me moral support throughout the process, embodying what the true Assumption spirit is all about. I had the endorsement and most importantly, the prayers of Assumption nuns the world over. That, in and of itself, was the grace and driving force.

Our event succeeded famously, for those in attendance had come from afar and walked away with their spirits filled with renewed vigor and devotion. From that event sprung a commitment to have annual retreats. The First Annual Assumption Retreat, held in Philadelphia in September 2015, occurred during the first US Papal Visit of Pope Francis. It was a wonderful gathering of over 200 alumnae who traveled and joined the millions of faithful Catholics in all the Papal activities in Philadelphia.

AAAA is committed to giving back to our alma mater by supporting the Missions of the Assumption. Additionally, wherever there is a chapter, it is also an objective to make a significant impact in the local community, for where we are planted, we bloom. As an Assumption woman, there will always be a voice inside whispering "Love never says: I've done enough!"

Be the Difference.

When I was in high school, I had a favorite sweatshirt with a silkscreen of a row of penguins, and one of them was in a Hawaiian shirt. I loved the shirt and the message that it delivered. Even when watching Sesame Street, one of my favorite segments was "one of these things is not like the other...."

I have never felt the need to conform. I was big on tweaking the norm. I am a graduate of Psychology. My original intent was to become a Psychiatrist but changed my mind when I had my unfinished Clinical Psychology homework in hand, and realized I preferred to party. Realizing that a profession in the medical field involved endless study, I simply worked enough to graduate with decent grades. I slid through my entire academic life in the upper part of all my classes, but never worked hard enough to top it. At that time, that was one of the ways I enacted being different.

After graduation, I swore off reading books. This was an intentional and different decision. I read a lot, but not books. I read journals, magazines, signs, newspapers, and newsletters. But books, I stayed away from. This was just my way of being different. I am so determined to live each present moment that I seek to learn from people, in person, instead.

Be the difference is the general maxim of my life. From my marriage to how we raised our children, we made an extra effort to be different. Circumstance led to our children spending their pre-school winter months in the Philippines. My mother who was widowed a month prior to my wedding lived with us from my honeymoon in 1986 to 2012. My mother living with us was a concept foreign to all my husband's circle of family and friends. I was the first Filipina they had ever known. Thirty years later in a climate of diversity, my family is still the only Filipino family they know.

From California to Oregon our lives were very "white," much like the TV shows I used to watch about American life. We were very *Wonder Years* for a while, and then *Knots Landing*, but not at all *Modern Family*. I had easily assimilated into my western life, bringing to that life only my Catholic faith tradition. Our children do not speak Tagalog, although they used to come home with heavy accents, depending on the yaya [nanny] assigned to them. By the time they entered school, they were the only Fil-Ams in all their classes, in all their grade levels. Only then I decided that to be different, I would start to instill Filipino values in them.

One of these values is respect for elders. This was very important to me because I found that to be most lacking in American life. I did not allow our children to call adults by their first names as I made it clear to them that people who are older have lived a much longer life to deserve the respect of the young. Therefore, my kids grew up calling our adult friends uncles and aunts, or acquaintances Miss and Mister, but using first names. In effect, these adults have appreciated this value and have grown to be our extended families. Now my children introduce friends as "this is my Uncle so-and-so, not by blood, but by respect." In fact, even as an adult myself, I cannot call decade-older people by their first names.

Another important value is hospitality, which fits in with service. Filipino hospitality is extraordinary in that we make sacrifices to make others feel welcome. It is our great ability to put others first. It is by putting others first that my children have grown to be very welcoming and inclusive, sensitive to making sure that nobody is left out.

As a non-practicing psychologist, I made conscious and deliberate effort to apply my education within my family by conducting group dynamics and counseling style meetings as soon as they were able to voice out their opinions and accept others. We had family conferences.

We were different all right. As adults my kids openly discuss with others how skewed I was in raising them, but that everything we did has made them the well-rounded, decent humans they are today. Our children's views are consolation enough for me, but additional affirmation has come from others who always compliment us on them.

Now, Just be Appropriate.

I find that as I have gotten older I now make sure that I stay appropriate even while being different. Appropriate is a big word in my life, and I find it a very difficult one apply.

Every day, everywhere, I come across inappropriate things. We live in a world that is all about disclosure to the point of too much information. Manners are sacrificed for rights, and there is a general state of mean-ness. Our world is in a global state of knowing and connection. It not only seems that there are cameras everywhere, there ARE cameras everywhere. We are all being watched, and we all need to be appropriate.

So what now?

I have learned that we live in a world of busy-ness, where we forget to stop and wonder and cannot find time to just sit and absorb and share happiness. I want to always effect infectious joy simply by serving, simply by sharing, and most importantly, simply by laughing.

I had a most wonderful friend who died of cancer many years ago. During her last year, we spent the time together almost daily, reviewing her life, living the rest of it as best she can, and planning her exit. She taught me so much about living. She was an atheist, but hands-down the kindest person I had ever known. She was a teacher. She noticed once that I kept buying bookmarkers, but do not read books. One day she gave me one that read the words of Martin Luther King, Jr.: "I may not do great things, but I can do small things in a great way."

I also read on another bookmarker the words of Gandhi: "The best way to find yourself is to lose yourself in the service of others." I now know who I am, with the labels that I claim for myself, and not dictated by others.

I am a servant leader.

Disrupting
the
Status Quo

AURORA ABELLA AUSTRIACO

PRESIDENT AND CEO, AUSTRIACO AND ASSOCIATES, LTD.
FWN100™ GLOBAL 2015

Being A Filipina Litigator
in a Sea of Dark Blue Suits

'What's A Nice Girl Like You A'doin in a Place Like This?' Sound familiar? It should. It's a quote from the Cheshire cat from Alice in Wonderland. The funny part is that I literally have been asked this classic question many times over albeit in different iterations.

I remember early on in my career as a young litigation attorney I showed up in court and appeared before a judge on a contested matter.I stepped up before the Judge when my case was called and opposing counsel stood next to me. He introduced himself but before I could even say a word, the Judge looked at me and said in a loud voice, enough for all the lawyers in the courtroom to hear, "I don't want any paralegal in my courtroom. You (pointing to me) get on the phone and call the attorney handling this case!" I have never been so embarrassed in my life and all I wanted to do was crawl under a rock, but I had a split second decision to make. Do I take this insult and leave or do I make a stand and make myself heard? I stayed and when the judge finally finished talking, I said in a loud, confident but respectful way "Your honor, I AM THE LAWYER. There's no one else to call." Then there was a long deafening silence in the courtroom. The room was full of dark blue pin striped suits; all white male lawyers who I could sense were just staring at what was going on. I watched the Judge's reaction; his jaw dropped and he was speechless. The Judge finally spoke in a profusely apologetic way and said "Counsel, I am so sorry for referring to you as a paralegal. I did not realize that you were a lawyer, please accept my apologies." I accepted the apology and then proceeded with my argument. After the hearing, the Judge asked if he could talk to me and opposing counsel. The Judge apologized again for his statement. The ending to that story is that the Judge became a good friend and to this day has become one of my closest confidantes. He did say that my speaking up was a catalyst for him to understand the unconscious bias he had against Asians that he never knew he had. Prior to me, he had not seen any female Asian litigation attorneys before in his courtroom. Remember, this was in 1990 when there were not that many Asian lawyers, let alone Filipina litigation attorneys. He also stated later on that my professional reaction to his statement impressed him and caused him pause to really think about his biases.

The point of the story is that I could have taken the easy route. I could have turned around and left the courtroom to avoid further humiliation but I decided not to. I decided to break the "silent minority myth" and spoke up to correct a wrong and I am glad I did. As Filipinas, we should not be afraid to speak our mind especially when it is warranted. When we do not voice our opinions because we are afraid of the reaction, or of what people would think of us, or for fear of ruffling feathers; this becomes detrimental. So my advice is...Be heard, be loud in a very professional way but do it when you have something valuable to say.

Why Write this Chapter?

First of all, I was asked to do it and it's truly an honor for me to do so. Second, I am always asked questions like: What does it take to be successful in the U.S.? How does a Filipina who emigrated to the U.S. when she was eighteen overcome many obstacles and become a successful litigation lawyer in a very male dominated field? Be the first Asian President in its 140-year history of one of the largest and most elite bar association in the world, the Chicago Bar Association? Be the first woman and first Asian President of the Illinois Real Estate Lawyer's Association? Be the first Asian to be appointed by an Illinois Governor to the Illinois Courts Commission? Be on the board of numerous Not for Profit organizations and yet manage to have a beautiful family? How does a Filipina who came to the U.S. at eighteen, twenty three years later be on the board of the one of the largest privately owned corporations in the U.S.? How does a Filipina who came to the U.S. at eighteen, thirty three years later be the CEO of a privately owned subsidiary of one of the largest privately owned corporations in the U.S.? How does she become the first on so many fronts? What advice can you give to other Filipinas? These are only some of the questions I have been asked over the years. And my answer is a constant: you succeed by taking risks versus avoiding risks; by speaking out and being heard; by getting out of your comfort zone and taking on challenges; by finding mentors and sponsors to champion you and your cause; by sticking to your priorities; by pursuing your passion and by making a difference; and most of all, by respecting and loving your family and friends. I have been asked to share my life experiences that have been game changers for me, professionally and personally, in the hopes that someone reading this may learn from my experiences. So here goes.

UNDERSTANDING MY PRIORITIES

I mentioned earlier that I came to the U.S. when I was eighteen and that was in 1983. What I did not tell you was that I am from a family of eight, 6 girls and 2 boys. My Mom was a nurse and my Dad was a salesman in the Philippines. My parents barely made both ends meet especially with eight kids. I remember my sisters and I walking 3 miles each way, in the morning and in the afternoon, in blistering 95-100 degree temperature every day to go to school because we could not afford to take public transportation. I remember having apportioned food for dinner because food was limited and what you were served was all you could have. I remember that having soft drinks, Coca Cola in particular, was a special treat because we could not afford it all the time. I remember not having "store bought" gifts every Christmas and "handmade" gifts were all we got but I also remember having the best Christmas celebrations every year with family. I also remember how important our family dinners were every night, chaotic but very fun as we were all together. I also remember going to church with the family every Sunday, rain or shine and then stopping by our favorite candy store after church. Honestly, I looked forward to going to church not because of church but because of the special treat afterwards!

Because we were not well off, times were very tough. But my parents were very smart and realized that they would not be able to send us to college if they stayed in the Philippines. So my Mom petitioned to come to the U.S. and back in 1973, there was a huge need for nurses. My Mom came to the U.S. first, then my Dad and then my older siblings next. Because of the strict immigration laws, my parents petitioned us one by one since the whole family could not go all at one time. It took over ten years before my two sisters and I were finally approved to come to the U.S. to rejoin the rest of our family in Chicago. Imagine that! Ten years without your children and only seeing them once a year. One does not realize how much of a sacrifice that was until you have your own children. Now that I am a parent, I realized the sacrifice that my parents endured just so they could give us a better life. I am truly so indebted to my parents, Pat and Jun Abella who both passed away in 2014. Without their vision, sacrifice, and love; who knows where my siblings and I would be now?Thanks Mom and Dad—I am forever grateful!

First, Family

Ingrained from childhood, family has been and will always be a priority for me. This is how my parents raised us and certainly this is how my husband, Dr. Jerome Austriaco and I are raising our two daughters, Danielle and Isabelle. Family comes first and everything else follows. The family values I learned from childhood are hopefully the family values we are instilling in Danielle and Isabelle. Our daughters are our driver for why we do the things that we do. We get involved in our community so that when they are older and they are starting their own professional career, there is less conscious and unconscious bias against them because they are women, they are Asians, they are Asian women.

Learning Values

Growing up with very little in the Philippines, it was difficult to navigate life, but we managed. Despite not having a lot, my parents truly valued the importance of a good education, hard work, honesty, loyalty, and respect. When you do not have much, you tend to appreciate things a lot more. When you do not have much, you do not take things for granted but you use them wisely. When you do not have much, many times you dream of things that you can have and, yes, I did dream a lot of those dreams when I was younger.

Big Dreams

So when I came to the U.S., I knew that I wanted to be successful in a country of opportunities. I had been told that I could accomplish great things in a country where your dreams can come true. I knew that if I worked hard enough, it would pay off. I believed every word of it! Maybe my naiveté propelled me to work harder and do better or maybe dreaming big gave me the drive to accomplish all that I have accomplished. Whatever my driver was, I knew for certain that I wanted to be a lawyer in order to make an impact on people's lives. I later learned after getting into law school that that was also one of my father's dreams that unfortunately he was unable to do since he started a family early. Family became his priority.

So growing up with very little made me understand the value of hard work, the value of money, the importance of being successful, the importance of a great education, the importance of competitiveness and being able to compete, the importance of relationships, and most of all the importance of family.

On Defying Expectations: Box Out

My Mom reminded us that we should finish college and as women we should learn how to fend for ourselves in the event our husbands leave us or something happens to them. This is very sound advice. I saw what happened when my uncle passed away and my aunt had no idea where everything was or even where to start with raising her family. With the help of my parents and the other aunts and uncles, she managed to get on her feet after a few years.

My parents told us to pursue a career of being a nurse, a doctor, or a health-care professional. Two sisters became nurses, another one became a psychologist, one a professor, one a restauranteur/computer whiz, one brother worked as a Quality Control Manager at a major hospital in Illinois, and another brother went to the Air Force and later worked at an airline company.

As for me, I thought I was going to be a doctor until I broke a nail, a little skin came off, and I saw blood. Guess what happened? I fainted. After that experience, I deviated. I knew I was bound to be a lawyer! My Mom thought that I should still go for nursing but I knew that that was not going to happen.

My point is, it is okay to pursue your passion and break out of the box that you were meant to fill. Box out of what is expected of you. However, if you do go for it, make sure it is what you want to do and that you excel at whatever it is you want to do. Only you can make your own decision and whatever the outcome is, be woman enough to accept the consequences of your action. But I caution you that mediocrity and complacency should never be a part of your DNA. You should always strive to be the best but realize that there will always be someone better than you and you will always be better than somebody else. As long as you understand this, you will be okay.

Be Yourself, Be Nice, Be Professional and Firm. All at the Same Time.

I was invited to be the keynote speaker at a Filipino event and I was seated at a table together with a group of Filipina VIPs. When I sat at the table, I said hello to all and all I got was a curt hello. Well, I was not going to sit at a table where no one wanted to talk to me, so I stood up and went around the table and introduced myself to each of them. I spoke to them in English since I did not know whether they spoke Tagalog or not. After I went around introducing myself, I sat down. As soon as I sat down, they must have assumed that I did not know how to speak Tagalog because they started talking to each other in Tagalog. And the conversation went like this but in Tagalog: "Who does she think she is not knowing how to speak Tagalog when she's a Filipina?" The conversation continued, "Why is she even sitting with us when she is not a VIP and trying to talk to us in English...!" As I was listening, I could not help myself but play along. I did not say anything and pretended that I did not know how to speak Tagalog and just let them talk to each other. A few minutes went by and before they could say any more embarrassing things, I leaned over and responded to them in Tagalog. Their jaws dropped and you could see the horror in their eyes. I continued to converse with them in Tagalog. Then of course, they stopped talking in Tagalog and only spoke in English. But I could still feel the question hanging in the air as to why I was sitting with them. The program went on and finally I was introduced as the keynote speaker. I addressed the group and when I was done, I sat back at the same table and lo and behold, the whole demeanor at the table changed. My table became so chatty and everyone wanted to talk to me all the time.

The point of the story is "be yourself." Do not just talk to people because they are VIPs or they are the keynote speakers or because of some stature. Respect every person whatever their profession or calling in life. Do not be rude to someone and be nice when you find out that they are of a certain stature. My mentor always told me "always be nice to people or the person sitting next to you because you never know who that person might be." So true.

I will tell you one more story. Many years ago, I used to work at this building downtown, on the corner of Dearborn and Washington. Every morning there was this older black homeless man named "Kenny" who used to sell the magazine "Streetwise." He was a very nice gentleman. He was always cheerful, always said hello and I got to be friends with him. He told me his life story: He lost his job and lost his home due to a foreclosure. As a result, his family left him. He has been trying to rebuild his life but no one wanted to hire him. Streetwise gave him the opportunity that he needed. Every morning I would give him a dollar for the magazine but never took the magazine so he can sell it to other people.

One day, Kenny and I were talking and as I was about ready to cross the street, I felt him grab me from behind and quickly pulled me from the street. Then I realized what had happened. There was a car that ran the stoplight and was going to plow into me if Kenny had not been there. Kenny saved my life.

So here is a homeless man who did more for me than most people I know and for who I am indebted. I thanked Kenny and would have returned the favor at any time. Unfortunately, a few weeks after that incident, Kenny stopped going to that corner. I waited for many months hoping that I would see Kenny again but never saw him again. I asked around, especially Streetwise if they knew where Kenny was but without a last name, they could not tell me any information.

Again, be kind, be nice, be true to yourself and most of all respect people from all walks of life. You will never know who might save your life.

REMEMBER THE "WHY?"

I mentioned earlier that my Dad wanted to be a lawyer but I did not know that until after I applied to law school. I could have gone for another post college education but something happened that made my conviction to be a lawyer stronger. Let me share that experience.

At a private tennis club (my husband and I love tennis) after a 2-hour tennis match, I sat at the club bar drinking cappuccino. One of the guys who played in the mixed doubles tournament sat a few seats away from me. We were both watching a college football game and then we started chatting. He started telling me about this exclusive tennis club on the north side with excellent clay courts and great tennis pros. I said "I would love to play at that tennis club-sounds like a great club." He looked at me and declared: "You can't, they won't let you." I was shocked at his statement. Instead of getting upset, I asked him why would they not allow me to play. And he answered: "Because they don't allow minorities in the club." I said "that's a stupid rule!" Then he looked at me and he realized that I was getting all uptight about it: "It's not my club, and I don't belong there. If I owned the club, I would let you play but I don't own it. Unless you change the rules, that's just how it is and how it will be." To which I retorted "Maybe I will." I was so mad but I realized that this guy was not really the bad guy, he was merely stating what the club policy over which he had no control. He also told me that he had not thought about the policy since no one really raised an issue with it until our conversation. Much to my surprise, he apologized for saying what he had said and agreed that that policy should be changed.

After that incident, I realized that this is just one of the many situations where bias exists, consciously or unconsciously. And since arriving in the U.S., this was my very first open experience of bias. And I can tell you that it was not a very good feeling. But I also realized that the way we respond to situations dictates how the ensuing response will be. As Newton's Third Law of Motion taught us "for every action, there is an equal and opposite reaction." I could have blown up and screamed at this guy for what he said but instead I opted for the high road and decided to get more information about the source of his statements. By engaging him in conversation about the policies of the club I could provide some education. So the lesson to be learned is: *Let's not be too quick to shoot the messenger because the messenger can still be influenced! And change happens one person at a time.*

This experience made me realize that being a lawyer would give me a voice and credibility in a space where the law was designed to enforce EQUALITY and JUSTICE FOR ALL. I quickly understood that being a lawyer in the U.S. would give me a license to serve the underserved, the minority communities, particularly the Asian community, and those who need protection the most. I quickly realized that being a female lawyer in the U.S. would allow me an equally loud voice in an otherwise male dominated society. And as I was processing all these, it became clear to me that in order to be heard, to be respected, and to compete in a male dominated society, I needed to do so at a level where I am at par with them. For me, being a lawyer was the medium to do it.

ON BEING THE FIRST ASIAN PRESIDENT OF THE CHICAGO BAR ASSOCIATION

If you had asked me in 1983 when I had just arrived from the Philippines whether I would ever be the first Asian President of one of the oldest and largest metropolitan bar association in the U.S., I would have told you that you are insane. Never in my wildest dreams would I ever have imagined that that was possible! How did it happen?

Learning from Mentors

I worked as an associate attorney at a small real estate litigation father and son law firm, Harold I. Levine, Ltd. for five years. I worked at least 60-70 hours a week, worked on weekends, and barely had time for lunch. The firm was so busy and with three lawyers handling the case load, there was not enough time in the day. As a result, I spent a lot of time in the office and ended up spending a lot of time learning and being trained by Harold. Harold became one of my mentors and became a second dad to me. He ended up taking me under his wing and taught me the nuts and bolts of what a good lawyer should be. He was a huge influence in the kind of lawyer I am today. I remember Harold telling me that "your job is a means to what you want to do in life so make sure you love your job as well."

Showing up 99 Percent

I remember a frame in Harold's office that had the saying "Success is 1% sweat and 99% showing up." I asked him about that and he said that it takes at least 5- 10 meetings for someone to remember you so it is important to be out there, be visible, and meet people. I remember him saying "It's when people know you and trust you that business will eventually come." I did not understand hi then, but as I moved on with my career I started understanding what he meant. Harold also pushed me to get involved in bar associations and organizations as well as pro bono service. I remember him asking me to go to bar association meetings and I finally said "something's got to give. Either I work less hours so I can go to meetings or don't give me any more pro bono cases, lessen my case load!" I distinctly remember him saying "someday you will thank me for pushing you to get involved." Not only did I become Chair of the Chicago Bar Association (CBA) Young Lawyers Section (YLS) but I also ended up being the first Asian President, eighth woman President, of one of the oldest, largest, and most elite metropolitan bar association in the country, the CBA! It is 140 years old and it has 22, 000 lawyer members.

Becoming President was no easy task. You had to be nominated into the leadership of the bar association and voted in by a very distinct Nominating Committee made up of Federal Judges, State Court Judges, Committee chairs, past CBA Presidents, YLS representatives, and Board appointees. The sole purpose of that Nominating Committee is to choose the future leaders of the bar association who will best represent the organization. As a result of my involvement in bar associations, I met and worked with partners of large firms, general counsels of corporations, Supreme Court Justices, Federal and State court judges, and the list goes on. While working with them on many programs and projects, they got to know me and I got to know them really well. My involvement with and constant exposure to well respected jurists earned me their respect and trust. "Success is 1% sweat and 99% showing up" was about showing up for people when you make a commitment. You show up and you do a great job. You show up when people count on you. You show up when needed and people will remember you. To date, I am always called upon to do work or projects with them because I have built up a reputation for honoring my commitments. These same folks became my supporters and encouraged me to become President of the CBA. Many times my reply was "You're out of your mind!"

Tapping the 94 Percent

So why did I decide to be President of the CBA? Why not the Asian American Bar Association or the Filipino Bar Association? I made a conscious decision early on to be involved with the CBA because the Asian community is only 6% of the population; there is a whole 94% of the population out there who are not as familiar with Asians.

In the early 1990s one of my dearest friend, the late Honorable Judge Sandra

Otaka who was one of the founders of the Asian American Bar Association asked me to chair one of the committees with the Asian American Bar Association (AABA). I was still a young lawyer then. It was a great honor to be asked to chair a committee but my heart was set on getting involved in a mainstream bar association. I had an in depth conversation with Sandra when I expressed to her that I was very grateful for the opportunity but I declined the invitation because I wanted to take a different route. I explained that I will always be there to support AABA but I would like to get involved in an organization where very few Asians dared to get involved at that time, the Chicago Bar Association. She asked why I would want to do that and my answer was simple. Asians know Asians and to get involved in the Asian American Bar where all the members are Asians was limiting our ability to be exposed to the mainstream population. Because we are only 6% of the population, there's 94% of people out there unfamiliar with the Asian Americans. I wanted to tap into that 94%.

Indeed, I was one of the few Asian Americans who got involved with the CBA. I was the only Asian American and only Filipina to be Chair of the Young Lawyers of the CBA. I was also the first Asian and only Filipina to be President of the CBA. As President of the CBA, I was the leader of the organization with a diverse group of Board Members consisting of Federal Judges, State Supreme Court Justices, appellate and trial court Judges, high profile lawyers, partners of large law firm, partners of small to medium sized law firms, elected officials, and the list goes on. Thus, as you might imagine running meetings of the CBA Board was no easy feat since I had to be clear, concise, prepared, knowledgeable, and firm but flexible. As President of the largest metropolitan bar in the country, I had to communicate with its 22,000 members and address issues affecting the membership and the legal profession. I was the organization's spokesperson as well as the face of the organization. As President, I answered calls from reporters, handled and managed crisis that came our way, and dealt with difficult decisions through my board. I encouraged the CBA to pursue a more global focus emphasizing the importance of globalization and building relationships with international bars. For the first time in CBA history, I brought a delegation of CBA lawyers and judges to the Philippines for a Business Conference and held joint meetings with Filipino lawyers. This was such a successful conference that to this date, lawyers who went remained in contact with each other and have partnered with Filipino lawyers for some of their cases.

The lessons learned from my presidency of the Chicago Bar Association are:

- Nothing is impossible, they're just difficult to achieve but if you put your mind to it, you can achieve things.

- Always believe in yourself and shoot for the moon.
- Always run an efficient meeting. Respect people's time and stick to the time schedule.
- If you want to be lifted, lift people up first.
- Surround yourself with very smart people.
- Create your own path to success.

MORE ON MENTORING AND SPONSORSHIP

I was lucky enough to have great mentors other than my parents. I mentioned one of them earlier in the chapter, Harold Levine. I also have another mentor who has become one of my dearest friends, Peter Birnbaum. Peter is the CEO and President of Attorneys' Title Guaranty Fund (ATGF). Subsequently, I forged another friendship with another mentor, Laurel Bellows, Past President of the American Bar Association. These are people who helped and guided me along the way in my career. They taught me the importance of: relationships and a good network, loyalty, honesty and ethics, and impacting people and/or outcomes. They taught me that life is short so seize the opportunity; they taught me that you are always marketing yourself so dress accordingly; they taught me how corporate America and organizations work; and they taught me the importance of finding and keeping your mentors and sponsors.

Always Be Ready

I once worked for one of my mentors, Peter Birnbaum as a law clerk and back then law clerks did the marketing to lawyers to get them to join ATGF as members. One day, Peter gave me an assignment to see this high powered managing partner of a large law firm and my task was to convince him to be a member of ATGF. I went to the law firm and this lawyer's office was a corner office that was the size of a penthouse. It had a spectacular view of the City of Chicago, all glass walls, and a high ceiling which made me realize that this lawyer was a very important man. I met him and I started giving him my traditional speech about becoming a member of ATGF, the benefits, etc. Before I could finish my speech, he started firing questions at me, one after another about the company, why he should join when he has everything, his objections, etc. The questions were not the typical questions I had been asked so I answered the questions carefully and those that I cannot answer, I admitted that I did not know the answer but that I would get back to him. This went on for 30 minutes but I managed to retain my composure and answer as best as I could. At the end of the meeting, this lawyer looked at me and said "Great job." I was a little puzzled but I replied "thank you." He then continued to say that my boss, Peter is a very good friend of his and that Peter called him before my meeting and told him to grill me with questions to see how I would handle myself. He proceeded to give me feedback. He stated that I did not get flustered and was professional. He said that I answered as best as I could and he appreciated my honesty in admitting when I did not know the answer but indicated that I would get to him. He said he would tell Peter that I passed. Whew! I did not realize that I was being tested and was glad that I passed.

The lesson here is to always be ready for whatever comes your way. Many times you have no control over what comes your way and it is your response that defines you. Expect that someone will throw a curve call and just anticipate it. As a result of that exercise, I decided to be the best marketing person that I could be. I attended seminars on how to be a great marketing salesman. I read books like *Getting Past No: Negotiating in Difficult Situations* (Ury, 1998). I put into practice all I learned. Again, remember you are marketing yourself every minute. When I leave my house, I make sure that I look presentable since you will never know who you might end up seeing at the grocery store, or in church, or at a coffee place.

ON BEING A BOARD MEMBER
OF A PRIVATELY HELD CORPORATION

I was asked to be on the board of one of the largest privately held corporations. This was an honor for me. They were looking for a female lawyer with my qualifications. They were also looking for younger board members and more diversity on their board and I fit the bill. It also helped that I was recommended by the CEO of the company who had become a really good friend of mine. Of course, there is nothing automatic. I had to be vetted by the Board Nominating Committee and since it is a private board, it was a long and lengthy process. I met with the individual nominating committee members, the nominating committee had to recommend me to the entire company board, who had to vote me in. The company board was made up of white male lawyers in their mid-fifties. I was voted in and elected to the full board.

My first meeting was very interesting. I walked into a huge board room and each seat was assigned. My name card was on the table. Around the room sat all my fellow board members who welcomed me as they introduced themselves to me. I have never met a group of really wonderful, incredibly intelligent, successful lawyers in their mid-fifties to early seventies who truly made me feel like one of them right away.

As the meeting convened, the Chairman of the Board said "Welcome Gentlemen to our Fall Board Meeting." I could not resist it so I raised my hand. The Chairman looked surprised and asked: "Ms. Austriaco, do you have a question?" I responded yes "could you also please add 'Lady' as well?" The Chairman of the Board smiled and replied "Of course! My apologies and I stand corrected. Let me try again, Gentlemen and Lady...welcome...." It was bold for me to do what I did but I certainly could not let him get by not acknowledging a woman on the board. I do have to say that because the Chairman was used to addressing an all-male board, it did not dawn on him to change how to address the board. Quite understandable but I had to say something in order to make myself heard. At the same time, I also used it to serve as an ice breaker for everyone which gave them a hint about who I am.

So, the lesson here is: do not be afraid to make a point or voice your opinion where warranted.

So What is the Measure of Success?

Success is a relative term that has many different definitions with different metrics for different people. For me, success is making a difference in someone's life. It is being able to impact people in a positive way such that their trajectory in life becomes upward and onward. It is being able to help even when no one is looking; the true measure of a person's character is knowing what they do when no one is looking. I define success as being able to accomplish things and getting to places while bringing my friends along with me to the top since I believe it does not have to be lonely at the top! I leave you with my favorite poem mistakenly attributed to Ralph Waldo Emerson entitled "What is Success?" This poem captures the essence of true success and I hope you enjoy it as much as I do.

What is Success?

To laugh often and much;

To win the respect of intelligent people and the affection of children;

To earn the appreciation of honest critics and endure the betrayal of false friends;

To appreciate beauty, to find the best in others;

To leave the world a bit better, whether by a healthy child, a garden patch or a redeemed social condition;

To know even one life has breathed easier because you have lived.

This is to have succeeded.

Only you can define what your success is. Only you can decide how successful you will be. We are on borrowed time in this world and the space we occupy is not infinite. You and I need to make sure that we use and spend it wisely.

AMELIA BARIA ALADO*

Attorney-at-law
Administrative Officer, Government Legal Department
Her Majesty's Government (British)
FWN100™ Global 2015

An Ilongga's Global Journey

What Happened?

On the 23rd of June 2016, I rushed home from work. I wanted to watch the results of the BREXIT referendum which was held earlier that day. You, like most of the world, are probably wondering what BREXIT means?

To truly understand what BREXIT meant, I needed to understand how the European Union came to be. England is just the island that is part of Great Britain. Great Britain is actually composed of three countries, England, Wales and Scotland. The United Kingdom (UK) is composed of England, Wales, Scotland, and Northern Ireland. The UK, in turn, is part of a larger political union, called the European Union (EU), which was comprised of 28 European states.

The EU was established after World War II, and based on the Maastrict Treaty, members of the EU enjoy the benefits of common economic, foreign, security, and justice policies. The EU and the UK have shown a commitment to the principles of democracy, human rights, respect for the rule of law, fairness by creating a level playing field, protection of workers, women, and the vulnerable, the environment, health, and safety. These are the same principles I subscribe to and why I decided to be a lawyer.

The establishment of the EU created the largest single market in the world, with more than 500 million people, until BREXIT. Simply put, BREXIT means

---

* The views presented are those of the author and do not necessarily represent the views of the British Government.

Britain's exit from the EU.

On the 23rd of June 2016, citizens from England, Wales, Scotland, and Northern Ireland; the UK; cast their vote on the future of the EU membership with the EU. The question on the ballot paper was: "Should the United Kingdom remain a member of the European Union or leave the European Union?" I confidently ticked the box that said "Remain a member of the European Union." I was fully confident that the remain votes would win.

I was wrong.

The leave votes won by 52% to 48%. This was a divisive referendum with England and Wales strongly voting to leave the EU while Scotland and Northern Ireland cast their votes solidly in the remain column.

What does this mean? What does it mean to me?

Before we get to the implications of Brexit, let me explain why and how I got to London.

THE FOUNDATION YEARS

My birth name is Amelia, but I have answered to many names, especially when I was growing up. At home, I am known as "Nene," sometimes "Inday," "Nora" (since I was a cry baby and an aunt nicknamed me after the superstar Nora Aunor), and "Bebang" or "Bebs."

After another five or six nicknames in school, I finally settled on "Aimee" as my official nickname.

My father, the late Andres Alado, was a very successful self-made businessman. My mother is Epifania Baria Alado, she was a public school teacher. Theirs was a "rags to riches" love and life story. Their families were against their relationship, so my father and mother eloped and started to build the family fortune with only their own hard work and industry.

I grew up with two brothers and one sister; my late brother Andrew who was 3 years older, my younger brother Antonio who is two years younger than me, and the youngest sibling, Andrea.

As far as I can remember, my father was into all types of business: retail, wholesale, industrial, agriculture, and aquaculture. My mother was always fully supportive of his endeavors, in addition to her teaching job. Andres and Epifania made sure that their children were a part of, and were appreciative of, the entrepreneurship culture.

My father instilled the value of hard work while we were children. We did find time to play, but he made sure we also worked and helped out in his various businesses. I was the cashier in our retail shop and a filling station girl at our petrol station. I also managed the payroll of our security business, sugarcane farm, fishponds, trucking service as well as the household caretakers and security personnel.

While working at all our different businesses, I had a front row seat and witnessed how my father managed people. He was tough when it came to business, but he was generous, kind, and cared for the people he employed. I saw how he efficiently handled problem situations and his staff. At an early age, I understood the virtues of honesty, fairness, doing the right thing, having a strong moral compass, being true to one's faith and self, as well as integrity and respect.

My father, through hard work and determination, successfully built his businesses and this allowed his family to live comfortably. As I look back, I appreciated the correlation between hard work and the fruits of honest labor. My father's work ethic and habits provided enough for us to have a comfortable life and enabled us to do many things in life.

We were privileged to have domestic help, drivers, and our very own nanny, Delfa, who is still with us after three generations. Yet in spite of the presence of household help, we were trained to do chores. These skills allowed me to be independent and were put to good use later in life when I lived alone.

My pre-school and primary education were spent at the elementary school in President Manuel Roxas' hometown of Capiz, and St. Mary's Academy in Roxas City. Secondary education was at the Assumption Convent in Iloilo City, an all-girls school. I was an *interna*, a student resident, staying in a dormitory with other girls. The nun who managed the residence was called mistress.

I remember being so miserable the first few months of my first year. I was homesick; I was alone, in a city 110km away from my hometown and in the company of people I had never met before in my life. It was traumatic at first, but then I found sports. I was not the academic type. I never aspired to be an "i-a-n" (valedictorian or salutatorian.) I was happy enough when I passed my classes. I found sports more interesting. Sports fit the image that I saw of myself; an innocent mischief-maker. I am unsure if my record of being the resident who got grounded the longest, six months, by Sister Mercedes still stands. My antics may have triggered the decision to change the management of the dorm from the nuns to an ultra-strict spinster named Ms. Lizares.

I had a difficult decision to make after high school. I needed to decide on what career to pursue.

I belong to a generation where our parents wanted traditional professions such as doctors, lawyers, accountants, and engineers for their children. My parents decided that my older brother Andrew was going to be a civil engineer. Thankfully, I was given the freedom to decide whether I wanted to pursue medicine or law.

My first choice was medicine. I saw myself as a healer, so I enrolled at the University of Santo Tomas (UST) in Manila. My stay at UST lasted one semester. I found the university environment was not for me. There were too many students, the campus was large, and the environment was too impersonal. I was used to the intimate, family-oriented Assumption Convent environment. I always felt, and still do, that the environment provided by Assumption was unique.

Also, I had a change of heart. The appeal of a career in medicine waned, and after one semester I doubted that I was cut out for it.

I transferred to Assumption College in San Lorenzo Village in Makati, and registered for a Bachelor of Science, with a major in Psychology. I thought that this might satisfy the requirements for a pre-med degree, in case I decided to go back and pursue medicine, and satisfied the requisites for a pre-law degree.

THE LAW AND I

Is a leader born or bred? Are leadership skills the result of genetics or are they learned skills? Recent studies have found that it is a bit of both; leadership is a complex product of genetics and environmental influences. My path to a leadership position in law is long and winding.

The first step was to gain the eight years of academic qualification. Then followed by at least a year of revision for the Bar examinations. The ultimate hurdle was to pass the Philippine Bar and practice law.

After my oath-taking, I received a letter from the office of then Secretary Manuel A. Roxas III, informing me that I had an interview with Attorney Amy Eisma. At that time, my mischievous streak was strong, and I was sporting bright, eye-popping, blue fringe (bangs). So I found myself sitting in front Attorney Amy Eisma, blue fringe hair and all, and being interviewed for a position in Secretary Roxas' core technical team at the Office of the Department of Trade and Industry. Atty. Eisma, who is now a good friend and mentor, must have seen something past the blue fringe as she offered me the position! Granted, before I officially started, I traded my blue fringe for a more standard color. This was my first adult job, and I needed to act, look, and project myself as a professional. Gone was the mischievous, cheerful, blue haired schoolgirl.

Aside from my job responsibilities which included research on trade policy, contributions to the development of the Implementing Rules and Regulations for trade laws, and being the representative of the Philippine government in round-table discussions with other nations, I also worked on Intellectual Property (IP) Law, including Patents, Designs, Trademarks, and Copyrights. I developed a firm friendship with the director of Trademark, Attorney Leny Raz, who became a valuable mentor. She was instrumental in my decision to specialize in IP law.

My next job was with the Court of Appeals. I served as a court attorney to Justice Marina Buzon where I researched precedents and legislation relevant to the cases being heard on appeal and helped draft decisions, orders, and resolutions.

While at the Court of Appeals, I accepted a lecturer post at the De La Salle University, College of St. Benilde where I taught Constitutional Law and Intellectual Property Law to groups of 40 university students.

I must confess. I am a rolling stone. I love to travel and explore new cultures and gain new experiences. I had been pondering the possibility of a trip to New York, U.S. to take the NY bar exam. For a lawyer, a foreign qualification in the Philippines means a qualification from the U.S. This was expected as the Philippines has closer ties with the U.S. than other countries. I made inquiries and got accepted to a New York University to review for the state bar. New York was my next destination.

In spite of my best laid plans, the Intellectual Property Office of the Philippines (IPO) nominated me for a six-month Fellowship in Intellectual Property under the auspices of the Japan Patent Office (JPO) and World Intellectual Property Office (WIPO.)

With the guidance and mentoring of Attorney Raz, I became the first Filipino, and the second in the world, after an Indonesian, to receive the award. I was told that I received the award because the stakeholders; IPO, JICA, JPO, and WIPO believed that I could make a difference in my ability to use IP as a tool for development, and not only for regulatory measures. They found that IP law could be leveraged to obtain a competitive edge. The fellowship was a prestigious position, with a lot of responsibility and pressure.

Move over New York. Tokyo, here I come.

Becoming Global: Turning Japanese

With the blessing of Justice Buzon, I accepted the Fellowship and was given a sabbatical from the Court of Appeals. This type of a break was unprecedented at that time and was unheard of.

While in Japan, I diligently studied and sought the best tutors from Japan's world-renowned universities, Waseda and Sofia. I attended training classes at the Japan Institute for Promoting Invention and Innovation and Asia-Pacific Industrial Property Centre. I visited government institutions, departments, and Japanese businesses. But it was not all work, as the naughty girl from high school who loved to play still lived in me. After work, my Japanese colleagues and I would socialize over sake and yakitori. Despite the language barrier, they only spoke extremely limited English, we always enjoyed going out, sometimes did karaoke!

I also networked with law organizations and associations such as the Foreign Women Lawyers' Association and the Roppongi Bar Association. One piece of advice, networking is a valuable tool in your arsenal. It was the catalyst for my being in London right now.

I packed a lot of adventure into my six-month stint in Japan, but it was not an easy transition. For the first time in my life, I had to learn how to survive a harsh winter. I had never felt freezing cold before, much colder than the winter I experienced in Australia. My insecurity would surface when I attended functions on my own. The language barrier frustrated me, and there was a strong hint of discrimination from my elderly female Japanese secretary. But in spite of the challenges, my Fellowship in Japan would lead to other experiences.

Expanding my Global Awareness: London Calling

"...Two roads diverged in a wood, and I—I took the one less traveled by, And that has made all the difference." "The Road Not Taken" by Robert Frost

At the conclusion of my Fellowship in Tokyo, I traveled around Europe for a month. I went to Paris, the south of France, London, Manchester, and checked out the Netherlands, Geneva, Switzerland, and Finland. I immersed myself in European culture, admired their history, and was fascinated with the new things I saw. I traveled by car, train, and plane; met old friends and made new ones.

After the wonderful break, I resumed my job at the Court of Appeals for six months before joining the Corporate Counsels, Philippines (CCP) law firm as an associate lawyer.

I was incredibly lucky and am most grateful to have been in the company of this great group of lawyers. Managing partner Atty. Arthur Ponsaran and senior partner Atty. Joaquin Obieta were like fathers to me. The culture at the firm was fun, and we were all supportive of one another, allowing each one to thrive. The firm felt like family. I would most likely still be working for CCP if the travel bug had not hit me, again.

I was still planning on going to London, so in the latter half of my time with CCP, I studied to secure legal qualification in London; London being a more practical choice than Paris. I also thought studying business French on top of law would be too much.

I remember a revered professor, Justice Alicia Sempio-Diy, giving a prophetic warning, "Law is a jealous mistress and the study of it is not for the faint-hearted."

Justice Diy is one of the authors of the Philippine Family Code of 1987. She became one of my mentors and educated me on the Family Code. Many years later, my expertise in this field was crucial in exonerating a Filipina from bigamy and perjury charges filed by the Home Office before the Crown Court of England and Wales.

Winning this case validated that I had made the right career choice, law over medicine. It reinforced for me that law can not only save lives, but the law can ensure a person's liberty and property.

For the next two years, I took the long-distance-learning course at the BPP Law School and traveled to London at least three times a year. I was the first and only Filipina in that elite institution. Some of my British and European classmates were working for big international firms in Hong Kong or Singapore. Sometimes they would talk about how wonderful their Filipina maids were in conversations with me. My classmates were delighted to find an ethnocentric Filipina who was confident and able to articulate her legal experiences from abroad.

All the traveling became physically and financially draining. I had to stay in London for at least four weeks each time. It made sense for me to relocate, but I was hesitant. I was uncertain about living abroad, and perhaps, I was also a bit insecure. If I relocated, I would leave a thriving practice, my built in support system of family and friends, and would need to start a new career in London. Could I do it?

My angels on earth, my mentors, encouraged me to pursue my dream. Friends from the world over, especially from the Philippines and London, gave me the courage, support, and assistance to make the decision. I owe my current situation in life to them. I must mention at least two persons who were the most instrumental in my move, Andy Zee from Singapore, and Valerie Gardner from London.

PRACTICING LAW IN LONDON

I moved to and settled in London in April 2005.

For the first three years, I immersed myself in the English culture. London is full of history, lots of parties, and there is always something to do year round. London is not a "love at first sight" type of city like Paris. It takes a bit more time to get to know London, learn its quirks, appreciate its culture, and slowly but surely you find yourself falling in love with your adopted city.

While doing part-time work for the Westminster City Council, I studied for the Graduate Diploma in Law and the Legal Practice Course. During the latter part of 2008, I was asked to temporarily cover an open position at the Crown Court for three weeks. A Crown Court only hears criminal cases such as murder, robbery, or sexual offences. Although criminal law is an area that I disliked and had never practiced, for some reason, money being one of them, I accepted the temporary offer.

The three weeks turned into months, and months turned into years. I would love to think that they must really like me, for my temporary three-week assignment, which started in 2008 morphed into an official position as a civil servant for Her Majesty's Government that I continue to hold.

Working for the court, I listened, argued, absorbed, learned, and most importantly, I learned to network. As I adjusted to my new environment, I had to tap into my emotional intelligence and learn how to work and interact with the Brits. Being genuinely friendly and light-hearted could only get me so far. I had to overcome my initial perception of the British "stiff upper lip" attribute; they are actually very engaging, sympathetic, personable and intelligent conversationalists. That is when you finally get the hang of their beautiful accent.

From the Crown Court, I applied for a parallel transfer to a County Court. This is a court that only hears civil cases like contract disputes or collection of sums of money. Once again, I turned into a sponge, absorbing knowledge and information, and continued to network, network, network.

Working at the Crown Court and the County Court under the Ministry of Justice gave me an excellent opportunity to learn and observe the workings of the British legal system. I would venture to say that the English legal system is the best. Speedy trials are held and dispensed with quickly. Resolution of the cases is not delayed. From what I have observed, their justice system is fair, and not corrupt.

A trial in England can be conducted and resolved from 1 hour or may last for a few consecutive days, depending on the complexity and volume of evidence. In the Philippines, a simple case can last for 30 years! I would like to push for the English system in the Philippines sans the jury.

Moving on from the Ministry of Justice, I have applied for promotion to work at the Government Legal Department.

It was a long and convoluted journey, but this is how I came to London, and why the Brexit vote was important to me.

While writing my story, I kept my eye on what the Brexit vote means for the people of England, British and European Filipinos especially myself. While the implications for the single trade system, for personal travel, for business, and for the financial systems remain unclear, the UK citizens are bracing for a long, drawn out exit process from a Union that was clearly beneficial to them.

GIVING BACK AND PAYING FORWARD

Living abroad, and traveling extensively, I developed a deep appreciation for the blessings and opportunities that I have enjoyed. Independent, strong-willed, intelligent, and secure, I looked around me and became more sensitive to the plight of others around me. I realized that I needed to give back.

During my time at the CCP, I convinced the firm to extend pro-bono services to indigent clients, and assisted claims of those who lived with HIV/AIDS and their families, who were associated to the Positive Action Foundation Philippines (PAFPI.)

PAFPI is a remarkable organization that touched my social conscience. I am grateful to Joshua Formentera, Founder for giving me the opportunity to help out. Hearing first-hand the accounts of the group's members or their survivors removed any stigma I held of the disease.

PAFPI has done so much in bringing the plight of Filipinos infected with HIV/AIDS to the awareness of the government and community organizations. Two of the most notable achievements of PAFPI were to incorporate HIV/AIDS awareness in the Pre-Departure Orientation Seminar of Filipino overseas workers and making cheaper medicine readily available.

My passion for volunteering took a back seat when I first moved to London but quickly got rekindled in 2012.

I volunteered as a games maker (GM) for the London 2012 Olympics. GMs make the Games happen. Thousands of volunteers were first used in the 1948 Games in London and the model using games makers has been copied in each Olympics after that. Volunteers were the lifeblood and were crucial in producing the two very successful Games in London.

There were around 240,000 applications to be games makers for the Olympics in 2012. I was one of the 70,000 fortunate people chosen to be a GM. I applied for one of three preferred roles and was lucky to be assigned to "Field of Play." This meant that I would be in front of the audience, working with world class competitors for the Fencing competition. I was over the moon, and it was one of the most incredible experiences I ever had!

Sometime in October, I received an invitation to a meeting of Filipino leaders at the Philippine Embassy in London. Curious about the invitation, I attended the meeting that was a report on the "Rome Declaration" by three UK attendees — Gene Alcantara, Sonny Laragan, and Daisy Bret-Holt.

The Philippine Government, through the Commission on Filipinos Overseas, launched a program called Diaspora to Dialogue (D2D) at the First Global Summit in Manila. D2D is a call to action for Filipino diasporas following the Sep 2012

European regional conference in Rome. Together with the Filipino-Italian community, the prime movers of the conference were Ambassador Virgilio Reyes and his wife Marie Luarca Reyes; Secretary Imelda Nicolas, Atty. Loida Nicolas Lewis, Atty. Rodel Rodis among others.

My involvement with D2D intensified my desire to volunteer and work with fellow Filipinos. I became involved and was one of the founders and legal counsel of European Network of Filipino Diaspora (Europe and UK).

Then Typhoon Haiyan happened.

Recorded as one of the strongest storms to ever make landfall, Typhoon Haiyan was the deadliest to hit the Philippines. It took at least three days for me to fully digest the seriousness of the situation as news of the devastation slowly trickled in.

I felt a terrible loss and intense empathy for the victims and survivors. My province of Capiz and the adjoining northern part of the province of Iloilo were two of the 44 provinces severely affected. My family and friends suffered financially, but thankfully they were all physically safe.

The French phrase noblesse oblige [nobility obliges] resonated. No matter our stations in life, we all have a social responsibility to contribute what we can whether it is time, money, skills, and connections, to humanity. My family founded the Work Environment and Lifelong Learning (WELL) Trust. This is our family's legacy to help the victims of Typhoon Haiyan. Our first project was to help my hometown of Capiz.

The Philippines suffered much devastation. I was so touched by the beautiful acts of humanity and compassion shown by the world, by fellow Filipinos at home and abroad, and by the British people. Everyone did all they could to help. To quote Oscar Wilde - "Behind every exquisite thing that existed, there was something tragic."

My involvement with the WELL Trust and the relief efforts for Typhoon Haiyan brought a profound realization of the vulnerable state of our planet. I started advocating for environment causes. The Philippines is vulnerable to the effects of climate change. In my own little way, I promote sustainable actions such as recycling, and using green or renewable energies.

In September of 2015, I launched "Appellation of Origin: The Philippines" (AoOP) with a gala celebration of Filipino creativity, culture, and talent. An Appellation of Origin in legal language is a "geographical denomination of a country, region, or locality, which serves to designate a product originating therein, the quality or characteristics of which are due exclusively or essentially to the geographic environment, including natural and human factors."

The AoOP launch highlighted the Philippines' rich and storied tradition of fabric weaving and embroidery, represented in the works of two artists from Manila. Behind the beauty and the glamour of their creation is a whole array of industries and a supply chain that sustains communities in the Philippines, especially women who are often the weavers.

After a hugely successful launch of the AoOP brand mainly showcasing our indigenous fabrics, AoOP intends to move on to the next industry that also involves other local community stakeholders.

In 2016, I accepted an appointment as a member of the Executive Committee for the ASEAN UK Business Forum (AUBF.) In May, I assumed the position of Executive Director and Secretary. I accepted the call to volunteer for this organization to further my advocacy for women's empowerment through entrepreneurship.

I spoke at the 5th Southeast Asian Studies Symposium (SEA Symposium) at the University of Oxford on Entrepreneurship Growth on Women, Business, and Economic Development, issues directly related to gender equality in Southeast Asia.

My speech explored women's intrinsic motivation to appear as empowered women; and the visible and invisible barriers for women to start a business. In the Philippines, Filipino women are active entrepreneurs and the country has the second highest percentage of women in business next to Peru.

The Department of Trade and Investment (DTI) data showed that Micro Small & Medium Enterprises (MSMEs) accounted for 99.7% of all businesses in the Philippines, and provided almost 70% of the jobs generated. In spite of this, Filipino women are in no better financial position than men and more women are in poverty than men.

WHAT I HAVE LEARNED SO FAR

- How do you eat an elephant? One bite at a time. When faced with what seems to be an impossible task, be organized, be strategic, take it slow but at the same time be quick. When the going appears to be tough, take a deep breath. Take a coffee break when you think you need it go back to the drawing board. Remember the motivational poster - Keep calm and carry on.

- Do not throw the baby out with the bathwater. In every experience we encounter, there are always lessons to be learned. Keep the good ones and let go of the not so good.

- Always have entry and exit strategies. Lessons learned from Brexit—there were rules on becoming a member state of the European Union, but none on how to leave.

- Be aware and validate emotions like frustration, sadness, and anger. These are all natural.

- Develop and motivate yourself. Attend training, seminars, and conferences. Join professional organizations, sports clubs, or adventure groups. Always work towards getting better. Be greedy, be thirsty, and be like a sponge. Absorb all the learning and knowledge that you can get out of any experience. Invest in education and advancement of your career.

- Be a social remitter. Share the best systems and practices you have learned back home.

- Be a game changer or change agent by getting involved. It maybe through politics, advocacy, or joining a group or organization. As Mahatma Gandhi taught, "Be the change that you wish to see in the world."

- Find a mentor, a sponsor, an ally, or an adviser. Get a tutor or someone that can be the wind beneath your wings. "You can't change the world alone - you will need some help - and to truly get from your starting point to your destination takes friends, colleagues, the good will of strangers and a strong coxswain to guide them." (William H. McRaven)

- Success has two components: skill and luck. Skill is learned and can be developed. Luck is about being at the right place at the right time. It's about timing, and seizing the opportunity when it presents itself.

- Travel when you can. Seeing places, meeting people, and immersing yourself in a different culture and life is fantastic. It is the world's greatest and most effective teacher. You learn a lot about people, and you learn things about yourself. Try to go someplace you've never been before but return, at least twice, to your favorite places and enjoy them. Heraclitus said, "No man ever steps in the same river twice, for it's not the same river and he's not the same man."

- Be a visionary. Always expect bigger and better. Prepare for contingencies. Learn from lessons, mistakes, and wins. Be aware and do not be a victim of your own success.

- Lessons from the EU Referendum. Be informed of the two sides of any argument. To be fair, each has merits but go with the argument that is more aligned to your values.

- Be bold. Be quick to establish yourself. Success never waits for anyone. There is no right time to do it but NOW!

- Read up or learn about random subjects. Keep updated on current events. You will never know when current news might arise during a conversation. You do not want to be caught left out of a conversation.

- Articulate your ideas and feelings, adjusting it to your audience and the circumstance. Learn how to engage different types of people.

- It will not be a bed of roses throughout your journey. There will be fun times and sad times and doses of challenging times. But always bear in mind; what does not kill you makes you stronger. Always be grateful even for those sad and demanding times and realize that your situation is always better than another's. Always hold the Serenity prayer close to heart.

- The decisions that we made in the past are in the past. No point of over thinking the what-ifs. If anything, take the lessons that would improve your decision-making skills in the future. Be content with your choice and thrive. Life is too short for regrets!

- Be charming, polite, and courteous. These do not cost you anything but will earn you goodwill.

- Network! Take time to invest in your social, political, and intellectual capital. Be an active networker but do not over-do it. Remember, a large city such as London is a melting pot of people, culture, and business. Opportunities abound. Be wary of cheats, frauds, and time wasters.

- Enjoy the ride now.

- Take pictures. Journal. Keep a record of the watershed moments in your life, but do not leave out the small ones. Believe me, you will not be able to recall them later.

- And finally, life is too short. Enjoy where you are, without losing sight of where you want to be. Live. Love. Have fun. Give back. And most of all, be true to yourself.

And, one final thought. Be grateful.

- My life's journey would not have been possible without the support of my family, friends, and mentors. To them, I owe my heartfelt thanks and appreciation.

- To the Filipina Women's Network, thank you for giving me the opportunity through this great platform of "sisterhood" to share my experiences, the lessons I have learned, in the hopes that my life's journey may ease the way for someone.

- Thank you for making the call to action so that I can look at my life, re-examine, re-assess, and find relevance in what I have accomplished and all the things that I have yet to do.

✳

VIVIAN ZALVIDEA ARAULLO

COMMISSIONER, CITY OF DALY CITY, CALIFORNIA
EXECUTIVE DIRECTOR, WEST BAY PILIPINO MULTI SERVICE CENTER
FWN100™ U.S. 2012

Rock the Boat but Stay on Course

As a new executive director of a community organization, I have learned so many new lessons in leadership, and have had more opportunities to practice the ones I had learned before, as a television news executive for more than 15 years. It has been my pleasure to observe community leaders in politics and in the nonprofit world do their work, no longer as a detached observer as I was during my many years as a journalist. I now have a front-row seat to the action, and many times, I have had to join in the mix. It is both exhilarating and nerve-wracking. And many times, I hear the voices of some of these leaders in my ear as I make some tough calls.

LEADERSHIP LESSONS

1. Reach Out, Reach Out, Reach Out.
Even if They Do Not Agree with You.

Over cocktails, Filipina Women's Network founder Marily Mondejar told me some of her war stories from her campaign for a seat on the Democratic County Central Committee. Marily told me how a particularly influential organization, the Teachers' Union, did not endorse her. Nonetheless, Marily reached out

and introduced herself and discussed her platform with them, even though she
that they would not support her. The teachers thanked her and applauded her for
her effort. The lesson is implicit in their interchange: We can agree to disagree
but that should not mean we cannot form a relationship. This, in my opinion,
is a dignified, graceful way to go about life in general. I have seen Marily facilitate the growth of the Filipina Women's Network to what it is today, a national
and now global network of hundreds of Filipina women all devoted to supporting
each other and Filipino causes in general. I can imagine just how much reaching
out Marily has done to both supporters and critics over the years to achieve this
impressive growth. It is sometimes easier not to reach out, but reaching out is a
valuable act of leadership in itself.

2. What do You Guys Think?

For the majority of my career as a news executive, I was accustomed to boardroom and staff meetings that reflected the hierarchical nature of decision-making
in the corporate world. The bigger boss conducting the meeting talked, the under-
lings and lesser bosses, like me, listened, then left knowing what my actions were
expected to be. Often, I have had the disagreeable, self-imposed task of having to
put the more dominant talkers, usually males, in their place: "Stop interrupting
me, please."

So I was particularly impressed at my first community meeting conducted by
Angelica Cabande, the executive director of the South of Market Community Action Network, a nonprofit whose mission is to organize the South of Market community in San Francisco. Angelica, a young Filipina woman who presided over
these community meetings, would ask her attendees very deliberately: "What do
you guys think?" I was struck and impressed by the respectfulness of Angelica's
approach, how she took time to make sure everyone did not only have a seat at
the table, but also had a voice. Her approach leads to more collaborative and con-
sensus-based decision-making. It is an approach I admire and try to emulate. This
young Filipina is, for me, a role model for a people-centered style of leadership. Ask
people what they think, and when they do tell you, listen.

3. No Personal Attacks. But Keep Fighting.

One of the perks of my job as head of a community organization and now,
as city commissioner, is having the chance to gather advice from people who go
through some of the toughest scrutiny—politicians. One politician I had the pleasure of having coffee with was San Francisco Supervisor Scott Wiener. Supervisor

Wiener's politics and mine are not the most compatible at all times, but I admire his tenacity and flexibility. Over coffee, I asked him for advice on how to deal with all the contentiousness in San Francisco. His most memorable advice was: "Just keep fighting for what you believe in. But not with personal attacks." I am happy to align with Scott on what is also my own preferred way. How often do we see people, in their personal and professional lives, reduce their arguments to *ad hominem* attacks? Attacking a person, not the issue, often leads to the absence of meaningful solutions because everyone becomes focused on defending their egos. As Scott also noted, doing so makes no sense because one day you will probably land on the same side of an issue and have to work together. And I have, since then, happily supported some of Scott's pro-poor, pro-family measures. I also happily disagree with some of his other measures.

4. Rock the Boat, but Stay on Course.

I had the good fortune of being at a Warriors game with fellow FWN awardee Hydra Mendoza, who is San Francisco Mayor Edwin Lee's Education and Family Services Advisor and San Francisco School Board Commissioner. Commissioner Hydra is the highest ranking Filipina woman in San Francisco City Hall. I was just months old in my position at that time, and West Bay Pilipino had just awarded Hydra as a Distinguished Citizen in the field of education. I asked her for some tips and her advice was simple: "Stay on mission."

Taking Hydra's advice, I assess everything I do as an executive director based on our mission. Does it relate to and support the people we serve? How close, or how far is this action to furthering our mission?

Months later, I found myself speaking before the San Francisco school board, opposing a budget proposal that would have allocated zero dollars to Tagalog language programs in the district. Hydra, who sits on the school board, was there.

As I alluded to discrimination against the Filipino community in the budget process, I felt myself hoping that Hydra remembered what she had told me months earlier. I was trying to psychically transmit a message to Commissioner Mendoza: *"Here I am, Hydra! I'm staying on mission, but sometimes staying on mission means I have to rock the boat! That might mean criticizing the school district you represent, I hope you understand!"*

Later, the school board ruled to fund the hiring of one full-time person who would oversee Tagalog language activities. I, and our allies, thanked Hydra for her support of the community. I felt proud to directly demonstrate to her that I did listen to, and learn from her. Stay true to who and what you represent, and rock the boat if necessary. Especially because in the nonprofit sector, you will likely represent many voiceless people.

5. Everyone's the Same, from the Homeless Guy to the Mayor.

The neighborhood where we serve, South of Market, is a traditional enclave of Filipino immigrants and also where many homeless individuals roam and seek refuge. During one event at the Victoria Manalo Draves Park, named after a Filipina-American Olympic hero, I met Kotton Kandy, a transgender individual who self-identifies as homeless. Kotton Kandy is usually dressed in glittery rainbow colors. She has asked me to marry her. I turned down that request, but continue to be friends. One day, walking down Howard Street, a bunch of men were shouting at me in a scary fashion. Suddenly, a person appeared by my side and said: "Don't worry, girlfriend. I'm here. I'll walk with you." It was Kotton Kandy! She had come to my aid without even knowing it was me. And from just that incident alone, I knew Kotton Kandy as a person of quality.

Meantime, I had the pleasure of meeting Mayor Edwin Lee at his office. The mayor was receiving very heavy criticism due to the housing crisis that was hitting San Francisco. When I met him, I felt comfortable and at ease. That is because in my mind, the mayor and Kotton Kandy, are at the most basic level the same. We are all just people with shared humanity.

I asked the mayor how he was feeling, knowing that he was the target of a lot of criticism. After the meeting, I wrote him a thank you note to tell him that I understood how tough his job is, to have to balance everyone's needs as head of a major city. I also asked him to help Filipinos who were being evicted from their South of Market homes.

We are all just people. This is a lesson I have carried over from my days as a journalist. I have spoken with heads of state, terrorists, celebrities, convicted murderers, young, old, male, female, and all kinds of people. I have never been worried about people's appearances. People just do not faze me, because everyone is the same.

Knowing that allows me to deal with everyone in pretty much the same way I would like to be treated. How people react to this egalitarian approach is a clue to their true nature. Some will enjoy a relationship of equals. Others might be offended because you do not seem to be intimidated by their stature. Others will abuse your accessibility.

But their reactions are not your problem. In fact, it is a good way to determine who you want to closely associate with, or not. Do not be intimidated by power, fame, or poverty.

Remember, after everything is said and done, we are all just the same.

6. Build Permeable Boundaries.

This esoteric- and paradoxical-sounding sounding piece of advice comes from a woman who has been my mentor and spiritual teacher for more than seven years, Victoria Austin. Victoria is a Buddhist priest and leader at the San Francisco Zen Center. I have come crying to Vicki many times, confounded by the sometimes mean and harsh world from members of the community. Yes, it is not all *kumbaya* as you might think it is. It can get very competitive and downright ugly at times. Vicki knows it too, because the San Francisco Zen Center has had its own share of controversies in the past. A former executive director in the Chinese community once told me that nonprofit people can sometimes be just plain mean, likely because they are so passionate about their causes, and their passion sometimes shows up as anger and drama. "Okay, I'll respect that but I refuse to participate," I replied.

Some of my cry sessions with Vicki revolved around a leader who regularly dealt with our conflicting views by screaming at me, both in public and private. This was the board member who seemed intent on burying me alive by humiliating and screaming at me during board meetings. Yes, these things happen in the nonprofit world too.

Vicki taught me how to build better boundaries so that these aggressive behaviors would not cause me to crumble. But the boundaries, she said, have to be permeable, a seeming paradox. The principle is simple enough to understand. It is like building a wall but including a door. We do not shut people out completely, but we do not allow them to come in and destroy us whenever they wish. To do so would really help no one.

Vicki taught me to call out the offending behavior, with an eye for correction. For example, calmly state: "You are screaming at me. We can't talk that way. But we can talk when you are not screaming." Walls up, but door still open for improved behavior.

Sometimes it worked, sometimes it did not, but at the very end, I made it very clear what behavior was unacceptable, and screaming at me would yield no results. It is hard to keep screaming at a wall and a closed door.

For the hostile board member, I built a boundary by appealing to the other board members to help me stop the animosity during board meetings and to help keep discussions on track. I learned to meet his potshots with calmness, and the other board members did not pile on to join the drama. I still engaged but did not allow myself to get carried away by his behavior. When the board member realized that everyone else was also tired of the drama, he resigned.

Frankly, it is easier to build a wall with no door and just shut off people.

But the beauty of the permeable boundary, as Vicki taught me, is that it allows those people to still work with you; if they can respect your boundaries.

Since then, the screaming leader has stopped contacting and attacking me, and though I hear he still says negative things about me from time to time, he has at least not joined in other hostile activities that have been launched against me. Yes, the nonprofit world is just another reflection of life. We suffer, but there is an end to suffering. Build those permeable boundaries when you need to.

7. Collaborate; but only if it Feels Right.

One wonderful feature of community that I enjoy is collaboration. Even in the corporate world, I enjoyed collaborating with other departments or companies to create win-win solutions that ultimately delivered better results for the end users. Why work separately, when we can work together on mutual objectives and create something so much better?

In community, it is the same thing. I clearly see how collaboration makes sense for the people we serve.

Some collaborations work like magic. I like to bring whatever resources I can to the table for a greater cause. I found it fulfilling to work with other community organizations in the South of Market (SoMA) to prevent the eviction of Filipino families, to speak up with others for a Filipino Heritage District, and to oppose forces that would lead to the decimation of the Filipino community in the area. I enjoyed bringing together the Asian Pacific Islander (API) community and labor allies to take on a corporation whose past CEO called its workers "Filipino pigs." This last one is still a work in progress, but we are aiming for a successful result.

But not all attempts at collaborations work. What I have discovered is that collaborators must have a similar way of approaching change. In the corporate world, we call it synergy. In community work, I would call it ideological compatibility. We all work for change, but oftentimes, it is in how we approach change-making where the big differences lie. For example, I was in a collaborative that worked for multi-ethnic causes. I began to realize that the Filipino and Asian causes were not high on their list of priorities. They claimed it would be too expensive to respond to the Filipino and Asian American concerns. Their position truly mystified me. After some soul-searching, I had to end my relationship with them. It felt disempowering, rather than empowering, and that is a red flag to watch for in joint efforts.

I respected the work of one of its founders so much, but found that their organization's methods and beliefs no longer matched ours. Collaboration is meant to empower others. If it does not feel right, then go. It is not unlike dating. No regrets or rancor, but consider it a lesson learned. Which brings me to my next point.

8. Follow your Gut. Do not Second Guess Your Instincts.

The dating reference is just so easy to expand on because we have all done it; dated someone we thought was absolutely right for us, only to later realize what a stupid match it really was. As we process the pain and kick ourselves for allowing all that to happen, we look back and realize that early on, we actually had an inkling that this might not be the right person for us. We flash back to that first dinner out and remember how this person was rude to the wait staff: "But look at his accomplishments and how attentive he is to me!" How his social media status is alarmingly full of cuss words and hate speech: "But oh, he's so charming and nice to me, and so talented!"

We then kick ourselves even harder for not heeding the signs, that little alarm bell ringing inside our head, that red flag waving right in front of our eyes, and so on and so forth. We ask ourselves, "Why didn't we trust our instincts?"

The same thing applies in the professional world, but substitute the word "dating" for "hiring." I have made only two hiring blunders in my professional life, but I paid for those mistakes dearly. I have made the mistake of being overly impressed by résumé and accomplishments, but ignored subtle hints that came out even during the interview and probation period. The person said mean things about their former employer and co-workers: "But a magna cum laude from a reputable school! Maybe he/she won't do it to me because I'm different." Oh, how we pay for ignoring the hints. People and situations actually announce themselves to you in so many different ways the very first time you encounter them, but you must learn to listen deeply, because the announcement is being made in the place we have been taught to ignore; in our gut.

We have been trained so much to use logic and reason, but truly, this anti-intuition stance denies the built-in radar we were all born with. In some instances, we are like animals that seem to instinctively know. Why are we so comfortable with the idea that dogs can spot friendly or dangerous strangers and situations? We have the same skill. So in decision-making, listen to that small voice inside you. Do not be afraid to lead with your gut.

9. Introduce Everyone to Each Other.

As a new executive director, in a new chapter of my life in the nonprofit sector, I was an unknown entity in San Francisco community. I was not a community organizer or a volunteer. But I practically knew every one of the personalities and their causes, because as the former head of news production and executive producer of a news department, it was my business to know who the people in the community are, and it was my job to decide what was important to merit airtime on the news. And so, as a news executive deluged with requests to cover news, I deliberately hid myself from the public we were covering to avoid offending the people whose requests for coverage we had to unfortunately reject. My reporters could just tell people, "Our boss sends our regrets that we cannot cover your event or put you on the air." They could just blame the nameless, faceless boss that was me.

I relished my behind-the-scenes role. As a former newscaster and TV reporter, it was refreshing to be out of public view and indulge my introvert side.

But when I finally joined the community, I had to leave my comfort zone and get to know everyone. I felt shy and awkward, like the new kid at school. Then, during a community event, the most popular woman came over and introduced me to other people. The popular woman, who also barely knew me, was Supervisor Jane Kim, who serves in the district where our agency is located. That simple, gracious act of introducing me to people in her district when there she had the opportunity to do so was profoundly powerful in its impact on me and I have copied her. I found myself introducing people who had already known each other for years.

It is a very kind thing to do, to help smooth the way for new people in your sphere. We take it for granted during social occasions, where it is good manners to introduce our friends to each other.

But in community and public life, the same act takes on a different meaning. You meet people you could work with, or people whose causes complement or match your own, and your network begins to build. It makes work so much more enjoyable and fun, to meet new people. Oftentimes, it all begins with a simple introduction, like how Jane did it for me and continues to do so for others. As Maya Angelou famously said: "People will forget what you said, people will forget what you did. But people will never forget how you made them feel." Make new people feel welcome. It is a simple, gracious act of leadership.

10. Progress not Perfection. Celebrate Victories.

One thing I have always been, as a journalist, and as an executive, is too hard on myself. I thought that this brutal self-honesty was healthy, because then I could achieve even more and motivate myself to shoot for higher goals.

But my inner critic can be so harsh, I can demoralize myself to the point of paralysis. This is what my teacher Vicki pointed out to me. Yes, I can be quite the overachiever, but I also make myself so unhappy over mistakes that I fail to see how far I have gone. This is not a right way of seeing things.

It is a very miserable outlook on life, and can make it rather uninspiring to be around.

Vicki taught me a valuable lesson: that we treat others the way we treat ourselves. Therefore, if we are harsh with ourselves, we will be harsh with others.

I have since learned to cut myself some slack, because I finally realized I cannot achieve perfection. Yes, this is how deluded I have been. The most we can hope for in life and at work is progress. I have forgiven my many stumbles and have started to realize my own successes. I have not been a very good celebrator of victories. My tendency is to just get things done and move on, without really patting myself on the back for jobs well done. It is something I am still working on. I now realize that we *need* to celebrate the good things we have done. It is our duty to do so, because in celebrating victories and progress, we inspire ourselves and others to do well.

If we are unable to inspire ourselves or others, we are unable to lead others to victory. It can be a small victory, like finally finishing that invoice. It can be a big victory, like helping others find a job, ending a violent situation at home, or preventing them from taking their own lives. To lead, we must inspire. To inspire we must celebrate progress. To be able to celebrate progress, we must stop measuring everything against perfection.

HEARING THE LEADERSHIP TIPS OF OTHERS

So many people have come to be friends, advisers, and mentors. There are too many people to thank, people whose words of wisdom and guidance I will treasure always.

Everyone has a great tip, and do not hesitate to ask people you feel you can trust for advice. But even as you do so, remember that whatever you receive is just advice. I will once again quote my most important mentor, Vicki Austin, who once told me, when I asked her, for the umpteenth time, what I should do next: "You can't ask the car where it wants to take you, Vivian. You need to decide where you want to go, get in, and then drive the car."

※

THELMA B. BOAC

San Jose Berryessa Union School District Board of Trustees
Filipina Women's Network Board Member *2014-2016*
FWN100™ U.S. *2007*

From My Two Mothers:
A Legacy Borne

'W hat happened? Why are you crying?' asked my stunned husband seeing me sobbing in front of my computer. I answered, "I don't think I can do this, writing about myself, remembering my childhood. It's too emotional, and I can't even get past the introduction." He said empathically, "Oh, yes, you can! Just remember, it's not just about you anymore, it's beyond you. We're talking about the legacy you're going to leave your children, especially, your grandchildren. Your grandchildren need to know who their grandma really is and who she has become. This is the legacy you will leave behind. So, let's go and write your story!" Wiping away tears and letting out a big sigh, I begin to write.

In my childhood, the thought of flying alone across the Pacific Ocean was never in my wildest imagination. But I have always known that somehow there was something out there for me. I remember whenever I walked along that long pier in my town, I would look across the water as far as my eyes could see and think that America was just on the other side of the horizon. At night, I would hold the flashlight and shine it into the heavens just to see how far heaven was. I just wanted to touch it. What I did not know then was my mother's strong belief from the day I was born that I was destined to do great things in life.

In this chapter, I reflect on the leadership qualities that my two mothers instilled in me that helped me discern my purpose in life and gave me strength to adjust to being given up for adoption, travelling to America by myself at age 10, and acclimatizing to life in a strawberry farm. These leadership qualities that I practiced early in life served as the building blocks for my subsequent leadership roles in my chosen career; first as an educator, then as an administrator, and as the only woman member of the Board of Trustees of the Berryessa Union School District in San Jose, California.

"Mimi, you are going to America!"

My life's journey began in a village on the island of Bohol. It was there that my parents gave me up for adoption to my mother's older sister – Auntie Crispina, also called Auntie Pining, who lived in America. Sadly, Auntie Pining lost her two young children and her first husband during World War II. After the war, Auntie Pining who was a risk-taker journeyed by herself to the U.S., met and married Uncle Diego in California, and because they had no children of their own decided to adopt one of my birth mother's nine children.

I remember one afternoon in 1958, when I was only eight years old, while walking home from school I saw my mother in the distance walking quickly towards me and calling out my name "Mimi", which was my family nickname. She seemed excited but somewhat sad at the same time. She said, "Mimi, you are going to America. You are going to school and live with your aunt and uncle in California. Isn't that wonderful?" My response was one of innocence and ignorance. I did not know where America was and how far away it was, but I had heard it was a beautiful place; rich, with streets paved with gold. So I said, as I hugged my mother, "Wow, I am going to America."

Auntie Pining picked me to go to the United States to live with her and my uncle since they did not have any children of their own. Another reason was Auntie Pining wanted to help my mother and her family with the hope that one day I would be able give back to the family. It was not easy to feed a family of nine children plus "Nanay," my beloved grandmother. Certainly, sending all nine children to school and giving them a good education was an additional challenge. We lived a simple life and there was harmony at home. Prayers played a critical part in our daily lives. The sound of music was everywhere with the men and women playing guitars and banjos. My own mother had a beautiful voice; she had the gift of song. Music is one of the most cherished gifts I inherited from her. Moreover, my own exposure to leadership and politics came quite early since my mother was very involved in politics. She pretty much took the leading role in many of the social activities and fundraising events in the town. Thus, she was always in the "public eye."

Why Me? Discerning My Purpose in Life

I asked my mother why I was the one picked to go to America and live with my aunt and uncle, especially since there were nine of us, including my six brothers and two sisters. My mother showed me the letter my Auntie Pining wrote to her and my father. My aunt wanted, first and foremost, a little girl. But, this little girl had to be old enough to dress herself, be able to help around the house, and be old enough to not forget the family and life she left behind. This was the reason my mother and my aunt chose me. This little girl was to have a mission in life, and that mission ultimately was to get a good education and help the family back home. All this was instilled in me. My mother revealed, as well, that when I was born she knew I was destined to do great things in life. She had kept this secret to herself. But when it became apparent that there was now an opportunity for a better future, she decided to share the secret.

I was born with the umbilical cord wrapped tightly around my neck. The midwife thought I was stillborn. I did not cry, and I made no sound. I was barely breathing. My own mother prayed and prayed for me to live. Then all of a sudden, I gave out a loud cry. Right then and there, my mother said, she decided to give me the English sounding name of "Thelma." It was the name that came to her mind first. She confessed that she did not know why she thought of that name, but the name "Thelma" now seemed to be a foreshadowing that I would end up as the child chosen to live in America. "Destiny" she said. "The stars are aligned just for you, sweetheart." Of course, at my ripe young age of eight, I had no inkling of what any of this meant. But the expression on my mother's face told me that it was something wonderful. I did not realize until later that this destined "mission" would become a lifetime commitment for me. My mother was a deeply religious woman. She told me that it was God's will that I was chosen to go to America because God had a purpose in life for me. Whether to go to America or not, was not my choice; it was my choice to discern my purpose in life and to act accordingly.

Everyone knew I was soon to leave for Manila and then to America. Our relatives, friends, and neighbors all told me I was the lucky one, the one destined to go places. I was reminded that amongst the three sisters I was the most vocal, the most argumentative, and the most likely to be in the middle of children's disputes. There was something uniquely different about me, I was told repeatedly. I had a spark. I was not afraid to speak my mind to anyone including adults. I was someone special. At a young age, I was told that I was already demonstrating leadership.

Off to America Alone: Finding my Strength

It was time to prepare my papers to go to America. The plan was for me to go on a student visa, and upon arrival in the U.S. my aunt and uncle would process the adoption papers. The criteria for a student visa was very clear: excellent student and a high grade point average (GPA). Thank God, I was an honor student! I loved being in school and cherished learning. The spirit to excel was always in me. I carried that spirit throughout my years as a student, an educator, an administrator, and as a trustee.

I remember how proud I was of my mother who was unafraid of the interviewers at the American Embassy. She was fearless and confident. Despite the fierce and sometime tricky questioning, my mother convinced the interviewer to give me a student visa. I was amazed at what my mother had accomplished. Without her "raw" courage, I would not have been able to cross the ocean to the U.S. I was in awe of her, a woman filled with deep faith and conviction. This image of her made a lasting imprint on my soul. It made me emulate her. I, too, became fearless and confident.

Now it was time to leave for America. My little sister, who was 7 years old at the time, and I had to say goodbye. She and I did not really comprehend what was happening except for the fact that I was leaving. I think we both thought I was coming back the next day. The scene at the airport was something I will never forget for as long as I have breath left inside me. I knew full well it was extremely difficult for my mother to let me go, though she did not show it. There was a great deal of drama and a lot of haggling between the airport officials and my mother. She was busy negotiating who would be watching me the entire trip until we reach San Francisco. In those days it took three days to fly to San Francisco with stop-overs in Guam, Wake Island, and Honolulu. At last, another family with a little girl, a year younger than me, agreed to watch over me. It was time to say goodbye to my brave and relieved mother who was already exhausted from the intense discussions. The plane had been delayed for an hour due to the negotiations. My mother looked at me, touched my face and hair, and kissed me. I never felt so alone. Confusion filled my heart and mind. My eyes swelled with tears, my mother looked at me and signaled "No". Then I followed the family to the plane. I did not look back. It was best. With three long days of plane travel, I had plenty of time to think. I was pretty much alone. As I looked down on the clouds below, I thought of my mother being brave, skillful, and assertive. I thought about my entire family. Would I ever see them again? As I looked up above and saw a sky full of bright shining stars, I recalled my mother saying to me back home, "The stars are aligned just for you, sweetheart. It is God's will." She was, indeed, an inspiration to me in all aspects of my life. I learned from her example to use my instincts to capital-ize on my strengths to respond to new situations whenever and wherever it was required.

LIFE IN THE STRAWBERRY FARM

I arrived in San Francisco on June 6, 1960. I was ten years old. Arriving very early in the morning, I felt as if I was being poked with needles on my legs. I real-ized later on it was the cold weather that was affecting my bones.

My 10-Year Old Self: Coping with a New Environment

My soon-to-be adoptive parents, Diego and Crispina de Vera, met me at the airport. I had never seen them before except in photographs, so I was not sure what they really looked like in person. As I was passing by a line of many greeters, a woman grabbed my arm and asked me a question in English. She resembled my mother. I said nothing. Then the man next to her said something, and she asked me again, this time in my dialect. I nodded my head. Then the lady who was with me on the plane verified that I was indeed Thelma. My new parents had a big smile on their face and a huge sigh of relief. This was a huge comfort for me as I stared at my new mama. She looked so much like my mother. She took off her coat and placed it on my shoulders. She held me close to her as we walked to the car. That very moment I made a pledge to myself to be a good girl, to be obedient, and to study hard.

After four hours on the road we finally arrived in Oceano, a small coastal town located between San Francisco and Los Angeles. For the first time I saw my new home, and for a ten-year old it was quite a sight to behold. The gate was open for us to enter. The white colored house was right in the middle of a strawberry farm. There were people picking strawberries, three dogs barking, and one beautiful cat named Patsy sitting on the porch as if waiting to greet me. I had no idea what a strawberry looked or even tasted like. During dinner that evening I had it for dessert along with ice cream. My taste buds and my stomach could not handle it. I threw up right then and there. Then deep loneliness sank in, and I cried at the dinner table. Seeing me, my aunt and uncle cried with me. I do not think anyone ate dinner that first night.

At the farm I learned how to pick beans and fruits including strawberries. My new dad paid me fifty cents per crate for the strawberries. That was my typical job during summer. Later on, during summer my classmates would join me so they could earn some extra money to buy clothes for the following school year. My dad would gather all of us during the break and give us punch and cookies. Then he would lecture us that farm work is hard work and not for girls like us. "Go to college and get a good education," he would tell us. We all did go to college; some took the two-year path and the rest of us the four-year path. I chose the four-year path.

Learning about Living with Prejudice

My dad told me about how he came to the United States at the age of 16 along with his older brother and several cousins, boarding a boat bound for America to search for a better life and a better future. The year was 1926. They worked in farms throughout California moving from one to another while experiencing discrimination every step of the way. Furthermore, not too long after that, my dad and many others experienced the Great Depression of the late 1920's and endured different types of hardships. They were not allowed to marry or socialize outside of their ethnic group. They were banned from restaurants and public places. There would be signs at these restaurants that said "Dogs and Filipinos not allowed." As though "Dogs" equated with Filipinos. Since Filipinos are social in nature, socialization was pretty much limited to Filipinos and other people of color. Socialization was mainly weekend dances and events held at "dance halls." The laws in America in the 1920's, 1930's, and 1940's were not kind to Filipinos and to other people of color. Hatred and prejudice were a part of their lives. And yet, they loved America very much. Many became World War II veterans. Many of the manongs [older brother] married later in life after World War II to young Filipinas and brought their young brides to America. These evolving families became my aunts and uncles throughout my childhood. The phrase "it takes a village to raise a child" was already ingrained in the Filipino.

Despite all the hatred and prejudices my dad had to endure in America, he was never bitter, never held grudges or blamed anyone for the discomfort and pain of being discriminated against. One could only admire his positive attitude towards mankind. Today, I do not waste my energy on people who may not like me. But make no mistake, I always treat everyone with respect, even those I would refer to as possible "saboteurs." These are people who would want to block one's agenda and would be resistant to change. My dad only had a sixth grade education, but he was wise. His positive approach to life has guided me throughout my years as an educator and, now, as an elected official.

Learning to Cope with Disruptions

My adoptive mom finished first year-college before she got married. World War II broke out; her first husband was reported missing in action in the Battle of Bataan, and her two very young children died just before the Americans liberated Manila. Though devastated, she moved on with her life. Fearless, and a risk taker, she journeyed by herself to the United States after the war.

Extending Family Values

My adoptive mother and father met in California and married eventually. They had no children. Both were very social and civic minded. For years I watched their participation and involvement in the community. As I was growing up, there was hardly a weekend where my family was not at a birthday party, a wedding, or a christening. We were all one family. This became my model for how I treated my staff when I became a high school principal; like family.

Presenting Your Best Self

My dad loved to dress up and was always impeccably dressed during events. This was how the men dressed on weekends as they prepared to go to "dance halls" to socialize during their early years in America. From both my dad and my mom, I learned how to dress and conduct myself in public, how to address people, and foremost, how to communicate with the public. To them appearance was extremely important, and to this day I am always cognizant of my appearance, demeanor, and language whenever in public.

THE LEGACY OF TWO MOTHERS

In the summer before my senior year of high school, my mom and I travelled back home to the Philippines. She herself had not returned to the Philippines since the end of World War II. The reason for going back was twofold. She had promised my biological mother that I would come back to visit; the other was for me to be reminded of the life that I had left behind. My mom was fearful I had become too "Americanized." My birth mom's family continued to struggle with life on a daily basis. The experience of the visit filled me with a combined sense of compassion and humility; two leadership qualities that define who I am today and what I have become. Humility, as in self-restraint from excessive vanity and compassion, sympathy, empathy, and concern for others have guided my professional life as instructional leader, high school principal, community leader, and public official. I thank my two mothers who were exemplary models of these qualities.

EXPANDING MY HORIZON

My mom and dad recognized I had a talent for music even at a young age, so I was given piano lessons. To please my mom, I decided to continue my music studies at San Francisco State University together with a major in Spanish.

Right after graduation from high school, I had the good fortune to travel all over the United States and Canada. It was a gift from the parents and family of my best friend, Kathy. It turned out to be more than a vacation; it was an education. Visiting the southern states left a lasting imprint on my mind. The signs outside the bathrooms that read "Whites Only" and "Colored Only" were shocking to me. The year was 1968. I had thought that discrimination disappeared after President Lyndon Johnson signed the Civil Rights Bill in 1965. Apparently not. It was a sad reminder of the hatred and prejudices that my adopted father and many other people of color experienced from the 1920's through the 1950's. And, sadly enough, there is still discrimination even today in the 21st century. My trip to the southern states made me even more committed to the idea that discrimination of any kind has no place anywhere and, most certainly, not in education. I believe diversity is a strength, and educators must be sensitive and embrace the differences between cultures. They must work towards eliminating all prejudices and biases.

As part of a study abroad program, during my senior year of college, I attended the University of Granada in Granada, Spain, (La Facultad de Filosofia y Letras) to continue my Spanish Language studies. Studying in Spain fulfilled my dream to go to Europe, a dream that started when I was a sixth grader after one lesson on Europe. The study abroad program was a life-changing experience. It made me get out of my comfort zone, forced me to challenge myself and opened my eyes to the world. Most importantly, I discovered that we as a people have more in common than we are different sharing one world.

THE EDUCATOR IN ME: MY CAREER PATH

Passion for Teaching

After completing my studies abroad and obtaining my California Secondary Teaching Credential from San Francisco State University, I got married to Dan

Boac, now my husband of 42 years. We first lived in Sunnyvale, California, where I began my teaching career, and then moved next door to Santa Clara. Eventually we settled in San Jose, where I began my administrative career. I had taught for twenty-years before becoming a school administrator. I loved being in the classroom and was comfortable in my little "kingdom." It took a colleague to convince me to become an administrator. Before that I served on different positions such as Department Chair for English Language Development, as well as Bilingual Coordinator and Coordinator of Testing and Assessment. This colleague of mine asked me this question, "Thelma, where do you see yourself ten years from now?" I never really gave it much thought and could not give her an answer. So I just said, "Here in my little kingdom." She said, "No. Get your administrative credential. Everyone you work with respects you. You have what it takes, and you have the right stuff to be a leader. We want you to be Principal. You have become a wonderful role model to our community, especially the youth. They look up to you with admiration and respect. What a great way to leave a legacy for our students, especially, the Filipino students."

Becoming an Administrator

Though I was reluctant to leave the familiarity of being with students and working closely with staff, I decided to become an administrator. I thought that I could truly make a difference in students' lives by the critical decisions I would be making. I completed a Master's Degree in Education with emphasis in Administration and Supervision, followed by a Professional Clear Credential.

Afterwards, I was promoted to become the Villa Principal at Independence High School in-charge of the entire 9th Grade program. Shortly thereafter, the first woman ever selected became the new superintendent of the East Side Union High School District. During the superintendent's first year, I focused on my work and did the job I was required to do. I had no idea I was being noticed. During her short tenure, the superintendent was courageous in promoting women into leadership positions.

Staying True to My Core: Integrity

In a surprise move, one evening the superintendent invited me to have dinner with her. I thought, for sure, she was going to fire me. I was wrong. Her plan was to remove my head principal before the school year was over. She wanted me to take over as Principal of Independence High School. I was dumbfounded! After giving my reasons, I said "No." She told me to think it over and give my decision the following morning. I suggested to the superintendent to wait until the school year was over, letting the principal preside over the graduation ceremonies in June and I would take over in the fall of the new school year. My suggestion was rejected. Removing the head principal before school was over was something I could not swallow. I was not about to strip her of her dignity. Moreover, I was concerned with the morale of teachers and students and the entire learning community if there was a sudden disruption just before the end of the school year. I understood the impact and how it could affect everyone. I was committed to a smooth transition and more concerned with the stability of the learning environment than advancing my own ambition. I stuck to my decision and preserved my integrity. Not having compassion for another human went against every fiber in my body. I understood very clearly that being a leader does not guarantee everyone will like you. The head principal was concerned my administrative career was over because I did not obey the wishes of the superintendent. I told her I was content and comfortable with my decision. That day we became more than colleagues; we became friends.

A year later, I received a phone call from the superintendent again. This time she offered me the position of Principal at Silver Creek High School. I accepted the offer and remained in this position until I retired. My promotion as Principal of Silver Creek High School was announced in the July 2005 edition of the *Evergreen Times*, the community newspaper of Evergreen Valley:

> *Boac, a long-time East Side Union High School District (ESUHSD) educator, has been at Independence High School for 24 years. Since 2001, she has been villa principal for the ninth grade program at Independence High School, handling the full gamut of administrative responsibilities required to lead a school of 1,200 students. From 1981 to 2001, she taught ELD, English as a Second Language, Spanish, and World History; served as literacy coach; coordinator for Federal Programs and Department Chair throughout two decades of service there. She was also a club advisor for various student organizations. She holds a bachelor's degree from San Francisco State University and a master's degree in Education with emphasis in administration and supervision from San Jose State University.*

My years as Principal at Silver Creek High School were the best years of my professional career. As an educational leader I was able to use everything that I had learned and experienced in the past. Having the ability to observe people and accentuate the good that is in them is a gift. My goal was to lead a staff and treat them as members of one family. I used this skill in my relationships with people in building a unified and collaborative learning community. In order for me to move my agenda forward, I could not be a leader without followers. This could only occur when the leader sets the tone and example. It's all about "relationship, relationship, relationship!" This can only be the result of being skilled in relating to many different types of people, being sensitive to people's feelings, and treating people with respect regardless of their rank or position in the organization.

Leaders sow seeds in everything they do whether good or bad, and those seeds will eventually bear fruit. There is a saying, "what we sow is what we reap." I believe that with all my heart. Every time a leader acts with kindness and respect and integrity, the seed is planted. Building positive relationships with people is similar to cultivating and sowing seeds that will grow and bear fruit. It does not happen overnight. It is a process that needs to be nurtured.

An important lesson I learned as a leader is that a leader cannot do it alone. A leader must have support at all times. You need to cultivate a network of support that can provide encouragement and energize; and who can be your confidante and sounding board. It is also critical to bring "enemies" closer to you. Do not just have the "yes" people around you. Surround yourself with people who have different opinions and who can be honest with you. These are the people who can keep you focused on your mission and point out ways where you can be more effective as a leader and help you see your blind spots. I made it a point to have a communicative relationship with members of the teacher's union and included its president among my circle of advisors. We never agreed on everything, but I valued his opinion for I felt he had his hands on the pulse of the entire staff and this helped me see what I might not see. Again, this is being cognizant of the blind spots that I might not otherwise be aware of.

In my first four months of being a high school principal, an emergency occurred, and the high school had to be placed on a lockdown. It was timely that the president of the teacher's union happened to be in my office when I received the phone call from the police department. He reminded me of the steps as I acted quickly and calmly. He stayed with me as I was making decisions throughout the ordeal advising me and keeping me focused on the priorities of keeping our students and staff safe. Nervous parents were waiting outside the police barricaded area anxiously waiting for news on their children. After two hours the lockdown was lifted. He advised me to go outside and address the parents, which I did. The incident was handled successfully, and for a rookie principal his presence helped me deal with a difficult situation. This vignette goes against the notion that school administrators and the teacher's union are always at odds with each other. I am a firm believer that "enemies" can work together for the common good, and this incident was one great example. Working together as one family was my theme in achieving the goals and objectives for Silver Creek High School.

COMMUNITY BUILDING

Mirroring my parents who were active in community organizations, I too became active in community affairs after moving to San Jose, California. Being an educator in the community was an asset. I got invited to functions and important events. I became the "go to" person for advice and counseling for many Filipino families and families of color. I was humbled, and still am, by their demonstration of respect and admiration. I was sought after to take leading roles in many organizations, such as chair of the Santa Clara Valley Philippine Professional and Business Society (PPBS) Scholarship Committee and board member of the Doris Prince Foundation at San Jose State University where I assisted students to enroll in its Educational Leadership Program. I became involved in community centers, especially the Tony Siquig Northside Community Center, creating programs for ethnic groups interested in English Language Development (ELD). I assisted in providing tutorial services for high school students in Mathematics and English and helped prepare students for the SAT college entrance exams. I have always believed that education is not limited to the school grounds but extends to the community as well.

In 2002, I became the President of the Silicon Valley Filipino American Movement in Education (FAME). This organization was started in 1972 by a group of very dedicated educators. The group influenced the East Side Union High School District policy of recruiting teachers from the Philippines to mirror the student population of the district. FAME succeeded in bringing fifty teachers to the district from 1999 through 2002. The majority were Math, Science, and Special Education teachers, fields that were in short supply in California's public school system. During the three years the program was active, the new teachers were assigned to all thirteen high schools within the district including Independence and my own at Silver Creek. My role in the program was to provide staff development and prepare teachers for their new experience in America's public school classrooms. I was their mentor then and still am today. I am very proud of their accomplishments and the challenges they have overcome. They continue to thrive and have become a great asset to the school district.

My advocacy in nurturing environmental consciousness is reflected in my involvement in the Philippine-based non-profit organization, Human Development International (HDI). HDI is part of the United Nations' endorsed "Call to Save the Mountains of the World" initiative, an initiative focused on helping to improve the lives of indigenous people around the world. I am also on the Board of Directors for the Children's Health and Education Fund (CHEF) Foundation, another non-profit organization focusing on helping students succeed in school in the needy areas of the Philippines. I have been instrumental in providing books for the classrooms, as well as supplying books and reading materials to empty libraries in the cities and provinces of the Philippines.

As a former child in the province, I have not forgotten the thirst for learning of so many children yearning to have a book in their hands. I was one of those anxious to learn. This is an on-going effort to keep supplying books to the needy places in the Philippines. I have been fortunate to be the recipient of many awards and to have been recognized by many organizations, including the California State Legislators, for my commitment to community service. They include: Marquis Publications Who's Who Among America's Teachers (1996), Dr. Martin Luther King Jr. Good Neighbor Award (2005), Filipina Women's Network (FWN) 100 Most Influential Women in the U.S. (2007), Marquis Publications Who's Who of American Women (2007), Filipino-American National Historical Society (FANHS) Filipino Community Pioneer Award (2010), San Jose Local Hero Award by California State Assemblyman Bob Wieckowski (2011), Kalayaan Hero Recognition by Philippine Consul General (2015), Community Hero Award by California State Assemblyman, Kansen Chu (2015), and 2015 Distinguished Women Awards by Ivy Rose Community Foundation, and members of Eta Rho Omega Chapter of Alpha Kappa Alpha Sorority.

My involvement with the Filipina Women's Network since 2007 has been more than an asset and a blessing. It has encouraged me to continue my passion for helping others and has taken me to new heights as well as provided opportunities that I otherwise would not have entertained. The premise that Filipinas have the qualities to be leaders and to be influential continues to be the fuel in my veins. I cannot help but think of Eleanor Roosevelt who said, "Always look fear in the face." And Meyla Roberta Gbowee, a Nobel Peace Prize awardee, who said, "One can never leave a lasting footprint if we are always walking on tiptoes." From the legacy of my two mothers to the goals of the Filipina Women's Network, I will never be walking on tiptoes. My feet are firmly planted on the ground. I know where I have been, and I know where I am going.

FROM EDUCATOR TO POLITICIAN

After nearly four decades in education, I decided to retire. I was looking forward to my retirement when San Jose State University, the National Hispanic University, and the Santa Clara County Office of Education recruited me to train, supervise, and coach new teachers and newly appointed principals and school administrators. There went my retirement!

Politics never entered my mind, although the issues involving education were always in the thick of politics. Due to a sudden resignation on the local school board, my name was thrown around for appointment to the Board of Trustees of the Berryessa Union School District in San Jose. I became one of the finalist and was one of seven people interviewed for the position. Lo and behold, I got appointed to the governing board to serve the remaining two years of the term of someone who left. After serving two years, I decided to run for a new four-year term. I had become convinced that my work was not finished and there was still much to be done. I found out quickly that running a campaign was not that easy. Time was of the essence, and money was critical.

Reciprocity Based on Respectful Relationships

Since I knew my community well and they knew me, people were willing to volunteer and donate to my campaign. The seeds that were sowed bore fruit. I am now reaping the respectful relationships I had built for many years. My campaign manager was an eighteen-year-old who had just graduated from Independence High School, where I had been the former Villa Principal. The students heard about my campaign, and they readily volunteered to walk precincts and spread the word throughout the district. The students were savvy in the use of technology. Thanks to the youth in my community; I can easily say technology played a role in my re-election. Being respected and highly regarded as a community leader and an educator is a treasure. The result was re-election to a four-year term in the November election of 2014.

Setting Educational Policy

Education has always been my passion. I have dedicated my life to teaching, encouraging, inspiring, and empowering youth to reach their highest potential; giving them access to the best education possible so they can compete in the 21st Century global economy. I have come to the realization that I cannot turn my back on the important issues of education. I have to be a participant in the critical decision making process impacting students and student success. It is interesting being the only female on the Board of Trustees, "the rose among the thorns." I am the most experienced of the Board members in dealing with educational issues having been active in this field for almost four decades.

Keeping the Dialogue Going

But what I am learning now is that change does not come quickly. What I am discovering is that listening is a critical part of the process. There are many ways to improve education. But if we truly want to make change, we need first to understand what is involved. We cannot be arrogant about our own ideas; first we need to listen and to listen to those we disagree with and engage those who disagree with us. My job on the Board of Trustees is to make things better for all students. In order for me to do that, I have come to realize that we as leaders need to be active participants at the table and be part of the discussion. This is never easy given the obstacles and the people who disagree with you. But at the same time, we also need to let others speak and listen to them, yet have the confidence to challenge them with our own ideas. Most of the time it is more important to listen than it is to talk. How else can we learn about what needs to be done or to change to improve a situation? No one ever stops growing and evolving, and one of the ways to learn is to listen to others. As we gain an understanding, little by little we can consolidate our gains so the next time we can start from that position. As Epictetus, the Greek philosopher, wrote: "We have two ears and one mouth for a good reason." In this way, listening can take one's leadership to the next level. It can help to create a healthy culture. In this age of instant communication, we are often in such a rush to communicate what's on our own minds that we fail to realize the value of everything that can be gleaned from the minds of others. The purpose of communication is not only to message but to engage. It is not a lecture or a monologue. It is the first step in building trust and rapport, and with that as a basis we can begin to make progress.

On to New Horizons

As I consider where to go next, one area in the field of education I am drawn to is exactly how public education is currently being financed. It is my belief that the needs of students, teachers, parents, and community members must be taken into consideration as critical choices are made regarding the state's funding priorities. My hope is that as I begin to build relationships with various stakeholders, I will be able to have a platform to influence policymakers to find a more consistent means to fund education at the level that is needed. Education must become a priority so that students and teachers can thrive. With an adequate source of funding in place, educators will not have to concern themselves with struggling to have enough resources to do their job well. As an elected official, I am often asked by legislators what concerns educators most. Since I am intimately familiar with the pulse of the learning community, I can be the voice for students, parents, teachers, and the community. As a young girl, I was very fortunate to have parents who were my voice. At this point in my life it would be a blessing for me to have this opportunity to be a voice for others.

THE CIRCLE OF LIFE

After sixteen years of marriage, my husband Dan and I were not blessed with children of our own. I never thought that my adoption story would be repeated. Dan and I adopted the two children of my youngest sister, Nene, who had passed away suddenly, leaving the children without a mother at such young age. Not too long after her death, the father also died suddenly; this time leaving the children fully orphaned. In 1989 we became parents to a teen-age boy and a teen-age girl, Roland and Maria Rosalie. Today, we are blessed with four grandchildren; three little girls and a young boy. The legacy of my two mothers lives on. It is indeed a gift from God. My life has come full circle.

GLENDA TIBE BONIFACIO, PH.D.

Associate Professor
at the University of Lethbridge in Alberta, Canada
FWN100™ Global 2015

Legacy in the Academe:
Integrated Activism for Social Justice

The university is a contested space; a place to belong and a place of exclusion. As an undergraduate and graduate student at the University of the Philippines, the liberatory agenda of freedom, equality, social justice, and activism were central values that shaped who I am today. The combination of scholarly and voluntary activities opened my eyes to the schisms between the ideal and real in society, first in the Philippines and then in Australia and in Canada.

In this chapter, I examine the real and potential legacy of Filipina academics in transnational context. The first section offers a glimpse of my trans-Pacific journey from the Philippines to Australia and the ways in which differences in academic social systems affect scholarly practice. The second section situates my present reality as an academic in Canada and the manner in which subjectivities define global-local interactions in course delivery and engagement. The third section positions the concept of situated feminist leadership as a form of integrated activism against racism and discrimination for social justice through my research on Filipino women's lives in diaspora. Finally, the fourth section posits the view of an unfolding legacy as I am one of only eight tenured Filipino academics in Canada in 2012 (Coloma et al. 2012).

TRANS-PACIFIC ACADEMIC JOURNEY: PHILIPPINES TO AUSTRALIA

I completed an undergraduate degree in Political Science with honours in the 1980s. My awakening into critical thinking, sometimes viewed as radical by conservatives and conforming peers, is a product of the interplay of personal, social and political context of my generation; the so-called "martial law babies" growing up during the Marcos regime. I was the first female elected chairperson of the student council at the University of the Philippines Tacloban College in 1983-1984. I served as vice-chair of the alliance of student councils in the province of Leyte during this time, with massive rallies organized to criticize human rights violations and the dictatorship. The school-sponsored award to an honour society in recognition of my academic accomplishment as magna cum laude was withdrawn because I rejected the order of the college dean to pull out the students from a protest rally before the graduation ceremony.

As a university student, I was selected to join the Task Force for Youth Concerns of the Asia Alliance of YMCAs based in Hong Kong, the only Filipino student in this group tasked with empowering young people in the lead up to the International Youth Year from 1982-1984. I travelled extensively to other Asian countries including Australia and Canada, once as the invited speaker of the YMCA associated world youth congress in Canada. I represented the Eastern Visayas Region in the ASEAN-Japan youth program in 1984 that allowed me to travel to Malaysia, Indonesia, Singapore, Thailand, and Japan. These international opportunities to meet people from different countries was a factor in my decision to pursue a Masters in Asian Studies at the Asian Center, University of the Philippines, Diliman. I received a scholarship and presidential grant for my graduate studies.

The transition from student to academic came very early. Immediately after graduating with a bachelors' degree, I was asked to teach a course in Political Science at the University of the Philippines, Tacloban College. Within one semester I found myself teaching my friends and peers from student organizations. I was teaching Political Science concepts concerning civic engagement for restoring democracy that were as real as the socio-political environment at that time. In 1991, with a master's degree, I returned as an assistant professor in Political Science to the University of the Philippines, Tacloban College. From 1991 until 2000, life as a UP academic was challenging due to administrative politics. I heard colleagues say "once a rebel always a rebel" when my student activism days were entangled with faculty politics. I embrace certain values and principles that can never be compromised because my sense of justice and fair play is paramount. Holding on to principles and fighting for what I believed in took a personal toll and further threatened the economic security of my own family. I prevailed and matters were resolved in my favour. I learned that academics are not only facilitators of acquiring concepts and knowledge but also activists who can apply what they teach. Leadership is developed through experiencing problems and finding the best solutions, and the ability to take risks along the way.

Conflicting discourses are often viewed by Filipinos as personal conflicts with no separation between the idea and the person. When I disagree with an idea, it does not mean that I am against that person. But Filipino academics and the parochial nature of Philippine social system suggests otherwise. This often leads to division in departments and with administrators. Teaching in an environment of personal discord is difficult; and professionalism is replaced by personalism. In this environment, teaching is not only a vocation but a form of leadership. Teachers are ideally viewed as models of learning and an example to emulate. In the academe, professors need to show leadership on matters where they are considered an expert.

Pursuing a PhD in Australia opened me to a different system where merit took precedence over personal matters. I observed in the Australian setting that some professors have heated exchanges about a particular issue but shake hands after, often with a smile. In the Philippine setting, I remembered my colleagues snubbing me after we disagreed in a meeting. If I adopted the cause of students then I was assumed to belong to their camp and such identity continued to live on even when the issues have changed. However, my home department in my university in Australia during the three years of postgraduate scholarship offered the freedom to pursue academic rigours of research without the nasty politics of smaller campuses in the Philippines. As a postgraduate student, I devoted my time to research and my family who accompanied me to Australia; five daughters and a husband.

While searching for a "doable" topic for a doctoral thesis, I was pulled into the lives of migrant Filipino women in Australia. Living in Australia in 2000 and thereafter for the next three years provided a view of what Pyke and Johnson (2003) consider the racialization and subjectivities of Asian women. At that time, Filipino women were thought of as "mail order brides" imbued with high sexuality and exoticism and prone to violence (Saroca 2006). I interviewed Filipino women who were married to Australian men to examine their perspectives on their lives as wives and workers. The leadership, volunteerism, and activism of these women in Australia are very different from their social construction as "mail-order brides." I came to the conclusion that in the racist and exclusionary paths of Australian immigration, all non-white women married to Australian nationals are lumped together as "mail-order brides" even if the intimate relationships started as co-workers, students, and the like; the very same interactions experienced by women anywhere in the world. White women married to Australian men are not labeled as "mail-order brides," unless they are from Russia (Morgan 2007).

Concerned about the lack of scholarly work on Filipino women beyond the victim cliché, I completed my doctoral thesis in 2004 to better understand the socio-cultural contexts of the construction of the idea of the Filipino woman both in the Philippines and Australia, and how these ideals are practiced at home, at work, and in the community. My thesis was approved by external examiners without revision. The thesis was original in its transnational recognition of migrant lives now rooted in Australia. Putting my own study in the scholarly milieu of most foreign academics writing about Filipino women inspired me to write from a more nuanced perspective. Scholarship and research are, thus, avenues for leadership.

Filipina scholars, particularly those who completed the terminal degrees for their profession, have the responsibility to pursue holistic perspectives to understand the specific histories and realities of Filipino women whenever possible. Many research projects and scholarly works have emerged in the last two decades about Filipino women by non-Filipinos and these have tended to focus on particular aspects of their lives as migrant workers, as brides to foreign nationals, as caregivers, as nurses, as domestic workers and the like. These studies tend to contribute to the negative construction of Filipino women in the countries of destination. It is as if what matters most in the lives of Filipino women in Australia, for example, is to be a wife and nothing more.

Life is complicated and migration is a life changing journey. Often nationals in countries of destination have their lives affected by stereotypes. Holistic studies are still at the margins of the scholarship on immigrant women despite the ever increasing social divisions based on religion, race, ethnicity, and immigrant status in the 21st century. As a Filipina scholar, the sense of urgency to add sources of knowledge about gender and Filipinos in the diaspora to the scholarship on dominant populations is reflected in my published works (Bonifacio 2003, 2005, 2008a, 2009a, 2009b, 2009c, 2010a, 2010b, 2013, 2015). I find that activism is not only demonstrated by organizing solidarity groups and joining protest rallies in the Philippines but also continues in teaching, research and scholarship; areas in which leadership can grow with students and colleagues in the academe.

Research and scholarship are, indeed, pathways to leadership in certain subject areas. There are many aspects of Filipino women's lives that need attention, beyond the dominant representation as "servants of globalization" (Parreñas 2001). Histories of colonialism and imperialism have tied the Philippines to the western world but it does not mean that there will always be a general narrative of submission and subservience. Through leadership in scholarship and critical discourse from the Philippines to Australia, but multiple stories and each is unique.

My trans-Pacific academic journey increased my awareness as a Filipino, as a woman, and who I can be amidst a sea of whiteness. I had an awakening that race is a huge qualifier for inclusion and belonging in western society. Sharing opinions on matters of public policy and providing information to those who ask for it is indicative of leadership. Informal leadership among Filipino women may have far greater impact than leadership with formal authority seen as too distant to bother.

Australia is the closest predominantly white Anglo country to the Philippines. Australia was my first country to live in where racial differentiation is rooted in its history and immigration policy. Living in Australia gave me and my family not only our "baptism of fire" of exclusion and belonging but also a deeper awareness of where the Philippines is situated in the global context. The international position of the Philippines relative to the countries in the western world demonstrates the rights and privileges accorded to its citizens. Instead of going back home to the Philippines after my doctoral studies, the family consensus was to leave for Canada.

GLOBAL-LOCAL INTERACTIONS: TEACHING IN CANADA

My family of five daughters and my husband left Australia to permanently migrate to Canada in late 2003. Finding an academic job takes time; positions are filled for the next semester or academic year. While waiting for an academic post related to Political Science, I worked in odd jobs in the service and manufacturing sectors, jobs dominated by racialized immigrants in Canada. This short non-academic venture offered direct experience of the real lives of immigrants in Canada in the 3D sector; "dirty, demeaning, and dangerous." Writing about gender and immigration seems more real because of my personal interactions with other immigrant women in the non-academic sector. My work with foreign-trained medical doctors, licensed nurses, and other professionals on the assembly line provided an introduction to the globalized economy.

In 2004, I received an unexpected message about a sessional lecturer post at the University of Guelph in the Department of History to teach a course on Asian women. A semester in Guelph, Ontario opened the nature of contractual relations between the teacher and the student in Canada quite unlike in the Philippines where the relations are tipped in favour of teachers. The syllabus is the contract. Nothing can be changed in the course without the support of the majority of the students in a classroom. Students in the Philippines tend to cower under the authority of teachers. This is mainly not the case in Canada.

For over ten years, I have worked as academic with the University of Lethbridge in southern Alberta, the so-called heart of the "Bible belt" where social conservatism is the dominant language in politics and social life. To a predominantly white student population, faculty, administration, and staff , I have an accent. Some of members of the university community have peculiar accent, too, coming from Quebec or other provinces, and outside of Canada. As a Filipino academic, I am the "other" and "outsider" in almost any social group in the university.

I needed to find inspiration and connection with the course topic and myself. Teaching women in society and the gendered structures and practices to mainly white female students is a bit daunting. How could these students connect with me, talking about feminism and the women's movement when we are separated by so many barriers? I used a global-local approach to teaching, in women and gender studies, globalization, religion and sexuality, activism and advocacy, and research methods. The global represents the entire universe of humanity, not only of Canada as the centre for students' learning. By looking at the global perspective, I find a sense of connection as a Filipino academic in a Canadian university. The local is represented by Canada, or Alberta, or Lethbridge.

Teaching is often class-based; but learning comes in different modes like community exchanges, symposia, conferences, public exhibits, dialogue and the like. I integrated an 'open class model' of learning (Bonifacio 2008b) at the University of Lethbridge to allow students, mostly white, to engage with the wider community about the impact of their research. Aside from developing confidence in public speaking and offering an opportunity to interact with others outside the classroom, students in my classes explore issues of wider significance and tend to connect to the lived realities of women around the world. The goal is to enable students to gain a more critical analytic lens for understanding the theoretical concepts and their application in gendered lives.

In 2015, I offered an intensive summer field course in the Philippines for a month with 14 Canadian students. We were based in Tacloban City in the province of Leyte in Eastern Visayas. We were there two years after super typhoon Haiyan (local name, Yolanda) had devastated the region. There were significant risks to bringing these students to the Philippines. Accommodations in the ladies dorm in Tacloban City did not guarantee functional air conditioning, the security of their belongings, and persons. While this was the University of Lethbridge's first field course to the Philippines, it was very successful in terms of accomplishing course objectives and teaching pedagogy. In practical terms, living in the same dormitory with your students 24/7, although a nightmarish challenge, was very fulfilling.

The field course is the quintessential experience for teaching global-local intersections. It is only with direct exposure to coastal communities in a developing country like the Philippines where Canadian students can fully grasp the impact of climate change, the effects of the global economy on domestic economy, the influence of western culture in Asia, and how concepts are grounded in the lives of island people. My interdisciplinary background inspired me to develop a field course where Canadian students could appreciate their place in society, the links between countries, and how policies in the global North affect the global South. What was especially inspiring to conduct this field course is that the Philippines is among the top ten countries in the world with the smallest gender gap index despite its developing status compared to Canada (World Economic Forum 2015).

Leadership is not only exercised through positions of power but also through innovation. Academics need not follow the usual lecture format all the time, and non-conventional modes of teaching like a field course are opportunities to increase learning in a different manner. The field course provided an environment in which learning could take place on the ground, and provided students with direct community interactions. Filipina academics like myself in Canada have transnational linkages that are useful in developing courses that offer Canadian students varied opportunities for learning. In this way, Filipina academics enhance global competencies of Canadian students for learning about their position of privilege.

INTEGRATED ACTIVISM: SITUATED FEMINIST LEADERSHIP

The feminist dictum that the "personal is political" has guided my understanding of leadership as a form of integrated activism for social justice. As a Filipina academic I am positioned differently in terms of gender, race, and migration history in Canada. These social identities are marked in my daily interactions with the community, including the academe. What is personal is political, and what is political is personal as racialized academic. I experience racism and discrimination based on visible markers of identity like race or Philippine ancestry as I tread public spaces. Almost every day I have to answer the question, "where did you come from?" I am almost tempted to say, "women are from Venus."

At one time in a shopping mall I met another Filipina and we bumped into her former white employer. The former employer asked where I worked as a nanny, and I jokingly informed her that "I sweep in the university" to which she replied, "really?" It is as if a Filipina working as a janitor in the university is unheard of, apart from working in home care or in seniors home. In response to her amazement that a Filipina works in a university as a cleaning person, I said, "I sweep the minds of students." This encounter may be brief but it speaks of the long held view that Filipina women in Canada work only as caregivers and nannies. To get people to think beyond the stereotype that Filipinas are lowly paid live-in caregivers is a call to action. A Filipina can be anyone she would like to be, anywhere, and at anytime, like other immigrant women in Canada and elsewhere.

Policies increase hyper media attention to the plight of Filipina women in Canada. Filipina women as migrant workers seem to be on the limelight for protesting racism, discrimination, exploitation, or as lifeless bodies returning home after tragic death in the hands of employers. In many of these reports Filipina women are represented as coming from poor background, linking poverty to crime and others. These cases appear normal in any society, but when migrant status is added to the equation, then the representation becomes especially appealing to the media.

Filipinas around the world, especially academics like myself, are uniquely positioned to contest inaccurate assumptions. Our contributions worthy of media attention are not predetermined. Projects like the Filipina Women's Network (FWN) are remarkable in demonstrating the positive contributions of Filipino women worldwide. While the FWN list of women is limited to certain categories this does not discount the fact that there are millions of Filipinas around the world making a difference in their communities. The FWN list is only a sample of them.

In my experience a feminist situated leadership of Filipinas is expected. As racialized minorities in white-settler societies in Europe, North America, and elsewhere, Filipinas occupy a position of marginality that define their abilities to engage in their host communities. By feminist, I mean belief and acceptance of women's equal rights regardless of race, class, sexuality, religion, and other identities. These identities situate realities that shape their experiences with others. Hence, a feminist situated leadership suggests that based on where we are coming from, Filipinas are called to strive for social justice. For many of us, we are already doing this unconsciously: fighting for what we believe is right, pointing out injustices, sharing information to empower others, etc. Filipinos in diaspora, in general, are the most highly organized group for social action. Filipinas are an integral part of any solidarity groups, both with Filipinos and with non-Filipinos. There examples are easily found online. Their online visibility provides an alternative view of Filipina lives, not that of plastered photographs in dating sites.

Through the years I came to the realization that if matters do not feel right, then they must be wrong. Leadership is uncalled for. One does not need to be in a position of authority to exercise leadership. Leadership is fighting for the principles you believe in despite the risks involved. A situated feminist leadership is a daily dose of leadership; it is exercised anytime, anywhere, and with anyone. We occupy different positions and roles in society with intersecting identities that cannot be separated from our realities. From this vantage point, we exercise leadership in formal or informal ways. Millions of Filipino women, including those in the Philippines, take part in this form of leadership.

LEGACY AND THE UNFOLDING FUTURE

Despite living away from the Philippines for the past 15 years or so, I have always found time in the summer months to visit my hometown, Tacloban City. As noted earlier, Tacloban City was the main site of super typhoon Yolanda in 2013. I have connected with other schools and organizations for projects even prior to this natural disaster, considered as the strongest typhoon to hit landfall in human history. I find benefit in making my teaching and research grounded in the realities of Filipinos locally, nationally, and internationally. Perhaps Filipina academics like myself can articulate connections that will make the global-local perspective more significant in people's lives, especially in my case, students in Canada.

As a result of super typhoon Yolanda and the lack of immediate government response to help survivors, in 2014, I founded the ReadWorld Foundation together with a small group of volunteers, mostly professional Filipinos in Lethbridge. The main goal of this foundation is to provide library resources to public schools, including elementary, high school, and universities, affected by disasters. Based on information from family and friends in Tacloban City, relief goods coming from overseas were resorted and repacked for distribution to survivors. Corruption was widespread. Instead of sending goods that could be resold in the black market economy, I decided to launch the "adopt-a-school" project linking schools in Lethbridge with schools in disaster zones. The activity to collect used books and school supplies followed an email request from a former colleague in the Philippines asking for me to donate my own books to the library. As of March 2015, ReadWorld Foundation had shipped nearly 100 boxes to over 20 schools in Visayas and Mindanao.

The adopt-a-school project has been embraced by public and Catholic schools in Lethbridge as an example of civic responsibility. Our limited fundraising events are complemented by school support and I foresee more sustained efforts in the future through them. The activities of ReadWorld Foundation bring hope and provide an example of young people getting involved to help others. I gave birth to the idea for this project based on a situation that I felt needed to be addressed and the limited options I had at that time. What happened next was a surprise for the better, and continues to be so.

I am not sure what the future unfolds. My daughters are now grown up and are independent enough to carve a path on their own. Perhaps I may stay in Canada, perhaps I may be in another place. The possibilities are endless. But wherever life leads me as a Filipina academic, I am confident a legacy will unfold.

SALVE VARGAS EDELMAN

FOUNDER AND PRESIDENT,
RISING ASIAN PACIFIC AMERICANS COALITION FOR DIVERSITY (RAPACD)
FWN100™ GLOBAL 2015

To Dream the Impossible,
Begin to Make it Possible

SVE Productions, in partnership with VAsianTV and Vegas TV, invite you to watch our new Television Show, ISLA VEGAS, The Ninth Island, a cultural and performing arts show! This new TV Show will be launched on Sunday, September 30, 2012 and will simultaneously broadcast on Vegas TV Channel 14 and VAsianTV KTUD 25.3. It is a unique TV Show that will include various Asian Pacific American communities in Las Vegas, hence the title; ISLA VEGAS, the Ninth Island.

So read our promotional invitation to Isla Vegas. Our purpose in producing this show was to celebrate diversity that is uniquely Las Vegas, exciting, colorful Las Vegas, by bringing together and showcasing the talents of a multi-cultural group of people. And in the process, we wanted to learn to appreciate, understand, and embrace our different and unique worlds. My 17-year dream became a reality because of my passion for the cultural and performing arts which lie at the heart of how I continue to utilize my God-given talents in various leadership roles.

This chapter explains how this dream came true. The dream had begun with a commitment to a vision and with engaging the local Las Vegas communities to buy into the vision of a Rising Asian Pacific Americans Coalition For Diversity (RAPACD). I drew on the performance skills I learned as an international crooner, the management and organizational competencies I learned while working for the corporate world in insurance and financial services, in real estate, and with the

Bureau of Census. Living in Las Vegas made me aware of the many Filipinos and Hawaiians who moved to Las Vegas and nicknamed it the "Ninth Island." Hence, the title of the show "Isla Vegas, the Ninth Island."

I also discuss how this vision gave birth to another vision, the Twin Lakes Community Clinic. Responding to a call to care for my mother meant immigrating to the U.S. and giving up my career as a crooner. It was a blessing in disguise because by doing my duty, I learned other skills, including being a successful real estate agent while continuing to pursue my passion for the cultural and performing arts. Moving to Las Vegas presented an opportunity to achieve a seemingly impossible dream. How that dream became a reality also shows how I grew my capacity as a leader. Leadership for me is the ability to care passionately and communicate that passion by inspiring and motivating others to take action. My leadership philosophy is best summed up by John Quincy Adams. "If your actions inspire others to dream more, learn more, do more, and become more, you are a Leader."

A DREAM COMES TRUE

At the launch of the Isla Vegas in 2012, I declared, "To the cultural differences that bring us together as one people of Las Vegas—*Cheers! Mabuhay! Kampai! Gun bae! A'kale ma'luna! Manuia! Chok dee!*" The Chinese proverb states that "When you learn a new language, you gain a new world!"

The path to making a dream come true requires the leadership competencies of persistence, perseverance, patience, commitment, dedication, diligence, and unwavering faith that others will share your passion. Isla Vegas showcases the multicultural talents of Asian Pacific Americans living in Las Vegas. These multicultural talents include the Tendo Baikoki Japanese Cultural Dance Group, Tevakanui of Las Vegas, Maori Volcanics, Heart of Polynesia, Las Vegas Hawaiian Civic Club Chorale Group, Polynesian Rhythms, Filipiniana Dance Company, Shirley Chen and Dancers, Philippine American Youth Organization, Vietnamese Mutual Associations, Isla Vegas Young Stars, Isla Vegas Band, and many more. The show also features various international Asian Pacific cultural performing dance groups such as Kahurangi Dance Theatre of New Zealand and the Aborigines Playing Didgeridoos from Australia.

The show was produced specifically by Asians for the Asian-Pacific American market in Las Vegas. The Asian-American Pacific Islander community saw a 116 percent growth from 2000 to 2010. This show was meant to celebrate the diversity that is uniquely Las Vegas. The exciting, colorful Las Vegas, by bringing together the various talents of multi-cultural groups of people has helped everyone learn to appreciate, understand, and embrace their different worlds. Each episode focuses on an Asian or Pacific community. Each featured community brings its own performers to show off their unique culture and tradition via dances and music. Performers are all volunteers who enjoy not only performing but also the camaraderie with other Asian Pacific members while filming the Isla Vegas show. Making this dream a reality builds on my experience as an international performing artist for over four decades. Traveling around the world and living and performing in Asia, Europe, and the U.S. provided me with the right stepping stone to create a cultural and performing arts television show.

Producing the show required meeting production challenges including budgeting and paying for expenses for filming, editing, equipment rental, lighting, set decor, make-up artists, scriptwriter, camera men, and other production crew. Despite these production challenges, I continued to believe that a unique show like "Isla Vegas, the Ninth Island" will not only survive but flourish as it offers a different genre of entertainment. I brought people together with different talents and resources to see the importance of what we, as a collective, were doing.

The show accepts donations and sponsorships via TV commercials and is currently seeking a grant to continue production in the years to come. At present, the show survives with the help of various volunteers sharing their talent and time. It is the passion for performing and sharing their unique culture and tradition that spurs their commitment. The show aired on MyNews3's DT3.2, Cox Cable 123, COZI TV, an NBC Network. It can also be seen on Isla Vegas Channel on YouTube, where our third season will be broadcast globally.

CREATING THE DREAM

The show is produced under the mantle of Rising Asian Pacific Americans Coalition For Diversity (RAPACD), a volunteer non-profit educational and cultural organization, which I helped establish in February 2012, and which later became a 501c3 Non-Profit Organization in 2013. RAPACD programs are designed to help the youth develop interpersonal skills and promote friendships among its diverse cultural members. RAPACD raises awareness of Asian Pacific American socio-cultural, economic, and civic issues by educating and engaging members of various communities to embrace and celebrate diversity. It joins with mainstream and other minorities in building cross-cultural understanding of these issues. Programs are designed to educate the community on civic and economic issues in order to bridge cultural differences among various cultural minorities. An Indian Shaman has stated that what we do now will affect seven generations from today. And that is what motivates my leadership.

LEADERSHIP COMPETENCIES

Working to make dreams come through is merely the first step. Sustaining and nurturing that dream to grow fully requires firm leadership, passion, skills, and competencies. I showcase the key leadership competencies below by examining how I made my dream a reality.

Commitment to a Vision

To lead, you need to express your exceptional and positive vision for the future. A leader with a plan is the easiest leader to follow. Once aware of the team's goal, each member will strive to do her part to aid in the completion of the objective.

After I moved to Las Vegas, I began looking for an Asian Cultural Center or a Filipino Community Center in order to make new friendships and establish a network. I found a sign on the I-15 Freeway and Spring Mountain Road that said "Asian Cultural Center." I found the same sign on Flamingo and Wynn and I looked around for the building. Unfortunately, it was just a sign despite several attempts to create an Asian Cultural Center. So, my personal mission became to find a way to have our own venue for an Asian Cultural Center in Las Vegas.

Beginning in 2012, I started sharing my vision with numerous elected officials, but nothing happened. Then in 2013, RAPACD officers and members and I met with our local Congressman about a proposal to acquire a city-owned building for our cultural center. The Congressman supported our proposal and within a month, the City of Las Vegas Parks and Recreation Deputy Director contacted me about two vacant buildings. My officers and I checked it out and we put together a Business Plan. We met with one of the City Councilmen about our proposal and in November 2013 the City Council of Las Vegas granted RAPACD two neighboring buildings in historic Lorenzi Park in Las Vegas. Indeed, it was a historic day for RAPACD! In December 2013, we celebrated the grand opening of the RAPACD Cultural Center. We celebrated as a community that persevered together.

Coalition Building

Success in acquiring and renovating the building required uniting a host of local community organizations not only among the Filipino-American community but also with the American Asian Pacific Islander (AAPI) groups. Mastering the art of community building had happened while I worked for the Bureau of Census as a Community Partnership Specialist for the Asian and Pacific Americans in

Nevada. I received training to engage and mobilize various Asian and Pacific Islander community leaders and the members of their organizations. I visited various temples, tribes, wards, mosques, and churches. I mingled with the community leaders and their members. I learned to to say hello, thank you, cheers, and other greetings and respect terms in their languages. My attempt at learning their languages was very much appreciated. It is said that when one learns a new language, one gains a new world!

Learning about the 116% growth in the AAPI Community from 2000 to 2010 was key to recognizing the need to establish an AAPI organization. The groups that finally united to work together included more than 32 organizations. This was the beginning of RAPACD. RAPACD started with three countries but soon expanded to include 51 countries, including Latin America, European, Middle East and Southeast Asian countries.

Communicating Effectively

Clear communication is an integral part of excellent leadership. I have learned to express my ideas clearly, and to make sure everyone understands the vision. At the same, I encouraged RAPACD officers, members, and volunteers to create a conversation-friendly environment and give everyone the freedom to express their thoughts and concerns. By doing so, we were able to engage the community, share our vision, and engender trust among the community. As a leader, I try to encourage creativity by asking everyone to participate. By being open to hearing ideas, suggestions, comments, I have inspired others to think outside the box, take more chances, and not be afraid to make mistakes. Doing so has led to the creation of better, more innovative ideas.

Engaging the Community

Since the inception of RAPACD, we have successfully encouraged our diverse community stakeholders to showcase various cultural events, job fairs, youth activities, workshops on professional development, health and senior wellness, performing arts, voter registration, fundraising, and art exhibits. Our center has also served as a venue for meetings by other groups, such as Pacific Islanders Network, International Christian Church, District Governor's Joint Visitation of the Lions Club International, Charter Night for the Las Vegas Legacy Lions Club, Las Vegas Twin Lakes Lions Club, Twin Lakes Community Center, and Charter Night of the Las Vegas Twin Lakes Lions Club.

Sharing the Passion

Leaders need to share their passion for their work with the Board of Directors and volunteers. If a leader is enthusiastic and believes in the project, while recognizing the hurdles that the team will encounter, everyone will continue to do the needed word. Do what you love and love what you do! This is especially true in an environment where there are so many cultural differences and language barriers, and where results are not easily quantifiable, such as the work of non-profit organizations. As a leader, I constantly reiterated my strong belief in the organization's role in impacting the lives of the people we serve. This was to unite and inspire the organization's officers, directors, members, and volunteers, even when faced with many challenges.

Translating Vision to Action

Devising an effective strategy to translate vision into action is an incredibly difficult task. Yet it is also a vital part of being an effective leader. By following a strategy, RAPACD and I were able to focus on the organization's collective success. Since I have been involved in connecting with community since the early 1980s, I made use of the lessons learned from that experience. For example, I was the founder and president of the Calolbon Civic Association, USA. We built a public library, sent balikbayan boxes filled with books, magazines, newspapers, various reading materials, supplies to the library, and paid for a librarian. With RAPACD, we focused our action on giving back to the Philippines and improving our local community in Las Vegas.

GIVING BACK TO THE PHILIPPINES

In May of 2009, as President, I formally launched the Catanduanes International Association, Las Vegas Chapter. Our Mission was to provide medical, dental, and surgical services to the indigent families in the island of Catanduanes, Philippines. My parents were born and raised in Catanduanes and were among the founders of a Philippine-based civic association to provide the medical services in Catanduanes. I led the effort to organize and raise funds to send 188 doctors, nurses, dentists, volunteers, and lay people for our medical mission in Catanduanes in 2011. That medical mission served over 10,000 indigent people in five days. It was the most meaningful, gratifying, rewarding, and Mother Teresa-like medical mission I have ever experienced. I highly recommend this humbling experience to Filipino American community leaders living in the U.S.

Improving Life in Las Vegas:
Twin Lakes Community Clinic

As Charter President of the Las Vegas Twin Lakes Lions Club, I spearheaded Health and Wellness Fair, vision screening, and foot screening. I am proud of influencing the Lions Club to support the Twin Lakes Community Clinic as a RAPACD project. From listening to the voices of various communities in Las Vegas, we learned that one zip code area had been designated as a medically underserved area with shortages of primary care, mental health, and dental care and that many of the people in this area faced socio-economic, cultural, and linguistic barriers to health care access. The community also has a large uninsured population with the highest unemployment rate in the country.

RAPACD submitted a proposal to start a Community Health Center inside the historic Lorenzi Park area with the objective of increasing access to comprehensive, culturally competent, quality primary health care services. Given that RAPACD has two buildings in Lorenzi Park with almost 5,000 square feet, we proposed starting a clinic to complement our other programs in youth development, economic development, and civic engagement. The leadership of RAPACD recognized the dire need for access to primary care, and is committed to addressing this need. We anticipate opening the clinic within 12 months. We are working on fund-raising to supplement fund generated from services and to ensuring the activity will be sustainable. It is anticipated the clinic will provide services to more than 450 patients. RAPACD is committed to enrolling 50 percent of the uninsured in Insurance Exchange or Medicaid programs while continuing to provide other services to the residents of the area.

Enlisting the Help of Allies

I have consistently sought the help of community leaders and worked on creating business plans that can be submitted for funding to government agencies. We have ensured the timely response to questions about our proposals and attempted to keep all the key players informed of our activities. Recently we proposed renovating our RAPACD building and have received approval. Our major fundraising event is now underway to support the Community Clinic. We have a vision to improve our community. Now, this is our opportunity to bring our vision to life!

Wearing my other community hat, I have taken the lead in enlisting the help of other community organizations to provide disaster relief aid for the Ondoy and Yolanda Typhoon Victims. We collected 60 *balikbayan* (large 20 in. square) boxes filled with gently used clothing, shoes, medical supplies, non-perishable food and canned goods, blankets, towels, and linens. The boxes were distributed to over 300 families in Tacloban City in the Philippines in 2015.

Developing and Mentoring Future Leaders

In 2012, I attended the Leadership and Networking Program conducted by the Central Intelligence Agency (CIA). The Keynote Speaker, a senior officer, discussed the importance of diversity and inclusion along with leadership insights and perspectives from her over 20 years of federal government service. I met with the Program Director, and shared my dream of organizing an Annual Youth Leadership Conference as a partnership between the CIA and RAPACD. After several emails, meetings, and proposals, we organized our First RAPACD Annual Youth Leadership Conference. The first Conference in 2012 was attended by over 50 high school and college students. In 2015 the attendance increased to over 100 high school and college students.

Every year, we select student leader speakers, business leader speakers, community leader speakers, and keynote speakers, to join CIA staff to make presentations to the youth. This is a very successful annual youth leadership conference held at various venues in Southern Nevada. The fourth RAPACD Youth Conference in 2015 was attended by over 100 high school and college students.

To Thine Own Self Be True

Leaders need to identify their strengths and weaknesses. They need to ask for feedback from their Board of Directors and members. This helps leaders pinpoint exactly where they excelled and where they fell short, so they can improve upon their shortcomings. Leaders need to have patience, perseverance, persistence, and resilience. To have the tenacity to go after dreams no matter how hard it is and how long it takes is what makes me who I am. That is why and how I lead. I believe that eventually, the universe conspires to make success a reality. My smile is my logo. My personality is my business card. How I make people feel after I help them is my trademark!

Maintaining my Passion for the Cultural and Performing Arts

Music is a universal language. I am blessed to have God-given talents and passion for singing, performing, entertaining, dancing, speaking, emceeing, hosting, producing, directing, organizing, and pioneering in the cultural and performing arts. I share my talents wholeheartedly and unconditionally every day in every way. In 2016, I emceed and performed at the Chinese New Year, the Las Vegas Spring Festival Parade, the Grand Opening Celebration of the Filipino American Heritage and Arts Museum, and the Talent and Me International Reading Alphabet Recitation Contest, and NAFFAA'S Mabuhay Expo.

Utilizing my Talents

God has always orchestrated everything in my life. I have been singing since I was five years old. I was a professional folk singer in the Philippines in the 70s. I was recruited by a Japanese talent scout in 1975 and performed in Okayama, Japan, and mostly sang in Japanese. Then a Filipino and German couple recruited me while I was in Okayama, Japan, as a lead singer for Conti Production to perform in Western Europe: Germany, Holland, Spain, Switzerland, France, Italy, Portugal, and Finland. My last performance before migrating to USA, was in Agana, Guam. I sang in Spanish, German, Italian, Tagalog, and of course in English.

Upholding The Dignity of Labor

As a little girl I was taught by my Mom to "uphold the dignity of labor." Growing up, I remember being very entrepreneurial. I learned to harvest our fruit trees and go to the market and barter my harvested fruits for fish and vegetables. I embraced the entrepreneurial spirit and implemented it in every area of my life. For over 45 years in the work force, I have been a working leader, manager, supervisor, CEO, founder, and president; I love to work in the trenches with my team members. As founder and president of RAPACD and Twin Lakes Community Clinic, and Executive Director of the RAPACD Cultural Center, I mop the floors, vacuum the carpet, set up tables and chairs, clean up the kitchen and toilets, cut the grass, wash dishes, cook food, and throw away the trash before and after the events. I take pride in the fact that we have a place that we can call our own. We have a poster at the Center that reminds me of why I do what I do: "You have the vision to improve your community. Now here's your opportunity to bring it to life."

A Blessing in Disguise

I migrated to San Francisco, California to take care of my mother in 1980. My Mom, Rosario Santelices Vargas was a Public Teacher for 36 years in the Philippines. She petitioned me as an immigrant in 1976, but I chose to go to Europe first to pursue my career as a crooner and singer. When she got sick, being the youngest of eight children and single at the time, I was designated to take care of her. I could have stayed in Europe but it was my duty and responsibility to take care of my Mom. I am so glad I did. Even though, I sacrificed my career as a crooner and singer, I knew, even then, that things happen for a reason.

Learning other Functional Skills

I worked for Bechtel Corporation in 1981, where I met my best friend and my first husband, Leo Stanley Spensko, a Mechanical Engineer, Quality Control Engineer, and Quality Assurance Supervisor. I worked in various positions at Bechtel, such as, administrative assistant, office manager, senior buyer, project administrator, and senior contracts administrator. Projects I worked on while at Bechtel included the SOHIO Project, the Susquehanna Nuclear Power Plant Project, and the BART Project. I attended Bechtel's various in-house supervisory, office management, administration, and procurement training and development courses. Because of the glass ceiling that limited my advancement, I left Bechtel after I got my license in insurance in 1992. I also worked for AL Williams, World Financial Group, and New York Life. I became a unit production manager for Bankers United and later became a financial advisor for Berkshire. When I moved to Las Vegas in 1996, there was no reciprocity in the insurance industry between California and Nevada so I moved into financial services. I became a banking center manager for Wells Fargo Bank and US Bank. I then went into the mortgage industry as a loan officer and later became a unit production manager. In that position I supervised 25 loan officers, 2 processors, and 1 assistant. Then, I studied to become a real estate professional and had been a Realtor since 2003.

Pursuing my Dream

At the same time that I was learning new functional skills, I pursued my singing career and became the lead singer for Roy Leano and his orchestra for 16 years. I also started an entertainment business, Salve Vargas Productions, where I teamed up with my husband, Leo. We provided DJ and Minus One Music to many community events, festivals, and special events in San Francisco and the Bay Area. In addition, I also established a Performing Arts Studio and taught performing arts for 10 years to about 100 students. Some of my performing arts students made it big on Broadway (Miss Saigon Canada) and the Disney Channel. This is one of my biggest achievements and provided for one of my proudest moments. I'm very proud of my students! I carried this passion for the cultural and performing arts with me when we moved to Las Vegas in 1996.

Finding Life Partners

My husband, Leo, who had retired in mid-1999, passed away later that year. I was devastated when I lost my best friend, mentor, advisor, business partner, and husband. This was the most difficult time in my life because I felt I had lost everything. We had been married since 1981. As a widow, I went through many trials but I became a much stronger person. Not only did I survive. I thrived. As the saying goes, "In every adversity lies an opportunity." I met Paul Alan Edelman, a widower from New Jersey in 2005 and we got married in 2006. He had 20 years of experience in casinos in Atlantic City, New Jersey. After he lost his wife in 2004, he moved to Las Vegas. In addition to his music as a professional drummer and a percussionist, he is a Concealed Carry Weapon Instructor for his Nevada Marksmanship Training Business. Paul, like my first husband, has become my best friend, business partner, advisor, and mentor. Paul is the drummer and I am the lead singer for the Isla Vegas Band featured on the "Isla Vegas, the Ninth Island" TV show. We have a very happy, fulfilling, meaningful, and well-balanced life.

Meditation Is Vital

I have created and updated daily a personal vision board. I put all the photos of my dreams, goals, projects, wishes, and aspirations on my vision board so I can see them every day. I write in my "Gratitude Journal" 10 things I am grateful for every day. I write all my dreams, wishes, goals, wants, needs, aspirations, achievements, and ambitions in my personal "Dreams Journal." I meditate on God's Word, God's Promises, and Jesus' calling and have an unwavering faith that God will provide whatever I need to fulfill my Divine purpose according to His Divine Plan. I serve as a Lector and Extraordinary Minister of Holy Communion on Sundays at St. Joseph, Husband of Mary Roman Catholic Church, which is very rewarding for me.

MORE DREAMS. I AM NOT YET DONE.

I have more dreams to pursue in order to make a difference and have a positive impact in my community. My goal is to leave a legacy for our youth. I have another impossible dream, inspired by a recent development in San Francisco, California. I want to establish a "Filipino Town" called SoVegas Plipinas in Las Vegas to serve as a center for the Filipinos, the fast growing ethnic group in Las Vegas, I believe this next impossible dream will soon become possible.

❋

MICHELLE FLORENDO

Founder & Principal, What if You Could
FWN100™ Global 2015

The Old Rules No Longer Apply

S tudy hard. Do well in school. Go to college. Get a good job. Do a good job. And then you will be set for life.

That was the formula for success repeated in so many immigrant households like my own as I was growing up. It made sense. After all, it was that very formula that enabled my dad to go from a poor subsistence farming family in rural Ilocos Sur in the Philippines to raising his own family in an upper-middle class neighborhood in the United States.

I still remember the day in the first grade when I came home with my first report card. "Wow," my dad said. "Good job! Keep studying hard so that you can go to a very good school—maybe even Stanford! Be sure to do well in school so that you can go to college and get a good job. That way you can live a good life and be happy."

So I did just that. I studied hard. I got good grades. I earned my Bachelor's degree from Stanford University with a concentration in Decision Engineering. And then I got myself a well-paying, respectable job in management consulting. I moved out of my parents' house and was able to support myself, living in an apartment in San Francisco. I traveled abroad to vacation in far off places and bought designer clothes. I had made it. Or so I thought.

After a short time, I had a feeling that something was not right.

The Need for Vision

I watched those ahead of me work hard and get promoted. Promotion came with a nice bump in salary, but it also came with an even larger bump in workload. As I looked higher and higher in the organization, I saw people who made more and more money, but had less and less time to actually enjoy life.

All of a sudden, I was not sure if that was the future I wanted. In fact, I knew it was not.

I had blindly followed a formula for "success," but the life I saw ahead did not feel like it fit me. The vision of success that I had adopted was someone else's. I could not say that I even knew what success looked like for me. For the first time, I had no vision.

As a person who had grown up always planning at least two to three steps ahead, not knowing the next step was jarring. I was a planner without a plan. I felt completely lost. On top of that, not only did I feel like I lost my direction, I felt like I lost my identity.

For months I felt alone, and stuck. It was not until I started reaching out to others for guidance that I was able to move forward. One of the people I reached out to astutely pointed out something that I had not been able to see for myself. He said, "Ok, Michelle. Let me get this straight. You currently work in a job where you use your background in decision analysis to help companies make the best decisions for themselves, right? Well, why not use that same background to help you make the best decision for you?"

Funny how it often takes someone from the outside to point out what's been lying under your nose the entire time. My training in decision analysis emphasized the fact that it is impossible to make good decisions on how to proceed unless you first define your objectives. What is it that you ultimately want to see in the outcome?

When people do not know what they want, they end up looking outside, even when the answers are actually within. My entire life, I had defined success according to what other people said it looked like. It was time to start to do the hard work. I needed to sift through all of the layers of what I had thought success meant and get to what was really at the core. What is it that I wanted? What did I enjoy? What did I find fulfilling? How did I want to feel at the end of each day?

It was time to articulate my VISION for myself. I wanted to use my analytical abilities to solve problems. I wanted to be able to tackle problems in a way that allowed me to see how all of the moving parts fit together. I wanted the ultimate purpose of my work to be linked to a positive impact on people. And I wanted my work to be able to support the type of lifestyle I enjoyed.

THE NEW MODEL FOR CAREER PATHING

For me, there were many things wrong with the old approach to career pathing. "What do you want to be when you grow up?" is such a common question to ask children, we hardly think of the implications this has on the problematic way we have historically thought about careers. When we ask that question, we often expect one answer, as if people should have just one vocation over the course of their lives. On top of that, we often expect the response to come in the form of a job title; as if that job title held the same meaning across time and space.

That way of thinking about careers may have been fine for my dad's generation, but the occupational landscape has changed drastically for Generation X and Millennials. My dad has essentially worked in the same line of work, with periodic increases in pay and responsibility, for my entire life, and likely will continue to until he retires. For my parents' generation and my grandparents' generation, that kind of career trajectory was not uncommon.

Now, however, things are different. Stability is no longer the norm; inevitable change is. Entire industries can rise like the technology sector or fall like journalism in a single decade. Companies may rise and fall even faster, creating even more volatility with the possibility of layoffs. There are job functions that existed years ago that no longer exist today, and jobs that will be invented years from now that no one has ever heard of today.

I do not blame older generations for passing on this old way of thinking about careers. That is the only reality they knew. However, I have seen that those who are unprepared to deal with the dynamic nature of the new economy are likely to get thrashed by it. So I have learned to adopt a new model for career pathing.

In order to find a fulfilling career in such a dynamic environment, I have found that it is far more useful to seek out opportunities that fit our ourselves, rather than try to fit ourselves to a particular job. What that means, though, is that we need to have a clear picture of what it is that we want. To do that, in addition to formulating a vision, we also have to be open to using our current situation to SEEK NEW INSIGHTS that may inform the evolution of our vision.

In a dynamic environment, it is impossible to have perfect information from the very beginning. The best we can do is start with an initial vision, and then continue to learn from new experiences in order to refine that vision. Just as it is impossible for a child to know with certainty what they want to be when they grow up, it can be impossible to know what we want, and what we do not want, until we experience it.

Because I had taken the time to learn from each of my experiences and to use this information to refine my picture of what I wanted in my career, I had the good fortune of navigating my way to a dream job on more than one occasion.

After I graduated with my MBA, I had spent dozens of hours reflecting on what I had liked and disliked in my previous roles, and spent even more hours speaking with professionals in my new field of interest to get a sense of what types of organizations and roles would be a good fit with my skills and interests.

I remember sitting across the table from the Chief Operating Officer of an organization I wanted to work for. At some point in the conversation, he asked me, "If you could design your own dream job, what would it look like?" Because I put in the work thinking on that very subject, I told him. I told him what skills I wanted to use on a day to day basis, what I wanted to be responsible for, and how I envisioned spending my time. I told him what kind of people I wanted to work with, and the way I liked to work when part of a team. I told him what kind of organization I wanted to work for.

Two days later he called me back to say that he wanted to interview me for an opening they had. It was unexpected because I had been checking their website every day for openings and as of the day prior to our conversation, had not seen any current openings. He sent me the job description for the position and it looked strangely similar to what I had described would be my dream job. Within three weeks of the initial conversation with the Chief Operating Officer, I was working for the organization in the very job I dreamt up.

WHEN YOUR JOB
IS NO LONGER YOUR DREAM JOB

It can be tempting to think that once one lands a dream job, that is it. To think that is the finish line. But that rarely is the case. Why? For the same reason the old rules of career pathing do not apply; the inevitability of change. As it so happens, my dream job did not stay my dream job. The role changed. My boss changed. The leadership of the organization changed. And consequently, so did how I felt about my job.

As the job that used to excite me deteriorated into one I dreaded to face, the old way of thinking about careers flooded my mind:

"This was supposed to be my dream job! What happened?"

"I must have made the wrong decision. But what do I do now? How can I trust myself to make good decisions going forward?"

"Why am I not happy? I should be happy... after all, I chose this."

"Not long ago I told everyone this was my dream job, how can I possibly reach out to my network now to say I'm looking for something different?"

"Maybe I should just put my head down and stick things out."

I see the same thoughts and feelings in the clients I now coach. Regret. Self-doubt. Guilt. Shame. Resignation. It's bad enough when a job becomes draining. Dealing with all of those additional negative feelings can be paralyzing. Yet, all of those feelings are a product of the old way of thinking, where you are supposed to know with certainty what you want to do, and then stick with that linear path for the duration of your working life.

In this new state of the working world, characterized by inevitable change, it was not my fault that my dream job was no longer my dream job. Many of the things I had previously loved about my job changed. That does not mean I made a bad decision; I made a good decision, aligned with exactly what I wanted, given the information I had at that point in time. And then the situation changed so that it was no longer ideal. It was fine to be unhappy with how things changed, there was no need for me to feel guilty about that. Also, if people understand, as I did, that often, things change, we should not feel ashamed to reach out to say that we are looking for something else. And we should only choose to stick things out after we fully evaluate other options and decide what is the best course of action.

In an environment of inevitable change, it is important to EMBRACE FLEX-IBILITY. There was no reason to feel like I had to stick with a particular course of action even when I found that it was no longer aligned with my vision. Whenever one's objectives, options, or information change, there is an opportunity to make a new decision. There are often many ways to get to where you want to go, and every decision is an opportunity to correct your course.

I owed it to myself to make a new decision that would realign my career trajectory with my vision and what was important to me.

THERE HAS TO BE ANOTHER OPTION

As I progressed in my career, I knew I wanted to have children someday. However, I saw many women ahead of me having children and then facing the dilemma of choosing between spending their days at work or spending their days with their child. Most career-oriented moms I spoke with admitted neither option was ideal, but felt they were stuck making a choice between those two. Either choose to stay home with my child and put my career on hold, or choose to go back to work and sacrifice the ability to build my schedule around the needs of my child. The decision did not feel like it fit me. It was like a flashback to the moment in my first job when I realized "this is not the future I want." There had to be another way.

In decision analysis, the foundation of making good decisions is to examine all three of the core components of a decision: (1) the objectives, i.e. the vision of what you want in the outcome, (2) the options, i.e. the various courses of action you can decide to pursue, and (3) the information you have on how each option may help you achieve your objectives.

When someone feels like they are limited to just one or two options, what is really happening is that there are in fact other options that exist, but they have been subconsciously written off as undesirable or impossible. What was it that I was reluctant to consider?

If those were the only two clear options that existed when working for an organization, what would it look like if I did not work for an organization? What if I worked for myself?

That option was initially scary. I never pegged myself as an entrepreneur. I went to business school at UC Berkeley, a school well known for its entrepreneurial spirit, but I always felt that starting my own business was something for my classmates, not for me. Perhaps it was a remnant of the risk aversion that many children of immigrants are raised with: just go down the known, safe path. Why risk everything we/you have worked for?

I reminded myself of my vision. I wanted to be able to tackle problems in a way that allowed me to see how all of the moving parts fit together. I wanted the ultimate purpose of my work to be linked to a positive impact on people. I wanted my work to be able to support the type of lifestyle I enjoyed, the type of life where I could dedicate myself to both my career and my children, whenever I chose to have them.

Whether leading yourself or a group, there will be times when you will have to create new options. You will have to innovate. By definition, innovation means doing something few have ever done before, which means there will be uncertainty, and where there is uncertainty, there is risk. And it may be scary.

Yes, striking out on my own would be risky. It may not work out. But, as I tell my coaching clients today, when dealing with risk, we must look at both sides. The tendency is to think of the risks of action, but there are also risks of inaction. What would I risk if I did not consider starting my own business? I would risk a lifetime of regret for not trying. I would risk the chance to spend more time with my children and my career. I would risk the chance to achieve exactly what I envisioned.

I remind my coaching clients that especially in an environment of inevitable change, it can be riskier to stay still than to take action. There are risks on both sides. So, one of the critical things to develop in order to survive and thrive amidst change is the COURAGE TO TAKE RISKS. My favorite quote attributed to Franklin Delano Roosevelt encapsulates what courage really is: "Courage is not the absence of fear, but rather the assessment that something else is more important than fear." The key to moving forward, even in the face of fear, is not finding a way to eliminate the fear. The key is to make your dedication to your vision larger than your fear.

INSPIRING OTHERS TO TAKE ACTION

I have now been coaching high-achieving professionals concerning their career decisions for almost a decade, and whenever I share stories about how my clients have been able to transition from roles where they dreaded going to work to ones where they felt energized and excited, people inevitably ask, "How do you do that?"

What is interesting is that helping others to navigate change is rarely about telling them what to do. Sure, I may provide them with tools and strategies that help prepare them for transition. But really, the critical part of the work I do with my clients is getting them from a place of knowing what to do to actually doing it. What that requires is helping them to see differently.

To really break through, I help them decide to craft a clear vision, that is authentic to themselves and not just a compilation of what others want for them. It is about helping them understand that inevitable change does not have to be bad, and that they have the power to use change to their advantage. It is about helping them identify when they may need to make a new decision. It is about helping them see beyond the obvious options in front of them to imagine what other options could exist if they summon the courage to create them. Ultimately, my job has been to help them unlearn the old way of things that keeps them stuck, and paint a picture of what could be possible in this new, dynamic, reality of career pathing.

LEADERSHIP TIPS

I believe that effective leadership is the art of moving yourself and others toward a goal, even in the face of uncertainty and change. In order to do that, good leaders master the art of making good decisions and empowering those they lead to make good decisions as well. Early on in my career I applied the principles of decision analysis to helping companies maximize the outcomes of business decisions. Now, in my work as a career coach, I have had the pleasure of teaching those same principles to individuals, so that they can practice good decision making in their careers.

Regardless of where you are in your career, whether you are in an entry level position simply leading yourself, or you head an organization leading thousands, I encourage you to use the following tips to practice effective leadership and decision making in dynamic environments:

1. Articulate your vision

Perfect execution of a plan is worth nothing if what you are working toward is not the right goal. Think critically about where your current vision for the future came from. Is it truly congruent with what you want, or is it more of a compilation of what others want? Take the time to articulate your vision, and then use it as your compass for decision making.

2. Seek out new insights

We never have perfect information from the very beginning. Effective leadership, whether of groups or yourself, is partially driven by vision, and partially driven by the ability to refine that vision based on learnings and insights you draw from situations as they unfold. Incorporating something new into your vision does not mean you were wrong, it simply means that you now see/know something you may not have been able to see/know before.

3. Embrace flexibility

Change is inevitable. Like waves in the ocean, you can either let a wave of change throw you off course, or you can learn to surf. As long as you have your compass (your vision) and are willing to make new decisions to course-correct where necessary, it's ok when everything doesn't go according to plan. In fact, being flexible may open doors to other paths to your goal that you may not have considered otherwise.

4. Have courage to take risks

Often, we think about the risk of doing something. Also consider what would be the risk of not doing something; sometimes it may be riskier to do nothing. When faced with risk, it is natural to experience some fear. Remember that courage is not the absence of fear, but the recognition that there is something (your vision) more important than your fear.

❇

ARLENE MARIE "BAMBI" A. LORICA, M.D.

CEO, TRANS-PACIFIC INITIATIVE
FILIPINA WOMEN'S NETWORK BOARD MEMBER (2007-2016)
FWN100™ U.S. 2007

SHE-pherding: Leading from Behind

S he "stays behind the flock, letting the most nimble go out ahead, whereupon the others follow, not realizing that all along they are being directed from be-hind" (Mandela, 1995, p. 22).

Mandela used the pronoun "he," but was explicit in including women in the struggle. I believe Mandela would have appreciated the modification of the quotation and the use of the term SHE-pherding. According to Hill in the Harvard Business Journal (2010), within the next decade, "the most effective leaders will lead from behind, not from the front (p. 1)." In my life, I had to learn the value of leading from behind the hard way as my 'flock' was tested, suffered, and ultimately triumphed over adversities both large and small.

INHERITING CAPABILITIES

Having been born to a family of healers and spiritual leaders, I knew at an early age where my future lay: I wanted to be a pediatrician. As a doctor for children, I would make the world a better place one little life at a time.

My mother, Consuelo Rosales Asuncion Antonio, was an accomplished and loving woman. A pioneer during her time, she too wanted to be a physician. Her older sister, Natividad Asuncion (Sor Naty), was one of the first females admitted to the prestigious UP College of Medicine. However, she changed her mind during her freshman year, after being assigned to illustrate the male and female genitalia and discuss in detail the procreation process. A sheltered girl, she was completely naive about the birds and the bees. Wishing to protect my mother from the same experience, my grandfather, Jacobo, a respected businessman, discouraged my mother from attending medical school. Frustrated, my mother took up pharmacy, topped the Pharmacy Boards in 1954, and went on to obtain her master's degree in the U.S. as a Fulbright scholar. Upon returning to the Philippines, she first worked as ascientist at National Institute of Science and Technology before becoming the first chief pharmacist at Cardinal Santos Memorial Hospital in San Juan, Metro Manila. She was later appointed to the Pharmacy Board of the Professional Regulatory Commission.

Learning Capabilities
through Experience and Education

As a child, I grew up being part of medical missions that provided free medical care to poor barangays. I also helped with gift giving, and fundraising drives, as well as preparing food for the indigent. It became second nature for us to be aware of the plight of the less fortunate and do what we could to alleviate their suffering, even if it was at a distance. And yet, it was only after my mother's untimely passing in 2006, and I found her CV, that I learned that she was the past President of at least half a dozen professional, alumni, and service organizations.

Having a cardinal for a grand uncle, Julio Cardinal Rosales, several bishops and priests in the family, and two of my mother's sisters as nuns, it was preordained that I would go to a Catholic school for girls. I remember little about those elementary school years except that I felt unchallenged. Having tiny bones, I was subjected to bullying by bigger and tougher girls whose families had local "mafia" connections. I also recall being teased for my small feet and skinny legs.

As the oldest child, I was taught early on to take the initiative in finding a solution to any problem on my own. I decided to transfer to a different school after sixth grade. I took the Philippine Science High School (PSHS) entrance examination without my parent's knowledge because I did not want to go to the all-girls Catholic high school my parents had chosen for me. As luck would have it, I passed, becoming one of thirty two out of thousands of aspirants from the Metro Manila area. My father, who had never considered any school other than a Catholic girls' school, was shocked. It disrupted my father's plans for me, but he eventually saw the sense in it. I was proud to be a Science scholar.

I learned about life at Philippine Science, but, maybe not in the way you would think. For starters, I learned that there was a much bigger world than the sheltered slice I had grown up in. I had never even crossed the street without adult supervision. But now, with my dear friend and future priest, R.V. Baylon, I learned for the first time how to use public transportation around the city. I was able to see the marginalized people of Cubao first hand in an unfiltered setting. I saw how people, some with disabilities, young and old, tried to make a decent living selling food and other necessities. I marveled at how they were able to get by with so little and yet outwardly appear happy.

At PSHS, I thrived in more ways than I could have at an all-girls school. I explored my athletic side and even finished first place in the freshman 'mini marathon'. I was a tough cookie playing basketball and soccer. I became an officer in the Citizen's Army Training and secretly loved being saluted by the nonofficers. I headed the Math Club and Photography club and was the managing editor of our school paper. I had a blast! Life was good.

The college application process was straightforward for me. The only logical choice then was the University of the Philippines (UP) in Diliman and, eventually, the UP College of Medicine in Manila.

Although a great uncle, Justiniano Asuncion was the founding president of the Upsilon Sigma Phi fraternity, I was not allowed to join any Greek societies in college because my father wanted me to focus on my studies. Perhaps he also thought that I was not mature enough. Interestingly, a few years later, when I decided to join the Mu Sigma Phi sorority in the UP College of Medicine, I was pleasantly surprised when my father did not voice any objections.

Like my aunt, Sor Naty, I also had my own challenges in medical school that had little to do with academics. For example, as part of the initiation process for our sorority during our freshman year in 1984, we had to go through a gauntlet wherein upperclassmen asked trivia questions related to medicine. I was well prepared and felt confident until I was stuck for almost an hour in a station manned by my friend, Dr. Dave Deloso. Soon I was the only one in my group left, and everyone gathered around me while I sweated, unable to answer the question. As I struggled to recall the skeletal system from top to bottom, I was deeply embarrassed that I did not know the answer to the question. The loud taunting of the upperclassmen brought me to tears until they finally let me go, without revealing the answer. It took me a few days to figure out the correct response to what turned out to be a trick question:"What is the name of the bone in the penis?" (Answer: There is none.)

THE AMERICAN DREAM

After graduation in 1989, I helped my husband apply to numerous hospitals in the U.S. for fellowship and residency training. I took a year off, and with two young children, I joined the SUNY Buffalo/Children's Hospital Pediatric Internship program in 1991 followed by and the Pediatric Residency program at Georgetown in 1993. This experience taught me a lot about competition, tenacity, and emotional intelligence.

Working full time as a pediatrician with four children in private schools and having a relatively nice house in the suburbs of Washington, DC was my American Dream. My husband had to work several moonlighting jobs so that we could pay our mortgage and tuition bills. Money was tight, and we could not afford a nanny so we all worked very hard which instilled the same work ethic in our children. I was proud of how independent my kids were, a big improvement from my upbringing in the Philippines where I personally had a nanny until I was 21 years old. In keeping with Filipino tradition, our older kids helped take care of their younger siblings. Looking back, I felt this arrangement brought the family closer together especially during tough times.

Although we were far from perfect, to the community we lived in, we looked like the model family. We were struggling but thriving, getting things done well, excelling in our respective fields, and having a blast living the American Dream. That was true until the delicate balance was disturbed.

UNINTENDED CONSEQUENCES OF DOING GOOD

Having been supported by the FilipinoAmerican community when we first arrived in the U.S., the time came when we knew it was our turn to give back. We understood the hurdles and struggles of being an immigrant family and we recognized when we had reached the point where we could help others in similar situations. Aside from helping financially, we were also there to provide mentoring and emotional support.

One of our classmates was struggling with four young kids while his wife was studying for the board exams. He would visit us from out of town, and with open arms, my husband and I welcomed him into our family on occasional weekends. The occasional weekends, however, turned into every weekend for more than a year, and, as the visits became more frequent, I would be burdened with caring for his four young boys along with my own four children.

Without support, adding four more children every weekend turned out to be too much for me. Constantly caring for eight children while working fulltime as a pediatrician took it's toll on my health. I began to suffer from severe headaches. In September of 2001, immediately after 9/11, I was diagnosed with temporomandibular joint dysfunction (TMJ), a condition that causes intense pain and limits movement. As doctors often do, I ignored my symptoms until they became debilitating.

The stress made my TMJ even worse. I underwent traditional treatment with little relief, so I started exploring nontraditional methods such as energy healing. I went to Sedona, Arizona to learn more advanced healing energy treatments, including touchless energy healing. Energy medicine recognizes the power of our thoughts and our environment. Using the principles of energy medicine, anyone can be trained to utilize the body's natural capacity to heal.

Our energy system regulates millions of processes in our bodies every second. In energy medicine, energy itself heals, and is used to treat or prevent disease, while also giving life to the body. Negative or troubled energies lead to illness. Pollutants, stressors, and information overload overwhelm the energy system. Energy medicine aims to restore a harmonious balance which is the key to good health.

Healing Energy: Self and Family

"The way you help heal the world is you start with your own family."

Blessed Mother Teresa of Calcutta

Our family life balance was disrupted and my marriage suffered. Aside from my patients, I had four children that needed me. I knew I needed to do something to help myself. My family was counting on me. As a physician, I knew that there were a wide range of factors that influence healing. I investigated several, and looked at ways to utilize my own healing energy on myself. Through yoga and meditation, I felt the energy of my inner body circulate again. My body felt lighter as I slowly regained my inner and physical strength through daily meditation and focused intense physical exercise.

Eastern tradition teaches us that the energy called chi is the bond that connects the body, mind, and spirit. The energy used by martial arts students, using the flow of chi to maximize their strength, is the same energy I used to strengthen my spiritual body. With intention, and by actually experiencing a direct connection to life giving energy, feeling it with every power of my being through meditation, I was able to heal myself: my body and my spirit.

According to Nobel laureate in Medicine Albert SzentGyorgyi, "In every culture and in every medical tradition before ours, healing was accomplished by moving energy." In Sedona, I learned to be aware of the energy that constantly surrounds us and attune my senses to it's presence. I developed the ability to harness this energy, which I believe is more effective than any existing western medical treatment modality. I learned that powerful energy intervention is an innate gift. As I continued to master the use of energy medicine, I was able to slowly heal myself of TMJ. Little did I know that a much greater challenge lay ahead.

Testing our Family's Resolve and Resilience

In 2004, I was deeply involved in social justice ministry and advocacy for Our Lady of Mercy Parish and the Archdiocese of Washington, while also serving as the community service chair for the Holton-Arms Parent Association. Working full time with four active kids, I wanted to mirror my own upbringing for my children because growing up, my parents, both working full time, were actively involved in service to the community. Having no household help, I was under a lot of pressure, but I enjoyed working with kids as a pediatrician in McLean, VA. My husband, Victor, a nephrologist, was the President-elect of the Philippine Medical Association of Metropolitan Washington, DC. Back then, I could not have been more grateful for all my blessings. I loved my job, I had wonderful kids, and I had a successful husband. It was around this time in my life when the challenges started.

The first hurdle I had to face was preparing my oldest daughter for college. I knew about tenacity, competition, and emotional intelligence. But, I was not prepared for the college application process for my oldest daughter Michelle. In 2004, she was graduating from the Holton-Arms School, a prestigious all-girls school whose alumnae include Jackie Kennedy and Christine Lagarde and other outstanding women. Michelle was an excellent thespian, a talented singer, and a graceful dancer. It gave us great joy to watch her perform onstage. She was a strong athlete and she excelled academically. Even as a child, she was able to diagnose simple ailments and provide a therapeutic solution to a medical problem almost intuitively.

She wanted to be a doctor and it seemed natural that she would want to go to Princeton. Most of the girls at her school had professional help applying for college. I personally thought that was excessive and unnecessary, but I was humbled when I realized I had much to learn about the extremely competitive college application process. I realized then that my emotional intelligence was not as high as I thought, as it almost felt like I was living through an earthquake. She settled for her fallback school, Georgetown. God in his mysterious way had provided the best school for her, and for us, a mere 20 minutes away. The proximity of George-town turned out to be quite important for what was to come next in our lives.

To nurture our marriage, my husband, Victor, and I regularly attended an-nual retreats for married couples in West Virginia. In March 2004, while on retreat, our next hurdle began. Victor started having severe abdominal pains and diarrhea. His physician prescribed an antibiotic, Flagyl, early on and recom-mended a colonoscopy if the symptoms persisted. Even as he took the medication, we both knew this was more than just a case of complicated gastroenteritis, espe-cially when the pain became so severe that it woke him up at night and he started losing weight. We were hoping that it was just a case of inflammatory bowel dis-ease and his symptoms did seem to improve with the elimination of caffeine, processed foods, and sugar from his diet. I later found out that for the entire year prior to his illness, Victor's diet consisted mostly of rainbow colored skittles daily for lunch as he rushed from one hospital to another to see his patients and still be home in time for dinner with the kids and me. Because his symptoms persist-ed, he eventually scheduled a colonoscopy in May 2004, two months after his symptoms started.

Dr. Bob Morton, a friend, was one of the top gastroenterologists in Northern Virginia. We were not feeling very optimistic going into the colonoscopy suite but I did not really feel the impact of what was going on until the doctor came out and talked to us after the procedure. Victor had colorectal cancer. The doctor said it did not look very good. That hit me. Hard. I felt like my world had fallen apart. How was I going to take care of him and the children at the same time? I knew that we would have to work on being more efficient in our lives.

We had adequate health insurance, but the medical expense were just the beginning of the costs of cancer. Victor needed to take time off to heal. How were we going to get through this financially with just my meager income? How were we going to pay all the bills? Michelle was scheduled to start college that year and Leia, my second daughter, was a year behind her. And what about the younger two, Andrew and Christine? They were so young. Would they grow up scarred? Would their memory of their father be tainted with the smells of hospitals and medication? I had to snap out of these anxieties if I was going to be of any use to my family. I simply could not afford the luxury of spending time on these worrying questions. I needed to focus and concentrate on the most immediate problem: my husband's cancer. Victor needed support while he underwent further testing. We sought the opinions of several oncologists and surgeons, and scheduled him to start radiation treatments as soon as possible in order to stop the progression of the disease.

The colorectal surgeon we chose was a very warm, caring, practical person.

He explained the procedure in great detail and I recall holding on to every word that he said. He asked us to keep our blinders on and focus on the goal of obtaining a cure. He told both of us to take our doctor hats off and allow him and his team to do their jobs. We all had our individual roles in Victor's holistic medical management and I knew what my role would be. In order to leave no stone unturned, I decided I would fill in the gaps in his treatment with energy medicine. My previous experience with TMJ had taught me a great deal about the value of healing energy.

My husband was one of the best students in our college of medicine class. A classic physician trained in western medicine, he wanted a treatment plan that was evidence based, had undergone clinical trials and had proven peer reviewed therapeutic protocols. Lacking these traditional standards, energy medicine was almost a form of quack medicine for him. Thus, a major stumbling block to his holistic management was his intellectual resistance to it. The laying on of hands, balancing of energy, and the use of healing oils was nothing short of voodoo medicine to him. His western medical training made him skeptical because at that time, the evidence was not strong for this eastern approach to treatment. I later learned that healing and medicine was not a calling for him initially, but was something his parents wanted because he was the smartest in the family. Raised by parents who were both scientists meant his upbringing was geared more towards debunking eastern and faith based medicine which were not highly regarded in his family. At the height of his illness, I decided that this was not the time to convince him of the merits of what I was going to do. I just had to do it, with or without his knowledge. The day after his diagnosis, we proceeded with a planned 18th birthday celebration for Michelle. Being in the company of friends, he was able to recharge and optimize his body's capacity to heal. It helped to take a break, and boost morale before we had to take on the daunting task of dealing with the cancer.

Learning to Delegate and Work as a Team

My active role in his treatment affected our whole family. I could no longer be hands-on with the children. I had to delegate. There is a five year gap between my two middle children, effectively splitting my children into two different families. We affectionately called my two older daughters "Family A" and the younger two children "Family B." My two oldest daughters were in their teens at the time of Victor's diagnosis.

Michelle was preparing to enter Georgetown, while Leia was preparing to apply to Stanford. My older daughters lent their Godgiven gifts to the challenge.

Michelle and Leia offered to help with their younger brother and sister who themselves filled in whenever they could. Their hard work helped me focus on my husband and my job. Andrew would take care of Christine, while Christine would take care of Daddy, acting as his personal nurse.

Everyone had an assigned task. I felt this would minimize the impact of the illness and treatment on the kids while providing a venue for the whole family to grow closer as a result of this challenge.

Keeping Hope, Faith, and Love

The treatment plan called for three months of debulking radiation therapy for the colorectal lesion prior to the main surgery. The goal of high-energy radiation was to shrink the tumor and kill cancer cells by damaging their DNA. Once their DNA (molecules inside cells that carry genetic information) is damaged beyond repair, cancer cells stop dividing and die. After they are broken down, they are eliminated by the body's natural processes.

Victor's PET scan, a type of imaging test that uses a radioactive tracer to look for disease in the body, revealed a lung lesion, highly suspicious for metastatic cancer. Thus, while undergoing radiation, in July 2004, he underwent a pulmonary lobectomy, the removal of part of the lung that contained the lesion, a procedure that is both diagnostic and therapeutic. I cannot forget the gloomy look on the thoracic surgeon's face as he came out of the operating room. He immediately told me he was sorry, that although the surgery went well, he was disheartened by what he had found and that he was 99% sure that it was malignant tumor that likely spread from the colorectal cancer. He immediately changed the diagnosis to Stage 4 which carried a significantly worse prognosis for Victor. For some unexplained reason, I remember feeling strangely hopeful. You can call it gut feel or faith but I felt peaceful after Victor's surgery despite the surgeon's bad news.

In contrast, I was not very confident prior to his surgery. When morphine refused to take the pain of cancer away, I would use my healing energy to augment Victor's pain medications and he would sleep like a baby afterwards. I came to understand the real power of healing energy: it is deep love. I simply could not imagine a world without my husband. So I focused all my love and faith into his healing. Radiation, surgery, and chemotherapy are the mainstays of cancer treatment and I thank God that we have them. But love has its own indomitable power that cannot be denied and should never be overlooked.

We were also able to squeeze in about half a dozen voice lessons prior to his surgery, an out-of-the box way of increasing his lung capacity and boosting his morale at the same time. Together we learned the duet "The Prayer," popularized by Celine Dion and Andrea Bocelli while he was undergoing radiation therapy. Thus, when the day of the surgery finally came, I felt like we had done the best we could do to prepare and I left the rest up to God. I sang a church hymn repeatedly "*Nada te turbe*" as he was in the operating room. That day, I felt that no bad news could break my innermost calm. The surgery went well and the following day we got a call from his lung surgeon. He was retracting his initial bleak prognosis after reading the cytopathology report, which stated that after further analysis of the specimen, what seemed like malignant cancer cells on gross examination turned out to be fungal cells under the microscope. The cancer had not spread after all. I watched as Victor's despair turned into joy and gratitude. God is good.

His next operation was the main colonic tumor resection at Inova Fairfax Hospital on August 30, 2004. Afterwards, the surgeon commented that it was one of the biggest tumors he had ever had to operate on and we later learned 6 out of 14 lymph nodes were positive. This meant that he would have to undergo at least six months of chemotherapy.

This was the next hurdle. Victor was ravaged by the chemotherapy treatments designed to save his life. I went with him during his first few chemotherapy sessions and it was draining for me to watch him become ill and weak. The healing instinct in me did not allow me to just watch him. The next time he went for his chemotherapy, I stayed behind at home. I set up our bedroom for his IV fluid infusion. Then I set up the bathroom to be like a steam room, meticulously cleaning the tub where he would detoxify from the energy draining effects of the chemotherapy. I meditated at home while he got his treatment so that I could more effectively deliver the energy intervention that would help him maximize the benefits of his chemotherapy. This was another way I would help fill the gaps in his cancer care.

As soon as he came home from chemotherapy, I would hook him up to receive an extra 1 to 2 liters of IV fluid in addition to what he had received at the hospital. This IV treatment allowed for added detoxification through his kidneys. As he slept, while receiving IV fluids, I would perform the touchless energy healing method I had learned in Sedona.

When he woke up, I would put him in a whirlpool tub with 12 lbs of magnesium sulfate in a makeshift steam room so he could further detoxify the chemotherapy through his skin. In addition to IV hydration, I would give him oral hydration as necessary. After a simple organic dinner and a good night's rest, he would bounce back the following day.

TRANSCENDING SELF

While Victor was undergoing chemotherapy, we got a call from our friend Dr. Ted Gancayco, who was the President of the Philippine Medical Association (PMA) of Washington, DC. The PMA was chosen to lead the 2006 Philippine Festival in Washington, DC, which would be the centennial anniversary of Philippine migration to the United States. Ted asked Victor if he was up to the challenge of leading the Festival during the centennial year. I was thrilled when his face lit up while he was on the phone. He realized it was a large undertaking that required a great deal of work and he asked me and our four children for support, as this was a huge responsibility that was going to affect our whole family. The project required more than a year long commitment. With our family's blessing, he accepted the challenge.

Prior to his abdominal surgery, in August of 2004, the PMA deferred his term as president from 2005 to 2006 to allow Victor to complete his treatments. On behalf of the PMA, Ted and another past president, Stuart, asked me to be president of the PMA but I declined because I had placed Victor's care and that of the family above everything else. Even our decision to accept the chairmanship of the Philippine Festival of 2006 was part of being in tune with his holistic therapeutic regimen. Working on this service oriented project gave my husband and children something to look forward to. It was no longer just a way to celebrate the strength and resilience of the Filipino community. It also became a way to celebrate the strength of one Filipino family, ours.

FIRST THINGS FIRST

As I let go of my fears for my family, I found the strength to work with others to lead part of the June 2005 Festival which turned out to be a huge success. For 2006, we chose the theme *"Isang Daang Taon—100 years: Proud History, Lasting Legacy."*

Our family had been through so much already at that point, what would this new challenge bring? I hoped for the best, but I knew that it could also bring out the worst. The previous year, I had watched as another leader in the community handled just such a challenge. He and his wife had seemed just as strong as Victor and I. They took on the challenge of leadership with great joy and while both in good health, not after battling cancer. Yet after a year or two, the pair was divorced. Victor and I had already been through so much. Just as I decided that I would not lose him to cancer, I decided that I would not lose him to this daunting project. My husband was still recovering from cancer. To protect us, Victor and I joined a *"Bu-kas Loob sa Diyos"* [open self to God] retreat. Here we both learned how important it was for us to work as a team. We needed the strength of relying on each other before anyone, much less the entire FilAm community in Washington, DC, could rely on us.

Leading from Behind:
Sharing the Vision and Inspiration

As Michelle went off to college and while Leia was preparing to move to Stanford, Victor was recuperating well and was able to go back to work, but he still got tired often. In September 2005, we had our first of many festival planning meetings. Victor presided over these meetings, while I made sure that we had everything we needed at hand. I was able to see each event as a moment to get through one step at a time. Letting go of the anxiety over these planning meetings freed me up and made me available to all the volunteers who needed my help. Eventually, I learned to just do my best and trust in my team.

The Centennial Celebration of 2006 was a huge affair requiring more than a year of meticulous planning and work by a dedicated team that we thoughtfully formed. The month long celebration in June in multiple venues engaged Filipino-Americans from all walks of life in the tristate area and brought out the best and, unfortunately, a little of the worst in our volunteers. As we emphasized our goal to strengthen our shared sense of community and ethnic pride, I was able to identify those volunteers who would be most helpful in achieving the goal.

The Philippine Independence Gala Ball was well attended, star studded, and was by all measures, a resounding success. The festival's showcase event, the Philippine Fair and Parade on Pennsylvania Avenue near the U.S. Capitol was also widely successful, and, for 2006, as estimated by the DC government, 40,000 people attended.

Being physicians, we added a Health Pavilion that focused on the growing epidemic of diabetes affecting our community. I also initiated the FilAm Centennial Idol, an open singing competition that capitalized on the Filipino's love for singing. Our Grand Marshall for the parade was Congressman Tom Davis of Virginia. Other festival events include a series of Senior Citizens dialogues, an Art Exhibit "Filipinos in America: Through the Eyes of Artists", the Dr. Jose Rizal Youth Awards, and golf and tennis tournaments. The festival concluded with the Annual Community Picnic and SportsFest, both of which focused on camaraderie and unity through friendly competition.

Planning such a large series of events took more than just hard work on the part of our team and myself. There are always obstacles that pop up when you least expect them and one incident occurred while we were planning the fair on Pennsylvania Avenue. A restaurant along the route repeatedly refused to sign the permit we needed and my team became increasingly anxious and frustrated as the date approached. I decided to go to the restaurant alone, and, after eating, I asked to see the manager who was very pleasant and immediately signed the form without any hesitation. Getting all the requirements needed for the fair affirmed what had been impressed upon me as a child: when you see a need, fill it. Take the initiative. Confident optimism helps too.

On the day of the fair and parade, word came that there was a big group marching that had not registered ahead of time. Some feared this could lead to a disruption or ugly confrontation. After taking time to meditate on a Bible passage, I calmly reminded everyone that we are all part of one community and soon enough, everyone started working towards a solution. If I had walked into that situation without meditating, I doubt we would have achieved such a positive outcome.

Today, ten years later, I remember the lessons learned from these trials. By the grace of God my husband is healthy as we continue our journey. I believe that the work we did together for the Centennial celebration was a positive factor in his recuperation and healing. Working towards a goal gave him something to look forward to during the gloomiest times of his treatment, like a beacon in the darkness.

SHEPHERDING: ENVISIONING, ENGAGING, AND EXECUTING

Since the festival, I have stayed involved as a community organizer and advocate, supporting political, artistic, humanitarian, and environmental causes. I have used the lessons I learned about love and courage, challenges, and leadership, while being at the background or forefront of global community concerns. Since 2011, one of the biggest causes I have been involved in is the protection of Philippine territory within our Exclusive Economic Zone (EEZ). By creating global awareness about China's troubling activities; massive militarization, artificial island building, and the unconscionable degradation and destruction of the environment in the West Philippine Sea; we have managed to rally and engage regular citizens, as well as get global support for our cause. In an effort to help stop the expansionism of China, I have personally worked to influence, quietly recruit and bring key players together to help come up with nontraditional soft power solutions to the ongoing conflict.

I believe that the rule of law is supreme, and that international commitment in the UN Convention on the Law of the Seas (UNCLOS) should be honored. Aside from settling maritime territorial disputes in this militarized area, at stake is the freedom of navigation in a region that is vital to the stability of the global economy. As a peace advocate, I support a multifaceted solution; diplomatic, legal, credible military deterrence, extensive coast guard development and training, territorial waters vigilance, tight mineral and marine resources management and protection, ecotourism, and an economic boycott of noncrucial goods made in China. At the same time, it is crucial that we continue to develop Philippine-China relations. To quote military strategist, General Sun Tzu, in *The Art of War*, "To subdue the enemy without fighting is the acme of skill".

Often, I think about the SHEpherd Nelson Mandela implicitly talked about. She knows that every flock is different; that every pasture has its sweet spots and its rocks. She knows that even though the sheep may look the same from a distance, each one has its own personality, strengths and weaknesses. She knows her own trials and triumphs. But the SHEpherd uses her own imperfections as much as her talents to help her sheep get everything they need and meet the needs of her community. Ultimately, she knows that her flock, like any family or organization or country, is a work in progress. And she knows that sometimes, the best way to lead her flock is from behind.

❋

MUTYA SAN AGUSTIN, M.D.

RETIRED PROFESSOR
PEDIATRICS, CLINICAL EPIDIMEOLOGY, SOCIAL MEDICINE
ALBERT EINSTEIN COLLEGE OF MEDICINE
FOUNDING PRESIDENT, PHILIPPINE AMBULATORY PEDIATRIC ASSOCIATION, INC.
FWN100™ U.S. 2007

Revolutionizing the Health Care
Delivery System

During my 35-year professional career in the Bronx, New York City, I struggled to make radical changes in the community and hospital based health care delivery system, with a focus on primary care. Over the years I have returned frequently to the Philippines. During those visits I nurture my professional connections, lecture to faculty and staff in the department of pediatrics, University of the Philippines, College of Medicine, and make presentations to professional groups in other medical institutions and the Philippine Pediatric Society. During these visits to the Philippines I have noted a professional barrier between specialist and generalist pediatricians. I provide advice on public health issues when appropriate. My goal is to effect changes in the Philippine primary health care delivery system along with corresponding changes in medical education and post-graduate training. My vision for the Philippines is based on my experience with the primary health care system in the Bronx, NY. In this chapter, I reflect on why I decided to focus my medical career on primary health care, the leadership actions that were instrumental in achieving this vision, and the leadership qualities I have learned from my upbringing and experience. My medical career has shaped my leadership philosophy: "Knowing is not enough; we must apply, Willing is not enough; we must do." (Goethe) It is my belief that health care is a human right. I have disrupted and helped transform the health care status quo.

BUILDING A LEGACY

In June 1994, during one of my visits to the Philippines, I founded the Philippine Ambulatory Pediatric Association, Inc. (PAPA). PAPA is an organization of diverse pediatricians and general practitioners from different parts of the country, engaged in private practice, or in hospitals and government health facilities. The objectives of PAPA is to advocate and support the establishment of training programs that will increase the number and distribution of general pediatricians whether they are involved in clinical practice, teaching, or research. The goals are to enhance the quality of medical care provided to the general pediatric population; to improve the organization and delivery of pediatric health services in ambulatory settings; and to increase research activities relevant to ambulatory pediatrics. PAPA also promotes publications and advocates for public policies that support children's health. Since its inception, the organization has collaborated with national and international groups to develop initiatives that impact the work of pediatricians, especially initiatives that benefit families and children. The advocacy programs of PAPA on Community Based Tuberculosis Control Program in Children; Brief Advice for Smoking Cessation: Tobacco Control in Children and Adolescents; Health Supervision Guidelines for Infants, Children and Adolescents and Reach Out and Read Program, an innovative evidenced based early pediatric literacy program are nationally and internationally recognized and acknowledged. Currently, PAPA has chapters in Cebu, La Union, and Bulacan.

Developing Others to Share a Vision

I initiated the establishment of PAPA working with four pediatricians in the Philippines. Three were graduates of the International Pediatric Fellowship Program, Department of Ambulatory Medicine, Montefiore Medical Center, Albert Einstein College of Medicine, of which I was the director.

The International Pediatric Fellowship Program offered one-year fellowships to physicians from other countries opportunities for education in Primary Care in the United States. The fellows were mostly junior faculty members of teaching institutions, or departments of health. Fellows were selected for their organizational skills and potential for achievement in the academic world as primary care clinicians, teachers and researchers. Fellows were required to return to their home institutions. All 16 graduates of the International Pediatric Fellowship Program from the Philippines returned to the country and have assumed leadership positions in medical schools, teaching hospitals, the Department of Health, and non-government organizations.

Returning to the Philippines for at least two to three months a year has been personally and professionally rewarding to me. I left the Philippines in 1957 when I was 22 years old and had completed medical school at the University of the Philippines. I went to the United States for postgraduate residency training in pediatrics at Sinai Hospital Baltimore, Maryland and at Johns Hopkins and Baltimore City Hospital. Whether I was in a hospital setting or outside, adjusting to life in the United States was not easy for me. Being separated from family and being a minority in a foreign country was a learning experience that at times was depressing and stressful.

LEARNING TO BE RESILIENT

I believe that my childhood during World War II in the Philippines helped me learn to endure hardships and made me tough. I was seven years old when the Japanese invaded the Philippines. We vacated our house in Manila when the Japanese commandeered it, making it one of their official headquarters. We were forced to move in with relatives in the province of Rizal. Food was scarce, and we ate mostly coconuts and yams. Everybody in my family had to work. My job was to deliver carabao [water buffalo] milk to village houses early in the morning. When the defeat of the Japanese seemed imminent in late 1944 we returned to Manila, walking through the mountains. We prepared for the journey by putting on three layers of clothing. As the top layer became torn and dirty we took it off and threw it away. Memories of the long march, being constantly aware of dangers that I did not fully understand, dodging American bombs, and running into the forest to hide from retreating Japanese soldiers left me with nightmares that lasted long into my adult life. Despite these hardships, I learned the courage that is required when one must persevere in the face of obstacles.

Family Values

I am the youngest of seven in a family that values higher education. Among my siblings, the oldest became an educator and principal of a public high school. There were two lawyers, a dentist, a pharmacist and another physician with whom I spent most of my summer vacations. My mother was the quintessential Filipina mother: always there for us, taking care of our needs and keeping us together. My father was a writer, journalist, and editor-in-chief of *Taliba* and of *Bagong Buhay*, both Tagalog newspapers. My family was central in my upbringing. They nurtured my motivation to achieve, determination to face challenges, resolve to overcome obstacles and resilience in dealing with stressful situations.

SETTING VISION

Early in my career as a medical doctor, I was determined to create a community-based primary care facility. This vision was influenced by my medical school experience at the University of the Philippines, and my experiences at the Philippine General Hospital and pediatric residency training at Sinai Hospital, Johns Hopkins, and the Baltimore City Hospital. At that time, medical education and residency training was oriented toward inpatient care and medical specialties. Most patients were seen in overcrowded emergency room and outpatient clinics. The health care delivery system was fragmented, episodic, and specialty care oriented with no single person responsible for providing comprehensive, continuous and coordinated medical care.

Finding the Courage of My Convictions

My eyes would not shut. Lying in bed that night, scenes from the emergency room (ER) killed my sleep. ERs always smell like sickness. They smell of blood and vomit, followed by gusts of alcohol and Lysol from someone cleaning up a mess before another erupts. It was the end of 1966, I was alone in bed and the house was silent. My body felt heavy and dull, but I could smell the ER. Interrupting the chaos in my head of sick and wounded patients and frantic doctors was the voice of the secretary of the Chairman of the Department of Pediatrics at Montefiore Medical Center: "The Chair of the Department of Pediatrics , Montefiore Medical Center wants to see you first thing tomorrow morning." A simple phrase, one that would have evoked excitement not long before the call from the secretary. The secretary had said that he wanted to talk to me about my future. He and I had spoken about it just a few months before, so I knew what this meeting meant: he was offering me a pathway to join him in the upper echelons of academic pediatric medicine. He would give me my own laboratory and help get grants to carry out my research on carbohydrate metabolism in the newborns of diabetic mothers. Any sensible young doctor just a few years out of residency would have jumped at such an opportunity.

That night, in those hours before the meeting with the chair of the department of pediatrics, my mind skipped between memories of patients, dysfunctional medical establishments and what on earth I wanted from being a doctor. My gut said what the chair of the department was offering was not right for me. Tossing in bed, I questioned myself, how could I be stupid to think of throwing away such sure success?

What made that night especially hard, and what made my thoughts so fierce, was not just the imminent meeting with chair of the department, or that my identity as a physician was in crisis. I could not rest because I was alone. My three children Emmanuel, aged five; Ariel aged three and a half; and Angela, aged two years, were in their rooms sleeping, and it was just me there in that bed. Normally, I would have talked about this with my husband. We would have figured it out together. Should I forgo my ascent in academic medicine or should I stay in clinical medicine? But that night I could not do this because my husband was gone. Eight months earlier, he died of liver cancer at age 31. We had been classmates in medical school and both had done residency training in the U.S. I became a pediatrician and he became a surgeon. I could not sleep that night, thinking of my late husband, my children and the patients whom I cared for in the hospitals in Baltimore, Maryland and in South Bronx, New York. I weighed the risks and consequences as I decided on the future direction of my career.

Doing Whatever It Takes; Compassion and Commitment

It was 1958, some eight years before I faced a decision on my future in medicine. I was doing a rotation at Baltimore City Hospital during my residency training in pediatrics. Late one night, on my way out the door to go home after more than 20 hours of treating patients, I happened to glance a woman holding a small baby that appeared to be about six months old. The infant's body was stiff and puckered. I bent down. He was barely breathing. The mother had been sitting in an overcrowded ER lobby waiting for someone to call her number. I grabbed the infant and yelled for the mother to follow. We ran up the stairs to the pediatric intensive care unit where I worked. I called to the staff, "Code!" The baby was given oxygen. The intern and resident checked the vital signs. They pulled back the baby's eyelids hoping to find a response. I said, "Let's start an IV. We have a severe dehydration here!" I needed a vein to start the IV. Feeling with two fingers along one of his arms I searched for some slight throb, but dehydration shrinks the veins. I found a spot and stuck the needle in, but nothing. I kept prodding one withered arm, then the other. The resident reported the baby's vitals were not good. The oxygen started to flow, so at least he was breathing. My fingers dug into a spot on his leg and found a vein. Some blood beaded up, but the vein collapsed. I was so frustrated! Why was this baby on the threshold of death? Why did the baby not get help from someone in the ER hours earlier? None of this needed to be happening, I kept thinking. My fingers continued to probe his flesh. Finally, I hit a vein in his leg and the needle stayed put. The nurse turned on the IV and everyone breathed as if we all shared the baby's lungs. I stayed through the night with the baby and he recovered.

Understanding the Context

In the spring of 1966, within months of my husband's death, I had to start moonlighting because I did not earn enough at my job as an attending pediatrician at a hospital and a faculty position at Albert Einstein College of Medicine. After my regular weekday shifts as a specialist in neonatology, I worked weekends at a public hospital in the South Bronx, the borough's poorest section. The Bronx sprawls north and east just across the East River from Manhattan. It has middle class enclaves and working class areas but most notoriously, it has poverty. The South Bronx in 1966 had buildings that had been gutted by fire. There were garbage-strewn lots instead of parks. The streets were desolate and weeds grew from buckled sidewalks. Crime was rampant. Hard drug use was endemic. Sideswiped by unemployment and municipal disinvestment, residents lacked basic services and the resources to move away. At the time the South Bronx had one of the country's highest rates of drug addiction and crime. Its children suffered from high levels of infant mortality, lead poisoning, and malnutrition. It felt like a developing country.

I remember one time I called the cops when I saw a man breaking into an apartment. "What are you doing in the South Bronx, doc," the policeman on the phone said. "Get the hell outta there!"

On the contrary, the more time I spent as a doctor in the Bronx, the more I wanted to stay. I know it seems crazy, so let me explain. Moonlighting for the hospital in the South Bronx entailed making weekend home-visits to premature babies and their mothers. We would usually see two newborns on Saturday and two on Sunday. The driver would take my nurse and I through the South Bronx streets looking for the address the mother had given. That was when I truly began to see the poverty. The burned out apartment buildings had giant black sockets where the windows used to be. Sometimes people lived on the lower floors of rotting buildings. Weeds grew through holes in the roofs. Front steps were crumbling. At that time, a quarter of all New York City's structural fires flared in the Bronx. No one hung out on stoops, the streets were too dangerous for anyone but the gangs. I would walk into an apartment building and up the stairs; pitch black, littered with garbage and shit; animal or human, I could not tell. A fetid smell would fill my nostrils and stay for days. I always wore my white coat, like a flag of surrender that could be seen, however faintly, in the bleak surroundings. On one visit, we knocked but no one came. I turned the knob and the door creaked open. The nurse and I stepped in, softly calling, "It is your doctor from the hospital." The mother answered from a doorway across the small living room. There were no windows and no lights were on. It was morning but we could barely see our way to the bedroom. She was under the covers with the baby, who was faintly grunting. I pulled back the sheet to look at him. My job was to make sure the preemies were clean and fed and healthy. But my eyes having adjusted, as I looked at the baby lying there, I saw dark spots on the bed: cockroaches. They scattered, running under the sheets and onto the floor.

The nurse and I washed the baby in the cramped kitchen sink. There was a window, the only one in the place that provided a tiny respite from the gloom. We fed the baby. I talked to the mother about how to keep him clean. We turned the lights on and swept the floors; we told the mother that a brighter apartment would make everyone feel better. She just looked at me and said, "Who is going to pay the electric bill?"

It was this experience that planted the seed, and on that sleepless night alone in my bed, the seed began to sprout into a vision. If I could understand my patient's life circumstances, what happens outside the hospital, then I could provide them with health care that mattered. If I simply give them treatments and prescriptions, they might take care of themselves, but they might not, even if they wanted to. It might be that they are so depressed, they cannot get out of bed to clean the apartment, or they cannot get a job to pay the electric bill. It could be that no one has ever treated them with the kindness and respect they need in order to know how to delicately and lovingly wash a baby. Believe it or not, this is what gave me hope during that torturous night alone.

As part of my duties moonlighting at the hospital in the Bronx, I worked nights in the Emergency Room. At the end of one of my shifts, as I crossed the street toward my car, I spotted the silhouettes of four young men, teenagers sitting on the hood of my car. The car was low on the ground, all four tires slashed. The boys were waiting, not for me in particular but to see the shock and fear on the face of whomever owned the car. It made me angry but I was not afraid. I headed back inside the hospital knowing I would have to stay the night. I could not go home, no tow truck would come to the neighborhood so late at night and it was not safe to ride in a taxi alone. I could have called the police but I did not. Even though I was still new to the South Bronx, I knew that if I, the doctor, called the cops, then these kids would not trust me. Even though I did not know the boys, they would know the doctor got them in trouble. Their friends would hear and all this would do was sow even greater distrust. I called home to tell my babysitter I would not be back home that night. I found a stretcher in the emergency room and wheeled it into an empty examination room and slept.

FINDING MY SENSE OF PURPOSE

You might think that since I had recently and suddenly become a widow and single mother that I would want comfort and not this intense, insecure career alternative. Yes, indeed. Security is what the chair of the department could give me. But it became more apparent that that was not what I wanted.

Yes, I was unsure, but I embraced the challenges of being a physician in the South Bronx. After only a few months, I had already begun to feel a sense of purpose I did not have before. I could not say no to the community I had begun to discover and turn away from my promising ideas about a better kind of health care. Maybe I did not need a prestigious career. Other doctors may have wanted to retreat from the South Bronx, but I could see a role for myself as I never had before. The challenges of giving health care in the poorest neighborhood in the biggest city in the United States excited me. The people called me.

The 1960s and early '70s were the time of the war on poverty. President Lyndon B. Johnson's program created Medicare and Medicaid and allotted new funding support for community based health care centers. Money began to flow into neighborhoods like the South Bronx. At that time, I was an attending physician, and a neonatologist, conducting research on carbohydrate metabolism on newborns. Administrators at Montefiore Medical Center and the Albert Einstein College of Medicine collaborated on a proposal to open two community health centers in the Bronx, one affiliated with Albert Einstein College of Medicine and other with the Montefiore Medical Center. As my research funding on carbohydrate metabolism was running out, I took a job as an attending physician at the newly opened Montefiore Morrisania Comprehensive Child Care Center serving the South Bronx. Initially what attracted me to the job was the salary. It paid more than my attending physician salary at both hospitals where I was working. I was surprised by how much I loved the new job. I had not expected that my role as the primary care pediatrician of their children would mean so much to them and to me. Providing care on the front lines in this ravaged community, in contrast to the rarefied wards of a traditional hospital brought medicine to life. But I knew that the chair of the department would not like this. He wanted me to leave the Montefiore Morrisania Comprehensive Child Care Center for an academic position in the department of pediatrics at the medical center. However, when I thought of the mother of the baby in that apartment I had visited, I realized that as I was teaching her to care for her baby, she was teaching me how to be a better doctor, one who

integrates the bigger picture of her patient's lives. Primary health care means having a specific primary care physician, who can provide comprehensive, preventive,
acute episodic care; and coordinate all medical services on a longitudinal basis. It
also means paying attention to the neighborhood and the resources it can provide.
It means valuing the customs and cultural beliefs that at first may seem ignorant.
Primary health care prevents unnecessary visits to the ER and hospitalization. Primary health care shows patients who do not think they can do it how to take care
of themselves. It nurtures within them self-confidence.

When I kept my appointment with the chair of the department, I informed
him, "I want to stay at the Comprehensive Child Care Center in the South Bronx.
I am happy there. I am a people person." Surprised by my decision, he said, "You
know that if you stay there, you will have less chances of moving up, of being
promoted to full professor." He reminded me how important it was for my future
to become an academic physician and how the institution would benefit from my
research and teaching. I had made up my mind. I chose to follow my heart.

Leading Innovation

In March, 1967, I was appointed director of Morrisania Montefiore Comprehensive Child Care Center, six months after I had joined it as an attending physician. I organized the medical services as a non-profit HMO (Health Maintenance
Organization) with an emphasis on primary care. Most people, especially the poor,
go to the doctor only when they are sick. In the South Bronx there were almost no
private doctors so all the residents had access to were hospital emergency rooms
and walk-in clinics. In medicine this is referred to as episodic care. This is when
someone waits until they feel so bad that they have no choice but to get outpatient
treatment at a hospital. Thus there is no continuity. No specific identified primary
care physician to track their medical status over time and help manage their illness
with an accumulated knowledge of their health. In addition, there is fragmented
care, when patients are seen by different doctors each time they visit the ER and/
or the outpatient clinic. It was obvious to me that this health care delivery system
needed to be changed along with corresponding changes in medical education
curriculum and postgraduate residency training.

It was at this time that a larger segment of society had begun to view health
care as a human right. I did not consider myself a political activist, but I understood what I did as political. For me, the federal funding for the community based
comprehensive primary care centers in poor neighborhoods and the awareness
of inequity created fertile ground for new ideas and unorthodox actions. As required by the funding agency, I created a community board composed of parents of

children registered at the center. The community board met with the administrative staff at least once a month to discuss issues regarding medical services provided at the center and how the center could address the health issues in their community, such as lead poisoning, teenage pregnancy, HIV. The core of the delivery system was the primary care practice teams composed of the pediatrician or internist, nurses, nurse's aide, and clerk.

Children were assigned to a specific team with one physician responsible for the provision of comprehensive and coordinated medical services on a continuing basis. Patients were seen by appointment, and by the same physician at each visit. A complete range of services were available, including speech and hearing, eye testing, dental, laboratory and x-ray. Psychological consultations were made available for both parents and children.

The Morrisania Montefiore Comprehensive Care Center departed from the fragmented service pattern of the past and found ways to provide health care geared to the needs of children as whole human beings. On December 2, 1969, I testified before the Senate Appropriation Sub-Committee on Labor, Health, Education and Welfare, chaired by Senator Warren Magnuson, on the need for continued funding of community health centers throughout the country. Funding was granted.

Directing a Neighborhood
Family Care Center (1973 - 1976)

Morrisania Neighborhood Family Care Center (NFCC) was designed to operate as the outpatient facility of Morrisania Hospital, a municipal hospital. In 1973, when the NFCC opened, I was appointed as director and given responsible for program planning, implementation and coordination of all services provided at NFCC, including pediatric and internal medicine primary care and the subspecialty services surgery, obstetrics and gynecology, ophthalmology, otolaryngology dentistry, as well as the hospital emergency room services, home care, and employees health services. As director, I was responsible for the recruitment, appointment, hiring and firing of medical care providers. The functional independence of NFCC facilitated the establishment of priorities for the different components of medical services provided to the patients of NFCC.

Expanding the Concept:
North Central Bronx Hospital (1976 - 1997)

When Morrisania Hospital closed in August 1976, I was asked to open the new North Central Bronx hospital and to serve as the director of the Department of Ambulatory Care Medicine, also known as the outpatient department. The Department of Ambulatory Care Medicine was an autonomous department with its own budget, occupying the first four floors of the hospital, including the emergency medical services (ER), all the specialty and subspecialty services and primary care teams.

Comprehensive primary care services were provided by teams. Each team had a pediatrician or internist, nurse practitioners, nurses, nurse's aides, and clerks. In addition, there were the social workers, psychologist, speech and hearing therapist, early childhood educators, nutritionists and laboratory technicians. Subspecialty consultation was provided within the primary care teams by the subspecialist to minimize unnecessary referral to the subspecialty clinics.

Community Outreach Programs were established, including the adolescent pregnancy clinic with two years follow-up after delivery for both adolescent mother and baby; breast feeding promotion; HIV/AIDS; a program to provide Graduate Education Diploma (GEDs) in collaboration with the Department of Education; after hours telephone services; child abuse services, and linkages with schools for health care promotion.

Transferring Lessons Learned:
Montefiore Medical Center (1997-2002)

In 1997, I moved the entire Department of Ambulatory Medicine, including the medical staff, nurse practitioners and some nurses and program structure to the Montefiore Medical Center. The move to Montefiore Medical Center gave me the opportunity to establish the Department of Primary Care Medicine at a non-profit voluntary hospital. The lessons learned from North Central Bronx Hospital were put to good use, including the administrative arrangement of having an autonomous department with its own budget, responsible for program planning and implementation; the structure of the primary care practice teams; and the Community Outreach Programs.

The success of the Department of Primary Care Medicine demonstrated that it was possible to establish the primary care model in a hospital-based outpatient setting in both private and public hospitals. The idea was replicable and scalable.

Ensuring Sustainability: Medical Education
and Postgraduate Residency Training

Both the North Central Bronx Hospital Department of Ambulatory Medicine and the Montefiore Medical Center Department of Primary Care Medicine became the site for education and training of medical students from medical schools in the U.S. and from abroad. Albert Einstein College of Medicine residents in training and other health-care professionals, from the U.S. and from international organizations.

My Legacy: Giving Back

My medical career in the Bronx set the stage for my sustained involvement and leadership over 35 years. I was able to develop a successful alternative primary health care model for the poor. I was successful in changing power structures. Planning and implementing a new health care delivery model included sharing the vision and subsequent collaboration with various internal and external teams, as well as working with diverse stakeholders. My leadership demonstrates that changes can bring about results in a health care model that provides comprehensive patient-centered, family-oriented care that benefit the poorest of the poor. What I learned about leadership in the Bronx is now being tested with the Philippine Ambulatory Pediatric Association.

❋

JOSEFINA "CHEF JESSIE" SINCIOCO

RESTAURATEUR
FWN100™ GLOBAL 2014

SAYING "YES" TO GOD'S WILL

When I was told that I would be preparing the Pope's meals, I went down on my knees, in joy and gratefulness for this blessing. This is what I said in an exclusive interview with the *Inquirer* on January 20, 2015. For the Pontiff's first meal in Manila, I prepared saffron risotto, pan-fried sea bass with potatoes and vegetables, and a dessert of flambé mango with mantecado ice cream. I also served him *turon* [a Philippine snack made of thinly sliced bananas and a slice of jackfruit, dusted with brown sugar, rolled in a spring roll] and banana cue since I had been told he had a sweet tooth. To cook for the Pope was the ultimate honor of my 24-year culinary career. Since then, people have been calling me the PAPAL CHEF, a title that I am very proud of. A title that cannot be matched.

In this chapter, I discuss the role of family in developing my self-confidence and the hands-on training in purchasing, budgeting, and the culinary basics. Pivotal to my career as a chef that eventually resulted in my becoming the Papal Chef while he visited the Philippines was winning a baking contest with "My Tita's Special Treat." Winning that contest led to training at the Inter-Continental Hotel in Manila, travel to Vienna, Hungary, and London. After I returned to the Philippines, I resigned from the Inter-Continental because of their discrimination because I was a woman. I discuss my process of discernment as I considered my options and the consequences of my decisions. Finally, I explain why I talk about my life as a living testimony of God's plan.

The Role of Family in Developing My Self-Confidence

I was born and raised by a poor but very hard working couple in Sulucan, Angat, Bulacan.

My father, Juanito, the fourth in a family of nine siblings, was a farmer. His parents were my *Lolo* [grandfather], Pablo Capistrano Sincioco, and my *Lola* [grandmother], Maria Nicolas.

My mother, Carmen, was the eldest in a family of 14 from my Lolo Donato Castro Cruz and my Lola Rosita "Puti" Cruz.

My Lolo Pablo, "Ambo" as he was fondly called, was a very good story teller. What I remember most was when he told us that the property of the Sinciocos reached as far as your eyes could see. However, they had to sell most of it so that his only brother, Nicanor, could study law. Lolo Canor became a very prominent lawyer during his time.

My Lola Maria was a petite, pretty young woman. When visitors from Manila would be seen in Sulucan and asked where they were headed, they would respond, *"Dadalaw po sa magandang dalaga!"* [To visit the beautiful miss]. They were referring to my *Inay* [mother} Maria, as we all called her.

My *Tatang* [father] Juanito was short, like his mother *Inay* Maria, and was very good looking, too. He was always jolly, a friend to everybody. A lot of people call him Jack.

What I fondly remember of my childhood was when my Inang Carmen and I would sell *bilaos* [a flat round-shaped rice winnower, a traditional basket implement in the Philippines, usually made from woven wood or rattan] of freshly harvested vegetables. We would each have one bilao on our heads and shout, *"Bili na kayo ng sitaw!* [buy beans] *Bili na kayo ng kamatis!"* [buy tomatoes] as we peddled. My mother liked bringing me along because I entertained our customers. They would ask me to either sing, dance, or play the hula-hoop in exchange for a purchase.

Looking back, I realized, those times primed me for sales and thoroughly developed my self-esteem. I was able to rid myself of shyness.

First Lessons in Purchasing and Budgeting

When I was almost nine years old, a big change in my life happened. My Aunt Lita, my father's sister, brought me to Manila, with my parents' consent, to stay with her and her husband, Uncle Eddy. This was a fulfillment of my Aunt Lita's promise to send me to school as soon as she was settled in Manila, as I was her favorite among her nephews and nieces.

I started my life in the city as a third grade student at The National Teachers' College, in close proximity to where we lived in Arlegui, Quiapo, Manila. My aunt and uncle were newly married at that time and were working at my uncle's family business. My aunt was the Accountant and Treasurer of six of their corporations, and my uncle, the Export Manager.

It was at this time that I was taught to do household chores; cleaning the house, washing clothes, going to the market, and cooking. My Aunt, aside from being an outstanding office Manager and Accountant, was also an excellent housekeeper, a very good wife and mother, and a fine cook.

After a few years, when I was a secondary school student at Manuel Luis Quezon University in Arlegui, Quiapo, Manila. My uncle, aunt, and I had to move to another house closer to their office. My uncle's family owned half the block of the property where the house and office were situated. It was a few blocks away from my school and Quinta market. My Aunt and I would go to market every Saturday. This activity was my first lesson in purchasing and budgeting. I was able to familiarize myself with finding the freshest produce in the market and at the same time, bargaining for the best price. We would go home with baskets filled with fresh fish and seafood, meat, vegetables, fruits; the finest of the lot. This were more or less our week's supply of food.

Learning Culinary Basics

On occasions, when we did not have house help, I had to lend a hand in the kitchen. This included: cleaning and sorting out what we bought from the market, cooking, and doing household chores.

My Aunt, being an excellent cook, would always prepare a complete meal of salad, soup, main courses of fish and meat, and desserts. We would all be at the dining table every meal time. This was a daily routine!

Looking back, I now realize that this was probably how my palate was developed for impeccable taste. That was something I could not have learned from any school.

My Aunt Lita, being an excellent accountant, wanted me to follow in her footsteps. So, I enrolled in a Bachelor of Science in Commerce in College at Manuel Luis Quezon University in R. Hidalgo, Quiapo, Manila; a 15-minute walk from the house. Initially, I enrolled in subjects leading to a major in Accounting. However, during my second year when I took advanced accounting, I realized I was not meant to deal with numbers.

My aunt was not aware that as early as my primary school years, every time we passed by Ayala Avenue in Makati, I yearned to work in one of the buildings there. Tagged as the Philippines' "little New York," corporate buildings lined the street, with banks situated on their respective ground floors. As a child, I thought the Banks owned the whole building, so I would always tell myself, "I want to work in one of those banks in those tall, beautiful buildings!" That was enough inspiration for me to shift to Banking and Finance, and I graduated with that degree. I applied for work in almost all the banks along Ayala Avenue. Unfortunately, I was not accepted by any of them. My aunt, seeing my anxiety, suggested that I go to China Banking Corporation. She was familiar with the company, and had a few connections there. I applied, went through the process of interview and exams, and got the job. I was assigned at the money market division of their head office in Binondo, Manila, not Ayala. I was dissatisfied. I was supposed to replace somebody who was resigning in a month's time but while waiting to start my career, another major twist in my life happened.

Winning My First Baking Competition

The Great Maya Cookfest of Liberty Flour Mills was ongoing. It was then the most prestigious baking and cooking competition in the country. My aunt was enrolled at the Maya Kitchen for lessons and easily became a favorite of her teachers. She was then prodded to join the competition as they were still searching for the last monthly finalist for the baking category.

Instead of joining the baking competition herself, my Aunt pointed to me! I obliged as I was not doing anything at that time. We practiced day and night until we were able to concoct the perfect mango cake that I called "My Tita's Special Treat."

I won and became the sixth monthly finalist in the baking category!

After a month, the grand finale was held at the Grand Ballroom of Hotel Inter-Continental in Makati. On the day of the competition, the ballroom was filled to the brim with baking and cooking enthusiasts. All the finalists had to prepare their entries from scratch in a span of two hours.

While we were doing our entries, judges were not allowed to watch the process. Only one of them was allowed to observe, Mr. Siegfried Schoeber, an Austrian, the Hotel's Resident Manager. Mr. Schoeber looked intently as we went about preparing our entries. He was the front judge who assessed the contestants' ability in terms of knife skills, organization, proper cooking techniques, to name a few.

At the deadline, we creatively presented our finished products on our respective tables ready for judging.

My entry "My Tita's Special Treat" won the grand prize in the baking category!

Aside from a complete line up of kitchen equipment and a lot of other products, a major part of our prizes was a trip to Japan, where all the six winners would represent the Philippines as culinary ambassadors. The most important surprise of all was when Mr. Schoeber approached me, alongside the top six winners lined up with our trophies, and told me, "Young lady, I am offering you three months of training in our Pastry Department!" That was like winning the grand lotto! I was ecstatic!

After the trip to Japan, in July of 1983, I went to the office of Mr. Schoeber and claimed the promised training.

ON-THE-JOB TRAINING TO BE A PASTRY CHEF

My aunt made me a beautiful pink sailor-style blouse with mini skirt and matching floral scarf. She also got me a 3-inch wedge shoes with a matching bag. I was dressed like I was going to an office!

Mr. Schoeber accompanied me to the kitchen and I was introduced to the Executive Chef. We passed the main kitchen and I was led to the pastry section. I noticed the staff were all men! I was introduced to the pastry chef, a Swiss national, Chef Roland Lutz, who became my mentor. That was my first introduction to a professional kitchen.

I was so amazed at all the things around me, it was like I was in a pastry wonderland! That same day, I started my training, from 9:00 AM until 5:00 PM in my girly outfit and high heels! My back and legs were so painful but I did not mind the pain. I felt that I was in the best place on earth! I had found my niche!

Working diligently and having been the favorite assistant of my Pastry Chef, I was asked to replace one of my colleagues who left for a job on a cruise ship. On September 3, 1983, I was hired as a third Commis, the lowest rank in the kitchen.

In 1985, as my Pastry Chef claimed, for the first time in the history of Inter-Continental, I accelerated to first Commis skipping second Commis. After another two years, in 1987, I rose up the ladder again to become a Demi-Chef de Partie. Being competitive in nature, I was tasked to join contests and was instrumental in bagging the L'Assiete D'Or, the most coveted award at the yearly Chefs' competition of Chefs on Parade.

In 1988, I joined the Plated Desserts Category of the same competition, held at the Manila Hotel, and bagged the Gold Medal with Distinction Award for my entries.

I was then promoted to Chef de Partie and was sent as the sole representative of our country to Food Hotel Asia's Salon Culinaire in Singapore.

Professional Development in
Vienna, Hungary, and London

In 1989, upon the recommendation of our Executive Chef, Billy King, I was sent for training at the Inter-Continental properties in Europe. I was sent to Vienna, Hungary, and London. That was a tremendous break in the culinary world! I was offered the opportunity to stay and work in there but I told them I have to go back to my country and share what I learned with my staff.

Saying NO to Discrimination

Upon my return, the Hotel made an announcement in the newspapers on my new title as "The First Filipina Pastry Chef!"

Unfortunately, when I got my promotion paper, I was stunned to see that my title was still the same: Assistant Pastry Chef, reporting directly to the Executive Chef. This caused my resignation from the hotel. Being a woman, I could not help but think that discrimination hindered my attainment of a hard-earned promotion.

Considering my Options:
The Consequences of My Decisions

I received offers from the neighboring hotels but I did not accept them. I was interested in the offer of the Hyatt Terraces in Baguio as a Pastry Chef but when I asked permission from my Mother and my Aunt, both of them vehemently objected.

I chose to obey.

Soon after, Baguio experienced a strong earthquake that brought Hyatt Terraces to the ground.

In the meantime, I helped a friend open the first bake-off shop in Manila. The concept of a bake-off shop was very good but its location was off.

While engaged in this temporary project, I signed up for a two-year contract to work as a Pastry Chef in Sara Hotel in Beijing, China. This did not materialize because it was during this time when another amazing opportunity happened.

LEARNING TO PARTNER

My former executive Chef Billy King called and invited me to be one of his partners in setting up a restaurant in Greenbelt, right at the very heart of Makati City.

The restaurant became Le Soufflé Restaurant-Wine Bar. Le Soufflé Restaurant-Wine Bar officially opened its doors for business on October 4, 1991. It was a partnership between Chef Billy King, Chef Andreas Katzer, and Mr. Lester Harvey.

Le Soufflé became the favorite restaurant of Makati's *creme de la creme* for business meetings, birthday parties, anniversaries, product launches, and other special events. It was the only fine dining restaurant outside of a hotel at that time and had a big round bar where people became instant acquaintances. It was viewed as a lucky place by business people for negotiations. Le Soufflé became a byword to the elite and famous. It was the only place that satisfied everyone's craving for fine food.

During this time and in between, we were able to open other restaurants like Top of the Citi, Papermoon Mediterranean Restaurant and Bar, Poppies Dining, Blarney Stone Irish Pub and others.

EXPANDING PARTNERSHIPS

Midway through 1998, we received advice on a plan to demolish all the buildings in Greenbelt where our first Le Soufflé was located. Therefore, we decided to work on the next "Le Soufflé at the Fort" in Taguig City. That was our biggest outlet! We spent all our savings in building it, plus, we had to sell 15% of the company to prospective partners. It was at this time when Mr. Ariel de Borja, the late Dona Chito Madrigal, Mr. Johnny Litton, and Mr. Iñigo Zobel became our new partners.

On December 1998, though not 100 % finished yet, we opened Le Soufflé at the Fort for an exclusive wedding event. From that time on Billy King and Andreas Katzer ran the show at the Fort while I was left to handle Greenbelt.

Our last day in Greenbelt was New Year's Eve of 2000. With all my staff from Greenbelt, on February 14, 2000, we opened Le Soufflé at Wynsum Corporate Plaza in Ortigas Center, which I single-handedly ran for five years.

Six months before our lease expired, we were advised that our rent would be raised by 25% effective with the new contract. I had to look for possible venues for a transfer. It was at this time when Mr. Manolo Lopez, a regular client of the restaurant, approached me and asked if I would be interested in running

"Fernando's," the fine dining restaurant of the Rockwell Club.

The following day, Mr. Lopez arranged for my meeting with Ms. Buda Nubla, the General Manager of Rockwell Club. I went alone and when I saw the place, I was speechless! It was such a beautiful restaurant! The size of the dining room was perfect! It could accommodate about a hundred people, with high ceiling, overlooking the majestic pool, garden, and the tall buildings around the area. I told myself, that this was a perfect place to which to move.

Ms. Nubla and I had a one on one meeting and the deal was done that same day.

With around 50 staff from Wynsum, Le Soufflé opened its doors in Rockwell Club, Rockwell Center, Makati City on February 8, 2005.

At this time, with Andreas running the show at the Fort and I, handling Top of the Citi and Rockwell Club, we were providing the livelihood of about 150 employees and their families.

Until that historical day in September 2009, during our board meeting, I had to announce that I was quitting the board of Le Soufflé because I opposed their decision to close the Top of the Citi. I had to defend my staff, because they would lose their jobs, and it was almost Christmas time.

SETTING UP MY OWN COMPANY

Obviously, God was on my side. We had a smooth transition, I chose to set up my own company to retain the employment of 46 employees.

On November 2009, JCS Gastronomie Incorporated, was officially created with the help of my good friend, Atty. Louie Ogsimer.

That outlet, now became Top of the Citi by Chef Jessie, and is still very much present providing excellent food and service to its loyal clientele and still is the source of employment for 50 employees.

December 2009, Le Soufflé at the Fort closed for business.

That left Le Soufflé with just one outlet, Le Soufflé at Rockwell Club that I had headed since it started in 2005. When I informed the Rockwell people of what has happened, they wrote the board of Le Soufflé and told them that Le Soufflé was in Rockwell because of Chef Jessie and therefore she should continue running it! Le Soufflé had no choice but to give in. I wanted to continue using the name of Le Soufflé but I was told I would have to pay to get the name. I felt very bad. Aside from the fact that I did not have enough money to pay for it, I thought I worked so hard for 18 years to keep that good name and now they are asking me to pay.

AND NOW, CHEF JESSIE!

When I told Mr. Manolo Lopez, now Ambassador Manolo Lopez, about this, he told me right away, "You don't need that name, we will think of a new name for you!" The Ambassador was actually on his way to the private room upstairs for the Rockwell Club's board meeting.

After a few hours, Mr. Jay Lopez who was looking for me announced that we had a new name already, I was excited! He announced the new name of the restaurant, he said the restaurant would be called "CHEF JESSIE!" We were all so happy! It was the Ambassador himself who thought of that name!

On February 8, 2010, Le Soufflé in Rockwell Club was officially launched as Chef Jessie Rockwell Club.

I never considered that in my best attempt to save the employment of our dedicated staff, I would be in this kind of a predicament. God knows how I loved and sacrificed a lot, and had given my all for Le Soufflé.

Le Soufflé had brought us the fame and honor of being the most sought after fine dining restaurant and caterer for 18 years!

I never, even in my wildest dream, ever wished that its existence would end. My biggest consolation though was, I still had everybody with me. We all still carry the Le Soufflé spirit with us everyday!

Moving forward and with the addition of another outlet, 100 Revolving Restaurant, in Eastwood, Chef Jessie now provides employment to 165 regular employees.

With my new partners, Chef Jessie is in good shape and still is the top choice of the elite in the business community, including diplomats, top government officials, celebrities, and people with great taste!

BEING PAPAL CHEF: DISCERNING GOD'S PLAN

My most remarkable accomplishment and the summit of my career as a Chef and Restaurateur was when I was tasked to prepare and cook all the meals of the Holy Father Pope Francis, during his visit to the Philippines in January 2015. Since then, people have been calling me the PAPAL CHEF, a title that I am very proud of. A title that cannot be matched!

Looking back, when my dream was to become a banker so I could work in one of the tall, impressive buildings along Ayala Avenue, and having become an accomplished Chef and Restaurateur, I am amazed at how God's miraculous plan played out in my life. I am so grateful that God bestowed His love and blessings on me this way. I have come to realize what has happened in my life from the time I was offered that opportunity for training in the Pastry Kitchen of Hotel Inter-Continental, might not have been achieved if I were a banker.

My childhood ambition of working in Ayala Avenue came true when I trained and eventually worked at Hotel Inter-Continental Manila whose address was No.1 Ayala Avenue, Makati City!

Even my dream of working in one of the banks along Ayala Avenue was fulfilled when I started running the operations of Top of the Citi in Citibank Tower at Paseo de Roxas, Makati City in 1994.

I thank God that He led me to the right direction in life.

Whenever I get invited to talk at commencement exercises, seminars, team building activities, or asked to do simple cooking demonstrations for students, housewives and household helpers, my message is that my life is a living testimony of God's goodness and greatness. My hope is that the message will be a source of inspiration. Yes, we can plan our life and dream of being somebody someday, but if this is not part of God's plan for us, we will never feel accomplished and be happy! At first, I was hesitant to speak and share about my life. I always preferred to be a silent worker at the back of the house but then I came to realize that God needs testimonials that will affirm and firmly establish His presence and hope to His children! I have to be heard so that people who hear my message might be enlightened and live their life in accordance to God's plan for them so that, they too, will be happy.

My life is really a good showcase of careful discernment and obedience to God's Holy Will. I thank God that He made me develop this kind of personal relationship with Him. He is an extremely supportive, understanding, forgiving, and very loving Father. The three beautiful restaurants that have been entrusted to me are more than enough proof of God's wonderful love and blessing! They are concrete manifestation of His unquestionable goodness!

I never sit and rest on my laurels. I have to make sure that whatever was given to me is very well cared for. This requires hard work, dedication, sacrifice, and study that I do not mind because I know this is my only way of showing my sincere gratitude to God who is the source of all.

I often encounter people who comment on the success that I have achieved but I always tell them that these are God's blessings!

Every night before I sleep and thank God for the day, I surrender my whole life to Him and pray that I may be able to fulfill His holy will and plan for me; nothing more and nothing less.

I thank God for the recognitions I have been given, including:

- October 7, 2014: Was recognized as one of the 100 Most Influential Women in the World by FWN100.

- July 9, 2015: Chosen as BRAVO Awardee as one of the eight Most Empowered Women in the country.

- November 28, 2015: Was awarded as one of five HUWARANG ANAK NG BULAKAN 2015 by Club Bulakeño

- March 2016: Was voted "Best Chef of the Year" by the Faculty Staff and students of Lyceum of the Philippines.

THANK YOU DEAR LORD FOR ALL YOUR GOODNESS AND LOVE!

Becoming Strategists

ISABELITA M. ABELE

President & CEO, US Lumber Inc.
FWN100™ U.S. 2009

Going Against the Grain

As an Asian American leader in what I consider the "second part" of my life, what I am today has been determined by the "first part." My life's challenges began in my home town of San Pablo City, in Laguna, Philippines. As a young adult and mother I had become a Catholic school teacher. Even with a degree from a university, I had very few resources and the salary as a teacher was inadequate to meet the needs of several generations of my impoverished family. I HAD to make a better life and a better future for my family.

Fast-forward to 2016, I, Isabelita Marcelo Abele, am President and CEO of the family-owned and Southern New Jersey-based U.S. Lumber, Inc. I have successfully gone "against the grain" and positioned my certified woman and minority-owned lumber and building materials company as a regional leader in sales. As a woman in a field dominated by men, I have not let my gender, accent, or my 4-feet, 11-inches height deter me from making my dreams for the company a reality. This chapter is about the major disruptions and adjustments that have marked my transformation from Catholic teacher to a leader in the corporate world. I was able to draw on inner strength, fortitude, risk-taking, and competencies from my cultural heritage as well as from the active pursuit of new skills, knowledge, and expertise.

DREAMING OF AMERICA

The most exposure I had to a different world was from watching television. Television showed an affluent life in the United States. I can remember that, like many others around me, the soap opera 'Dynasty' captured my imagination. I was intrigued by the female lead, Joan Collins. Were people really living like that? Could it be possible? My Philippine family is very humble, but I dreamed of having more opportunities and a life just like Joan. I dreamed someday I would open and run my own company. It was then that I set my sights on America and did everything I could to get myself there; no matter what it took.

With relentless tenacity I had applied to every recruiting agency that came into my small town. Again and again. Again and again my applications were dismissed. The risk of not achieving my goal was high and the strain on my emotional stamina was getting thin. Nevertheless, I did not veer from my path. I kept my focus on my dream.

UNMET EXPECTATIONS - DASHED HOPES

At last, I finally landed my ticket to the Big Apple in 1981, with nothing but hopes and dreams in my pocket. I was sadly and suddenly disappointed by the circumstances within which I found myself. Upon arrival in America I took my first job as a maid, cleaning girl, and nanny. I expected to work in a big "homey" house surrounded by wealth, jewels, and food. What I had not expected was to become a mistreated domestic worker and held against my will by that first employer. It took months of planning and praying, but eventually I fled one afternoon, quite literally, while the employer was out. Making a dash to the nearest phone booth with a quarter in my pocket, I sought the assistance of a gracious friend who allowed me to hide in the safety of her home. This initial experience became my next major disruption on the long road to the anticipated 'Joan Collins lifestyle'.

DEVELOPING LEADERSHIP COMPETENCIES

The struggle to escape still seems unreal and is seared in my memory even though that was many, many years ago. I reflect on those days with sadness until I remember that I triumphed in the end. My journey took me through many bends along the road; some of them joyful, some of them laborious; however, none of them stopped me. I learned to show gratitude, perseverance, open-mindedness, and respect for tradition that I now use to lead my new life. In fact, from the perspective that I have developed throughout the years, I believe that leadership itself is a collection of learned skills that increases your ability to guide those around you. For me, the most important piece of becoming a true leader has been the ongoing growth of my own open-mindedness and learning to avoid considering challenges as personal, aside from absorbing their lessons. There were days that seemed like an endless exercise in perseverance and a test of my commitment to my life-long goals of becoming a business woman. Other days helped me feel gratitude and appreciation for the role models of my Philippine heritage. What is the bottom line? All lessons are learned and earned but must be applied to move forward.

Working Smarter

The first of those lessons is that starting a new life can be full of hardships. Specifically, emigrating from another country with the intent to build a better life can be a long and lonely journey, no matter where you are coming from. Critical to persevering that dream of a new life is reminding yourself that there will also be endless joy and possibility. What does that mean for those attempting to break through the barriers and avoid being taken off-course? Sometimes it could mean having to work harder and smarter than people who do not have the extra challenge of being from a diverse background. In my case, I never dared to doubt the outcome.

Living and Sharing Our Cultural Values

The journey itself has taken me very far from the place where I began. I am not talking about San Pablo City; I am talking about the traditions and lessons that our Filipino ancestors taught their children and then their children's children, and so on. Each of us has a responsibility to continue teaching new generations so that they too can reach for those dreams of learning, growing, and climbing corporate ladders if they choose. An important part of the effort to make change in the lives of those we love is to pass along all the culture and values that many of us grew up with in our homeland. Heritage relies on people like you and me spreading the lessons we were born into so that new generations, whether born here in US or back home in the Philippines, can benefit from our rich cultural traditions and legacies.

Showing Respect

Simply put, I learned from my parents and they learned from their parents, and so on. I can remember that as a child, one of our consistent messages was to show respect toward everyone, not just those that are older than you are. This was something my parents, grandparents, aunts, and uncles always insisted on without fail. Children were taught social guidelines at a young age; only speak when spoken to, use your 'pleases' and 'thank you's and never, EVER interrupt a grown-up; the usual constructs of good manners. The difference was, that these rules were never to be broken, no matter what! Sometimes all it took was a stern glance from my mother, and we, kids, knew not to do whatever "bad thing" we were thinking of doing. That look on her face said everything. You know the one? My kids know it too. But even more importantly, so do my clients!

Valuing Family

I am sure that my fellow Filipino-Americans have much in common with the way we grew up. And if I am right, most of us probably came from homes that also believed that "family" and "respect" were two of the most important building blocks in the foundation of our culture. As a Filipino-American female entrepreneur, it is this core of Filipino values that I recognize have helped me achieve what I have achieved. In fact, after years and years of learning from different people and different sources, I have come to value what my culture has provided me. The family values have stayed with me in my voyage from a struggling teacher in my hometown of San Pablo City to a mistreated maid in New York City to the executive role of President in a multi-million dollar US corporation.

Using Family Values to Grow My Business

As the baby of four children in my family, I am the only one that made my way to the United States and a career in the business world. Of my three siblings, my older brother and I were always more similar to each other than the others were. Family values were instilled into all our lives, but somehow my oldest brother and I had a special connection. In fact, when we lost him several years ago, I tried helping as many of his 10 children as I could at the time. While I was certainly no Joan Collins, I was fortunate to be in a better position to help financially than many of my other family members. Coming from a background and culture that places importance on close relationships has taught me this is the most valuable thing we can learn and teach each other. The kinship and security that a big family can give you means very little in the business world without truly embracing the lessons about helping one another, supporting relatives and community, and showing respect to all people, young or old, family or otherwise.

Being Strong and Persistent

I truly believe that my culture and heritage gave me the strength and persistence to move away from distraction, to embrace the struggle, and to go against the grain when necessary. I use many of those foundational social constructs that we learned long ago to directly help build good client relationships. Truth, honesty, and open-mindedness are key factors for creating and maintaining respect from colleagues and customers. A consistent practice of telling employees, vendors, and clients exactly what the company needs from them, or what I expect from them, creates a fair and genuine starting point for lasting relationships. On the flip side, I make it a practice to listen to employees, clients, and other industry stakeholders. I believe that it has been my family history that provided the good habits of setting expectations and creating strong two-way line of communication where questions are always welcomed and are considered important. As a result, building trust is a vital piece of maintaining my good reputation with customers and business connections. We proclaim this loudly as our company slogan. "We're fast. We're reliable. We care."

Building Relationships

Building good relationships with my clients has not always been easy. I struggled for many years, and sometimes still do, with the challenge of speaking English as a second language. I felt disrespected by some clients and vendors who thought they had the right to make negative comments. "Here comes the tiny woman in a hard hat that can't pronounce her words." Sometimes they were even rude enough to pretend not to understand what I said and to make me repeat it, over and over again.

I may never lose the accent with which I learned to speak English, but there was never a reason not to READ, READ, READ. I would read anything I could get my hands on and let myself be immersed with new ideas, thoughts, and information. The more I learned and became fluent in the specialized vocabulary I needed to run my company, the more confident I became with my knowledge. Perseverance was the key. The rude clients and vendors did not get to me. They only made themselves appear to be less professional and more like bullies. My integrity, resolve, and manners are always intact. Remember, the voice that speaks to you in your own head does not have to speak perfect English, and neither does the one that speaks to everyone else.

Turning a Negative into a Positive

At times, it would have been easier to just run away when I experienced challenges. It was important to remind myself that if I allowed someone to get me off-course, I would be handing them my hard earned power and respect. Each day required that I be stronger than the day before, look adversity in the face, and remind myself that 'ignorance has no first language.' I refused to allow these experiences to make a negative person of me. Eventually, my accent became my calling-card to some very unique relationships. My voice can never be mistaken for someone else's. After over 30 years, my accent is still the best part of me; my friends and clients never question who is calling on the phone! Consequently, this also differentiates me as well as my business proposals from others and I do not hesitate to point this out. I remain proud of my differences and teach others about me and my culture whenever I have the chance. This sharing of backgrounds only makes everyone stronger and smarter, along with the relationship itself. The people in my life may never forget who I am because of the accent; it is up to me to give them a favorable impression of the rest of me. Open-mindedness was the key to turning relationships around, language barriers or not.

Being Different is a Positive

One of the greatest gifts I learned to share with the different people in my life is that it is okay to be different. I have always held that being different truly means that each of us has a variety of experiences and knowledge that no other individual has. Whether it's a prominent accent or a family with a rich heritage, being different provides the opportunity to use your unique perspective to drive a new life. When I came to America, I promised myself that I would never hide my talent and abilities. In fact, not hiding my abilities is central to my personal philosophy as I am now also better able to celebrate and nurture the talents of others.

Improving One's Self

Ever since I gave birth to my BIG dreams based on what I had seen on television, I have always tried to remember who I was. No matter how difficult the struggle, I never lost sight of the idea that something better lies ahead. What helped me to focus on the end goal was the belief that we should do more than just work on our businesses, but strive to work on ourselves. International organizations like the Filipina Women's Network, along with my local Asian-American Chamber of Commerce and the National Association of Professional Asian-American Women, have been important resources for me. Not only are they able to offer educational materials for an entrepreneur, but they also provide support, role-modeling, and inspiration from some of the great women that have come before us.

Being Role Models

Another aspect of our business is helping our community by being role models. This belief in being role models has been the driving force behind much of my participation in business, local and national association boards, fundraisers, and projects along the way. Of the many core lessons I have learned from my ancestors and the Filipino culture, is that helping people in all facets of their lives is what creates a strong and diverse community. It is our responsibility to pass these lessons along to the next generations.

I am certain that this is how my parents and grandparents felt when they taught us to embrace "the spirit of being hospitable to guests." It is part of the Filipino culture to be open and ready at all times to share your heart and your home while making people feel welcome. This means everyone, whether they are family, friends, neighbors, out of town guests, or even business associates. It is because of this belief in opening myself to community that I put so much of my own effort into fundraising and volunteer activities. My family is often right by my side since I volunteer their time as well as my own. Because my family respects me and my leadership actions, they happily participate and engage with the community.

Building Community

My husband Merrill and I have hosted many business events in our home. We go beyond the annual holiday party, where each of our employees, their spouses, and even the children, are welcome at a family style feast and celebration. We extend invitations to events to the wider community throughout the year. The intent is to establish partnerships, craft new agreements, and to allow for multi-national endeavors to drive toward new collective goals while paving the way for our youth to learn from others. My family and I call this 'supporting community from a personal perspective.'

Going Beyond

By multi-national endeavors I mean that we must think BIG. After all, it was a big dream that brought me to where I am, and only big, shared, dreams will take us to new heights. My family and I have hosted at our home, for example, the staff of the Philippine Consulate General of New York in order to work on the relationship between Rowan University, a large New Jersey state college, and the University of the Philippines, College of Engineering. By working closely with the University Board of Trustees and academic leaders, we are supporting collaboration between the universities that will improve both. We have also hosted at our home receptions for the Girl Scouts of America to support their mission of "helping build girls of courage, confidence, and character, who make the world a better place."

Accepting Help

We know we cannot do it all alone. Having the perseverance and drive to achieve your goals while staying on course are often only one piece of the recipe. Learning to accept assistance from those around you who are willing to contribute to your success is a critical lesson.

For the contemporary female entrepreneur, businesswoman, and mother, learning to ask for help is not always easy. There is no shame in asking for assistance but no one can help if you remain silent about your needs. Most people actually seek ways to help others because it feels good to make others feel good. Take advantage of opportunities to join forces, and create partnerships.

CO-CREATING: GROWING U.S. LUMBER

Meeting my husband Merrill Abele profoundly changed my life. When we married in 1984, he was operating a lumber business called Silver Lake Lumber. Besides working with my husband to learn the business, I studied accounting and went to computer school at night. In 1985, I launched my own business, the US Lumber and Plywood Corp., a lumber brokerage. I was the sole employee. US Lumber and Plywood grew to $2.7 million in sales by 1992 at the same time Silver Lake Lumber was experiencing a downturn. Upon my suggestion, my husband sold as much of his company as he could and we merged what was left into US Lumber in 1993. I own 51 percent of the company, while my husband owns 49 percent.

U.S. Lumber holds several certifications in Pennsylvania and New Jersey. It is also Forest Stewardship Council (FSC) Certified and is able to supply FSC Certified products and satisfy all of the sustainable forestry origin requirements for projects that require Leadership in Energy and Environmental Design (LEED) Accreditation. We attribute our success to our exemplary customer service. We are proud that our customers include companies such as Boeing, DuPont, Merck, Peco Energy, PSEG, and Philadelphia Gas Works. Our products have been used in many notable projects, including several Atlantic City casinos, the Phillies ballpark, and Morey's Pier. US Lumber's past and present clients include: DuPont Company, Philadelphia Gas Works, Exelon Peco Energy, Merck & Company, Madison & Carson Concrete, Mumford & Miller, Atlantic City's newly opened Borgata Casino and most recently will supply materials for the upcoming Freedom Towers redevelopment project. When Philadelphia Eagles fans walk into the team's two stadiums, US Lumber's plywood is throughout the stadium, and our company was part of the Septa Transit Project built by PKF Mark III. For several years, US Lumber will continue to supply lumber and plywood for the Driscoll Bridge repairs funded by the New Jersey Highway Authority. The Trenton Route 29 Tunnel, the US Postal Service Project, and construction at Temple University constructed by B. Peitrini and Son all include US Lumber materials. The New Jersey School Construction Corporation (NJSCC) contracted with an approved construction company that retained US Lumber as one of the project suppliers. Building trust, according to Business Week (2006), is key to earning customer loyalty, which in turn is essential for building and maintaining a customer base. I am proud to say that U.S. Lumber excels in building trust in our company, our products and services, our marketing, our industry, and our customers. Equally important to the philosophy of U.S. Lumber is to give back to the community.

Many of the opportunities that came to me after fleeing that abusive 'first employer' are because of Merrill. With him came gifts of love and confidence in my abilities, perhaps more confidence than I had in myself at the time. It was his patience and perseverance, alongside my own, that offered opportunities to learn about business, about commerce, production, and about the building supplies industry. Given that the industry is all about creating a foundation for new construction and that the new construction requires an architect; it provides a metaphor for creating a new life. I have often felt as if Merrill was creating a new foundation for my life as I myself was the architect for my world.

I often reflect on how far I have come in nearly 36 years of living in the U.S. My experience has proven, to myself and to the world, that a woman with endless drive and a warm, compassionate heart can succeed in business, raise a family, build community, and have Joan Collins' life style too.

✳

SONIA LUGMAO ARANZA

President/CEO
Aranza Cross-Cultural Strategies
& Global Leadership Development
www.SoniaAranza.com
FWN100™ Global 2015 & U.S. 2007

Transformational Leadership
Begins Within

Transformation requires change. Change is disruptive. Inconvenient. Frightening. Even for the stouthearted. My journey examines lessons learned from disrupting a comfortable life, confronting inconvenient truths, and facing fear in order to transform. The experience is not unique to me. Many summon the courage to push their limits and create lives they prefer. What I humbly share are the lessons learned from my personal journey. I do this in the spirit of service and in the spirit of making a positive difference. My hope is that someone out there, no matter where they are in their personal or professional life, will dare to disrupt their comfortable habits of thinking and take a closer look at the many disguises of fear that have taken root in their lives. Transformation is about disruption and evolution. We share our stories to encourage one another. Reflecting on my journey helps me to be open to new adventures, reminding me that the journey continues. I aspire to always evolve. Like nature, continuous evolution is necessary to achieve higher forms of life. It is exciting to know that evolution can take place in any season of one's life. I believe you are never too old and it is never too late to evolve.

I was born in the Philippines and immigrated to the United States when I was eight years old. Upon our arrival in 1969, it was evident that I needed to master English in order to communicate. In those early years, native English speakers, both children and adults, ridiculed how I spoke. Today, corporate giants and global organizations pay me to speak. I design, develop and deliver innovative keynotes and seminars to top Fortune 500 companies and organizations around the world on the subjects of global leadership, cross-cultural communications, and diversity & inclusion strategies. My sessions utilize multimedia including cutting edge videos, music, and innovative activities to engage audiences. I love what I do! Never in my wildest dream as an immigrant little girl did I imagine I would be doing this.

Although adopting a new language was a component of my early set of challenges, it was simply a beginning. Confronting much larger and more challenging habits of mind are what transformed my life from a simple immigrant girl struggling to master a new language to using the language I eventually mastered as a vehicle to bring ideas alive and share with the world. Today I often ask myself, moments before I step foot on a stage, "how did I get here?"

When I was a little girl, I heard adults use the Filipino term "*Pwede na*" which is generally translated to mean "that will do" or "it's acceptable." It implies that something may not be the best but it can get by. Adult relatives, acquaintances, and people in public places would use the term as though it was an ointment that provides comfort. The term has specific applications for people. Some are driven by guilt, thinking they ought to be more grateful for what they have. Others adopt the term to put things in perspective, reminding themselves that "it could be worse" so they might as well accept things as they are. Often, it is an acceptance of mediocrity, believing that what is at hand is "good enough."

Individuals who are transformers dare to defy the "*Pwede na*" mentality. They refuse to accept the notion of simply getting by. They engage in transformation and transformation requires disruption. The answer to the question, "how did I get here?" involves defying "Pwede na" and it involves the willingness to disrupt things as they are.

What is transformation? Transformation is a process that brings about radical change. In animals, it's a metamorphosis in the life cycle like a caterpillar transforming into a butterfly. In humans, it can mean a complete shift in the trajectory of one's life, a dramatic alteration in appearance or a complete change in character. In organizations, it can mean a profound move in direction. There is plenty of evidence in nature that shows what happens when species do not transform. Without transformation or evolution, they perish or die. In people and in organizations, lack of transformation and evolution is like a slow death as the author Henry David Thoreau suggested in *Walden* (1854) "The mass of men lead lives of quiet desperation." As human beings, we learn to mask our desperation and manage to function in spite of it. We generally do not like change, yet change is required to confront our desperation. So what do we generally do? We avoid it! We are masters at avoiding feelings that require action. We shop, we eat, we work, we exercise, and we turn to whatever our drugs of choice may be in order to escape and avoid what really requires our attention. Conscious or sub-conscious, we find ways to delay the work of transformation. We are good at designing and maintaining attractive fronts, displaying things that people will admire. We practice self-deceit by showing off a great appearance, masking the pain, covering up the truth, and hiding the brokenness. We generally continue to do this until an external force, such as death, divorce, illness, termination of employment, bankruptcy, etc. demands that we change. If we are fortunate, an internal force; awareness, change of heart, etc. confronts us.

If we muster the willingness to transform, how do we begin? How do we continue? Looking back at my personal journey, it was not easy. I began with awareness which came by way of being exposed to ideas I had not known were available to me. The awareness led to a bit of courage which helped me to confront my self-limiting beliefs. I wanted to be fully known to myself. The process was uncomfortable but I persisted. I wanted to understand my fears and how they prevented me from unleashing my potential. Transformation is hard work and no one can do the work for you. Transformational leadership begins within. Leaders fail when they fail to lead themselves. It has been 20 years since I embarked on my transformational journey. Knowing what I know today, I would say to my younger self, "Jump in! Be bold! There is nothing to fear! An amazing life awaits you!"

MY FOUR PILLARS OF TRANSFORMATION

Looking back, there are four leadership competencies that helped me. I consider them as my four pillars of transformation:

1. Increasing Self-Awareness
2. Taking Risks and Innovating
3. Setting Vision and Strategy
4. Developing Adaptability

1. Increasing Self-Awareness

The fist pillar of transformation is increasing self-awareness. Self-awareness involves self-observation in an effort to fully be known to one's self. Observing the good, the bad, and the ugly in ourselves is uncomfortable and disruptive! Part of the human condition is that most people go about their daily lives unaware. Self-awareness does not happen automatically. Often, it does not happen at all. Even if self-awareness happens, it does not guarantee change because change is hard and we avoid it. It is like the story about a dog on a porch who was moaning. The dog was apparently laying on a nail. A visitor asked why the dog did not just get up and move away from the nail. The dog owner said, "it's not hurting enough." Like the dog, most of us just moan and groan where we are. Since it does not hurt enough, we do not move. As stated earlier, we generally do not take action until an external force demands that we change. External forces include death, divorce, illness, termination of employment, bankruptcy, and so on.

For me, self-awareness came when I was exposed to ideas I had not considered before and the possibilities haunted me! It was like a jolt that woke me up and I could not go back to sleep. The year was 1996 and I was Director of Constituent Relations for a Member of the United States Congress. Six years earlier, I was hired in Hawaii where I grew up and moved to Washington, DC for the position. It was quite an adventure. Working on Capitol Hill was intoxicating. It was quite the scene, surrounded by people in power and those who enabled them. The architecture of the experience is designed to be addictive. Even idealistic politicians who arrive vowing to make changes end up intoxicated by the grandeur, making countless compromises, coming back for more. The reaction people had when they learned I worked on Capitol Hill reinforced the idea that it was a special place. Everything about it fed my ego. For an immigrant born in the Philippines and raised on the island of Oahu, being in the nation's capital was exciting. Yet, the excitement did not translate to fulfillment. It reminded me of junk food. It fills you up but it has very little nutrition. I tried to convince myself *"Pwede na"* and that it will do. I even felt guilty, thinking I should learn to be more grateful, imagining countless individuals who would love to take my spot.

I survived the early years on Capitol Hill by tapping into my passion for civil liberties and civil rights of immigrants. As an immigrant myself, the issues were close to my heart. In the midst of immigrant bashing and the introduction of anti-immigrant legislation by conservative forces, I utilized my position to clarify complex legislation for immigrant community organizers. I laid out the details in simple terms such as who the proposed legislation would hurt, who it would benefit, and the long term effect on families. I utilized my position to provide access to Capitol Hill for community organizations that gave voice to immigrant rights. With the help of like-minded staffers, I organized community dialogues on the topic of immigration and inspired community groups to take action. At every opportunity, I utilized my position to influence my boss, other members of congress, and their staff to vote on immigration legislation with compassion and constitutional fortitude no matter what the conservative dissenting opinions presented.

My work on immigration took a foothold. However, as time marched on, it was evident that the toxic environment and artificial nature of relationships were not healthy. I decided to augment my work life with a healthier activity and went to school to earn a second master's degree. During the day, I worked full time on Capitol Hill. At night and on weekends, I went to American University. Indeed, going to school provided fulfillment but it also gave me something unexpected. It exposed me to amazing possibilities I had not considered before! I attended classes with fellow professionals who were committed to striking out on their own. They were excited by the idea of entrepreneurship. I had never thought of working for myself. I never considered the idea of getting paid to do what I love. It was thrilling and frightening all at once! It stirred in me wild imaginings and created a restlessness that I could not stop. Each day I went to work on Capitol Hill, I could not help but think of the world of possibilities waiting for me. Like Plato's allegory about a cave dweller who left the dark and saw the light, I could no longer stay in the cave knowing that a big wide world exists outside. The idea of creating my own luck and doing what I love was stunning! The possibilities danced in my mind, day and night!

Increasing self-awareness moved me to take inventory of my life and answer important questions. Where had I been and where was I now? Do I like what I see? What's working? What's not working? What do I need to let go? Where do I want to be? How do I get there? Increasing self-awareness meant taking an honest inventory and being fully known to myself. Armed with what I found, I challenged the "*Pwede na*" mentality. I decided to strike out on my own. I wanted to create a life that I preferred rather than one that came by chance. Increasing self-awareness opened the drapes in all the rooms of my life and turned on the lights!

2. Taking Risks and Innovating

The second pillar of transformation is taking risks and innovating. Fear is the biggest obstacle to accomplishing this. The great Sufi Master Hafiz wrote "Fear is the cheapest room in the house. I would like to see you living in better conditions." This pillar of transformation requires leaving what is familiar and comfortable which is not easy to do. Part of the human condition is that we are afraid of uncertainty. We want to know how the movie of our life will end! We crave certainty like how we crave air. We want reassurance that everything will be alright. Taking risks and innovating requires letting go and finding comfort in the discomfort.

In my journey, taking risks and innovating began with the willingness to make friends with my fears. It takes practice to do this. It involves cultivating compassion for one's self. I learned to be patient, giving myself time to understand my concerns and to come up with practical solutions. For example, when I was afraid to leave my position on Capitol Hill to become an entrepreneur, I gave myself time to consider different options. I decided to save six months' salary before I gave notice to my boss that I was leaving. The six months' salary would serve as my initial capital. I started my consulting business on the third floor of our house. It needed only a dedicated phone line and a computer. The rest of my saved salary served as cushion to experiment with product design, development, and marketing. Taking risks and innovating were less daunting when I took financial responsibility for the investment that my adventure required.

To further alleviate my fear of taking risks, I sought out entrepreneurs to learn from their experience. I reached out to others and developed relationships that would help me build my consulting business. I soaked up everything they had to offer. I listened to stories about failure, success, and lessons learned. I also invested in my knowledge by attending educational seminars on how to successfully start a business. In other words, I dealt with my fear of taking risks by showing compassion for myself and taking concrete action steps. The more I did this, the braver I became.

One of the tools that was helpful to me is called a SWOT analysis. The idea behind a SWOT analysis is to perform a self-assessment in order to get a realistic picture of yourself and make informed decisions. "S" in the analysis stands for Strengths. In my experience, listing strengths requires asking the ego to take a backseat. The ego wants you to think of yourself as greater than you actually are. The ego can cause blind spots! An honest list of strengths require evidence. This could include results from previous experiences as well as feedback from others. "W" in the analysis stands for Weaknesses. The ego can wreak havoc here too. It can deny the fact that you have gaps you need to fill. It can minimize areas that require your attention. In listing weaknesses, the other extreme can also happen where you exaggerate things. For example, in my initial list of weaknesses, I listed 'lack business experience' and quickly turned that into a self-made obstacle. The fact is, there is nothing about business that you cannot learn from others and from the numerous books available! Yes, experience is a great teacher but you cannot get experience unless you begin. "O" in the analysis stands for Opportunities. This speaks mostly to opportunities that we waste because we are not aware they exist or we ignore them. In listing opportunities, I created a "dream list" of potential clients and the people I thought could connect me with them. I also included opportunities to heighten my visibility and increase my knowledge. "T" in the analysis stands for Threats. The biggest revelation about threats is that most are internal. This includes anger, impatience, and procrastination. While threats may include some external forces such as competition, I found that most threats are the ways we sabotage ourselves.

Taking risks and innovating are like muscles that must be developed. The more you work it, the stronger you become. The same is true with courage. Each time you face fear, the more courageous you become. The inner-self has a memory that says, "I've been here before. I don't have to be afraid."

It is important to acknowledge that 'innovating' is sometimes a lonely experience. As you innovate to create your own luck, others will cast doubt. This is especially true with loved ones. As you formulate ideas about the future, they will try to convince you to stay on more familiar grounds. They appear to want to protect us from failure but in fact they are projecting their own fears. It is during those times when it becomes important to be your own ally. Armed with self-awareness, trust yourself. Innovate and create your own luck! The risks you take are worth the dreams you want! When I left Capitol Hill, I marched forward and did not look back. One day at a time, I kept taking risks and innovating. Twenty years later, I am so glad I did! In fact, I wish I had done it sooner! With hard work, determination and grace from above, the exciting possibilities that I imagined became a reality. Exciting possibilities are waiting for you too! Take the risks and evolve.

3. Setting Vision and Strategy

The third pillar of transformation is setting vision and strategy. This requires knowing your purpose, your reason or your "why" for doing what you want to do. My purpose is to make a positive difference in people's lives through leadership development, to communicate ideas that uplift and inspire, and to do work that I love. This purpose shaped my vision and served as my beacon. It helped me to stay focused. It informed my goals, objectives, and plan of action.

Setting a vision is powerful. For some, the vision develops over time and does not come in one big flash. As things unfold, the vision becomes more clear. Vision not only helps to imagine the possibilities but it serves as a guide in making sure your actions align. My vision, my purpose, became my navigation system. It helped me to stay on track and avoid diversions. For example, when I left Capitol Hill, several individuals tried to convince me to sell their products "to have income on the side" or to join their company and help accomplish their goals. Having a purpose and setting a vision helped me to avoid these diversions and stay on course. When people ask me how I have successfully stayed in business for 20 years and continue to aim for more, the truthful answer is that I do not give in to diversions! No matter how tempting the diversions may be, I stay true to my vision and purpose. It is like driving with a GPS to a specific destination. You can take rest stops, maybe explore nearby areas, but the destination is clear.

What happens when there are unexpected detours beyond our control? Similar to driving, if you follow the detour signs, you eventually get back on the road that leads you to your destination. Detours are different from diversions because with detours, the intention is to still reach your destination with a few adjustments. Diversions set the stage for you to neglect your vision, causing you to abandon your destination. Like most businesses, I made adjustments as circumstances changed but I stayed true to the vision. One example comes from the early years in my business. I started my business in January 1997 and my son was born in November 1998. I was on a roll building my consulting practice and I was also excited to be with my young child. I wanted to do both! What I learned in those early years is the powerful lesson of embracing detours joyfully, without fear. I did not want to miss the privilege of raising my young son. I wanted to be around for his first word. I was feeding him soft rice with Filipino *sinigang* [soup] and I kept repeating the word sinigang. After a pause in eating, he said "gang" with a short "a" sound as in sinigang! He saw my thrilled reaction and that prompted him to keep repeating "gang" over and over to my delight! I wanted to be around for his first step. I remember my son and I were in the family room as he was attempting to go beyond standing up by himself. When he took his first step, I screamed with delight and ran for the video camera. He kept on walking without stopping! I kept on crying with joy! Twenty minutes into the video, you can see us both filled with glee! These were priceless moments that I experienced because I was willing to embrace the detour without losing sight of the destination. The detour I took was to keep my business 'local' rather than global which had been my original intention. In those early years, I did my best to keep work close by in the Washington, DC area. As my son grew up and attended school full-time, I made adjustments to my business, accepting engagements outside the area. I learned to be selective, choosing business opportunities that contributed to my growth rather than squandering my energy. I made sure I had enough quality time with my family. Also important in the early years, I found trustworthy child care providers to support me as travel and business increased. The detour proved to be rewarding. Setting a vision and keeping it at the top of my mind gave me the confidence to know that I was still on track. The timeline was adjusted but the destination remained the same. Today, my son has a robust schedule of his own and I travel worldwide. I have the privilege of conducting leadership development sessions for top Fortune 500 companies from China to Costa Rica. As I travel the world, I use technology to stay in touch with loved ones. Detours happen. Setting a vision and having a clear purpose will keep you on track to reach your destination.

Developing long-term objectives and regularly updating plans to reflect changing circumstances are also important parts of setting vision and strategies. In the tenth year of my business, things seemed great. I had established my brand, regularly received referrals and reaped financial rewards. Suddenly, circumstances changed. The economy took a downturn. For me, it hit around 2008. Contracts were getting fewer, shorter, and paying less money. I updated my plans but stayed true to my long term objective. I saw it as another detour and remained confident. Instead of riding the economic tidal wave alone, I decided to build alliances and to collaborate with others. I partnered with fellow consultants to go after contracts. I teamed up with firms who had multi-year engagements. I reminded myself that I still got to do what I loved and I still made a positive difference. I accepted how the changing circumstances affected the financial rewards and I learned to be grateful for the resilience it developed in me. Like all detours, this one was temporary. The economy eventually shifted and companies were ready to spend again. Soon enough, I was going after my own contracts once more. Overall, the detour enriched my business and my life. I enjoyed the relationships that helped me to grow. I still collaborate on many contracts today. I still partner with firms who are innovative and raise my game. I carefully choose individuals and organizations who share my values and who want to make a positive difference in the world.

Strategy is also an important element of transformation that requires attention. One of the strategies that made a big difference in developing my business is how I chose to market myself. Since the best way to experience my work is to hear me speak, I decided to compete for coveted speaking spots at large conferences. This exposed me directly to big buyers. The price point I set for my products (leadership development training, executive workshops, keynotes) commensurate with the quality of my work and the return on investment for the client. The price of my products had to match with the pocketbooks of the buyers I identified. Early on, I stayed away from people who wanted my work for "free" or in exchange for something of little value. Normally, one would not walk into an art gallery, point to a work of art and say to the owner "Hey, I want that one for free!" So why would I accept that in my business? I demonstrated respect for myself and for my work by staying away from people who did not want to pay. Also important, I limited my time with people who undervalued my worth or did not have an appreciation for the time and imagination it takes to develop my presentations. In other words, I treated my business like a business!

Once my business was profitable, it gave me the freedom to give back to the community and to causes that I support. Each year, I accept a number of *pro bono* engagements from organizations that serve underprivileged groups, those fighting for justice, and for immigrant communities. Success helps me to be of greater service to others.

Another strategy I employed was branding. Early on, I was intentional about branding myself as distinct. Relatively speaking, there are very few people with similar background in my business. I utilized my distinct background: born in the Philippines, immigrant experience, raised in multicultural Hawaii, academic degrees in cross-cultural communications, travel to Russia as a student, work in the United States Congress on complex legislation including immigration, cross-cultural perspective, etc. to differentiate myself. This is key. In business, you must set yourself apart from the competition so buyers know you are unique and worth the difference in price.

Over time, I learned that setting vision and strategy is about being true to who you are. It is about focus and shutting off the noise around you. There are lots of people eager to tell you what to do and how to do it! Remember, it is your vision, not theirs. Be clear on the direction you want to go. Be willing to do the work even when it is hard. Do not be afraid of detours. Be open to different ways of moving forward. Believe in yourself. In the end, "To thine own self be true."

4. Developing Adaptability

The fourth pillar of transformation is developing adaptability. This involves the ability to adapt to changing circumstances as previously discussed, openness to the influence of others, and interpersonal savvy. What is interpersonal savvy? I would describe this quality as instinctive, but it is possible to learn over time with constant practice. Interpersonal savvy is about your ability to engage effectively with others. It requires humility. It is about taking yourself out of the spotlight and paying attention to others. It is about being aware of how you impact others and making necessary adjustments as needed. This can be perplexing because it requires enough presence of mind to not get "triggered" by others while being able to sense their needs and adapt to it. Take negotiations, for example. What to give, what to take, what to let go, are all very fluid. What part of it is your fear of rejection and what part of it is your gut telling you this one is not worth it? In the heat of the moment, they are hard to distinguish! This is true no matter how long you have been in business. Be aware that interpersonal savvy and your inner voice can be convoluted with your own neuroses! Developing interpersonal savvy in the context of "developing adaptability" takes time and experience. In negotiations, it is hard to know when the other person is bluffing. Should you ask for a higher fee from someone who claims they have a small budget or do you accept the lower fee? Only time and experience can teach what questions to ask in order to find the truth about what they really have. And yet, time and experience guarantee nothing! You can still get it wrong! In such situations, just make sure the lesson is not wasted. Interpersonal savvy includes learning from the experience. As the saying goes, "the lesson keeps repeating itself until the lesson is learned."

Developing adaptability involves being a student of other people's needs, motivations, and agendas. Human beings are complicated! Developing adaptability involves learning the art of communication, understanding how your way of engaging and interacting impact others. Whether you are aware of it or not, you are an "experience." How you speak, how you listen, how you act. You are an experience! Your ability to tailor your communication based on others does not mean you are abandoning your true self. It simply means that you are adapting based on the circumstances. For example, in certain cultures, it is expected that I speak in the position of authority when I deliver my presentations since I am the speaker. In other cultures, I am expected to yield and just be a facilitator. In another example, there are business environments where I set the tone and can expect others to follow. However, other business environments expect me to co-create the path in a collaborative effort with others. Developing adaptability means strengthening your ability to flex. How do you reach your goals without harming relationships with others? How do you adjust your communication and leadership style to the demands of ever-changing situations? How do you accept feedback, even criticism, and incorporate it into the adjustments that need to be made? How do you make sure power does not go to your head and you remain open to the unique perspectives of others even if it means things will take longer? When is it time to let go of the "tried and true" in order to innovate? The answers to these questions lie at the heart of developing adaptability: Learn how to relate to others while learning how to relate to yourself.

EPILOGUE

Transformation is not easy but it is necessary. Transformation is about evolution. Like nature, we must evolve to fully live. We are born and we die. In between, we have this adventure called life. One would think that the impermanence of life would motivate us to live with gusto and seek to continuously evolve. The sad truth is that many of us do not evolve. Even the ambitious among us settle. Certainly there are things beyond our control that we must accept but that is not what I am talking about. The challenge I raise is about confronting the many disguises of fear that show up in our lives such as the *"Pwede na"* mentality. Whether we admit it or not, we say "*Pwede na*" or "that will do" to many aspects of our lives including our careers and intimate relationships. To confront this, we must be willing to transform. Transformation requires change. Change can be scary. Change is also disruptive and inconvenient. The good news is that we have tools to help us! The four pillars of transformation I shared with you are Increasing Self-Awareness, Taking Risks and Innovating, Setting Vision and Strategy, and Developing Adaptability. There are many more leadership competencies, thoughts, and ideas available to help guide our transformation. All we need is the willingness to begin.

Looking back at my journey, it would have been easier to stay where I was rather than to step into a future of uncertainty. There was no guarantee that the disruption would all work out. As an immigrant Filipina to the United States, there was much to be grateful for. Even if I decided not to continue to work on Capitol Hill, I could have applied for another job that had more "security" instead of becoming an entrepreneur. To top it off, the entrepreneurial work I chose is not easy. Creating my own luck and doing work that I love were thrilling ideas but they were also frightening. Years later, with 20-20 hindsight it is clear to me. The famed physicist Madame Marie Curie was right when she stated: "Nothing in life is to be feared. It is only to be understood." I learned that the fear of transformation is self-imposed! I would not live the life I have today if I had stayed where I was. I am immensely fortunate to get paid to do what I love! Not everyone gets to do that. The immigrant little girl from the Philippines who was ridiculed for how she spoke now speaks for a living worldwide. I have the honor of making a positive difference in people's lives. I have the privilege of helping to develop leaders in Top Fortune 500 companies and organizations. I experience joy and fulfillment in witnessing others transform. "*Pwede na*" would have prevented all of this.

When my father recently died, it was both a heavy and light experience. Heavy, because death is so final and irreversible. Light, because I was reminded that no one is exempt from death and that life is for living! My hope is that we fully live our lives before it cease to exist. "*Pwede na*" will not do. I hope the reflections I shared from my journey will inspire someone in a small way. No matter where you are in your personal or professional life, my hope is that you dare to disrupt comfortable habits of thinking and take a dive into discovering who you really are, what you really love, what matters most, and what you want to do with this impermanent life. You are never too old and it is never too late to evolve. Be open to new adventures and new beginnings. Dare to disrupt!

❈

JUDY ARTECHE-CARR

with

JOSEPHINE ROMERO*

CEO, Arteche Global Group
FWN100™ Global 2014

LEADING BY EXAMPLE

My life story is a like a maze fraught with twists and turns, seemingly endless, yet replete with interesting and surprising events as though an end unto themselves. I see my public persona as a thought process leader who influences information technology (IT) in global business, relationships, and academe. My colleagues in the information technology industry appreciate me as a self-described evangelist who makes things happen in the best possible way, and who encourages people to work together in unusual situations. While my associates on Wall Street experienced me as a maverick with unexpected analyses and solutions, co-workers in multimedia entertainment and advertising decades ago knew me to be serious and exacting. My oldest friends saw me as gregarious and irrepressible.

How does one delineate the essence of a multifaceted person as I seem to be? Friends have teased me to ask if somehow I bring to mind that incorrigible "nun-to-be." Surmounting challenges while facing fearful odds has always been the story of my personal and professional journey in life. I had to reinvent myself from a shy Catholic young girl from Tacloban City to a global leader in New York City. I hope that my story of leadership and diversity is an inspiring one that many younger Filipinas may want to emulate.

---

* Author's Note. I asked my friend Josephine Romero to help write my leadership story based in part on interviews conducted by Karen Morris.

Youthful Path to Leadership

Always having excelled in school, I found myself branded a leader because I consistently did very well academically. It was assumed that I would lead; from conducting the national anthem at the school assembly in the morning, to being head of the class and all the extracurricular activities I joined, to performing as a member of the Leyte Filipiniana Dance Troupe, dancing Itik -Itik, and playing the rondalla, a Filipino string instrument. I was a female renaissance person in far-flung Leyte Province, accomplishing all of this where the assumption was that I was nurtured by the entire village. Additionally, I was a pixie-looking graceful girl with feminine features and a soft voice. And to top it all, I came from a family of six siblings brought up by a single parent who had been widowed at a time when women were dependent on their husbands for economic support and whose main source of livelihood had nothing to do with her training.

So from the very beginning, the pressure from everywhere; school, family, peers, the town, the province, pushed me towards success with no if and or buts. There was no choice but to succeed, to be the best in whatever I did.

"What I want to be when I grow up ..."

Apart from my strong Catholic heritage, I realized in later years that this desire for success was unconsciously inspired by the attraction to the power and mystery of the religious orders, and most especially to the iconic status of nuns. Nuns were, to my mind, professional women who had a special standing. At an early age, I was introduced unconsciously to my second perspective of women in leadership.

I claim my initial and ultimate inspiration was my mother. After my father's tragic early death at the age of 42, I witnessed my mother's transformation into the strong, brave, and loving person she was and continues to be to this day.

My mother evolved and adapted from being a housewife to the sole bread-winner for six children aged 2 to 13 years old. While she earned a Baccalaureate degree as a Pharmacist, consistent with the time, she had chosen not to work when she got married. Courageous, resilient, and proud, she did not take any handouts. She opted to sell insurance and became a top producer in her geographic area. Eventually, she became the branch manager of Philamlife Insurance Company in Tacloban.

Life Lesson #1: There is a real life lesson here about the importance of education and associated options for women and girls, whatever life choices they make. But the real, real life lesson that I will carry in my heart forever is that my mother is the superwoman from whom all inspiration emanates; and what this was what I wanted to be when I grew up.

EARLY LIFE TRAUMA

My father was campaigning for his brother Elmo who was running for Mayor of Tacloban City, Leyte when he suffered heart pains. He was brought to Bethany Hospital overnight for observation where he died of a heart attack. This changed my family's life.

My mother, Luz, tried to overcompensate for the family's loss, and my siblings and I knew we had to do our part by studying very hard to help by getting scholarships that would free us from school fees and tuition. I was the eldest at 13 years of age, and a freshman high school student when my father died. He did not plan for the future and this is what motivated my mother to believe in life insurance, which she knew she could have used. We had to move from a big house to a smaller one, although within walking distance of the school. The big missing piece was the loss of my father who doted and spoiled us. We no longer had a car or luxuries, but enjoyed abundant love from relatives and friends.

Life Lesson #2: It is the way you live your life that counts. Don't take anything for granted. Family is important and being secure in the love that surrounds you makes one well-grounded.

EXPLORING THE WORLD

In my senior year, my family hosted a Rotary Exchange student from upstate New York, Nancy Nonnengard-Bouchard, for the summer. I learnt a lot from the experience, and had a lot of fun too! I found that introducing her to the Filipino culture made me appreciate it and found the exchange of ideas from another perspective helped in my maturity of thinking. It definitely fostered the urge for travel.

When I graduated with honors from high school, I was nominated to be a Rotary Exchange Student to Melbourne, Australia. I did not realize at the time that my mother had to sell shares of stock that she had been keeping as a nest egg to fund my travel expenses.

The Rotary exchange trip was only the second time in my life that I had to travel by myself. I was so happy that one of my friends and cousin, Tess Astilla-Mendoza, was also on the trip, although we had different destinations in Australia. I was assigned to Glenroy, a suburb of Melbourne, and Tess to Euroa, Victoria where she stayed in a 150-acre Australian country outback estate.

Australia was a different world.

School was interesting, as it always had been for me, and more so in this new environment. We had uniforms even though it was a public school. While the accent was a little challenging in the beginning, in the end I did fine. I learned to listen well to understand the Aussie accent and slang by constantly turning to radio or "wireless" as they called it. I was asked to speak at various events. One of the questions I was often asked "Do Filipinos live in trees?"

Since I was the first exchange student of the Rotary club in Glenroy, everybody wanted to host me. I had 11 "foster" families in 12 months. So I learned to adjust to the foreign culture, the different family nuances, the various accents, and to many kinds of people. I was not only up to the challenge; I reveled in it!

All of the families were different in size, wealth, and personalities. The one thing stood out; they were all excited to host me, treated me like family, took me on trips to Tasmania, Canberra the capital, and more. One of my host families had a wine cellar, he brought out one of his prized wines for dinner and asked me if I liked it "Isn't it mellow and smooth?" Not knowing anything about wine that time, I said "it is wonderful." It was in Australia where I learned how to play tennis, one host family had their own private clay tennis court; and swim, where I had kids as my classmates in swim lessons. I was invited to the Philippine Embassy for a formal lunch by myself. It was a bit intimidating; being seated at a long table far away and with cutlery I did not know how to use. I just followed what the Ambassador and his wife used for each course so this was educational for me.

Life Lesson # 3: From my year in Australia as a foreign exchange student, I advise you to absorb all of the culture when traveling anywhere. A person can learn a lot about one's self that will definitely help one to rise up to life's challenges going forward.

NAVIGATING THROUGH DIFFERENT ENVIRONMENTS

Through the years, I have often spoken on leadership and coached executive leaders. Much of what I have shared on these occasions was inspired by my early experiences that formed my perspective on leadership.

My father, while gone too soon, was a dominant figure in my life before he died. He insisted that his daughters and sons should be strong and flexible. He wanted us to be competitive; so we had to run races and of course, all of us wanted to win! He wanted us to study hard and built a big library-sized table for us to study at. He wanted us to be well rounded and social and we had sit-down formal dinners with friends and relatives at home. If we misbehaved, the "look" enough disciplined us.

I remember being dispatched to distant relatives far away for a long holiday when I was about seven years of age when we were living in Manila (we moved to Tacloban the next year). Afraid and lonely, I was terrified. That was perhaps when I made what I deemed my first "leader-like" strategic choice: to either stay miserable or find the inner resources to adapt.

I literally learned how to adapt through that experience and since then my professional trajectory has been one of adapting to new environments, different cultures, and industries. I still remember returning home by myself on the plane. It imbued me with a desire to be on the move, to discover diverse environments. Since early adulthood, I have traveled widely, professionally, and personally. I get excited about diversity in people, outlook, and cultures. Opportunity resides very often in the new and different.

Life Lesson #4: In short, my next life lesson is to be adaptable and flexible; the choice is to stay miserable or find the inner resources to adapt and have fun.

CAREER EVOLUTION

My career has been marked by bold decisions that changed as the times changed. Early on, as a young, diminutive Asian woman my career evolved from the Children's Television Workshop (Sesame Street), to the testosterone turbo charged world of U.S. investment banking. My first stop was at the famous, or in-famous, Salomon Brothers which is now part of Citigroup. My second stop was at JP Morgan, now JP Morgan Chase. Tough playing fields in which I played quite well.

For someone like me who loves challenges and who had just finished my Masters in Business in Finance at New York University, I wanted to experience what it was like to work in this kind of environment. Interviews were tough and extensive. I remember as many as 10 interviews in one day. I was offered a job within a week. It was a great experience providing both substantive learning and another exercise in adaptability in an unabashedly male run world.

After stints at technology companies, Electronic Data Systems (EDS) now HP and Unisys, I did the boldest move of all by setting up my own management con-sulting company. My husband, Michael Dean Carr, encouraged and supported my decision and I thank him. The combination of marketing and advertising; risk, finance and technology management; and my reputation in the business world as someone who "gets things done" gave me an edge. I celebrate my 10th anniversary this year!

I remember in college being one of the lucky students to get a four-year scholarship with the All Nations Women's Group which gave me the opportunity to study at the University of Santo Tomas (UST), the oldest Catholic university in Asia, older even than Harvard University and also my mother's alma mater. At UST, I was a student leader but that all went away when Martial Law was declared in the early 1970s and most of the clubs, student groups, and any gatherings of three or more persons were disallowed. I remember being a bit upset as I had just been inducted to a scholarly sorority and underwent their horrible initiation; and then nothing because of Martial Law.

I studied very hard to keep my grades up to maintain my scholarship. I earned my Bachelor of Arts in Communications on time. I enjoyed a rich social life but had no boyfriends. Years later my male classmates shared with me that I had intimidated them!

After college, I felt lucky to get a job at a prestigious market research firm, Consumer Pulse, a firm that was sought after at the time by premier Philippine companies. My experience at Consumer Pulse taught me to make sure that whatever I say or claim to be able to do can be substantiated by facts. I learned early that deadlines had to be met since the research we did was the cornerstone of their clients' corporate strategy.

I had gone to work with a marketing and design company that was much sought after for its corporate identity programs. I learned about handling myself as a young account executive. A particular experience I still remember was a call to a cigarette manufacturer, where I made my presentation to a very prominent CEO whose team members spoke only Chinese. I was young and fearless and boldly expressed my opinions. My group won the account and I went so far as to ask when the client would send payment! At this, the CEO got up, opened his safe, took out a new ladies watch, and handed it to me. I was surprised at this unexpected gift and politely thanked the CEO. A Canadian executive who had attended the meeting asked me in private whether I thought I should return it. The Philippines is a mix of cultures, one being Chinese, and since I did not know if it would be an insult in Chinese culture to return the gift I decided to keep it. I went home thinking that I must have done something good or remarkable to get the reward. Although I never met the CEO again, I think to this day that probably saying the right things with some boldness was what impressed the executive.

The most memorable Philippine job experience was in Account Management at Minds Marketing Specialists, then a subsidiary of John Clements. It was an advertising startup headed up by women, except for the Art Director. I was in my early 20s and I took my role and responsibility as an Account Manager seriously-heading the division eventually after bringing in prestigious clients and managing key accounts. It was here that I learned a lot to manage relationships, listening to clients, basing creative ideas on well-founded research, and partnering with creative and production teams. It was such an exciting time, even with the account team fighting with the creative team, we won Philippine Clio awards. What did I learn most? Managing people and influencing outcomes can change one's perspective in life. My reputation as having integrity and a no nonsense attitude held me in good stead.

Life Lesson #5: One must never be afraid to speak up!

EXPERIENCING GENDER BIAS

My professional life may sound rosy but it was not always so. I experienced the gender bias that is usually experienced by many women executives, especially on Wall Street.

After a lunch meeting, all of the men were offered cigars and I felt left out so I spoke out, "what about me?" My comment elicited laughter from the group.

In any case, even though I experienced explicit gender bias, I was determined it was not going to stop my progress. I recognized that as a woman executive, and an ethnic minority, I had to contend with the phenomenon that the "only" woman at the table will become "one of the boys." This meant that I sat in meetings during which men expressed unadulterated gender biased comments or made excruciatingly dreadful jokes about other women. My dilemma was what to do or say about it. Interestingly enough, when my male colleagues and management got to know me, there were times when the men would swear, look at me, and then apologize! I had earned their respect.

As I climbed the executive ladder, I was able to make the business case for diversity and inclusion even before those words had entered the vocabulary. By heading up the Asian American Diversity Group at the investment bank, I had conversations with the CEO and Managing Directors. It was a start but, ingrained behaviors were hard to change. My contribution was recognized and I won an award!

THOUGHT LEADERSHIP

Some had wondered if my experiences with the world of finance was what pushed me into technology, but that was not the case at all. I made the change because I wanted to be in a fast moving innovative environment. I saw the combination of globalization and technology as the future. Someone said I was prescient about those macro trends but nothing surprised me even as the doomsayers were spreading rumors that a global information technology bust was at hand due in part to computer programs not being able to deal with the Year 2000 (Y2K) Millenium bug.

One thing I had not expected, however, was that technology firms in India that worked on Y2K projects were able to leverage these projects to become big global firms. The good thing is that competition was and is healthy for the industry. And eventually other countries followed the outsourcing trend, including the Philippines.

One of my predictions was featured in an interview with The Economist around 2008 where I suggested that the United States would become one of the top 10 sourcing countries in the world. This prediction was a stark contrast to popular pundits at the time, but I was proven right!

It has been less than 10 years since I said that the U.S. would eventually be one of the destinations for global outsourcing. This has happened much quicker than even I expected with companies bringing back outsourcing to the U.S. via insourcing within their own companies and/or looking at alternative sourcing solutions offered in depressed cities in the U.S. given advantages by local governments.

My story shows a pattern of innovation, informed risk taking, experimentation, adaptability to change, trend identification, executive action, and an optimistic lens on change. This is probably because I have always been an optimist about the use of technology in business and how it can transform people's lives for the better. During an interview with Karen Morris, a Founding Board Member of The Global Sourcing Council, I paraphrased Darwin by saying it is not the strongest of the species that survive nor the most intelligent, it is the ones most adaptable to change.

I went on to say: "One of the reasons why I moved to a tech firm was I saw an opportunity inherent in the differing pace of evolution and adoption within their client companies. Those least adaptable to change would need to turn to the tech provider firms who could offer a competitive advantage in terms of costs and productivity."

"Moreover, while tech continues to evolve at a rapid exponential rate driven by the consumer market and start-up companies, sourcing strategies will continue to demand constant innovation," I also added during that interview.

INNOVATION LEADERSHIP AT WORK

When asked about the information age world of endless data, a concept that baffles the minds of most C-level executives today, my analysis was that the world already has too much data but that we need to harness it. Even in our personal lives, we need to filter what is important and be more disciplined with deleting data not needed. It's like getting rid of clutter in your home.

With all these accomplishments through the years, I am honored to be recognized by many organizations worldwide through accolades and invitations to various boards.

In 2009, I was acknowledged and recognized as one of the Filipina Women's Network's 100 Most Influential Filipinas in the U.S., and in 2014, I was honored as a Global FWN100 Awardee. Some other awards include: 50 Most Outstanding Asian Americans in Business (2011) given by the Asian American Business Development Center in New York headed by John Wang <outstanding 50award.com> and the SIM Leadership Award (2014) at SIMposium in Denver, Colorado.

I am an advocate for women to be recognized for their talent and work. I especially believe in mentoring young women, and lately, much to my surprise, young men too. I sit on and actively contribute to many advisory boards and am a member of the Society of Information Management (SIM) Women, Womensphere, Global Sourcing Council's Women's Empowerment Committee, and the Women's Bond Club.

I am known for innovation leadership in many circles. I define innovation as consciously examining and changing the way you think and act, modifying behaviors to deal with the way the world is changing. It's a question of mindset as much as anything else. The problem that most suppresses innovation within our information technology industry is simply fear of change or nervousness based on snippets of information.

How innovation is manifested in global sourcing is one of the leadership issues that come up when I help shape a company's strategy. Understanding leadership for global sourcing can contribute to a business model for innovation. For others it is already part of how they do business and the question is how to make it better. However, some of the big firms and advisors need to move confidently forward with innovative practices. It is not easy given political debate and things like security breaches in the news but courageous solutions are needed. It is a complex digital world today with fast moving external changes and behavioral attitudes that make it difficult to make strategic decisions. However, it is doable as long as one can stay focused, think out of the box, and lead with confidence.

THE UNEXPECTED COME BACK: NEW YORK TO TACLOBAN

Volunteering on nonprofit boards and advisory boards of companies has led me on several paths including invitations to speak at global conferences and at the United Nations in New York, to teach and consult with universities, to be interviewed by the press, to judge global innovative competitions, to meet with CEOs of global companies and Presidents of countries; and most importantly, to expand my network of friends and mentors!

Being on the Board and Management Council of the Society for Information Management (SIM) <simnet.org> has reinforced my leadership skills in implementing programs with Chief Information Officers (CIO) and senior leader volunteers. They often have little time so the key is influence management and fast decision making. This garnered for me a significant amount of recognition in the industry that in turn paved the way for opportunities to learn and grow. Currently, as Board Chair of SIM NY Metro, I head up the Community Outreach program where we partner with the NPower Community Corps, a group that coordinates tech volunteers for social good. In the spring of 2016, I was one of the judges of Technovation- a Science, Technology, Engineering and Math (STEM) competition that encourages 12-19 year old girls in middle school and high school globally to develop apps for the social good and then develop a business plan to start their entrepreneurship. The teams were very impressive! I also led a SIM team to teach high school seniors soft skills at the Queens Vocational and Technical High School in New York City.

One of my most memorable experiences is meeting Dr. Osvald Bjelland, the dynamic Founder and Co-Chair of The Performance Theater <theperformancetheater.com>. The Performance Theater (TPT) brings together a select group of CEOs and world class thinkers, including young innovators to debate, with no holds barred, topics such as climate change. Dr. Bjelland has invited me and my husband Michael to several of the meetings from 2005 to 2013 in unique settings including: Oslo, Wolfsberg Switzerland, St Petersburg, New Delhi, Washington DC, Venice, and Istanbul. These meetings changed my way of thinking about the environment and innovation. Meeting the CEOs in these private settings where you can talk to them like ordinary people was mind-boggling and intellectually stimulating. Apart from serious discussions, it was a lot of fun and enriching taking in the culture of the countries and being introduced to their art and artists.

While attending one of the functions at the Outsourcing Institute, I met Josephine Romero then the head of the Philippine Trade and Investment Center in New York (Department of Trade) who convinced me to give back to the Philippines by helping form the Philippine Business Process Outsourcing (BPO) Advisory Council in 2007. To this day, I lead the Philippine BPO Advisory Council and the Advisory Board members have become friends of the Philippines. For example, Frank Sirianni, VP and CIO of Fordham University spearheaded the formal agreement between Ateneo de Manila and Fordham on internships and more. Another example is Frank Wadsworth, Head of Supplier Risk Management at Bloomberg LP who hosted the Philippine-based Business and Investment Team in February 2016 and Neil Brandmaier, VP and CIO of Capital District Physicians Health Plan (CDPHP) who has been an advocate and supporter of the Philippines. It has been a roller coaster ride since and I have been back to the Philippines almost every year. I organized an executive team of speakers for e-Services Philippines And in New York, I met President Gloria Macapagal Arroyo, President Benigno Aquino III, and other prominent Cabinet members. I acknowledge the partnerships with the Philippine Consul Generals in New York—Cecille Rebong and Mario de Leon who have paved the way in continuing this mission of making U.S. business aware of Philippine sourcing opportunities.

With a group of alumni, we started the HIC Alumni International in New York <hicalumniinternational.org> to award scholarships to needy and intelligent kids to continue their education at my high school alma mater, Holy Infant College in Tacloban City, Leyte. We have had about 17 scholars graduate since the program started. It was useful that we had in place a way to send funds to the school when it was devastated by Typhoon Haiyan in 2013. Through Fordham University, I introduced Sr. Carmela Cabactulan, the Head of the Sisters of Mercy Group to Catholic Charities in New York and Germany and they helped fund and rebuild the school. Now, as President of the HIC Alumni International, we continue to fundraise for a Women's Center and the scholarship program. In 2015, I also was able to get Broadway star Miguel Braganza to bring his Street of Dreams program from New York to Tacloban and thus to inspire 500 young kids to dance as part of the healing process from the typhoon trauma. At the end of the day, getting to know one's hometown again can expand one's world unexpectedly.

And finally, my introduction to the Filipina Women's Network <fwn.org> has given me the chance to meet many leaders of Philippine descent; I am so proud to be a Filipina! It was an honor to be nominated by Josephine Romero and awarded as one of the influential Filipinas. I have been an active member of the Nominating Committee, and have mentored young women, hosted events in New York and at the 2014 Manila Summit- participated as the moderator of the well-attended Millionaires panel consisting of Loida Nicolas Lewis and Angelica Berrie. I remember a young woman who was so moved that she started crying and thanking them for their inspiration.

So full circle from Tacloban to New York and back; it has been a great journey!

And it's impossible to name all I must thank for making me who I am today.

Life Lesson #6: Going back to your roots and making things happen is both humbling and satisfying. Volunteer for something you are passionate about! It is a good feeling and so rewarding to instill change, especially with the youth of today.

Final Word

My story through the years has included many twists and turns but consistently has depicted leadership anchored on adaptability and an inner strength inspired by early influences. I learned by the example of my late father and my beloved mother, someone whom I now care for in her sunset years. From their example, I have learned to live my life as a leader who leads by example. It is my hope that younger women and men can learn and be inspired.

I strive to continuously be involved in not-for-profit activities and act as a global ambassador of change.

My Life Lessons in Summary

Life Lesson #1: It is important to emphasize the value of education and related options for women and girls, whatever life choices they make. But the real, real life lesson that I carry in my heart is that my mother is the superwoman from whom all my inspiration emanates and that she is who I have always wanted to be when I grow up.

Life Lesson #2: It is the way you live your life that counts. Do not take anything for granted. Family is important and being secure in the love that surrounds you makes one well-grounded.

Life Lesson #3: Absorb all of the culture when traveling anywhere. A person can learn a lot about one's self that will definitely help to meet life's challenges going forward.

Life Lesson #4: Be adaptable and flexible; the choice is either to stay miserable or find the inner resources to adapt and have fun.

Life Lesson #5: One must never be afraid to speak up!

Life Lesson #6: Going back to your roots and making things happen is both humbling and satisfying. Volunteer for something you are passionate about! It is a good feeling and very rewarding to facilitate change, especially with the youth of today.

❊

ELIZABETH BAUTISTA

Operations Technology Group Leader
Lawrence Berkeley National Lab
National Energy Research Scientific Computing Center
FWN100™ Global 2015

Synergistic Change

Summer is my favorite time of the year. Not only is it warm beach weather, as much beach weather as we can have in the California Bay Area, but also because the students arrive at the National Energy Research Scientific Computing Center (NERSC). What we do is pretty impressive. We are the primary scientific computational facility for the Office of Science in the U.S. Department of Energy. We serve more than 6000 scientists across 800 projects and help accelerate scientific discovery. I help run the facility. Yes, that is pretty awesome. My team and I ensure that the facility is available for our users 24x7. We also serve as the Network Operations Center for the Energy Sciences Network (ESnet), the high performance global network that connects the 40 DOE research facilities, 140 collaboration sites including many universities and their instrument facilities like the Large Hadron Collider in CERN, Switzerland. Imagine what it is like to work here, or even to be an intern?

But, I digress. Let us get back to my point about the students. When the students arrive each summer, NERSC has much more hustle and bustle, a natural result of having young people around. There are the whispers of quiet discussion, or spontaneous laughter, or clicking away at their keyboards. This year's project is going to be interesting. My team and I have been preparing to move into the new building and we wanted a fresh start. We did not want the old bad habits to come into the new environment. There are going to be many opportunities to study the new systems, a new batch scheduler, energy efficiencies in the building, and Cori; the next supercomputer that will be arriving by the end of the year. A challenge we have wanted to overcome is automating many of our manual processes; out with the old way, prepare for the new. As Socrates said, "the secret of change is to focus all your energy, not on fighting the old, but on building the new."

ARSENAL OF EXPERIENCES

One of the team members had a great idea. We would use a module that would automate a small series of tasks, an "event handler." This would be software that can determine a series of actions based on certain parameters to react to an alert. For example, when we receive a message indicating a problem, the handler would open a tracking ticket, assign it to a person or a vendor, and dispatch an engineer the next business day, depending on the service level agreement. There are many events like this so we needed to create many "event handlers" that would function as small program modules that can eventually be duplicated by changing one to two lines of code. However, assigning the correct handler to the event would require hundreds of hours and with only one person doing this, it would take months. With summer approaching, I felt that we could assign students for this task, or perhaps even a team of students. As my team and I discussed the necessary skillsets, where to recruit, how many students would be needed, a light bulb goes off in my head and I decided this would be an all-female coding team. At this point, we had a ball and it was gaining speed down a very steep hill.

Much too quickly, summer was here and we had three female students from diverse backgrounds and diverse schools. We needed to bring them up to speed on programming in python. We started with a two-week python boot camp and invited other staff to join us since we had other projects within the division that required knowing how to code in python. When the students were done, I gave this set of instructions: "Ladies, I think you should come up with three modules per person per week. At the end of the next ten weeks, you should have a total of 90 modules. A team member will be working with you who will be responsible for testing, debugging as necessary, and then implementing the module." The students were shocked!! "That's too many, we won't be able to do it in time." I tempered the directive by saying if they cannot complete their quota in two weeks, we would adjust the requirement.

By the end of the second week, the students were each producing ten modules per week. My team member could not keep up with testing and implementation. By week 8.5, the students were done. My team member had prepared enough work for the team to code over 10 weeks but he had not anticipated they could accomplish so much so quickly. He needed to prepare more scenarios before they could do more coding. He was a victim of the coding team's success.

As a beginner, I believed that new responsibilities were best experienced with lots of hands on work. This was how I learned how systems worked and what programming tools I could create to automate repetitive tasks, for example, batch installation across the network instead of using CDs. Hands-on work gave me the opportunity to practice new skills, expand knowledge, and deal with people. This was certainly true for the female students who had some coding experience and working on this project provided an opportunity to see their coding project implemented. The team member who had to manage their work also practiced his skills in supervision, evaluation of the work, and dealing with people.

This project was not just coding for automation. I was building the next generation of staff and I was helping them create their arsenal of experiences. We are now in a better position to become more efficient as a group in diagnosing real issues in the facility, being able to correlate how one issue causes multiple ones, and at best, in performing higher level technical work. For example, we do not have to take as much time in opening tickets and filling out all the fields. What I wanted for the team was to have a high impact on the mission of the organization. That meant, we had to perform at a higher technical level, to be proactive rather than reactive, and to provide efficiencies that allowed processes to be improved, to increase cost savings, and to minimize downtime. While this role for the group was new to the organization, this was an opportunity for everyone in my team to improve their technical effectiveness, their interpersonal relationships with others, and to be recognized for the work they do.

In the beginning of the project, what I wanted seemed like a daunting task: that perhaps I did not understand the scope of the technical work, that perhaps it seemed only a great idea but not possible to implement, that perhaps I was asking too much of my staff and I was stretching them too much. On the other hand, perhaps it was just me being a visionary. A strategic vision provides a goal for a leader. It demonstrates that the leader can be innovative and think out of the box. It provides a path of what the end result needs to be. I had the idea, I had the staff buy in, and now we needed to execute and get to the finish line.

Focus on Milestones Then Move Forward

Agile software development (2013) "promotes adaptive planning, evolutionary development, early delivery, and continuous improvement, encouraging rapid and flexible responses to change." Part of helping the team get to the finish line is adapting an agile philosophy. The coding team came from different software backgrounds, so instead of focusing on the differences, we adapted and used the coding boot camp to equalize their experiences. They learned one process that we can work with but they also brought along other ideas from their prior experiences that we wanted to incorporate. We did not want to accept the old ways of doing things and encouraged change. When the team came up with an idea, we did not discount it, but rather we discussed it and determined what were the advantages in coding the solutions this way. We gave them short assignments with a deliverable so that they could immediately demonstrate success, which was a great motivator to continue to create more. As I explained, it was easier and quicker to get the version one out and create improvements in version two rather than to collapse the two versions. Also, the use of newer versions meant additional features and encouraged continuous improvement. After several modules, new ideas used in newer modules were used as upgrades in prior modules. Things were constantly changing for the better and because changes were small, the software continued to work. There was no huge overhaul but in the end, the final version was much improved and different than version number one. I used this technique as well with the staff for their individual projects.

As a manager, I could have set goals that seemed final. Because we were going through a transition, the team needed milestones. In project management, "milestones mark specific points along a project timeline and may signal anchors that focus on major progress points that must be reached to achieve success (Verzuh, 2008, p. 149). The goal was not to produce this small automation event in one area of our workflow, but to achieve this project so we could move forward in transforming the team.

LEADING THE TEAM EFFORT AND EARN THE ROLE

A team will rally around a leader whom they perceive knows what she is doing. To most people in high performance computing, it does not seem like I am very technical and that my educational background is not in hard core computing science. I also did not go to a famous school like Harvard or Stanford and I do not have a Ph.D. While my parents believed in educating their daughter, they also believed that I would have a husband who could take care of me and if I happen to have a job, it was just to supplement the family income. Instead of conforming and being the good daughter, I left home after high school, went to work so I can afford my rent and tuition. That was a lot harder than I thought and after a few starts and stops, and working at odd jobs, I even convinced myself that I could study accounting and become an accountant like my parents wanted, I finally enrolled in a local school studying Computer Information Systems. While it was a small school, it followed many of the methods that Harvard used so I was able to learn system administration, some programming, some web development, and even databases. I got the foundation of what I needed to work in the industry. I eventually went back to the same school to get an MBA in Technology Management, something else that differentiated me from staff who had masters degrees and Ph.D's.

Many factors influence staff perceptions of a leader. I have worked for NERSC for 16 years, transitioning from operations monitoring and reporting on systems, to supporting scientific workstations for staff, to helping manage a physics cluster and eventually a group lead of operations. I gained technical expertise across multiple areas, from storage, networking, to large systems and yet, because I do not fit the stereotype of a female system administrator, I was not perceived as a technical expert.

One afternoon, at the Oakland facility, months before we were ready to move to our new facility (Computation, Research and Theory building or CRT) in Berkeley, Oakland experienced a power outage. Some of the senior staff who would know how to handle this were at the new facility. Once I got the phone call confirming the outage, those of us in CRT headed to Oakland. When we reached our freeway exit, it was blocked by the police so we went to the next closest exit. The streets of Oakland seemed quiet but I did not really think of it at the time. I was on my cell phone, speaking to staff in Oakland, confirming that the uninterruptible power supply (UPS) was still running, staff were asking if they should do a graceful shutdown, the chillers in the basement that helped keep the facility cool were down, but lights were still on. It was controlled chaos. We reached our parking lot, each staff went to their areas and I headed for the machine room.

I asked for a status update, five people were speaking to me at once, and I could not process it all. I asked them to tell me one by one. The UPS was now down and we were dark. I asked someone to get PG&E, the local power company, on the phone so we could figure out what caused the outage and how soon we could get power back. It had been years since we had an unscheduled blackout. The facilities manager and the systems manager were asking me if they should switch off the power distribution units (PDU) so that we can control which systems got power when we got it back. I said yes. In the meantime, someone was saying we were having cell signal issues. I looked at my cell phone and had one bar, which was odd. Someone also mentioned there was police action in downtown. At that point I remembered that some exits had been closed on the freeway. I asked someone to get the news online.

There was much to coordinate. I convened a meeting in our conference room to discuss a plan. Our safety coordinator was already in touch with the Lab emergency operations center (EOC) and she was ensuring we had their support should this outage last much longer. At this point, I had no idea what time we would get power back. It was now around 5:00 in the afternoon when most staff would be thinking about heading home. At the meeting, I suggested we take shifts, that most staff go home and one representative of each area stay onsite to wait out the outage and perform the early restoration process. I soon received information that the soonest power would be restored was 8:00pm. I asked the remaining staff to get dinner and keep in touch, and everyone else to go home.

When I returned to the control room, my staff told me that the police action was a result of a police officer shooting a bank robber who was African American. Protesters were gathering in downtown, approximately seven blocks from us and some were blocking freeways. My concern was for the safety of the staff and engineers who needed to return to our facility later that night. I was also informed that the low cell signal was due to a cell tower being damaged from an explosion earlier in the day, which was under investigation. As I was processing this information, I thought of how protesters disrupted freeway traffic a few weeks prior and could prevent staff from reaching us. I could hear the helicopters circling above and I started to calculate how long it would take to bring up the computer systems. There was a possibility that I would have to ask that the big systems stay down until the next day depending on how much hardware damage had occurred. I was not sure I would be allowed to do it given that the Department of Energy (DOE) wants their facility running 24x7. At some point, my vision cleared and I saw what was going on in front of me. Staff were at their stations, waiting for instructions. Students were looking at me in shock. I looked at everyone and asked, "Is everyone ok?" At that point, the room broke into nervous laughter to be interrupted by the phone ringing.

To make a long story shorter, we did not get power back until 9:00pm. By the time the infrastructure was stable and we determined disk issues, it was very late. Staff and the vendor engineers were stuck in traffic. I called a meeting of the division leadership to ask if they would consider letting the computer systems stay down until morning given the actions around the neighborhood. My division director agreed and said that he would take care of speaking to DOE. I was not able to get everyone out of the building until 2:00am the next morning and we were all going to report back to duty at 5:00am, 3 hours later. I called a 6:00am meeting of the staff to plan out the day and we got started. It was the longest unplanned outage we ever had as a facility but we had only minimal damage.

There is nothing like a disaster to bring everyone together and I was appreciative of how everyone cooperated. From their side, they observed that I knew exactly what had to be done in the timeframe that was required. Prior to all this, I had a manager put into my performance review that I needed to develop deeper technical understanding on one area. He elaborated that I was really not an expert in even one thing and I should become one. This power outage event proved something to myself and I hope to those around me. While I was not an expert in one specific area, I have the expertise to bring the facility back to operational order. Maybe I can not do it all by myself, and that I do not have the engineering knowledge to do it all on my own. However, the sign of a good leader is knowing who you can count on to be your experts and getting them to work together toward your end result. I wanted my facility to be back in operational order as quickly as possible. That night, I laid out the timeline, I created the plan, and I directed traffic. In the end, it was a team effort.

Being in an emergency situation can bring staff together, but how do you do this when there is no emergency? Doing power work in the new building has taken weeks of coordination and planning. Then I had to tell the crew that they had to start at 4:00 am on a Saturday. Can you imagine the groans, complaints, and negotiations at this point? What can I do to motivate them to give up their Saturday? What are the buttons I need to push or what rewards can I offer to kick up their enthusiasm? Sometimes, all it takes are caffeine and sugar aka donuts and coffee. So that day, I agreed to bring in the good donuts, the ones with the creamy center and the strong coffee, not the weak stuff from down the hill. A good leader knows how to listen to their staff and execute on what is important. In this case, they wanted to be cared for and the gesture of care can be as insignificant as coffee. However, in very important situations like a performance review, a leader's listening skills can be the key to a good conversation. Sometimes, staff do not know how their career aspirations tie into the organization's strategic mission and it is the leader's job to help clarify and create a path for moving forward professionally. For example, there are skill training programs that are relevant to our area: linux system administration, programming, database, and so on. On the other hand, does learning about procurement, inventory, and travel have anything to do with our mission? Believe it or not, these skills are all relevant.

The flip side of motivation is to manage their expectations. If they understand the scope of what they need to do and they can perform that function, I can reasonably expect that they will do their best. The challenge is to make your expectations known so they can do what they need to do. For the students, I want to harness their creativity and apply that to their solution. One student said to me, "you make it sound so easy and when we get into it, there's a lot of layers." That is true, however, I also let them know that I do not really care how they got to the end result as long as it works and they document it. I hope by doing this that I have encouraged creativity, out of box thinking, and having an open mind. For the staff, it is more important to manage their expectations and be able to communicate what I want them to do. The dreaded performance review should not be done once a year in the sense that, conversations with staff should not happen only once a year. They should occur 3 or 4 times a year or every time a new project comes up or every time someone is discussing additional training. Performance review time can be the most stressful time of the year but there is no need for it to be this way. Instead, I propose to continuously have conversations with the staff. When my staff members do something good, I talk to them about it, tell them how much I appreciate what a great job they have done, and then remind them to note it somewhere for the performance review notes for the end of the fiscal year. When they are not doing so well, I talk to them even more often and offer to provide them with resources to make them successful. This constant feedback is a different way of working. There is a lot of documentation out there about the need for this but it is not easy to implement. Why? It takes time, lots and lots of time. It is also a decision as a manager, to make the time to do the process this way. The result of this time investment is that there are no surprises during performance reviews. Well, sometimes there are some, like when staff had not realized how much they had accomplished during the year, and how much those series of projects had made a big impact. Of course when staff are not doing well, I hope they recognize it too.

BRING FELLOWSHIP TO THE TEAM

There is nothing that brings together a group of diverse students and staff like a team activity. Every year, the Lab had an intramural softball league and teams come together from all over the Lab, the campus, and friends from outside the Lab to play. Staff in my division, were not that good at softball. Think of all the stereotypes of scientists and engineers and that would be us. One year, a staffer decided to form our own division team and she called us "the Petaflops," quite appropriate. This year, I decided to join much to the dismay of my friends and to the delight of my students. If I was going to do it, they would too. To tell you the truth, I suck at softball although I could catch and kinda throw but hitting that ball? Now that is a challenge in hand and eye coordination for me. After several practice sessions, we arrived at our first game, nicely outfitted in our freshly designed uniforms. After five innings we had not scored yet and the other team had six runs. That's ok, we cheered our successes whether it was getting to first, encouraging a runner to get to third, a nice catch, a good throw or even a bad throw as long as the person did something. We even celebrated just getting through the inning. That first game really brought both staff and students together. We lost that game but walking away from the field, it seemed like we were the winning team. In some sense, we won that day.

Amazingly, no one left the team. In fact, our team kept getting bigger. There were more people who wanted to play each week to the point where we had to share positions. Not everyone can be in the outfield at the same time. Back at the ranch aka, at the office, the students helped each other, they had lunch together, they would encourage each other, they even found a large space where they could work together instead of their respective offices or cubes. So what happened to Team Petaflops? By the end of the season, we won one game out of eight and we were the happiest team out there. The day we won, we texted everyone all over the place. I am sure there was something on social media about #AWin4Petaflops.

Back at the ranch, while Team Petaflops technically was not doing well as a softball team, in other areas they were doing fabulous. Every week, the coach, mentioned our successes by name and everyone cheered. Every week, those who did something positive for the team, were recognized by their teammates and other staff. Every week, there was a lot of love happening in that conference room with the staff in the Division. When that happens, staff work well together, issues can be discussed, new ideas can get generated. Success breeds success. This camaraderie has happened because they had found one thing in common outside of work that held them together through the tough times.

My team was going through a change. There were staff who were with us for many years who were going to do the job the exact same way, even though the job was changing. There were new staff who had fresh skills and wanted hands on experience right away to prove themselves on the job. In this complex arena, there is potential for interpersonal issues. The challenge for most of management is not necessarily to have a diverse staff but once they have the diverse staff, how to get them to work together. Knowing that a team needs one thing to rally around, I gave them something fun to rally around. One year I brought in a scientist who also worked with groups to perform improv as part of improving communication and group collaboration. Using the basis of improv, the instructor got them to be silly together in a safe environment, got them to speak about issues, and helped them through exercises to see what their co-workers strengths are and help them capitalize on those strengths. Just like two ballroom dancers, it is both their responsibility to make their partner look good. Sometimes, group physical activities help bond the team. Most managers do ropes courses as team building exercises. For my group, I wanted to do something different. One afternoon after a serious discussion about what new responsibilities we could potentially acquire, I ended the meeting with asking the team to stand up, stretch up and down several times, get the blood flowing, and put on Katy Perry's song, "Firework." Sometimes, silliness as a group also bonds the team.

There will be good times and bad times for individuals on the team as well as the team itself. There will be communication issues, personal issues, performance issues, and all kinds of other issues. As a manager, we have to think that we will be in this position for the long term and if we are to function effectively, we have to find out ways to bond the team and keep the fellowship going. I recall Aragorn's speech in front of the Black Gates before the big battle with the Orks when he said "a day may come when the courage of men fails, when we forsake our friends and break all bonds of fellowship, but it is not this day." This may sound too dramatic but a few months before we were getting ready to move to the new building, we were told by the management not to schedule time off during the summer and possibly into the early fall. The reality is we probably would have a lot of work to do until the end of the year. How do I break this news to the staff? I told them exactly that but also mentioned this line in the film. The next few months will take all of us to pull together to make the move a reality. We will be in two locations and making it all work: keeping one location going and putting together and learning the new location. There will be long hours but the reward is institutional knowledge within the group. This is valuable information we cannot regain once it has happened. As a leader, it is my responsibility to ensure my team carries their weight in this big deliverable by keeping them motivated, inspired, and bonded in fellowship.

RIPPLES IN THE STREAM

In a large organization, change is not easy. There are years of traditions to overcome, there are cultural roadblocks, and there are people who will tell you it was always done this way. In my case, I wanted something better for my staff, for my group. The way we work, in this case, monitor our systems and facility, has to change with the times and the upgrades in technology. We are constantly improving our systems to perform better, to compute faster, to be energy efficient and to move, read and write data faster, in order to reach exascale. Why then do we think that we can monitor these systems in the same archaic way as was done a decade ago?

Mother Teresa once said, "I alone cannot change the world, but I can cast a stone across the waters to create many ripples." I would like to think that I the type of person that is flexible to change and I encourage those around me especially my staff, that change is mostly for the good. I also like to induce the change. Being that my group is the center of what is going on, we should, as a group be able to affect synergistic changes, that impact not only us but all the groups in my organization.

Reality Takes People

My idea of an effective leader is a person that knows themselves well enough to demonstrate their personal values like hard work and taking serious responsibility for their actions. They should also be able to direct themselves, whether to keep up with a project, learn a new skill, or take risks. They need to know when to let others lead and potentially allow a staff member to move forward with what seems like an unlikely idea. Knowing yourself means allowing yourself to go beyond your comfort zone to get to know others, to be able to lead them. Leading teams needs effective communications, whether it is one on one or through various methods like performance reviews or just having a normal conversation. The team needs continuous professional development and leaders need to make this available whether that's letting staff take a class, having them try a new task outside of their normal operational area, or having them get involved with submitting articles for publication. Leaders should encourage positive interpersonal relationships, should set the example in valuing team members' diversity, and should create situations that allow the team to grow together. For effective teams to affect organizational change, there should be constant innovation, problem solving, and risk taking that aligns to the organization's mission. To make the vision a reality takes individuals working as a team, cooperating with each other. It takes people to make the ripples count toward synergistic change.

GLORIA T. CAOILE

Chair, FWN Advisory Board
FWN100™ Global 2013 & U.S. 2007

Beyond Our Dreams

Two years ago, I was in a photo studio with four generations of women from my family; me, my mother, my daughter, and my granddaughter. At that time, my granddaughter, Ciara, was only four months old; my mother, a mere 90 years old. My mother sat on a chair cradling Ciara in the crook of her arm, a bit tentative, unsure if the baby was comfortable. My daughter and I stood tautly behind them, both of us poised to catch Ciara should great grandma's arm tire out. Drowned in the background was the photographer's voice shouting smile.

The minute the camera clicked, time stopped for a second; and the lives of the four individuals in the photo converged at that moment; all four of us with different beginnings, circumstances, and opportunities, but bound together.

"Thank you, Gloria Caoile." President William J. Clinton was thanking me, Gloria Caoile, at the Congressional Asian Pacific American Caucus dinner on May 18, 1995. This moment is included in his papers (1995, p. 707). The memory always makes me smile.

Historical Influences

My mother was born in the Philippines, the daughter of an uneducated provincial girl from Pampanga and an American soldier who stayed behind after the Spanish-American war. My mother said it was not until she was eight years old when her American father, exasperated at not being able to communicate with his children, enrolled her and her siblings at a school where the medium of instruction was English. Access to education for Filipinos during the American occupation was much broader than it had been during Spanish colonization. My mother's education was cut short by the outbreak of World War II. In December of her sophomore year of high school, Pearl Harbor was bombed and her American teachers sent all the school children home. Schools would not resume until after the war. She spent her teenage years in a war torn country. At age 20, she was married. She witnessed her sister die from tuberculosis, leaving two orphaned nephews in her care.

My mother was among the first evacuees that left the Philippines right after the war. Being part American and pregnant, she was given priority and put on a military ship along with my American grandfather, who had been incarcerated at Santo Tomas. They joined my grandfather's family in Oklahoma. That is why I was born in Lawton, Oklahoma, an unusual origin for a Filipina American.

My father, a Filipino, subsequently followed. No offense to Oklahoma, but my mom said it was such a harsh and desolate place that my father could not imagine raising a family there. So they went back to the Philippines in 1947 and that was where I grew up. While I have lived here in the United States most of my life, my formative years were spent in the Philippines. So much of who I am is because I grew up there.

IMPARTING VALUES ACROSS GENERATIONS

My mother, of course, is a great role model. A feminist ahead of her time, she believed in the power of women. My mother was naturally gifted. She was intelligent, articulate, and opinionated. She never shared with us her unrealized aspirations. To her, it was a futile exercise to imagine what her life or career would have been had there not been a war. The reality of it is that the war ended her dreams. This is very similar to what is happening now to millions of women in war-ravaged countries. In my mother's thinking, the future was not for herself but for her children. She had two rules for her four daughters: get educated and do not be financially dependent on a man. Thus, we became working women. She gave me courage and independence and taught me how to reach beyond limits.

I have three sisters, all products of St. Scholastica's College, who are very much a part of the success I enjoy now. Strong-willed women, opinionated, loving, intelligent, and amazing individuals; they are a constant guide.

Not to be forgotten are the men in my family who have since passed away: A father who encouraged my ambitions, saying that "we could be whoever we want to be" and a brother who taught me to be a risk-taker.

My husband, Ben, and daughter Melanie, are at the center of my universe. As exciting as the work challenges were, my greatest pleasure was having Ben and Melanie to come home to at the end of the day.

I must have imparted the same values I learned from my family to my daughter Melanie. She found her way to a corporate job and successfully navigated through the labyrinths of corporate demands and rewards. Once she asked me if I could come to her company and speak about leadership qualities to a group of Asian and Pacific Americans. I was beyond thrilled.

What I said to the group bears repeating. These remarks have been previously published in my chapter Stepping Up (Beebe and Escudero, 2015, pp. 37-52). Since they are at the core of my life's experiences and beliefs I firmly believe that I must state them again.

1. Love what you do. Nothing substitutes for passion. Passion makes you believe in yourself. It is motivating. It is infectious. It is the key to long-term success.

2. Develop your people skills. Having people skills, being approachable, friendly, pleasant and respectful of others; requires that you actually interact with humans. Even in a technology-centric world, face time is essential to establishing relations. When you are able to make others feel at ease, they are more likely to cooperate.

3. Have courage. Resolve to go forward even when risk is involved. Have the courage to fight racial and gender stereotypes. Assert yourself and be confident.

4. Build competence. To be influential and have power, you need to be competent and bring value through your contributions. As a woman and minority, being good is not enough; you have to be excellent by putting in extra time and effort.

5. Step up and get involved. Work hard and work for others. Use your network to enable others and create the same pathways for them. Participate in civic life, whether it is community clubs or sports leagues. Realize that the bounty you enjoy is not free.

6. Don't wait for compliments. Work hard, show initiative, and good things will happen. But also guard against those who may sabotage you or demean your work.

These principles guided me throughout my working years. I spent the best part of my professional career at a labor union where I learned advocacy and where I accepted that working people have rights to good wages, health care, civil rights, and social and economic justice.

When my granddaughter, Ciara enters the workforce, I hope racial and gender inequality will be a thing of the past. My desire for her is that she will realize her full potential.

I have been involved in activities that encourage civic participation. I believe it is important for Asian and Pacific Americans, and Filipino Americans in particular, to be involved in public decision making processes. It is where one can influence the direction and future of this country. It just makes sense to me to continue to try to make the world a better place: for Ciara and her generation.

LEARNING LEADERSHIP QUALITIES

In addition to family, it was a Benedictine education that was the main influence in my life. Respect for others, recognizing the importance of individuals, and extending courtesy and kindness to all, regardless of station in life, are values taught at St. Scholastica's College. I learned to be confident, to become an effective negotiator among peers, and to be a trusted leader at school. All of these traits carried over into the real world. Having respect for different views and opinions, I got along well with diverse groups. Being able to accept people from varying backgrounds was fundamental to successfully engaging groups and achieving goals and objectives. Truly, the Benedictine values of respect, inclusiveness, kindness to others, and hard work, are key to what has made my life full.

Over 50 years ago, after I had finished high school, my mother and I boarded an ocean liner to return to the United States. At that time, the expectation was that women would become secretaries and men would become bosses. So my mother took all of her savings and invested it in a secretarial training course for me. Without going into a lot of details, I became an expert in business processes.

ALIGNMENT OF PASSION AND WORK ADVOCACIES

For 30 years I served with the American Federation of State, County and Municipal Employees (AFSCME), a union with 1.6 million working and retired members. AFSCME's members provide the vital services that make America function. Our members are nurses, corrections officers, child care providers, emergency medical technicians (EMTs), sanitation workers, and hundreds of other occupations.

AFSCME has always advocated for fairness in the workplace, excellence in public services, and prosperity and opportunity for all working families. These positions resonated with me and explained why I choose to remain with AFSCME.

I started as a Secretary in the Education Department. I fondly remember the interview process for this job. Apparently after several searches, I was picked because the HR person felt I could stand up graciously to my future boss who had a reputation for being difficult, demanding, and hard to work for. All of the boss's detractors were wrong. As the only woman director at that time, she needed to be 'loud, proud and lead without a doubt!' She was misunderstood. From her, I learned leadership qualities that helped me throughout my career.

Close to the end of my career at the AFSCME, I was in charge of the human resources department, convention and travel, facilities, and support services. I was once described as the "highest ranking Asian Pacific American in the labor movement." Today, many Filipina American Women have been elected to senior positions in their own unions.

BEING PASSIONATE AND FOUR LEADERSHIP PRINCIPLES

I have four leadership principles that I want to share with you in addition to being passionate about all you do. The first is about people skills. People skills may seem like an odd choice for a leadership principle, but success requires interaction with people. I am talking about the ability to interact. I know that in the workplace you have heard it often said "I don't have to like you to work with you," but it helps if you like people. You cannot hide behind your computers; you cannot simply rely on social media. You must have some face time. To be successful, you will have to spend a lot of energy mixing and interacting with people. I am not talking about just socializing. I am talking about building relationships internally and externally. Throughout my career, I spent time nurturing relationships. Your people skills need to be as good, or better, than your technical skills. I cannot emphasize this point enough. Today's work environment is so highly integrated that it requires cooperation, collaboration, and sharing of information. You need to be approachable, friendly, and pleasant. You need to make others feel at ease with you. I think for Filipino Americans, being approachable, friendly, pleasant, and, making others feel at ease, are easy skills to acquire. If you grew up in a Filipino American household, you learn at an early age to get along. In our culture, harmony in family, community, and society is emphasized.

At AFSCME, I was able to control the flow of information and access to president. That made me an important cog in the organization. I made sure I was approachable, friendly, and pleasant. I put people at ease. So when I had ideas on what our organization needed to do, I sold my ideas by going to the people who I thought needed to buy off on my ideas. I could have just easily gone to the president, got a yea or nay from him, and that would have been it. Instead I would take time to go to people who I thought would be affected by the decision and I would work with them in fashioning proposals that were workable for them but aligned with my concepts. It should not matter where you are in the hierarchy. If you know how to approach people, nurture relationship, and make people at ease with you, you will experience success. Oftentimes, relationships are overlaid with conflict and tension. You do not start out having the absolute right answer. You need to learn how to handle disagreement. Do not walk away from it; you must have the ability to diffuse it. Oh, one of my favorite techniques in diffusing tension is adding humor. But please, do not tell bad jokes.

The next leadership principle is courage. Courage is having the resolve to go forward even when there is risk involved. I am not talking about acts of heroism. I simply want to point out, you cannot be fearful. You cannot just keep ideas to yourself or downplay them. There is one sensitive point I want to make. In my view, race and gender are factors in the work place. So my advice to everyone is that you need to have the courage to fight the stereotypes. Oh, the list is long, we are meek, conformists, self-effacing, quiet, shy, technically competent but not managerial timber, and so forth. Although I believe our society has come a long way to leveling the playing field, bias in subtle forms still exists. Gender and racial disparities are real. So you need to have the courage to assert yourself and move forward. Learn to be confident and realistic about what you can do. It is a risk, but if you do not act, you will not advance. I always tell all, a horse that does not run is not going to win the race.

This leads me to my third leadership principle; be competent. To be influential in any setting, you need to know what you are talking about. How often have you heard the expressions value-added or value proposition? These are basically terms that ask "What is your contribution?" Work on your verbal skills. Become more outgoing, gregarious, and adopt more outwardly behavior. But if you lack substance, you will doom yourself to fail When I speak of competence, I am saying you need to be three times as good to be equal. Do not settle for being good. Be Excellent.

Please understand that I spent my life with organizations that fights for civil rights and social and economic justice, so my view is that race is still a factor in America. We have not gotten to the point where society is color blind. Until we do, people of color have to compete based on merit and competence. If there are barriers and obstacles placed in front of you, jump over them. You have to put in the extra time, the extra effort. Go the extra mile. You cannot just go with the flow. Yes, it requires hard work. In an article in Fortune magazine, researchers were trying to figure out what it takes to be great. Their conclusion is that natural talent is irrelevant to great success. Painful and demanding practice and hard work is what is takes to be great.

My final leadership principle is about respecting diversity. There are so many factors that make us different; culture, gender, religion, age, education, geography, political affiliation, occupation, and so forth. It is not only cultural diversity. Take into account all these other factors that make us different. But believe, 'being different, doesn't mean less than!" Just as we demand that the American mainstream respects diversity, we must also do the same. Thank goodness we are not all alike. Life would be so boring if we were. Respect different points of view. It does not mean you have to agree with them; but you must give them respect.

Although retired, AFSCME has continued to call on me for special assignments. In my most recent assignment, I led a disaster response and relief team to help 3,000 AFSCME survivors of Hurricane Katrina. I headed a similar effort on behalf of AFSCME a few days after the 9/11 terrorist attacks in New York. I personally managed the AFSCME September 11 Fallen Heroes Fund to assist members who were directly affected by the tragedy.

LEADERSHIP IN CIVIC ENGAGEMENT

My work has always extended beyond my involvement with AFSCME. I am committed to promoting Asian American and Pacific Islander participation in the political process. I have encouraged members of the immigrant community to vote, to volunteer in civic organizations, and to do their part in helping America maintain a healthy democracy. Civic involvement continues to be a lifelong passion and commitment.

I was a founding member of the Asian Pacific American Women Leadership Institute (APAWLI), the only national organization dedicated to nurturing and developing leadership skills among Asian American and Pacific Islander women. I was also a founding member of the Asian Pacific American Labor Alliance (APA-LA), a national organization of Asian Pacific American labor union members. I have served on the boards of several civil rights groups including the Filipino American Civil Rights Advocates and the National Federation of Filipino-American Associations. I was appointed by President Clinton to the White House Advisory Commission of Asian Americans and Pacific Islanders with the explicit mandate to advise the president and the federal government on how best to spond to the health needs of Asian Americans and Pacific Islanders. In addition to my work with the Asian American and Pacific Islander community, I have devoted a significant amount of my time promoting community and economic development programs that help the poor in the Philippines. I work with the Feed the Hungry Team as Program Director, Calamity Assistance and Rehabilitation Endeavors (CARE).

UNDERSTANDING MY IMPACT

I have been blessed to have received many accolades for my work in and engagement with the community I am very passionate about and I am totally appreciative of all of them. As leaders, we need to be aware of our impact and ability to inspire action. Consider the following statements:

"When Gloria T. Caoile joins a group, she unwittingly raises their energy level. Her effortless ways to direct, influence, motivate, and make things happen, are admired by many who have worked with her."

"Because of her energetic leadership in the community and in the political area, I and so many Filipina American women and men, inspired by her courage, dedication, passion for justice and equal opportunity; have joined her in working towards the vision of a fair and representative democracy in this country."

"Why does she inspire me? It's because Gloria exemplifies the best qualities in a leader; passion, commitment, a can-do spirit, positive energy that always radiates a room or a conference call, a multi-tasker, master of wearing numerous hats all at once and being very clear about not mixing up hats, selfless, humble, filled with joy, love and laughter."

My initial reactions? I reflect on it. It helps me continue the path I take. When you get a compliment, reflect on it.

The career I chose was that of a labor rights leader, which extended to advocacy for Asian American and Pacific Islander participation in the political process. It also involved special assignments such as leading emergency relief teams to assist union members in disaster-affected areas. I am now retired but my work with various Asian Pacific American organizations involved with fighting for civil rights and attaining social and economic justice continues.

Life has taught me that passion accompanies success. You have to be real. Everything that you do has to come from within you. Nothing can substitute for passion. It drives everything you do. It makes you believe in yourself. It is motivating. It is infectious.

Thank you, Lord, for making it possible for me to be a wife and mother. I am also a daughter, a sister, an aunt and the best of all a grandmother to Ciara.

So Ciara; this is dedicated to you!

EVELYN DILSAVER

INDEPENDENT BOARD DIRECTOR, MULTIPLE COMPANIES
FWN100™ U.S. 2011

Leadership. Power. Influence

Seven Eleven! Seven Eleven! What is that cry!? Were they yelling for the ubiquitous retail chain? No, it was my first foray into a leadership role. I was running for student body president of my high school and during the voting process, they botched my name. Someone had accidently morphed Evelyn into Eleven and the others took up the cry. I learned an important lesson that day...people can latch onto catchy phrases, slogans, and names and propel them to great heights. It was the first time I ever ran for an office and I honestly don't know what drove me to do that. I did have a leadership position in sports as co-captain of the varsity volleyball team, but this was different. I was the first female student body president and being first set a precedent for the future.

I remember telling my student body vice-president to give the talk to the booster club—mostly because I did not want to do it. I was too scared! Some years later, he told me he was so grateful that I made him do it and that I was willing to share my "power" with him because it gave him a huge boost of confidence. You know, sometimes we fall into lessons of leadership. I learned that "giving power away" to your colleagues and members of your team, grants you more power. They see your generosity as giving them career and leadership opportunities, which engenders loyalty and respect for you.

I remember my mom telling me, "If you don't have something nice to say, don't say anything." I stayed quiet for long periods of time. Others thought I was just poised! In retrospect, that comment has served me well in that I had to think about how I wanted to phrase criticism or disagreements in a way that respected the other person. This was re-enforced when I was Chief of Staff to a Co-CEO and his first words to me were, "Don't give me your opinion for the first six months". Well, I lasted three months, but I learned how to listen well. I learned that for the CEO to make good decisions, he had to hear multiple points of views, and I could help serve that role by listening well and being able to articulate those various views.

The other important lesson was how to influence without having authority. In my role as Chief of Staff, the goal was to free up the Co-CEO's time so he could focus on the strategy and major projects that would move the company forward, inspire the employees and find great talent. That meant I took on some of the other projects by helping to manage them, gave important feedback and made connections so that the larger perspective was taken into account. But I couldn't use the power of his office to make it happen as that would cause resentment. So I learned to create win-win situations by understanding the needs of the various parties and helping to make sure they were successful. Sometimes success just meant listening.

A LITTLE BACKGROUND: BORN IN THE U.S.A.

My parents emigrated from the Philippines to the U.S. in the 1950s after Dad joined the U.S. Navy. They were married in 1952 and my brother and I were born in San Francisco. My younger sister was born in the Philippines when Dad was stationed there for a few years, but we basically grew up in the States. My Mom and Dad never taught us Tagalog because they wanted up to grow up "American." Back then, having a second language was not as accepted as it is now. We were usually the only Filipinos in our communities and certainly in grammar school and high school. But we did learn to eat all the yummy Filipino foods!

My mom was college educated in the Philippines with a degree in accounting and after I started high school, went to work for the City of Oakland as an accountant. She represented a strong, independent female role model for me and my siblings. One Filipino cultural trait is equality of women. While that was not expressly communicated it played out in our everyday life. Mom and Dad had a partnership in their marriage. My parents encouraged us to get an education, a college degree was expected and I never thought there was an alternative either to getting a college degree or pursuing a career.

For the first time, my siblings and I had a chance to see where our parents grew up during a family reunion in the Philippines in 2016. Seeing this, I realized how lucky we were that my Dad came to America. While his family was considered "well off" by Philippine standards, they were certainly not raised in the same conditions we were fortunate enough to have experienced in America. It gave all of us, especially my nephews who were along for the trip, great perspective on my parents' courage to leave the Philippines and make America their home. Typical of most large Filipino families, they lived in a close knit community of aunts, uncles, cousins and friends. Giving all of that up meant our small family of five had to be close, look after and support each other and create our own community. Filipinos are known for their warmth, friendliness and generosity. Those traits helped us adapt to whatever city or military base we happened to live in during my Dad's twenty-year tenure in the Navy.

Making the move to Corporate Life

After graduating from college with a degree in Accounting, I first worked for a Big 8 CPA firm in the U.S., Ernst & Young (Ernst and Ernst when I joined). I was there for six years rising to Senior Manager and developed my own unique management style. I liked working with people who were self-motivated, ambitious, smart, and driven towards a goal. We did not have to "clock" in but were expected to get the job done on time. After Ernst & Young (EY) I was recruited as a controller for a bank, one of my former clients at EY. When I took on the role I was pregnant with my first child. At that time, there were no role models at EY for women with families and I wanted to be able to spend time with my growing family.

Not a Straight Path: Forks in the Road

I loved my job at the bank and I learned how to manage a diverse group of employees. Some were like my team at Ernst, self-motivated and ambitious while others just wanted to work from 9 to 5, stayed in one job, and loved what they did. Each group had different motivations for working. My challenge was to learn how to get the best out of each employee. During my time at the bank, I thought my career path would be from Controller to Chief Financial Officer (CFO). But two things happened: first, my boss told me I had a reputation for getting things done, but not enough strategic thinking. Second, I met the President of a company doing business with the bank who told me he was a prior CPA. Initially, I thought the only route for a CPA was to the CFO role but meeting the former CPA, now

President, got me thinking about what it took to be President. I recognized that I needed to develop strategic thinking and a broader set of skills.

After the bank, I was recruited by Schwab to be their Controller and I accepted the position. I reverted back to the career trajectory of Controller to CFO. After four years, I realized I really wanted to be in general management. After taking the summer off to participate in the Stanford's Senior Executive Program, I came back to Schwab with responsibility for managing several branches. While excited to learn something new and start building the skill sets I needed to be a general manager, it was very tough on the ego. I thought I was immune from having the job define who I was, but that was not true. When you are the Controller, there is only one of you in the firm. When you are a regional sales manager, there are many of you! And I kept getting compared to people who had been in their jobs a long time. Being the new kid on the block and still learning the ropes, I was always last in line for raises and stock options. I would see others who started with me get promoted into bigger jobs. I was not moving as fast as I wanted to. I had to keep reminding myself that this was a path I chose because I needed to acquire the skills for a bigger role. But it was hard!

FAMILY AND WORK

By this time, I had three boys and I really wanted to be involved with them. I started coaching girls' volleyball in their grammar school and eventually coached both boys and girls volleyball for over 10 years, while my husband coached them in baseball and basketball. My life was consumed by my family, coaching, and moving around Schwab to pick up new skills. You might wonder how I was able to move around Schwab. The Filipino trait of building a community was something I did unconsciously. To build community you build relationships and trust through fulfilling of commitments and promises. One of the big lessons I learned in my role as Controller was the importance of developing relationships with the other executives in the firm. Because I had a reputation for getting things done, the executives trusted me enough to give me opportunities in their organizations, even if I did not have the specific experience. I also learned to volunteer for new positions or "hard" jobs that were considered risky. As I mentioned earlier, I was Chief of Staff to the Co-CEO, Dave. This was also a risky role in that it was totally undefined. Dave had just been promoted and knew he needed help. He and I had worked together when he was President and I was controller. Dave became my mentor and as I mentioned, I learned how to manage at the executive level, how to listen and how to influence without using the power of his office.

Taking on Risky Roles

By taking on risky and new roles, I was learning how to create a vision, develop a team, and get everyone focused on delivering on that vision. One such role involved commuting weekly from San Francisco to New York for three years to help integrate a newly acquired company. I eventually served as the CFO and Chief Administrative Officer for the newly acquired company. That meant I was responsible for Finance, Treasury, Accounting, Human Resources, Project Management, and several small businesses. I was getting my wish! I was expanding my skill set.

After 9/11, I returned to San Francisco. I knew the family never wanted to relocate and three years of commuting to New York every week was tough on me and the family. So, I started interviewing for different roles at Schwab. I ended up interviewing for head of product development for the mutual fund group. I remember telling the head of the group that I had two of the four skill sets he wanted. I did not have mutual fund experience nor a classic product development background. But the other two skills were more critica—I knew how to get things done and I was a great builder of teams. I could create a vision of where we needed to be and get everyone pulling in the same direction. I was hired for the job!

Oh, and remember in the beginning I mentioned that I was scared to speak in public? I got over that. I had to give many speeches in my various roles, and I now really enjoy it. Public speaking requires figuring out who your audience is and what they need to hear to help them in the role they play. Public speaking combined my art of listening, creating a vision, and coaching into one integral competency.

After one year in my role as head of the mutual fund product group, I was promoted to lead the investment management group at Schwab. This was the proprietary fund group with about $132 billion in assets. The product group and sales group were moved into my organization. The challenge for us was that while the performance for these mutual funds were very good, the funds were not being promoted by the firm. The biggest category were cash funds and we wanted to grow the equity funds. In four years, we were able to grow the assets to over $200 billion and increase the amount of assets flowing to the proprietary equity funds from the total marketplace. We thought outside the box and created the demand from outside the company.

Every mutual fund has to have an outside Board of Directors representing the shareholders. I had my first exposure to an external Board as head of the mutual fund group. I enjoyed getting to know the board members, thinking strategically and critically about the business, and getting their points of view. Even then, I foresaw serving on a corporate board as a great future adventure for me.

Giving Back Through Non-Profits

By this time, my children were in college and I was not coaching volleyball anymore. Several years earlier I was introduced to Julie Abrams, the Executive Director of a non-profit called Women's Initiative. This organization helped lower income women become financially independent by helping them start and grow their own businesses. A year after joining the board, I became Chair of the board because the perfect storm hit. The founder, who was the main source of funding retired at the insistence of the board, and all but two of the board members quit. We brought in all new board members, found and diversified our funding, and built a great organization helping women start over 3000 new businesses annually. Working with Julie helped me continue my growth as a leader in the non-profit world and extended my coaching platform. While the organization eventually folded into another non-profit an important lesson remained with me: have the right people around you when things do not go so well and who will stay with you to the end.

I am retired from Schwab and now serve on several corporate boards, public, private, and non-profit. I really like the intellectual stimulation, the strategic and critical thinking, meeting fascinating people who I might otherwise have never met, and coaching and mentoring CEOs and their teams.

Lessons of Leadership

Along the way, I have developed a set of lessons about becoming a leader. What is a leader? Is one born a leader or can you learn to be a leader? Is a leader the one who has power because of their position, or because of their ability to influence others?

John Quincy Adams observed, "If your actions inspire others to dream more, learn more, do more and become more, you are a leader." There are many definitions of a leader, with some believing a leader has to have charisma, a huge personality that fills the room. Others believe a leader is one who serves their people.

My definition of leadership is best captured by Mark Mactas (2009), Chairman and Chief Executive Officer of global professional services firm Towers Perrin, "Management is power by position. Leadership is power by influence." In other words, a leader is effective in that they gather groups of people together to achieve a common goal, with a sense of urgency, fun, and excitement. Leaders build sustainable enterprises, that do not depend on just one individual for survival. I have my top nine lessons on becoming a leader. Yes, I do believe some people are born leaders, but I also believe there are many qualities that can be learned. These are the top nine lessons I learned about becoming a leader:

1. Learn to listen.

Listening well and hearing the other person's point of view allows you to come up with win-win solutions. This does not work when you have someone who is totally unreasonable, but that situation is rare.

2. Learn to have a voice.

This means learning to express your opinion in a constructive manner; not as a whiner but in a way that offers solutions. For women, this is critical because in many situations you will find yourself the only woman in the room. One of the Filipino traits that hold us back is the unwillingness to express our views, especially if they are confrontational. We are brought up to respect our elders or bosses and the hierarchy is important. The American culture values directness in communication. Be the "Voice of Reason" and you will break the stereotypes of women and Filipinos Pick your battles. If you find that you are always the agitator, then you need to look at your work environment. Some issues you need to let go and have others fight the battle. Which leads me to my third point:

3. You can accomplish a lot if you do not care who gets credit.

There are two parts to this. First, is to find others who share your point of view and let them take credit for the idea. That way, you aren't always the one out in front, and when it's successful, most normal people recognize your role in both getting it done, and supporting them. This can build tremendous loyalty and accomplish a great deal. Secondly, build a great team. Delegate. Ask questions. I know you have heard this before, but it's too easy for us to say, "Oh, I'll just do it. It will be faster". Or "It won't get done my way, so I'll just do it". And you find yourself putting in 14 – 15 hour days, feeling you are carrying the whole load and that no one is helping. So, how do you build a team? Find people who have skills you do not have, are smarter than you, and let them do what they do best. Give them the tools they need, the recognition, and rewards. Do not make it hard for them to do their job. This is also hard, because you have to have enough self-confidence in yourself in order to hire people smarter than you. But what this does for you is to leave you room to work on the next level of capability you need to advance to the next level. It allows you to think about the future and plan for it, so that you are prepared for what is coming up in a year or two, rather than reacting to the moment. And, if you have great people, it allows you to be promoted, as executives like to know that there is a successor who will allow for a smooth transition as you move up and on. I know I have been privy to conversations where we could not promote an individual because there was no one to take their place.

At times, you may have delegated and something untoward happened on your watch and so you reverted back to doing it yourself. Yes, this does happen. Here are a few things you could do that will help prevent big mistakes from happening before you have a chance to correct course. First, communicate with your team: If they are clear on the goal and you have frequent and regular meetings, once a week, every other week, to check in, then it becomes easier to catch mistakes and make mid-term corrections. Second, ask questions: What is your goal? How do you hope to accomplish it? What do you think the risks are and what do you plan to do to mitigate them? Today's worker is highly educated and smart and they don't necessarily want to be managed. You are not telling them what to do, but encouraging them to think and allowing you to understand how they approach a problem or goal. This also allows you to provide input along the way. And do not overreact if something does go wrong—business is all about managing risk and risk is the operative word. Real leaders seem to get their kicks out of seeing their own people succeed and their own organization succeed, rather than have their personal ambition take precedence. So to be a leader, be visible, be available and be a good listener.

4. Learn to have difficult conversations.

This is connected to "finding your voice" and being the voice of reason. Have you ever been in a meeting and felt the group was not talking about the "big" issue that was on everyone's mind, but dancing around it? That's called the pink elephant in the room. Everyone knows it, but no one is talking. Find a way to talk about the pink elephant—in a constructive way that encourages finding solutions.

Also, learn how to provide feedback to your employees that respects their dignity. Whether it is a tough performance review or you have to fire someone, learn to have those conversations that address their **behavior, not their personality or morals, good person, bad person.**

5. Do not compare yourself to anyone.

When you compare yourself to someone else, you become blind to your own talents and skills. I moved around the company because I wanted to learn new skills. It was tough because I was compared to others who had been in that functional role for many years. And I had wanted to kick myself as I saw others advance before me. But I reminded myself that this was a path I chose and I was learning new skills that would help me reach my eventual goal. You see, I wanted to be a general manager. I needed to obtain a broader set of skills. So, I moved around the company getting sales, product development, strategy skills, and the softer skills of listening, getting things done through influence, without direct authority, and building relationships. What I discovered is that I may not know the specific technical aspects of a new role, but I bring a very different perspective that opens up new questions, new ideas for doing the same thing. When I returned from U.S. Trust in NY and applied for a job again at Schwab, I interviewed for head of product development for the mutual fund business. As I mentioned earlier, I told the executive in charge that I met two of his four requirements. I did not know the mutual fund business, I was not a classically trained product development person, but I knew everyone at Schwab and therefore, knew how to get things done. He liked that and hired me, even though my predecessor was someone who knew everything about mutual funds, she did not have the other skills. With my team, we were able to grow the assets from $137 B to $210 billion by the time I retired four years later.

6. Be generous.

This is another aspect of an earlier point about "Accomplishing a lot if you don't care who gets credit". As you network and build relationships in your organization, ask your peers and your team, "How can I help you succeed? And then listen and act. Be the person who brings others together and makes the connections—you connect people and ideas. You get power by giving it away. This generosity of connection should apply not only to work but to your community. Volunteer, mentor others—believe me, you will get more back and it will enrich your spirit. When the kids were young, I coached girls' volleyball and the boys were the ball chasers and as they got older, they helped me coach. They learned to give back to their community and spent time with me from a different perspective than just "mom". When I returned from NY, I became involved with a non-profit, Women's Initiative, which is a one-stop shop to help lower income women with training, financing, and the support needed to start their own business and become economically independent. I served as Chair of the board for three years. The wonderful women I have met through that work has opened new doors for me. When I retired from Schwab, my network of colleagues and friends opened their own networks to me so that I had many options to choose from as I thought about my next adventure.

7. Build relationships.

Some may view this as networking, but if you look at relationships, it means getting to know the other person, what they like and do not like, what success means to them, and then understanding how you can help them achieve success. Through relationships you build trust and respect. Through trust, you get help, introductions, and opportunities.

8. Make time for radiant energy.

As women, we try to take on everything. Well, we are the ones who give birth to children, and for many, we take care of the home, work full-time, try to fit in an exercise class, try to make time for friends and family. Often, as a result of all this multi-tasking, we feel guilty. We have a tendency to separate our bodies from our heads and keep on going, refusing to say no. Finally, our bodies break down and we end up in bed with the worst flu going around. My point is, take care of yourself. Take time for that exercise class, with no guilt. If you do not take care of yourself, who will? We will live until we are 90, or certainly outlive the men so don't be in a rush to do it all. You can have it all, just not all at the same time!

9. Women are natural healers.

By this I mean that we have the capacity to design workplaces that are healthy and profitable. Respect the balance you and your employees need—we are in for the long-term, not the short term. We can build organizations where people respect each other, support each other for the common goal, have a healthy dialogue about business issues, have fun, and be profitable. Finally, have a sense of humor and don't take yourself too seriously.

The best way to tell if a workplace has a good leader is if you find a place where people come to work enthusiastically, they are excited to come to work, and they would rather work there than anywhere else. This type of workplaces does exist and more importantly, that is the kind of place you can create.

❈

JOSEPHINE ROMERO

CEO, Magpie.IM
FWN100™ Global 2013

15 to 51

This is a life story about 15 going on 51. At 15, I was in the midst of forming my views and shaping the values that define my kind of leadership and the way I walk the talk. I cannot change the past but I have always drawn upon my childhood memories as a guide for becoming the person I am today. In fact, I did put pen on paper as a teenager and wrote my 20-year life plan, a plan which I now realize falls short of my ambition of living life to the fullest since my life plan stopped at age 40! Nevertheless, this early plan guided the choices I have made up to this day.

As for 51, I am still some years shy of this age albeit already older and wiser, I now have made a plan as well for the coming decades because life, as I have seen it so far, is worth celebrating and the lessons are definitely worth sharing.

And so it goes...

BEGINNINGS

I was one of many Filipinos who grew up with a challenging family life. Not a unique situation, really, in a culture where soap operas take up more than half of all local TV programs despite the bitter truth that most of us live 'real-life dramas.' It is certainly not what I enjoyed because I have a no-nonsense attitude and prefer things as straightforward as can be.

And so there I was living in my own soap opera, growing up with three siblings in an, often, tense atmosphere but irrepressibly still kid-like and fun loving. We had other stimuli and external relationships to help us transform into well-adjusted personalities. Naturally, like a pot of water on an open stove, there came a time when the pot boiled over and the flame needed to be turned down to simmer. I learned early to take control of things I can indeed control.

It was during those times that I learned to handle housekeeping, budgeting, and other concerns that progressed to more complex issues as time went on. I learned to address matters that went beyond the usual friendship issues and schoolwork of a 12- or 15-year old. I learned to fill in what I deemed as gaps in our daily life.

I believe that my skills, values, drivers, motivations, and experiences since then have been consistent in reinforcing what I am at my core. At my core I am one who wants to do things right, who laughs a lot, who anticipates problems, and who thinks beyond self. Yet, some people might think I developed a sense of negativity: became critical of ideas, and was willing to cut off suggestions that might have worked. I claim my initial social and leadership lessons from my early life of "hard-knocks."

In retrospect, I ask myself if I was being raised to be 51 when I was exposed to all this at age 15. It did feel like I had my life on fast forward knowing that I was mature for my age then and how I always enjoyed interacting with older folks rather than my peers.

Life Lesson 1: Exposure to adult issues early taught me to cope with them. In the process, overcoming them as a child made me quite grounded.

FINDING MENTORS

A few years ago, I was looking at old photos with childhood family friends. We shared many nostalgic laughs but what struck us all was the realization that I was more often in the company of adults than with my contemporaries! We saw my younger self almost always seated with parents and other older folks during parties.

I remember enjoying hours and hours of my maternal grandmother's stories about life during the peace time before World War II and what it was like when the Japanese occupied the Philippines. As we sat by the giant mango tree at the farm in Care, Tarlac, I listened wide-eyed to my dad's dad's hair-raising anecdotes about the *tikbalang* [part horse, part human] and *kapre* [a giant who sits on trees]. I eagerly hung around my mom's dad to hear him crack jokes and play with us. I looked forward to the annual visit of my mom's aunt because she would teach me the traditional way of cooking *Capampangan* [from the province of Pampanga] delicacies like *leche flan*, *bringhe* [paella like dish], and chicken *galantine* [stuffed chicken].

I can recount many stories from my parents' parents, their aunts and uncles, their siblings and cousins, and others we called grandparents, aunts, and uncles even if we only had a smidgeon of blood relation. From spending a lot of time with them, I learned to relate naturally with people like questioning teachers and indulgent playmates. I learned that it was all right to be inquisitive because I knew my questions would be answered. It was all right to be curious because I knew I would be taught what I did not know. And it was all right to laugh and kid around because I knew my antics would be appreciated. I imbibed their values and way of doing, including listening to radio drama and waking up at the crack of dawn.

Apart from my grandparents, my uncles taught me to crave books, tinker with gadgets, and enjoy outings. They were the ones who introduced me to chord books like Moptop and Song Hits, songs of the Beatles and Kenny Rogers, and musicals like Lost Horizon and Pippin. Even before MacGyver became popular, I already knew what "doing a MacGyver" meant because my uncles had all been Boy Scouts. Their role model was their own dad and uncle whom I liked to watch while they tied knots or sharpened the *bolo* [large single-edged knife] for farming or clearing up around the yard. So, of course, I became a girl scout!

Life Lesson 2: All it takes is a mentor to set you off on the right foot. An encouraging mentor to teach you the ropes and to patiently answer a child's questions can instill a life-long love for learning.

HONING MY EMPATHY AND PEOPLE SKILLS

With Scouting, I enjoyed afterschool activities like climbing hills and fences with other girls and boys. All the extra to-dos energized me even more and I was out of the house seven days a week enjoying academic and extra-curricular activities. If I were not at school, I would be at my mom's shop interacting with other furniture sellers and customers, or my dad's craft shop chatting with carpenters and carvers.

As a Girl Scout, I was also introduced to the Scouts' ways such as the need to "do a good deed daily." This later on developed into my belief in living a life beyond myself. I learned from the lowland workers in our furniture factory, the highland tribal artisans who worked with my dad, the farmers and market vendors who visited my grandparents, and the physically challenged but smart kids who were my schoolmates. I learned up close and personal about their cultures and aspirations.

I appreciated the various ways by which my elders related to other town folk from both the lowlands and the highlands. And while attempting to bring my newly learned Scouts' values to life, I learned to empathize.

Did I mention tuning in to radio drama? Listening to radio dramas and singing to music, plus participating in Lola Basyang type of storytelling, must have been instrumental in making me like to listen and "watch" with my ears. To this day, I much prefer "watching" home movies by listening to the dialogue and imagining most of what is happening on screen. I suppose an offshoot of sharpening my sense of imagery is that I also learned to take an instant snapshot in my mind of a room or situation. This increased sensitivity to my surroundings and the people around me has been a blessing in many situations. It taught me to compartmentalize and to multi-task while using various senses at once.

Life Lesson 3: Empathy and better-honed sensory skills developed my capacity to relate to people across different levels of society or from different organizations.

FINDING MYSELF

It was in third year high school that I realized I wanted to study economics. But what to do with it after was not clear to me. All I knew was that it made sense to buy a bigger box of laundry detergent than to purchase small sachets, that industrialization would be a sure thing if the Philippines built a nuclear power plant to run large factories with efficient electricity, and that economics was more common sense than science.

Fast forward to the year I earned my economics degree. I neither joined the country's economic planning agency nor did I join a policy research firm to practice what I learned. Instead, I took a gap year to go to the United States at my mother's insistence. I did go back to an economics-related research job after the gap year but that is for another section of this story.

That gap period was liberating! The domestic tension in the home front had gotten worse over the years and had become almost unbearable. So moving to the city that never sleeps, and to a totally different career field working with fashion fabrics, was a refreshing change. I always considered the stint in New York as the finishing school that sealed my youthful character building process.

In New York, I learned many technical, management, and social skills. Among these are knowing how complex and interconnected the U.S. and European fashion fabric industries were how the Brooklyn Navy Yard and bonded warehousing worked; how Jews controlled the garment industry, shipping, entertainment, and many other industries in New York; how to use computer billing and accounting software; how to speculate in real estate and other non-cash investments; how rent control made it such a challenge for building management; how small doctors' clinics worked; and how the U.S. hospital system and medical records were manned mostly by Filipinos. I could go on and on. It was an amazing learning period and I was like a sponge that just kept absorbing and absorbing.

I remember crying in my first two weeks at work because my ill-mannered boss was rude and coarse. By the time I left the company, however, he was the one almost crying at the idea of the disruption my leaving would do to a well-run system that freed him up from operational concerns and allowed him to divert his energies to other more lucrative and enjoyable endeavors. We have remained friends over the years and continue to communicate.

Another thing that stayed with me from that period in the United States was the encounter with a cacophony of cultures and characters that somehow co-existed in organized chaos. While the financial chasm between the high net worth individuals and the regular workers was palpable, there was no visible difference in that they rode the same public transport system, shopped in their neighborhood delis, borrowed books from their community libraries, and played at their local ball parks. It was also during that time that I first encountered overseas Filipinos and how they worked hard to earn money for their families back home. All this was an eye-opener for me. Aha, I thought, the classic theorists were right! There was hope for the Philippines to eliminate class bias and mature into an egalitarian society after all.

Life Lesson 4: Mind the Gap! Time off can be very enlightening and liberating.

Saying Goodbye

I cut short my sojourn to New York when I learned of my dad's fatal disease. He had months to live and I took this as my chance to heal wounds. As a child, I enjoyed my dad's sense of humor and witticisms. I greatly admired his business acumen and street-smart solutions to life issues that stumped my genius uncles, his brothers. I looked forward to traveling with him when he went antiquing and mingled with locals in the Mountain Province and northern Luzon, or interacted with near and distant relatives. Regrettably, our family issues breached the close relationship we had and I missed out on getting to really know him and his thought process.

On several occasion over the years, I would meet friends and family who would share practical advice from my dad that had guided them towards a life of happiness and prosperity. It warmed my heart to know that he touched their lives so significantly. Nonetheless, it saddened me to realize that his children and grandchildren missed out on getting to know him the way his peers knew him.

I think it is very important to have role models. I have learned from the people I and many in the world admire: U.S. First Lady Eleanor Roosevelt, maverick businessman Richard Branson, lifestyle disruptor Steve Jobs, U.S. Presidential Candidate Hillary Clinton, and President Gloria Macapagal Arroyo. I have also learned from people I respect but have passed on: Apong Saling, my 99-year old paternal grandmother; Lola Sam, my 98-year old maternal grandmother; my colleagues Romy Borillo and Lita Madulid, Ambassador Cesar Bautista, and my dad.

Life Lesson 5: Strive to live a life worth emulating.

SHARING OF MYSELF

When people ask me why I am not married my reply is "I travel light." As to how I live in all other aspects, you read it right. Living with the basics makes it easy to move. It is also a reflection of my belief that we can live with just a few things and if we need anything else we can always get these wherever we are. What I do keep are books, photos, and things to hang on the wall; paintings, posters, plates, stamps, and three dimensional art work that I try to get as memento from each place I visit.

Traveling light makes me focus on the journey, the people, the learning, the fun, and not having to think about the baggage, the extra weight, and so on. Travel light also makes it possible for me to adapt to my new setting with very little adjustment.

Indeed, in keeping to the basics and collecting mostly memories, I get validation from the way the second richest man in the world lives. When asked by David Hanson of The Motley Fool why he still lived in the same house he bought in the 1950s, Warren Buffet replied, "for the $31,500 I paid for our house, my family and I gained 52 years of terrific memories with more to come."

Life Lesson 6: Travel light. Keep to the basics.

DEMONSTRATING BUSINESS ACUMEN

Professionally, I have been working as an entrepreneur, a researcher, an executive, and a public servant for more than 25 years; so far. In many of the roles I have taken, my responsibilities have generally followed the business development track; regardless of whether it was a startup, a corporate client, or the government. My employers and partners managed to harness my strengths and draw out the best of me whenever I was put to the test. I have delivered high quality and timely work, sticking to the job and not minding petty wars, giving more than what was expected, making sure our clients and constituents got the biggest bang for their buck or taxes. As a junior diplomat in New York with limited resources and instruction, I rallied local corporate partners, the Consul General and her team, the Presidential Protocol Ambassador and his team, my senior colleagues, and locally based Filipinos to support me in executing a complex business program during a three-day visit of a high level official. As the head of the office and the lead for program design, the substantive and relational aspects were my primary responsibility. In addition, I needed to oversee the logistics. In the end, with everyone taking their cues from one lead and throwing their weight in collaboration, we were successful in arranging two full-blown conferences, two exclusive luncheon meetings, 15 small-group meetings, and one 350-person sit-down dinner. To me, it was a singularly amazing human experience when everything that could go wrong did but for each failure, someone on the team turned it around.

Many of my career-related life lessons could be identified with either my stints in the diplomatic service and private enterprise. These two worlds are, in many respects, unique. Yet, my experiences and leadership from service in the diplomatic service and private enterprise tend to complement each other.

Being Strategically Focused

To begin with, I seem to have a knack for getting involved in technology start-ups that built some kind of tool or access for many people. In the late 1990s for instance, my college buddies and I setup Pinoymail.com, the biggest Filipino free webmail service at the time. We campaigned for the adoption of its use nationwide and grew our subscriber base to about a million by the time we sold it to an investor. At the same time, with another group of high school and college friends, I led the launch of the most comprehensive online tourism guide and travel magazine, TOURS.PH. It was widely accepted and we had numerous early adopters who advertised and subscribed to it in a big way. The times were not yet right for online payments, and we could not move to the next level of effecting financial transactions on the site. Years later, my partners from Pinoymail.com cracked this dilemma and so today, we are on a crusade to improve the Filipino payment experience through mobile payment solutions provided by our new fintech startup, Magpie.IM.

Expanding my Global Reach and Impact

I was building tools in addition to my entrepreneurial ventures. Returning from New York after my gap period, I helped the Women's Business Council of the Philippines articulate the policy agenda that would allow Filipino businesswomen to borrow capital from Philippine financial institutions in their own right and not as chattels of their husbands or wards of their fathers. At the Human Development Network, I was part of the team that facilitated the research and publication of the "1997 Philippine Human Development Report: Changing Status of Women." This report argued "initial steps must be undertaken to develop a system of gender-disaggregated data gathering, collection, processing and dissemination at the agency/firm, local and national levels to improve awareness and understanding of gender issues." Years before I ever became a public servant, I was already conscripted to build the country's first information technology industry promotion website to promote the country as a business process outsourcing destination at the request of a former associate from the University of the Philippines.

While working for the Philippine Department of Trade and Industry (DTI), I developed the ability to find the right intervention to address an issue with a creative, high quality, cost-effective solution that is also simple and timely. Interestingly, my stint at the DTI is the longest position I have held because the tasks there were designed as a series of projects. Going in, I knew furniture manufacturing and export, technology education and IT services. While at DTI, I learned about new industries, trade negotiations, and diplomacy.

I joined the Foreign Service bureau of DTI after over a decade of building experience in private enterprise and civil society. My main responsibility there was to act as government sales person by encouraging companies from the country I was then assigned to invest in the Philippines and to buy goods and services from Filipino exporters. In between overseas posts, I was given local assignments, including managing the office of the Trade Secretary and the Foreign Service bureau itself. I also took on local projects focused on capacity building for micro and small enterprise development.

At DTI, one of my major contributions was to bring industries and international trade negotiations to the next level. As an entry-level foreign trade service officer, I helped determine the key design and cost element for a winning proposal to a foreign government to fund a capacity building program for 400 government, industry, and civil society stakeholders on issues related to the World Trade Organization concerns. I was involved in multi-sectoral and interagency advocacies to deepen substance and widen reach in specific industries. Some examples: campaigning for public-private partnership to upskill Philippine engineers in semiconductors manufacturing in microelectronics integrated chip design; mobilizing Filipino-Americans and lobbying a foreign legislative body for favorable trade terms to save the Philippine garment industry; partnering with New York City industry pillars to establish the Global Sourcing Council and the Philippine Business Process Outsourcing (BPO) Council that would raise the Philippines' stature as a leader in the practice of business process management; and bringing together successful Filipino-American technopreneurs in northern California to share know-how and resources with Philippine stakeholders concerning Silicon Valley-type venture capital investment and requirements to be globally competitive.

I learned a lot from my 10 years at DTI. Stakeholder management became a leadership competency. For someone who was described by a Feng Shui master as an army tank when I was younger, I get a real kick out of people who now say I can be very diplomatic when I so choose.

Most importantly, I found it very rewarding to see small enterprises thrive because of a direct intervention I did or facilitated. I enjoyed participating in industry development and it fed my intellect and interest to be actively involved in developing and adding value to economic development programs.

Results Orientation

In hindsight, what I was able to offer DTI were novel and purpose-specific solutions that often went against the risk averse attitude of government agencies. My entrepreneurial spirit also was a real advantage for the work I did for DTI. I saw the business deal from the point of view of business owners and investors because of my entrepreneurial experiences at Josephine's, the family business. Josephine's that was first a micro producer and trader of Philippine indigenous materials and crafts and later graduated to be a furniture maker and exporter. I was also able to apply my experience to technology start-ups Pinoymail.com and TOURS.PH, and to multinational companies Sun Microsystems Philippines and Deutsche Bank Manila, among others. I quite understood and appreciated the goods and services I needed to promote. At the same time, I was able to accurately assess the buyers' needs or requirements so I did appropriate matches. And knowing about these new industries and business intelligence meant I also knew what the stakeholders' pains were, thus, I was able to recommend practical and effective solutions for their financial gain. That is the entrepreneur and problem solver in me.

Life Lesson 7: We live in a borderless world and regardless of where you have come from, how you have been raised, or what you have achieved; we can all make an impact.

MY LIFE SO FAR

To sum up life lessons from 15 to 51:

1. Exposure to adult issues way too early taught me to cope with these. In the process, overcoming these as a child keep me grounded.

2. All it takes is a mentor to set you off on the right foot. An encouraging mentor to teach you the ropes and to patiently answer a child's questions can instill a life-long love for learning.

3. Empathy and better-honed sensory skills developed my capacity to relate to people across different levels of society or organizations.

4. Mind the Gap! Time off can be very enlightening and liberating.

5. Strive to live a life worth emulating.

6. Travel light. Keep to the basics.

7. We live in a borderless world and regardless from where you have come, how you have been raised, or what you have achieved, we can all make an impact.

At 46, I have five years to go before the next milestone. Yes, I travel light and my boundless energy generates inner rays of light to shine my path. The best is yet to come. When I am 51, I would definitely be celebrating with more passion, risk, and adventure than I did when I was 15!

MYRNA YAO

*President, Richwell Trading Corporation
& Richprime Global Inc.
FWN100™ Global 2015*

Leading One to Many

One. One thousand. One thousand and one.

Numbers. Numbers, the all-important signifier of growth or demise. We count our age in numbers. We tell time in numbers. And in business, numbers can make or break you.

Let's start with the number one. The number one is very significant to me. I started a business with one employee, and in time, with focus, hard word, and sacrifice, one employee grew to more than a thousand.

One thousand and counting.

From small to BIG.

From local to global.

Indeed, it is possible. It can happen.

Just learn and do not stop learning.

To lead most!

Taking Initiative and Capitalizing Opportunities

My childhood dreams led me to where I am today. Looking back at my career path, I realize how much *self-awareness* helped me succeed. I was aware of my strengths and my developmental opportunities and worked hard to improve myself.

Since I was ten, I realized I had a knack for business, and my first venture was buying and selling small items, which I did on my own because I wanted to prove that despite being a girl, I can excel in a world dominated by men. I valued time and opportunity so I removed distractions while in college. While the rest of my classmates were enjoying their summer break, I stayed in school and took summer classes, I focused on my goal to earn a diploma at the shortest possible time and finished my degree in Bachelor of Arts in Business Administration in 3 ½ years.

My college years were not what you could call normal. I stayed away from parties and burrowed myself in books. Realizing that I may be deficient in social skills, I read books on etiquette, ballet tips, and proper posture. I improved myself by reading books in psychology, management, leadership, and biographies of successful people. A new phase in my life came when I met my husband in an August moon cake party. He was like a father figure to me. My father preferred a male child so when I was growing up I did not get that much attention from him. I thought that the decision to marry would somehow compensate for that missing fatherly love.

I pursued an MBA degree right after college, while married and raising children at the same time.

The tough times pushed me to be more driven and helped me realize my vision of building and leading a global business. When most of my classmates were enjoying summer vacation, I was learning my parent's business. While going to school away from my parents at a young age, I learned to make both ends meet with a meagre school allowance I shared with my sister. As a working student at the age of 18, I had to juggle my time between school and work. I will always remember how I mastered the art of standing in a bus while balancing and preventing any damage to the merchandise I had to deliver. The most important lesson I learned from these hard times is to dream and to not let the dream slip away no matter how difficult the situation. I knew what I wanted and poured all my energies into meeting that goal. Schuller might as well have written about me in *Tough Times Never Last, But Tough People Do* (1984). Being a woman, and a mother, I knew that I had to carve my own path. I decided not to leave my destiny in someone else's hands. I took charge of my path and seized every opportunity that came my way.

My buy-and-sell venture was going to be my entry into the business world. A small expansion was warranted. I hired an assistant, and my lowly business now grew a hundred fold. We were now a staff of two.

With one staff assisting me, I did all sorts of tasks, from the most mundane to the most critical. I answered phone calls while taking orders from the other line. I did not mind getting my hands and my face smeared with photocopier ink.

I personally attended to the complaints of our clients. I drafted and finalized letters convincing our prospective customers to try our products. I learned how to drive. There were numerous times when I had to deliver our merchandise to meet our commitments. My buy-and-sell venture expanded my network and this expansion provided new opportunities. My hard work paid off when I had the opportunity to become the distributor of Goodyear tires in Quezon City.

The tire industry was new to me, and I knew that I had a steep learning curve, but the will to learn was stronger than any doubts I had. I quickly mastered the technical knowledge necessary to do the job. My ardent desire to study the ins and outs of the trade bore fruit. Despite the recession at that time within two short years, our branch became Goodyear's biggest local distributor in the Philippines. Clearly, being a quick learner contributed to early successes.

With the growth of the Goodyear business, I needed to expand the office staff. And from two people, my company grew to 30.

Stocktaking: From Tires to Toys

The tire business was a success. We became the biggest distributor of tires in 2 years. I have reached the topmost place of the tire business.

While the tire dealership brought me a step closer to my vision of succeeding and making it big in business, in a world dominated by men, I felt I have to move on.

My affection for kids ignited the idea of focusing on toys. This love for children was developed early. My parents wanted another boy for their next child. Although they loved me, I did not get a lot of attention and nurturing from my parents because I was a girl. Although I understood and took the lack of demonstrable affection from my parents as normal, I grew up wanting to give care and attention to other kids. I wanted every kid to have a happy childhood.

I took a big risk when I decided to enter the toy business. In the 1980's, toys were only sold during the Christmas Holiday season.

Imported toys had been banned during the martial law years as all imported goods were very limited and strictly monitored. Stores had a toy section, but it was only a small part of the overall footprint and was only available during Christmas. Getting approval to import toys and finding the right store to sell the merchandise was one of the challenges I had to overcome.

At that time, they were considered a luxury item, like perfume, brands were limited, and duties was 50%.

As I researched, I found most of the stores directly imported their stock through the gray market. One thing stuck out. There were no toy distributors.

When the Marcos government finally allowed the import of toys, the taxes and fees were so high that one had to be a risk-takers to plunge into the business. And risk-taker I was.

I had to find a way to enter the toy business. I searched for a toy company with a manufacturing plant in the Philippines. I discovered that Mattel had a factory in the country, but the company had no plans to partner with a local distributor. Faced with this challenge, I knew I had to be resourceful if I wanted Mattel's business.

I planned to approach Mattel Toys, the makers of the world-famous Barbie dolls. But first, I used the information gathered from my research and prepared a proposal.

I competed with two major stores vying to get the contract and relationship with Mattel. Undaunted by my competitors, I set out to prepare a proposal that would eclipse theirs.

Preparation is essential, to any endeavor. My two competitors, major stores, had several outlets, which they intended to use for distribution. I offered something different. I was not tied to a base or a location, having no brick and mortar structures. I proposed to supply the brand at various stores around the country, thus providing for a wider distribution net. I turned the lack of not having my own stores into an advantage and impressed on Mattel that having no store of my own, would allow me to distribute to all stores. I impressed Mattel by personally attending the meetings while my competitors sent their managers. I could commit and close the deal right then and there as the owner of the company.

Who would think that a small business owner could win over big business. I proved that resourcefulness and dedication are paramount. I closed the deal. My company, Richwell Trading was awarded the exclusive distributorship of Mattel Toys in the Philippines in 1982.

THE CHALLENGE OF CHANGE

Closing the deal meant that changes were ahead, and I needed to find a way to successfully manage what was coming.

The shift from the tire business to toy business was a change that I compared to giving birth to a baby and enduring the child-birth pain.

The first difficulty I encountered was reversing the mindset that toys are only bought during the Christmas season. I knew that there had to be a way to sustain the demand for the Barbie brand year-round.

Stores pulled out the toys during the opening of the school year, that was in January at that time, as demand went down. The family budget often went to school needs like tuition fee, books, uniforms, and daily expenses. So I introduced special discounts for Barbie during school opening. The idea worked as our inventory showed increased sales on what used to be a slack season.

But I knew that the brand must be mainstreamed throughout the year. My next move was to introduce trade shows to showcase the toys. Changes in the market slowly began to develop. I tried working directly with retailers, but they would order only a few pieces every day. As an enticement to order more, I offered extra discounts to those who would place orders based on projected sales. This solved the pattern of retailers ordering on a daily basis.

I pushed harder and talked to the management of one of the largest chain stores in the Philippines. My goal was to convince them to have a dedicated Barbie corner in each branch. I explained that aside from dolls, this corner could offer Barbie shoes, bags, shirts, and other items that would definitely attract little girls. ShoeMart (SM) liked the idea and established their first Barbie Corner in 1989.

This was a milestone for Richwell Trading because it made the Philippines introduce the first Barbie store in the world.

It may appear that all went as planned, but this was not the case. I cannot forget the first day after I closed the deal with Mattel. Not one store wanted to buy the dolls. Christmas, they said, was the only time to sell toys. More so, they were intimidated by the high price.

I was worried and could not say a word when my salespersons came back empty-handed. But I had to show them that I can overcome setbacks. This was the first test of leadership.

I spent at least 2 days training and mentoring my staff in how to sell the Barbie Dolls. I would go on field visits with them to demonstrate how to convince storeowners. The next few days, my staff received orders for two or three pieces. Better than none I thought, and, I continued introducing the brand and the concept to the store owners until they were convinced.

PERFORMING UNDER PRESSURE

We all know that in business, it is not always a bed of roses, so to speak. *Building and maintaining relationships and managing conflict* is part of developing one's competency as a leader.

More than anything else, what tested my leadership skills of building and repairing relationships was the country's instability in the 1980s.

I was pregnant when I received a death and bomb threat that I knew was part of the national problem related to threats against businesses. The left-leaning unions had become aggressive in their attacks on businesses.

Our company was not spared. We were threatened and our employees were infiltrated by individuals trying to get our employees to join their cause. We were accused of unfair labor practices but I was able to prove them wrong.

Some of their demands were reasonable, and I agreed to them. An election was held on which union would represent the employees and the union that was more sympathetic to the management won. It was time for our company to have and to implement changes in labor management.

The episode with the union was a blessing in disguise. It showed we had gaps in our company's policies, rules, and regulations related to employee benefits that we promptly tried to address.

Up Next

Richwell Trading's impressive performance as the exclusive distributor for Mattel paved the way for acquiring distribution rights for other popular toy brands. The expansion of the toy distribution business would test my competency in *solving problems and making decisions.*

It well known that fads and kid's preferences of toys change. This is the nature of business. This is inevitable.

I had to decide to drop several brands after their popularity waned. The toy industry is volatile. There will always be new toys to edge out what used to be popular. I accepted the reality of how fast the toy industry changes.

In spite of pulling some brands, I continued to sell toys because I believed kids love playing with toys. Over the years, many toy brands entered the market. The best solution to ensure the company's continued success was to make sure that the products we offered were unique when compared to those of our competitors.

I also had to deal with the problem of copyright infringement. Imitators selling cheaper versions of our products increased. But I believed that over time consumers are wise enough to realize the danger of giving unsafe toys to their children.

I am actively involved in education campaigns about health issues related to cheap toys. My rallying cry was "patronizing unbranded and imitation toys is compromising children's health."

With over 40 toy brands now marketed by Richwell Trading, my vision of strengthening and expanding the company had come true.

I started training my daughters while they were still young, so when the right time came, they would be prepared to take over the company. I fused my career and family life by getting my four daughters involved in the business. My eldest daughter was my secretary, I started training her when she was eight years old, during the summer, she did office work. Other times, she would be at the warehouse, cleaning and tagging items.

After graduation from college, they worked for other companies to gain broader management experience before joining our company. Their contributions helped tremendously in the growth of our company as we brought the business from medium to a large corporation.

Giving Back: Leading the GREAT Women Project

One idea concerning economically empowering women has provided benefits to one thousand and more women. The idea of economically empowering women was inspired by my childhood experience.

I remember my mother running a small grocery while trading copra. The work of these women was very hard. Most of these women borrowed money from my mother to survive and I witnessed how they were economically disadvantaged.

I longed to free those women from the burden of poverty. I dreamt of being so rich I could help the women and children. I vowed to do this without having been encouraged to do so by anyone, not even my parents. This vow became a vision.

As Chair of the Philippine Commission on Women or PCW in 2004, I was responsible for improving the life of disenfranchised women through women's economic empowerment. I embraced the task, as it aligned with my vision.

My mission was to find a new concept to help empower women. We called the activity the "Gender-Responsive Economic Actions for the Transformation of Women Project" or the "GREAT Women Project." My vision finally had an identity.

The GREAT Women Project's goal was to transform the small or micro women's businesses into successful businesses by providing them with economic opportunities. The GREAT Women's Project was my opportunity to give back to women. These women reminded me of the women I wanted to help as a child.

I recall presiding over meetings, presenting reports to sponsors, and being deluged with questions. I am used to addressing questions, as board meetings in my private company are often an exercise in reasoning. I realized this project was no different as I took on the role of manager of a government project.

I will not forget the time, when I was presenting a report documented with graphics of forecasted project results, I was challenged by a comment that the goal we identified for the GREAT Women Project was too broad.

It is a common business principle to start with the product and to use market segmentation to target consumers. The usual strategy of market segmentation was difficult to apply to the goal of focusing the aim of the project. I settled on a strategy of clustering key activities and identifying those who were most capable of converting these activities into concrete "products" or "results" in government jargon.

I was able to apply my experience in business to successfully interact with various government and non-government organizations, our partners for implementing the GREAT Women Project.

The first partner I worked with was the National Council of Women in the Philippines (NCWP). The next opportunity came when I helped establish the Local Councils of Women. The Council is a non-government entity comprised of women's organizations existing in a locality and recognized by the local government. The Local Councils of Women represent the partnership between the women and the government in the local areas.

I increasingly felt the need to expand the reach of the women's grassroots organizations. I envisioned and founded the Philippine Federation of Local Councils of Women (PFLCW). The Federation is a national coordinating body of the local councils of women. Realizing the need to consolidate attempts to empower women for economic development, the PFLCW served as the link between the government, the private sector, and the women NGO in the community.

It was a challenge and a rigorous process to choose the project's partners that did not come easy. The selection process raised many questions. It was similar to choosing from the numerous toy designs. The selection criteria helped us reach an agreement as standards were established.

LESSONS LEARNED: PUBLIC PRIVATE PARTNERSHIPS

There is no absolutely smooth project, and I relish the moments of adjusting to situations as I managed projects. Just like adapting the fast-paced business environment with its quick transactions, to a bureaucratic setting where agonizingly long wait times are the norm. Of course, there were reasons for delays, so I tried to prioritize what adjustments needed to be done.

The on time delivery of reports, data, or projects is a strict standard in business. But I had to deal with government partners who were often late with their submission or completion of projects, factors that negatively affected the project timeline. Each delayed submission tended to push the project completion date further out.

The worst enemy of a business is the late delivery of a product or good. When a customer's expectation is not met, it leads to dissatisfaction and eventually a loss of trust. This was one of my most challenging adjustments. I managed by holding regular meetings with our partners and with the reminder that responsibility and accountability are inseparable if acceptable results were to be efficiently delivered.

The more complicated adjustment concerned fund management. One unacceptable consequence of late delivery could be unspent funds, and the overall project could be at stake. The responsibility fell on my shoulders to get things done. It felt like I was back to the days when we were struggling to market our toys and our sales inventory revealed unmoved items. As a solution, we channeled unspent funds to other collaborators of the GREAT Women Project, and this proved to be successful.

I worried about the late release of funds from the government. The bureaucratic processes that each agency had are a way of life, and one I had to deal with. I signed letters requesting the speedy release of funds that went through many channels. I sought an audience with agency officials and leaned on friends for counsel on how to legally expedite the process, but more often than not, waiting was always part of the process which to me was torture. I ceased asking how and why such situations happened. It was devastating to the process and the timeline, but it did not ruin me. Part of adjusting is learning to push hard until we are weary but not defeated. To adjust is to proclaim that you are not giving up but accepting the reality that you have to detour and try a new route.

Protecting the integrity of our institution while maintaining the partnerships that we built and the respect of the women who had started benefiting from the project was not an easy task. Always, I went back to the memorandum of agreement or the terms of reference, which made me sometimes reconsider my decisions but the provisions in the signed documents kept me firm. Our actions and decisions were guided by the rules. We kept our integrity, without sacrificing our relationship with our partners and our beneficiaries.

Soliciting support of government officials posed a different challenge. The heads of some government agencies were not keen on forging a partnership with us. They argued that the Philippines was already enjoying a relatively better status compared to those in other countries. Despite the fact that a grant was offered to them, the idea of having an additional source of funding for the agency did not seem all that appealing. The series of protracted negotiations threatened the project timetable but in the end, we prevailed, after many meetings and explanations.

Success Through Crab Mentality:
The Case of Aling Baby

A plain housewife working hard to make ends meet to survive, Teodora Aquino, popularly known as "Aling Baby," succeeded in sending all her kids to school and is now busy with leading fellow women entrepreneurs in managing their enterprises. According to her, all these were made possible by her faith in God, the assistance of the GREAT Women Project, and their crab mentality.

Their notion of crab mentality is a departure from the common Filipino attitude of hindering one's success. Aling Baby and the rest of the Cagbunga Crab Paste Producers' Association in Gainza (CCPAG) transformed the meaning of crab mentality and attached to it a positive image of continuous development of their crab paste enterprise.

The GREAT Women project assisted Aling Baby and the association in procuring a shared service facility to speed up the processing of their crab paste and ensure product quality. Through the project, the association's product passed the standards of the Food and Drug Administration. This allowed them to sell their produce outside the province of Albay. With the license from the FDA, more and more clients were placing orders, propelling Aling Baby and her cohorts to resounding success.

Competencies for Leading in the Private Sector

The accumulated experience from three complementary environments; the private/business, government, and non-government sectors built and strengthened my competencies as a leader. These are the very same competencies I try to instill in my daughters and my staff at Richwell. I believe these competencies are helpful for leading in the government and non-government sectors.

1. Forging Synergy

People are at the core of a company and thus we should encourage and practice collaboration because our goal is to build a team. I make sure that our Human Resource Development unit conducts activities, which allow staff to feel that our company is their second home.

Dynamism is sustained among the team by maintaining transparency. The status of our company is open to our people. Whether the news is positive or negative, I always inform them on how our company is doing.

2. Communicating Effectively

Open communication is the bridge that allows different personalities within our team to cultivate synergy. I call emergency meetings; in and outside of the office, during and outside of office hours, on work days and outside of work days when I sense that exchanges among staff have begun to deteriorate. During those dialogues, I am extra cautious, as I do not want to be accused of taking sides. Success is also fueled by effective communication.

3. Flexibility

The many instances of adjusting to changes had taught me the advantages of being flexible. I became a keen observer and learned the different working styles of my staff. By recognizing their differences, learned to adapt work and coaching techniques needed to drive them to be achievers. In business, we not only flex our muscles. We flex our minds and hearts to achieve excellent results.

4. Getting Information

I have realized that taking the small details for granted can cause big problems later on. I always assume that I am not given the whole picture or the complete situation all the times. When I ask questions, I ask it in a manner that is not obnoxious so as not to intimidate my staff. Asking questions in a subtle way to extract the information that I want is an art I acquired.

5. Listening

Conflicts will arise in any endeavor. The good news is, with every conflict, there is an answer or solution. It is my job as a leader to get into the heart of the conflict. My ears are my instruments for looking for solutions to these conflicts. I listen and avoid being confrontational. Lend an ear as the saying goes or otherwise the tendency of staff is to withdraw when summoned.

6. Decisiveness

While I try to be flexible and accommodating as a leader, I impress on my people that I manage the team, and I exude the confidence that I am in control whatever the situation is. I want results to happen, and trust in oneself has a lot to do with being results-oriented. My personal goal is to deliver results. But my team needs to embrace this goal, too. My team has committed to the objectives we have outlined as a family of resourceful individuals. I have built cohesive teams under my leadership by making my staff understand that without commitment and loyalty, the vision we created for the company will never be realized.

7. Developing and Empowering

As CEO, I do not have difficulty identifying who among our applicants and recruits have potential. I am convinced that everyone has a gift, and each one has the potential to succeed. It only takes the right opportunity to unfold for the person to show their strengths. Often, these possibilities are discovered when training sessions are conducted. But discovering possibilities require matching, too. What do I mean by this? One cannot be a good accountant if she does not possess the talent to be one. Training will be a waste of time, money, and effort if the staff member does not show an aptitude for analysis and numbers. I regularly conduct a skills assessment of my staff. Who is good in accounting? In marketing? In communication? Excellence in one's chosen field or specialization will uncover one's passion and interest.

I only ask a simple question to do a quick inventory of skills or competency: who can do what exceptionally? Once the inventory is done, each one is assigned a particular task, role, or responsibility.

8. Seek Opportunities to Learn

Starting a business calls for building knowledge and capability. Start by knowing the product, the market forces, the appropriate location, and the right people who can help in getting the business off the ground. Increasing knowledge about business, production, leadership, creativity, and positive thinking is equally helpful.

I read books, get updated on current events, and more importantly, I share my knowledge with my staff. I sought the help and counsel of people and institutions that have the expertise related to my business when I was a budding businesswoman.

9. Change Management

Life is full of change, and change happens in the business environment very quickly. Many times, changes are beyond our control. If there is one thing that I do is to shield my company from being stagnant. Stagnation is an indicator of instability. Responding to changes molded me to be self-reliant because I cannot leave things up to chance.

Most modifications occur in the demand and supply chain, pricing, marketing, business environment, customers, technology, suppliers, systems and procedures, competition, and government policies. Do not brush aside these changes because once you do, you stop being dynamic. My company grew because we faced the changes head on, and adapted as needed.

10. Knowledge of Job, Business

Developing a business plan that analyzes competition, customer satisfaction, employee management, and marketing adjustments were a challenge for my company but required to stay stable. I faced such challenge through self-reliance and having the determination to move forward and address any issues. The self-confidence, abilities, and experiences I built was my ammunition to face any changes. I can say that starting a business and making it stable takes time, and from my experience, it took one to two years before our business was stable.

11. Financial Management

My goal was to realize a steady profit, as I did not want to rely on outside funding resources for my company.

An unstable business is often associated with insufficient fund sources other than the company's profits. To finance our business, my target was to maintain a consistent increase in profit. I wanted to establish staying power in the market for our business to be sustainable. See Table 1 for tips on attaining financial sustainability and Table 2 for improving business knowledge competency.

12. Perspective Taking

Where is a determined, confident, self-reliant leader headed? No other course but to burst into bloom. And flourish. Believe me, these ingredient is a must to succeed.

Because I have been there; I have experienced it. And I will continue to be a business leader. When a company branches out, when business processes have been streamlined, when steady source of funds to expand production is established, when the demand for your product requires an increase in your work force and infrastructure, when a sizeable percentage of your projected customers has been captured, and when the thought of your competitors no longer strikes fear,

Table 1. Tips on how to attain financial sustainability.

- Go e-Commerce. Technology is powerful so take advantage of it. Make your enterprise visible through the Internet. Do not let the four walls of your small store or area confine your business. This limits your reach to potential clients. Let social media and the internet do the work for you. The probability of your product fetching global clients is within your reach, what with new gadgets and technology waiting to be used and applied.

- Register your products. Research the appropriate agency that would register your product to reduce, if not eliminate, the problem of infringement. Registered products, are more often than not infringed upon, and convey the message that these are quality products. Clients are always conscious about the safety and quality of the products they buy.

- Establish contact with entities that are potential users of your products to expand your market opportunities.

- Keep an eye on your obligations and pay them on time. Comply with government regulations and pay taxes and fees that you are required to pay.

- Innovate. I remember the shoes that I designed that other countries did not have. There are going to be hits and misses, but sooner or later you will discover the "innovative" product that will capture your clients.

- Polish your marketing strategy. Do not be content with your existing market list. Make that list longer. Make it grow. Be aware of the supply and demand and be nimble to move your products to those needing more supply. Create a niche market.

Source: Yao (2015). *The Gift Of A Dream – The GREAT Women Project*

Table 2. Tips to improve your business knowledge competency

- Know your business well. Limited knowledge on your venture can cause problems.

- Create robust marketing strategies. Competition is fierce and can ruin your market so continuously think of product innovation and promotion. Take them as a challenge.

- Carefully forecast your profit and expenses. Your cash flow should be sufficient to keep your business running.

- Devise an accounting system that gives you immediate information on income, profits, and losses. Such system will aid in monitoring how your business is doing.

- Maintain an operating budget that can be supported by sales.

Source: Yao (2015). *The Gift Of A Dream – The GREAT Women Project*

then you know you have grown and expanded your business.

Always remember to share lessons with other women, like I did. There is nothing more satisfying than seeing other women develop and succeed because of you.

13. Global Awareness

Make projections. Dream and visualize.

Engaging in business eventually means going global because there is no other route of expansion but to penetrate the market outside our regular clients. There is nothing wrong with being ambitious, determined, and persistent as these are essential characteristics of one desiring to succeed globally.

As I confessed, I started with selling small items, but I dreamed my business would go global. It happened because I thought BIG from the very start.

Going global is a difficult ambition, but this I have to say, "Think BIG... Start small..."

I started with two basic tasks; listing down what I would like to happen in my future and listing down what I am good at doing.

I knew what I wanted; for every child to have a happy childhood because mine, as I admitted was challenging. I wanted each child to own a toy; toys would always be part of unforgettable childhood memories.

I knew my strength and creativity. I used these talents not only in designing but also in running my businesses, leading my NGOs, and marketing my brand.

Unlike when I started, going global nowadays is easier. With the expansion of technology, women entrepreneurs are now able to conduct business online through e-commerce. Technical and financial assistance are likewise easier to access.

14. Leading Change

Social media has largely influenced businesses, large and small, to explore innovative opportunities to expand advertising as well as selling products and services online. I have maximized technology to put my company on the global map.

Social media has also allowed me to read complaints about products and all other mistakes that can ruin one's business. Negative comments and experiences happen and are reported on different social media channels. Sometimes, the comments can make or break a product, but tapping into social media could also erase these negative impressions. The same social media can instantly address the bad comments and regain people's trust in the company. If you are not using social media, you deprive your company of monitoring criticisms, acceptance, or rejection of of your products and services.

I spend time reading blog posts about our company products. With minimum cost, I get free reviews and announcements of what my company offers. What I find inspiring with technology is it provides a direct channel of communication with my customers. By interacting with them, they receive attention and know that their comments are being read by someone who appreciates their input. My customer feels that they are important and appreciated. Compared with newspaper advertisement where feedback is delayed; the Internet and the social media provide instant gratification, with only time and a few sleepless nights as investments.

Digital technology was a big unknown to me, but I am patiently learning because it is the name of the game today and tomorrow. In a digital world, I foresee every woman who is engaged in business owning a mobile device. Information is at her fingertips as she downloads applications that provide updates on industry developments. No small business owner will refuse the benefit of technology once they are trained and mentored on electronic mail marketing.

I have contemplated on teaching the skills in designing advertisements for products and services. I hope to be part of an online consulting firm and mentor women on all aspects of establishing a business, operations, and sustainability.

The objective of this intervention is for them to use technology as a door to win customers or clients and for them to be regularly updated on whether they provide excellent or poor products or services.

Leadership
for
Sustainability

EMMA MARCHA IMPERIAL

President, Imperial Homes Corporation
FWN100™ Global 2015

Leading for Sustainable Solar Powered Housing Community

After four years of promoting Solar Power for Low Cost housing through the company I own, Imperial Homes Corporation (IHC), I received wonderful news. I have been shortlisted by Financial Times London for the 2016 Financial Times/IFC Transformational Business Award in the Achievement of Low Carbon Urban Transformation category. Considering there were 155 entries from 219 projects in 92 countries worldwide, I was super excited. Here is the key part of the letter:

> *Dear Emma Imperial,*
>
> *I am delighted to inform you that you have been shortlisted for the 2016 FT/IFC Transformational Business Awards in the Achievement in Low-Carbon Urban Transformation category. Congratulations!*
>
> *The winners will then be announced at the FT/ IFC Transformational Business Awards dinner...on June 9.*

The award for Low Carbon Urban Transformation for Mass Housing Communities recognizes innovative projects that address challenges around energy demand and supply, environmental decay, and other climate change-related issues in urban areas in developing economies. The projects must show transformational impact, along with innovation, impact, replicability, financial viability, and sustainability. These are principles that I value and put into practice at IHC. Thus, my super excitement in being shortlisted for the reward.

The activist in me has always wanted housing to be easily accessible to every Filipino. I consider housing a basic human right. Under my leadership, IHC has succeeded as a mass housing developer, initially in Legazpi City. Then, I expanded my vision to the entire Philippines where there are increasing numbers of mass housing communities that are fully powered by solar energy. In 2015, after 30 years of being in the housing industry, IHC launched the first 24-hour solar powered system for 1,000 low cost homes in Sto. Tomas, Batangas. Now my vision goes beyond that of my own company to the bigger goal of making the Philippines the Solar Capital of Asia.

In this chapter, I reflect on the leadership context and the leadership actions that made the award possible. In terms of context, the environment under which Imperial Homes Corp operates includes external conditions, such as ecological, political, community which are beyond my immediate influence and internal conditions, as well as the housing industry sector and organizational reach which I can influence and change. The leadership actions I took included those that are internal to IHC, like strategic direction, and external to the company, like partnerships. I will also highlight the leadership competencies that have made me an effective leader in addressing sustainability challenges in the housing sector.

TRANSFORMING THE HOUSING INDUSTRY LEADERSHIP CONTEXT

Many in the Philippine housing industry believe that every Filipino family has the right to live with dignity in the comfort of their own home regardless of economic status. According to the website of the Philippine housing industry, the aim is to eliminate the housing backlog by the year 2030. Based on a higher demand in the market than the supply, the Philippine housing backlog currently stands at 5.5 million. Part of the backlog is to meet the demand for affordable mass housing market. Towards this objective, IHC has built more than 16,000 housing units mainly in Luzon.

The Philippine Renewable Energy Act of 2008 mandated that the government develop the country's renewable energy resources, including solar to promote a shift to more sustainable, reliable and affordable energy. According to the National Renewable Energy Laboratory, the Philippines' average solar radiation ranges from 128-203 watts per square meter, or an average of 161.7 watts per square meter, based on sunlight duration. The German aid agency, Deutsche Gesellschaft für Internationale Zusammenarbeit (GIZ) GmbH in cooperation with

Renewable Energy Developers Center (REDC) and World Wildlife Foundation (WWF) Philippines wrote the policy brief "It's More Sun in the Philippines." (2012) arguing for greater use of the sun as a free source of energy. IHC has led the way with its solar powered mass housing concept and delivery to homeowners.

Homeowners and small entrepreneurs can take out loans from the Home Development Mutual Fund (HDMF), more popularly known as the Pag-Ibig Fund, and other financial institutions to purchase solar systems. Through its performance and advocacy, IHC has paved the way for financial institutions to include solar systems in their housing loans.

IHC—Leading in Solar Powered Mass Housing

"SOLAR POWERED MASS HOUSING COMMUNITIES" is the new brand of IHC. The company is engaged in the development of modern villages, middle income as well as low cost housing projects. Properties for development are located in Batangas, Cavite, Nueva Ecija, Quezon, Sorsogon, Albay, and Laguna. Our investment properties and other expansion areas within the existing subdivision are being redeveloped into "Solar Powered Mass Housing Communities." Every home in our green community include the advantages of an eco-friendly lifestyle: (a) solar solutions with Lithium Batteries that save on electricity cost, (b) homes designed to conserve water and to allow for the air to circulate for cool comfortable living, (c) communities with wide open spaces for play and recreation, and (d) use of raw materials with lower embodied energy (see http://imperialhomescorp.com/).

The program provides the low and middle income segment of the community with convenient access to a more affordable green home. The green home does not just provide shelter to homebuyers but it also improves the family income through savings on electricity; savings that can be spent on more important aspects of living like education and health. Thus, improving over-all the quality of life and increasing the family's chances of success.

With the turnover of 500 solar houses to actual homebuyers, we have proven that our Solar Powered Mass Housing Communities can succeed. From a vision to create increased opportunities for a higher quality of life, we now have satisfied homeowners who are living in our built community. This is only the beginning. As we continue to grow aggressively as a company, we are sharing our concept with various stakeholders in our industry, both locally and globally. We are developing the need not just for a house but for a house that saves. We are influencing the real estate industry to be involved in mitigating climate change. We are conducting several awareness campaigns to emphasize that even people who have less; have the power to contribute to the war against climate change and poverty.

LEADERSHIP ACTIONS

Since we articulated our vision for solar powered mass housing, we have made several breakthroughs. For example, affordability of solar solutions has been always an issue. However, our properly designed solution matches the technical, cost, and convenience requirement of the Filipino homebuyers. Financing solar powered homes was another issue. With IHC's advocacy and influence, buyer-friendly finance options are now available. Affordability and financing have made a positive impact on the company's brand and sales. Below I would like to highlight the key leadership actions that have contributed to the success of IHC while helping Filipino families acquire their dream homes with solar solutions. These leadership actions demonstrate my leadership competencies, including alignment of employee rewards to company vision, sustainable product innovation, stakeholder satisfaction, shared commitment, financing options, performance accountability, marketing, international green standards, and scalability.

Aligning Employee Rewards to Company Vision

Within the company, my number one priority are our employees. Employees will come first in any of my decisions. As the owner of my company, I am hands on but allow my employees to decide and encourage teamwork. The value of each employee is recognized. Management incentives and rewards are given to those employees who perform beyond expectations. These rewards are well aligned with the objectives of the company. Each employee, however, has a clear understanding of his/her responsibilities making it easier for the company to operate efficiently. I allow my employees to make informed decisions and encourage teamwork.

Being a real estate broker myself, I share my knowledge and expertise with my agents. I train my employees to be entrepreneurial by giving incentives to all performing departments, thus creating small business units within my company. As a result, respect is reciprocal; I treat them with respect and they respect me.

Innovating with Sustainable Products and Services

The Tiarra premiere home and Delsey homes in Via Verde are Excellence in Design for Greater Efficiencies (EDGE) certified solar-powered homes. Our Solar

Powered Homes are equipped with 24-hour solar solutions. The roofs can be re-oriented to better absorb the energy of the sun. The homes are expected to save an average of 37 percent in energy use, 25 percent in water, and 32 percent in building materials. What this means for the individual homeowner is that the energy generated by the system may offset the homeowner's electric bill by as much as P1,800 to P3,300 [US$38.42 -US$70.42] monthly, based on P10-P12 [US$0.10-US$0.25] per kwh rate. We calculate that Via Verde's contribution to renewable global efforts will save the country fossil fuel amounting to P84 million [US$1,792,990] and eliminate 110k tons of carbon emissions per year.

Another innovation is the eSaver 3000 that use reliable lithium battery with an average lifespan of 15 years. An eSaver 3000 system can supply the basic electrical requirements of a typical home such as an electric fan, chargers for cellular phones, laptop, TV, and refrigerator. The engineering team cooperated with each other to make sure that the solar solutions address the typical needs of the homes we built and are available to everyone, not just the rich. We at IHC do not restrict ourselves to the rooftops of mass housing projects because our solar-powered solutions are flexible enough to be relevant to all types of development from low-cost mass housing projects to commercial projects.

Ensuring Happy Stakeholders

Our key external stakeholders include: (a) Homebuyers who will benefit from energy savings from the solar solution. Homeowners who live in solar-powered communities have expressed their satisfaction and enjoy a home without sudden and unplanned power outages; (b) Real estate developers who will be selling an added value to potential homebuyers; going from selling a mere house to selling a house that is beneficial for the homebuyer and for the environment; and, (c) Utility companies because homeowners are able to collectively support the utility's demand side management. By minimizing homeowner's demand during daytime peaks (between 10am-3pm), the utility is able to be more flexible in managing its resources without dispatching peaking plants which are typically the most expensive. In addition, the general public benefits as we share knowledge and understanding about solar and promote appropriate solar solutions.

Sharing Commitment

Imperial Homes expanded its business through a joint venture with Belgian-based Enfinity Global with whom we share a commitment to quality assurance sustainability, and social responsibility. With their expertise in solar energy, and our expertise in housing developments, we set up Enfinity Imperial Solar Solutions, Inc. (EISSI), a pioneering company that makes it possible for low-cost homes to take advantage of the benefits of solar energy. The EISSI partnership will build an unprecedented 5,000 solar homes in Batangas and other locations in Southern Luzon that can produce 5MW of solar electricity. From this partnership alone, we anticipate that the amount of fossil fuel savings may be increased to US$4.6Million and 3,600 tons of carbon dioxide emissions eliminated annually. Reductions in fossil fuel use underlies the importance of this initiative in the Philippines where buildings consume 63 percent of the country's energy supply, according to 2013 data from the Department of Energy.

Netsuite.Org (see http://www.netsuite.org/), the corporate citizenship arm of NetSuite, is committed to supporting capacity building efforts for non-profits and social enterprises around the world through their product donation and employee volunteer program. The transformational business concept became a role model when IHC became the first real estate developer to become a social enterprise grantee. As a social enterprise, IHC fosters a social purpose in a financially sustainable way.

As CEO, I demonstrated my commitment through participation in industry associations. I am a member of many real estate brokers and housing developer organization. I am one of the Founding members of Women in Shelter & Environment (WISE) composed of women developers who aim to provide greener homes in the Philippines. I was a Past Director of Subdivision Housing Developer Association of the Philippines and the Founding Director of CREBA in the Bicol Region.

Financing Solar Powered Homes

Completion of the Solar Powered Mass Housing Communities with built-in financing did not come easy. Since this is the first in the country, I had to sell the idea to banks. It took me one and a half years of follow up with Pag-ibig Fund whose technical people had to be convinced of the concept of the solar powered homes. In May 2015, the government's biggest housing mutual fund, Pag-Ibig Fund (HDMF), approved the solar solutions as part of the housing loans of its members. It also approved solar home improvement loan for its members who already own homes.

Partnerships with PAG IBIG and BPI Family Savings Bank had a snowball effect, garnering the interest of other banking institutions, such as Land Bank, BDO Unibank, Producer's Bank, and Security Bank.This made it easier for homebuyers to avail of solar solutions through bank loans.

Performance Accountability

On March 14, 2016, IHC, in partnership with a PAG-IBIG Fund, turned over to qualified homebuyers their new solar-powered homes. This was a landmark for the industry as it serves as proof that the PAG-IBIG Fund and other leading banks and financial institutions are now recognizing and supporting this innovation in mass housing development.

Marketing Locally and Globally

Part of IHC's strength lies in its aggressive marketing that is able to adopt to global changes. IHC currently has links with 50 local real estate brokers and 400 agents and has agents in US, England, Scandinavian countries, Italy, Spain, Singapore and Hong Kong.

Meeting Local and International Green Standards

The Climate Change Commission has recognized the Solar Powered Mass Housing Communities as a Climate-Smart Initiative under the Philippine National Climate Change Action Plan.

IHC received the International Finance Corporation (IFC) World Bank's first Excellence in Design for Greater Efficiencies (EDGE) Certificate for Green Building in the Philippines. This is a prestigious award given to home units that exemplify design achievements in the areas of energy, water reduction, and renewable materials. IHC's first solar powered mass housing project in Sto. Tomas, Batangas is currently the Poster Child for EDGE by the IFC World Bank. It is locally calibrated for the Philippines, and based on baseline and market studies. More information about the EDGE user-friendly tool is available at the IFC website.

Paying Attention to Scalability

Our vision has now become a reality. But there is still a lot that needs to be done. We encourage all mass and affordable housing developers and leaders in the real estate industry to promote and encourage solar powered homes in their development. In addition to offering and installing a solar energy solution, we are committed to educating homeowners and homebuyers on the proper use of solar. Action on the part of the developers will address the housing backlog in the Philippines. In addition, we will help alleviate poverty through savings in electricity, and we will contribute in combating the negative effects of climate change.

LEADERSHIP QUALITIES

The transformation of my company into a profitable and the leading company in mass housing and now in affordable solar powered mass housing required skills, talent, knowledge, and dogged persistence. I highlight key leadership competencies that helped me through this transformation. These competencies include being an entrepreneur, being passionate and positive, having a winner attitude, having a continuing desire to learn, finding inspiration, and paying attention to sustainability. Moreover, these are some of the same qualities I seek to develop in others.

Learning Leadership and Entrepreneurship

I learned how to be a leader and an entrepreneur from my father who was from Basey, Samar. Unable to finish his law degree, he moved to Manila with P9.00 [US$0.19] in his pocket. My younger years were spent at the busy port area of Manila where my father worked as a checker and a sub-contractor of stevedoring services. He eventually became a successful owner/businessman of one of the biggest stevedoring and trucking enterprise during his time. As a child, I was exposed to the business success of my parents and this developed my passion for entrepreneurship. At 8 years old, I started honing my entrepreneurial skills by selling to my classmates in Siena College different goods like roses I picked from our neighbor's garden, re-packed fruity candies from the nearby community store, and paper dolls. During my high school days in St. Theresa's College, I bought and sold second-hand typewriters. At age 16, I formed my first partnership with a friend to sell gold jewelry purchased in Bulacan.

I juggled work, studies, and business during my college years at the University of the Philippines where I graduated with a BS in Business Economics. While studying, I worked as an Investment Analyst in Ayala Investment and Development Corporation. After college, I continued working with another Ayala firm, International Heavy Equipment Corporation as a Sales Executive. My entrepreneurial skills and knowledge made me Ayala's top seller of heavy equipment. I was at the top of the game in a world where men ruled at that time.

Being Passionate and Positive. Having a Winner Attitude

In 1979, I married Legazpi City Mayor Gregorio Imperial, whose family is the oldest political family not just in Albay but in the Philippines. With my entrepreneurial spirit, I set up Albay's many firsts, namely, the Mission Montessori School and a 10,000 bird poultry farm. More importantly, as a Mayor's wife, I joined my husband in various social and civic oriented services. Out of this social and civil engagement, I decided to address the housing issue. Building quality homes for the poor became my mission in life.

In 1983, while raising two boys, I started Imperial Homes Corporation using my husband's land and about P200,000 (US$4,304.78) in initial capital that I borrowed from my mother. I developed single Spanish Style Homes in the City. I developed the first Public School Teacher Housing in Albay, an activity that became so successful it resulted in the development of more Teachers Villages in Legazpi City. With my skills and know-how, I expanded my real estate development to the remotest municipalities of the Bicol region. From 1986 to 1989 my family and I lived in California and worked as a partner of an independent American broker and later a financial firm. This was when I truly realized my passion for real estate. My company, IHC, has grown to become one of the country's respected home and community developers with the primary aim of providing quality and affordable homes to Filipinos. Since I started IHC, I have combined my entrepreneurship with a value of caring for the greater good of all.

I am passionate about growing businesses and my advocacy for solar powered mass housing. I nurture friendly collaborations with other mass housing developers. I call myself the friendly developer who partners with other well-known developers such as Ayala Land, and Megaworld Properties. I also reach out to women networks outside my industry; women whose main objective and common goal is to help the Philippines. Currently, I am the only CEO from the Real Estate industry who is a member of the Sylk women group, a group of powerful women CEO's from various industry sectors, such as the Business Process Outsourcing (BPO) call centers and IT sectors. The BPO sector has transformed the Philippines into the call center of the world. My success has been recognized in 2015 by Go Negosyo for Woman Entrepreneur and by the Filipina Women's Network as one of the 100 Most Influential Women in the World.

Continuing Desire to Learn

Before entering the University of the Philippines, I studied short summer courses on stenography and speed reading. At an early age I was eager to learn many things. I also tried learning languages like French, Spanish and Danish, but I was too busy to practice. I studied in Lumbleau Real Estate School to become the first Filipino Real Estate Broker in California in 1986. I topped the real estate broker exam in the Philippines in 1989.

Since my college years, I have desired to go to Harvard. When my company reached the US$10 million annual sales in 2005, I met a prerequisite of the Harvard Business School for the Owner President Management Program. The program is equivalent to a one year Harvard Business Executive course customized for Owner Presidents of companies who do not have time to study for longer period. Many top owners of big conglomerates in the Philippines graduated from this program. I learned a tremendous amount from the 132 Owner President classmates of global companies who were leaders of the best companies in the world. The Dean at Harvard inspired me to focus on my company's core competence.

Finding the Solar Inspiration

During my travels to Europe four years ago, I saw that even in cold and winter-heavy countries, the norm was solar-powered housing. That made me question why the Philippines which is a tropical country that gets a lot of sun all year round is not using solar energy. For some countries in Europe, homeowners either install solar solutions or place insulation in their walls in order to get a building permit.

Celebrating the Impact of the Solar Powered Homes

Success in building solar powered mass housing communities is a solution for better housing for the underserved segment of society. With the solar power model IHC is able to share innovative solutions that in the past, were only available to people in the higher income bracket. The solar powered homes community also helps alleviate poverty through savings for homebuyers on electricity bills. Moreover, solar power will produce cleaner energy, thereby contributing to mitigation on climate change and making the environment more resistance to extreme climactic events like typhoons and floods that regularly affect the Philippines. Not only will the 3.7 Million housing backlog in the country be addressed but also result in the elimination of 1,882,000 tons of carbon dioxide and savings of US$2.768 billion in fossil consumption per year.

TOWARDS SUSTAINABILITY

Driven by my passion in alleviating the housing gap for low and middle income homebuyers we created more dynamic and innovative housing projects. Even before the mass housing boom, IHC, under my leadership had collaborated with companies like Laguna Properties Holdings (an Ayala land subsidiary) for the construction of 2,000 socialized housing units and a joint venture partnership with Empire East and Suntrust Properties. Since then, IHC has built more than 16,000 housing units. In 1992, IHC reengineered itself to also develop environment friendly leisure development and develop middle housing market. Four years ago, IHC applied the innovative concept of Solar Powered Mass Housing Community to develop affordable green homes for low-cost and socialized mass housing. This is in line with our vision to promote equality of opportunity and shared prosperity. When I am passionate about something, I hold on to it. I work with passion to help others. I work with passion to work with others to help others.

IHC is a wholly owned family corporation. IHC currently has 11 on-going projects, 19 completed projects and will open 5 new projects. With new and innovative concepts, IHC has an inventory and investment in properties that could have a market value of P10-15B [US$200-320M]. As noted earlier, the company envisions to be the leader in affordable homes and leisure projects. It is our dream that other developers will follow suit and Philippines can be a leader and be the Solar Capital of Asia for Mass Housing Communities.

I believe that I am destined to provide shelter for low-income earners. I make sure that my housing materials and home features are sustainable and top quality. I also believe that low-income segment of the population does not just deserve a house but rather a sustainable home that will give them a sense of pride.

Four years ago, when I first thought of the solar-powered homes, a lot of people tried to discourage me. I bravely faced skepticism about solar solutions for low cost mass housing because, at that time solar solutions were not cheap. Unstoppable when I believe in something, I continued to retrofit my mass housing projects with solar solutions. I believe that the sun is free and solar will be a very good feature for low cost housing projects.

I share and encourage other developers to adopt my transformational business model to address around a 5.5 million housing backlog of the country which will create greater impact in the environment and in the economy.

I had a fixation on solar rooftops being solutions and part of real estate. It did not occur to me that this is going to be the future, providing savings to homeowners due to the parity of current electricity rates to solar rates as a result of declining solar prices in the world market. More importantly, global leaders are now pressuring the world to help mitigate climate change. I invite other real estate developers to adopt a solar-powered community in their projects, together we can make the Philippines the Solar Capital of Asia. That is the reason for my super excitement about possibly receiving the 2016 Financial Times/IFC Transformational Business Award in the Achievement of Low Carbon Urban Transformation category.

JANICE LAO-NOCHE

Sustainability Expert Professional
FWN100™ Global 2015

Disrupting the Stereotype:
Being You

The purpose of this chapter is to inspire young Filipinas that they can succeed by doing whatever they are passionate about. They do not necessarily have to marry a foreigner, or enter an occupation that is a priority of the country to which they want to immigrate. My story demonstrates to young Filipinas that if they stay true to who they are, if they do what they love, and do it very well: they will succeed. I will reflect on my early years as a second generation Filipino-Chinese, how I dreamed of working internationally, my early dreams of making a difference in people's lives, and how I remain committed to that dream.

My Early Years of Being Stereotyped

I am a second generation Filipino-Chinese. In the Philippines one would think that was common, but when I was growing up, there were not a lot of kids who looked like me. It was tough, and I would get teased a lot for having chinky eyes, or being "yellow-skinned", or be spoken to in broken English, or be asked if my parents were millionaires. Perhaps it was common for kids to say that to someone who looked different and immediately assume I fit a certain stereotype. For years I would try to fit in, try to look like everyone else, but there's very little one can do with their physical features when they are five years old. It also did not help that apart from my multi-race background, I was quite different from other kids: I loved to read, to debate with the grown-ups, and at that time, right between Ninoy Aquino's death and the 1986 People Power Revolution, wanted to know what was going on around me. But I was lucky enough to have a mom who knew how to harness my uniqueness; she was my Filipino side, so to speak. While she never understood what it was like to be Filipino-Chinese, she knew what it was to be different; because in truth, everyone is different. One day on my way home with her; I was crying for not being like everyone else in school and she told me that everyone was different in their own way and we are designed that way to contribute something unique to this world. To be told that at seven was a pretty strange concept to wrap my little head around. At that age, she also asked me a life-defining question: "So, Jan, what are you going to do with your life, so you can do something good for the world?" Of course, I rambled away and said I could be a nurse, or a doctor, the usual answers and then discouraging myself with reasons for why I could not possibly be those. But my mom pressed me with "You know, you can be whatever you want to be, do not let anyone tell you otherwise!" And at seven, I allowed myself to dream the impossible, to not allow definitions and stereotypes to stop me from being who I could possibly be.

Of course, it was easier said than done. I knew at that age that I wanted to experience the world outside the Philippines and that I wanted to make a difference in people's lives. I didn't know how it was going to happen. I had to contend with still getting teased in school for being different, no longer from a physical perspective, but getting teased for my dreams as I vocalized them to others. In hindsight, I am amazed at how I managed to stay true to my dreams. In fact if you look at it, it would have been so much easier to fit in with everyone else on this front because all I had to do was to keep my mouth shut. I could have stealthily gone through my school years with nary a soul knowing about my crazy and impossible dreams. But there was something about sharing with other people, as if claiming to the world and visualizing it aloud, that reinforced my belief that I was going to make it happen.

DETOURS TO MY DREAMS

Fast-forward to my eighteen-year old self; I had decided to apply for college in the United States. At that time I was already in my second year in Ateneo and I had heard about this new degree called biomedical engineering; a degree that would prepare one to formulate engineering solutions for when the body is weak, ill, or disabled. It was the perfect answer to my life-long question about how to make a difference and combine my love for all things math and science! At that time, only a handful of colleges in the world, mostly in the United States, offered this degree. I applied and got conditionally accepted at a number of colleges, however as I was deciding which college to accept, the Asian Financial Crisis happened. Before then, my family knew that they could afford to pay half my expenses, but with the financial crisis devaluing the peso, it was next to impossible to send me to the US. And this was incredibly heartbreaking. It felt like I was being pulled back from my dream and it was a harsh reality check for me. I told my mom "You said I could be anything I wanted to be, but it seems that's not true!" I had worked so hard at school to get excellent grades, worked so hard on my applications, secured the required professors' references, done well on my SATs, and then, this. I felt like the world was playing a cruel trick on me. I had to take a break from Ateneo as I was too shell-shocked from what happened and decided to go to Cebu, which I thought was as far as I could take myself from my normal life in Manila. I needed to re-think my life. I had not realized that I had created a stereotype for myself; a checklist for my life where I listed out: by age X, I would have done Y; by age A, I would have done B. I had turned into my own bully, and was harder on myself, than the playground bullies had been. So for two years I studied an engineering course, and also allowed myself to open up to whatever life had to offer. Surely being a biomedical engineer was not my only option to make a difference in this world? In those years I tried everything I could think of including learning Cebuano, German, and French; running for student council. I was a sponge, pushing myself to my limits and learning more about myself than I ever had before. It was a life detour about getting to know myself and understanding how best to harness my strengths. And I thank God every day for that detour, which I call my "veiled" failure years. I learned about tenacity, perseverance, but most importantly about acceptance and being my best ally. During my 18 months in Cebu, I had read an old Reader's Digest article about an engineer in India who was talking about the need for more people working on environmental issues. I was drawn to that story and my gut was telling me "this is it!"

RISING FROM MY PERCEIVED FAILURE

The thing about failure though is it can make you too cautious, and it took me a while to decide what to do about that nagging feeling in my stomach, that working on environmental issues could be my thing. I researched it and found that there was only one school in the Philippines that offered an Environmental Science degree and it was in Ateneo. So, with enough courage, I decided to write to the Vice President for Academic Affairs and the Vice President for Admission in Ateneo about my story and ask them if they would take back a former student without any additional examinations or references (by then the application period, including for transferees, had ended), and instead bank on my SATs, my previous grades in Ateneo, and my current ones in my school in Cebu which were all excellent. I did not have much family connections, and it was purely my grades, my then new-found passion for environmental issues, and the plea of a young 20 year old asking its former school to take her back. And I prayed to the heavens that was good enough. And it seemed it was; in a few weeks I received an acceptance letter from Ateneo. What a joy and a relief!

During my second time in Ateneo, what a great feeling it was to do the thing I had dreamt of for so long. Because I had worked so hard to get to where I was, I never took anything for granted. I was very active in the student council and other student organizations, taking a minor degree in Economics, as well as working with some of Ateneo's renowned science professors. By the time I graduated, three years after my original batch had done so, I was at the top of my degree class, and was the first in my degree to graduate with honors, ten years after the degree was introduced. It was such an amazing feeling to have overcome all the obstacles, made history, while staying true to who I was and what I believed in.

When People Believe In You

While I was in my junior year in college, six months before it was due, I started to work on my senior thesis. I chose as my advisor the then Dean of the School of Science and Engineering as I wanted to work with one of best science professors in Ateneo. I heard a lot of stories from alumni about how hard he worked his students and how he demanded excellence. The stories scared me but I knew from years in Cebu that if I wanted to stay true to who I was, that I should not be afraid. While heading to his office I chanced upon a poster about a scholarship program for post graduate studies in the United Kingdom. At that time, the UK was not exactly in my list of possibilities; I was preparing myself for eventually doing my post graduate studies in the US. I then forgot about the poster and continued on my work with the Dean. A few weeks after, while I was in the chemistry laboratory starting one of my thesis experiments, my Dean passed by to check on me. Since my experiments would take half a day to set-up, he stayed with me to help out and during the waiting period, he asked me about my plans for post graduate studies. I told him I was eyeing several U.S. colleges and preparing to apply. Then I asked him what he did for his post graduate and he mentioned Oxford.

I suddenly recalled the scholarship poster I saw a few months back and asked him what it was like to study at at Oxford and mentioned to him about the poster I saw. Immediately he told me, quite excitedly, "You should go for Oxford." He said "You would excel there, it's exactly what you need!" I was terrified to say the least, Oxford? Me? I'm not made for Oxford! I am not Bill Clinton, Margaret Thatcher, Aung San Suu Kyi. I was not even as good as my Dean. Oxford definitely was not what I considered in my realm of possibilities. And yet again, I found myself stereotyping and discouraging myself. But my Dean was adamant, he saw something in me that I had not seen in myself, that perhaps I could excel in one of the best universities in the world.

So a few days after I graduated, I received my acceptance letter from Oxford. I was surprised. Because I was not confident about getting into Oxford, I had not researched or applied for scholarships and other financial aid. So I requested a one year deferment on registration. During that year, while I was working as an environmental consultant, I applied for the scholarship that I had seen a year and a half earlier outside my Dean's office. In a few months, I was notified that I had been awarded a full scholarship to Oxford.

Confronting the Doubts

My Dean was right. I excelled and enjoyed my time at Oxford. I remember clearly my first bus trip from the airport and how awe-inspiring the place was. I was joining the ranks of its famous alumni. But as soon as I began my classes, the questions began. My classmates had never heard of the Philippines and when they had, they knew it as a very poor, underdeveloped place. I was often asked during the first few class sessions how I learned how to speak English so well. It was very frustrating having to answer their questions and I ended up questioning the place I came from, as if blaming people's perception of the Philippines for my own inadequacies. And as people were getting curious of the place I grew up in, I became scared that perhaps I was not good enough for this place, that they had made a mistake, and that someone was going to find out I was not right for Oxford. I had created this "reality" and stereotyped myself. It was a difficult adjustment at the beginning, the constant doubts in my head. Eventually, I decided to enjoy the experience and make the most of it. It is not often that someone like me from the Philippines gets this life-changing opportunity. It was a lesson to me about always reminding myself where I came from and the need to embrace myself for who I really am. Yes the Philippines has its problems and may not always create a great impression with foreigners, but it has shaped the person I have become.

My life will always be intricately linked to the Philippines and its recent history. The questions my classmates were asking me were less about stereotyping but more about an authentic curiosity of what they perceived as an exotic place. They wanted to know what it was like to grow up in a place with so much hardship, and yet thrive; how can people be so positive despite the poverty and corruption. I did not always have a full answer for them. It was in Oxford that I learned to love, accept, and be proud of being Filipino. I graduated from Oxford, to become the first Filipino to earn the Environmental Change post graduate degree. Since then, I have been supportive of several alumni, particularly another Filipino in completing that degree. It is my way of thanking my Dean for paving the way for me and pushing me further out of my comfort zone.

OPPORTUNITY IN EVERY SITUATION

Armed with my technical knowledge, I began my career working as an environmental researcher and consultant at an environmental think tank based in Washington, DC. Initially one would think that a research job involved going to the web and just searching, but it was more than that. I needed to understand the objectives of the task I was given and that the team I was working with was building a case to lobby international and multi-lateral banks to include more stringent environmental requirements before they invested or loaned to projects. But, there just was not enough information on the internet or even in libraries. I had to understand the banks' lending process and their ecosystem, their process for making loans, their rationale for making loans, the types of projects they would typically loan to, and the common environmental impacts. By breaking down the research into its smaller parts, I was able to identify alternative sources and tools to find the information required. It often involved cold-emailing and cold-calling experts about their experience and documenting the information the old-school way. This experience helped me to build my critical thinking, resourcefulness, and interpersonal skills. By default I am an introvert, and if someone had told me during my interview that I was going to have to cold-call people, that would have scared me enough not to continue with my application. But there I was, passionate about the cause we were pushing for, and driven to find the information we needed. My fear about disappointing my team was greater than my fear of cold-calling. When I was working on this project more than a decade ago, I could not even imagine the change it has created for some of the loaning practices of these banks. That experience demonstrated to me the importance of getting the right information and understanding the situation one is trying to change. While change does not happen overnight, it does happen if the case can be built in a compelling way.

After my stint in Washington, DC, I received an offer to work in Hong Kong for a world-leading environmental consulting firm. At that time, I had never been to Hong Kong and I wanted to try working in a place that was not too far from home, but also offered the challenge of being a new place and culture. When I joined, I was the most junior person in our team. While I had some experience, I did not have enough to be considered an expert at anything. My previous experience helped but I needed to learn from our senior consultants. The only way to gain the experience I needed was to job shadow and assist them. The moment I realized that this was what I needed to do, I jumped in with two feet and asked to work on different projects at the same time, not minding the long hours and the lack of my own work-life balance. I had decided that this was the time to get my hands dirty and learn from as many people, projects, and situations as I could. It was a decision I have never regretted and a decision that has paid dividends for my career.

In that position I saw an opportunity to build on the skills that I had gained in my previous job. Observing the consulting ecosystem helped me realized that to succeed in this career, one needed business development and client management skills. While technical skills were important, it was something that everyone in the company would eventually learn. But, the soft skills of business development and client management; understanding how the consulting business worked, knowing how to meet clients' needs; seemed lacking amongst my peers. That was an interesting insight for me, and I decided that I was going to work on the soft skills to stand out with my senior managers. Realizing that very few of my colleagues wanted to do this type of work, work that brought in business to the company, made me think that I had a higher chance of succeeding. I had seen an opportunity in an untapped market and I wanted to build on my skills of research and cold-calling. This time it came so naturally to me, that I did not have a problem lining up business development pitches. My tenacity and ambition surprised my supervisors and they provided support to my opportunity building experiments. For that I am very grateful. After eighteen months at this job, I was promoted to the next level and was tasked to train our new junior staff with technical skills while continuing with my business development work.

In one of my business development pitches, I heard of an opportunity to work in London for a boutique private equity firm. Since I graduated from Oxford, I had wanted to work in London but had not found the right opportunity. I submitted my application. In a few weeks, I found myself with an offer, and then moving to London with my new husband.

My whole story up until this time has been just about me without reference to my personal life, but my husband has been very instrumental in my career success. Back when we were still dating, he knew that my focus was going to be on building my career and he was very supportive of me. So when I had the offer to move to London, he decided to move with me as well because he knew this was a good move for me. He found a way to make it work for himself too. My husband then decided to take up a post graduate course. It worked out well for both of us.

Overcoming My Doubts

My move to London was not a straightforward move. The new role was less about technical knowledge but more about client management. However, my technical knowledge helped me explain problems and opportunities to my supervisors as well as to my clients. The combination of my technical experience and previous client management helped me succeed in that job. One thing I had been learning throughout my previous positions was the need to get buy-in from just about everyone. I had to learn how to seek support and approval from my project manager, my boss, my supervisors, my clients, the regulators, the government, and communities. Diplomacy and building relationship skill-sets were so crucial for my job in London, I was grateful I had the experience and knew how to do it. At this time, I already had a good reputation in the industry for my work ethic and resourcefulness. But I could not help but be intimidated by the new situation I was in, I had never worked inside an investment firm and had no impressions of what that this was going to be like. I also had to manage people who reported directly to me. I realized that while I wanted to work in a challenging environment, I always had this fear of not being able to deliver, of someone figuring out that I was not as good as they thought I was, or that I was not going to get the respect from my direct reports. This is the fear I have had to continue to work on even until today. My dad has a great line for this, whenever I feel afraid of being "found out"; "You have to learn how to be comfortable even when you feel uncomfortable". It continues to be a daily battle with my own doubting demons, but every day I remind myself of my father's words and my own words "I am good enough!"

Being "found out" is a ridiculous and un-founded fear because my achievements and career experience show otherwise. For this, I needed to remind myself about who I have become. This was the time I realized that I had grown into my own, as a woman and as a leader. For years I had focused on building my skill-sets and learning from others, and now finding myself in a place where I had become the person I had wanted to be and realized I had always been that person. But my resourcefulness, tenacity, drive, and passion never changed, it only grew.

After this position in London, my husband and I moved back to Hong Kong as we decided that we wanted to start a family and be close to our families for support. An important life lesson here; career is definitely important, but living one's life is more valuable. That means different things for different people; some may want to have children, others do not. But for me and my husband, we knew we wanted to have kids when we were ready to do so. With us in our early 30s, this was the right time. Moving back to Hong Kong also meant a move to a more senior role working on environmental issues inside a company, and this would be my first time to be an in-house environmental manager. That job required the combination of the different competencies I gained in my previous positions: resourcefulness, understanding context, interpersonal skills, diplomacy, client management, leading a team, and technical experience. While the competencies were not new to me, the company culture and environment was entirely different from what I had experienced. I had never worked for a big brand before, and it took time to get used to navigating and operating in a fast-paced, customer frontline environment, where everything we did was scrutinized by different stakeholders. We were held to the highest standards not only by the company, but also by our customers. This experience turned into a baptism of fire in more ways than one. Having children at this time complicated matters as well.

But as I had always done in the past, I jumped in with two feet and was willing to roll up my sleeves and learn from my staff about the company culture, and learn from my peers about the ways to get things done in the company. There was a lot of one-on-one coffee dates and lunches to get to know how the company worked. I had learned before that change does not happen easily to people, and in my job as environmental manager, I had to get the company thinking about more environmentally-friendly and sustainable ways to operate. That meant that I could not do it myself; I needed the support of many different teams. But I was new, had never worked in the industry before, and was much younger than most managers at that level. I was concerned about whether they were going to take me seriously. My fear of being "found out" crept in again, but all I had to do was take a deep breathe, look at the situation before me, and dive in. Building relationships took longer than I had thought, some of our projects failed, the number of people who had to buy into our projects would expand when we thought we had gotten everyone's support, requirements changed, misunderstandings with stakeholders escalated, etc. It was a perfect storm of things going wrong before you can figure how to make it right. But I realized that if we were going to enable change, it was going to take time and that what was needed was a huge dose of patience, humility, and perseverance. In the six years working for that company, I spent most of my time head down, with my team, trying to make as much progress as we could against what I felt were headwinds. I had realized working with different bosses in my previous roles that it was my responsibility as a manager and a leader to be positive even when the chips were down. Not a delusional kind of positivity, but a realistic type; where we would chart our strategy based on the constraints and work around them. After all "necessity is the mother of invention." Slowly but surely we were starting to see the outcomes of our efforts. At this time I had started to build my own leadership philosophy including embracing my own vulnerabilities, being authentic, and being open to change based on the ups and downs that I encountered.

CHANGE IS CONSTANT

Towards the end of my time in that company, I was approached by another large company about a potential role to manage its sustainability team. Initially I was hesitant, because I had invested so much of myself in the company and my role. I had made friends and it felt like family. It was the first time that I felt emotional pain just thinking about leaving my friends and my team. But my husband asked me a question "What are you afraid of?" I was afraid of leaving my comfort zone. I already knew how to navigate and work around the current system, and I knew how exhausting learning about a new situation would be if I moved to a new company. I was not sure if I was up for it. Or worst, I questioned whether I was going to succeed.

And yet, I decided to move and take the offer. I only had to look at who I was and who I had become; and I concluded that I had the competencies needed for the position. Most important of all was my tenacity to not only survive but to thrive in any situation where I find myself. The new position has been challenging, but this was not a decision I regretted. It has challenged me in so many ways in dealing with new experiences. All I had to do was tap into the self in me that is open to change, to learn from others and to be humble enough to ask help from others. I have been very blessed to have a great support at work from colleagues who are willing to help. I have been especially blessed to have great support at home.

As a working mother, it has never been easy to integrate my life and work, or even to try to balance both. There have been many occasions where I felt guilty for not always being present for my children. My mom stayed with us full-time and I knew the benefits that are gained in that situation. I often ask myself will my children lack in love or become less of who they can become I was not at home full-time? And I still do not know the answer to that question. What I do know is that I am doing everything I can to give them the best life and future that I can possibly give. I tell myself that it is normal to feel guilty, and this is a sign that I am trying to be a good mom. It is tough, this balance. But it is a balance I want to achieve.

FINAL WORD

Finally, when I look back at my life and see the many obstacles I was able to overcome, it is amazing, especially for a Filipina in Hong Kong, where the stereotypes can be challenging. I have the greatest respect for our overseas Filipino workers in Hong Kong, many who work as domestic helpers. I feel a sense of pride when people ask me where I am from and find it a bit amusing when they are surprised by my answer. Indeed, what a great privilege it has been to show the world what a Filipina can do, what she can achieve despite the odds, if she stays true to her calling, never gives up and never allows anyone to tell her otherwise. If there was one thing I could tell my daughter about my life it would be to disrupt the stereotypes, and be the best you you can be.

VINA LUSTADO

Founder of Sol Haus Design
FWN100™ Global 2015

Dream Big; Live Tiny

I do not remember much from my childhood in the Philippines. My fondest memory is of my family gatherings at my aunt's nipa hut located in a tropical jungle. Surrounded by palms, jackfruit trees, lush vegetation, and a nearby stream; this place was paradise to me. In our native Tagalog, we called this place the *linang*.

I come from a large family, five brothers and four sisters, ten children total. Often times my extended family would be included in our outings. To travel to the *linang*, my siblings, cousins, aunts. and uncles would pack the mules with straw baskets strapped on their backs. The baskets would be filled with food to augment what we could harvest from the *linang*. We would walk barefoot, about two miles into the jungle.

Sometimes it seemed like the entire town was coming along because there were so many of us. Upon arrival, we would go swimming in the stream. We were too poor to own bathing suits, so we would jump into the water with just our shorts and t-shirts. We would wash our clothes in the stream with a wooden paddle and beat our clothes against a rock. To go to the bathroom, we would dig a hole in the ground and use guava leaves for toilet paper.

The rest of the day was about being together, playing in nature, and cooking. Food preparation was the center of activity. We picked fresh jackfruit and bananas from the trees. My aunt, Tia Estelita, would climb the coconut tree barefooted. In her 40's, she never married and was a beloved member of the family. Her long flowing grey hair was past her knees. The meal was always cooked in a big pot over an open fire. We would eat with our hands. We made a dessert called **mi-nukmuk**; made in a big wooden bowl with mashed boiled bananas and *gabi* (taro roots) and coconut milk to make it sweet. I remember cracking the coconut open and straddling a wooden bench with a grater to shred the coconut meat. Then I would put the shredded coconut in water and squeeze the liquid out to create the coconut milk. When the food was ready, we all gathered together to eat by the stream.

In my memory, the excursions to the *linang* stand out as the most joyous occasions of my childhood. The English-Tagalog dictionary translation for *linang* is field under cultivation. As a verb, *linangin* means not only to cultivate and but also to develop a capacity by training.

I think the memories of the simple pleasure of the *linang* shaped my appreciation for the natural environment, for living simply, and for the sustainability principles that led me to the tiny house movement. The simple pleasures stayed with me, even as I immigrated to the US. I am grateful for how the *linang* has shaped my perspective and values as an adult.

IMMIGRATION TO THE U.S.

In search of greater opportunities, my father moved to Los Angeles, found a job as an accountant, and an apartment in which to live. One year later, my mother joined my father in the U.S. and found work as a seamstress. Over the next five years, they brought over all ten children. I was seven years old when I left the Philippines.

Our family of twelve lived together in a one-bedroom duplex. Needless to say, our family was cramped in such tight quarters. I remember sleeping in the closet, in the bathtub, and in the queen-sized bed with my siblings.

Because my parents did not have a lot of money, both worked long hours and had little time to spend with their children. They provided as much as they could, given the demands of a new environment and a new culture. My eldest sister, Rosie (or "Ate Salinda" as a sign of respect for the elder sibling), took on the role of caregiver while she finished nursing school. She started working as soon as she was able to help support the family. Mostly, my siblings and I fended for ourselves. As the third youngest, it was easy for me to pass unnoticed.

Being part of such a large family, I felt disconnected and longed for a deeper sense of belonging. Having left the Philippines at such a young age, I lacked a strong sense of my roots in the traditional culture we left behind. I was also challenged with learning a new language in a multi-cultural environment.

I was a third culture kid (TCK), neither Filipino nor main-stream American, and did not fit in with any specific crowd in school. Most of the kids were from different ethnic background with Caucasians in the minority. I learned how to build relationships with other folks from other cultures easily but I lacked a cultural identity of my own. My friends were from Korea, China, and Mexico. I had one Filipina friend with whom I remained friends throughout grade school.

Cultural homelessness is typical of third culture kids who grow up with a different set of values and standards than those with which their parents were raised. This lack of a cultural identity in Los Angeles left me feeling alienated.

At home, I also felt different from my siblings. As we grew older into adulthood, my brothers and sisters had stable jobs, got married, and had children; while I wanted to explore and travel the world. My siblings were guided by tradition and religion while I was guided by curiosity and adventure.

Without knowing it, I was searching for something from my childhood. It was the sense of simplicity from the *linang* that I remember so fondly. The transition to city living in Los Angeles was a stark contrast to where I came from. I was yearning for the connection to nature I had growing up in the Philippines.

ARCHITECTURE AND TRAVEL:
TOWARDS MAKING A DIFFERENCE IN THE WORLD

While adjusting to the new culture in Los Angeles, I worked diligently in school. At the age of thirteen, I moved out of my parents' house to live with my oldest sister in her apartment. I learned to become independent at an early age and got a worker's permit as soon as I could.

My diligence in school paid off. After high school I got accepted to UCLA and was proud to be the first in my family to attend a university. I was excited to take responsibility for my life as an adult.

Seeking New Knowledge

As a departure from math and science courses, I chose art as my major. After two years, I needed something more concrete and less subjective. Architecture seemed like a good balance so I transferred to USC for an architecture degree. I saw architecture as a balance of creativity and function, and a way I could make a difference in the world.

My architecture studies inspired me to visit in person the buildings I had studied about around the world. This led me to my first trip to Europe as a young female traveler on my own for three months. Architecture was a lens into different cultures and different ways of thinking. I learned how to make connections and was inspired by the different ways people live, work, and play.

With all my worldly possessions in my backpack, simplicity, mobility and freedom became very important to me. Living simply became my mantra connecting me to my modest childhood in the Philippines. I also became addicted to travel.

Throughout my adult life, travel has helped me re-assess my direction at pivotal points in my life. I went to Alaska with Habitat for Humanity to build affordable housing for disadvantaged families, to Italy to help build an artist residence, and to South America to trek Machu Picchu. Whether for personal or professional reasons, I welcomed the opportunity to experience other cultures and other ways of seeing the world.

While climbing the corporate ladder in architecture, I moved from Los Angeles to Chicago and then to San Francisco. I was working in notable architectural firms, gaining valuable experiences, and expanding my knowledge of the industry. I was able to position myself favorably on the corporate ladder and advance from one firm to another.

While working in a small firm in San Francisco, I was put in charge of a high profile residential project. With an estimated cost of over ten million dollars, the project was an exceptional opportunity for myself and for my portfolio. The scope of worked required travel to Germany and Italy to source building materials and furnishings. Since the clients were from Russia, I learned how to navigate different languages and learned ways of doing business with people from different cultures.

The project lasted for about four years. While it was certainly a wonderful opportunity, the project lacked a meaningful purpose for me. It was difficult to justify so much time and energy that did not have a positive impact on the world.

I saw that most architects catered primarily to clients with financial resources, and at the same time contributed to the pollution of the planet. More and more, I became disillusioned with the architecture profession.

INCREASING SUSTAINABILITY AWARENESS

I learned that the building industry is responsible for massive environmental degradation: greenhouse gas emissions, depletion of natural resources, and a major contributor to waste in the landfills. I did not want to be part of the problem. I wanted to be part of the solution.

Exploring the Connectedness of Affordability and Sustainability

In 2002, I pursued an opportunity that would prove pivotal to my career. I found an opportunity to do a research study on sustainable and affordable housing in a country that was on the leading edge of sustainability, Germany. This opportunity came from an international fellowship granted by the American Council on Germany (ACG).

ACG provided a stipend for me to live in Germany to gather data for the research. For three months, I was based in Cologne and traveled to various parts of the country to research three different housing projects. To communicate effectively with architects and homeowners, I chose to take an intensive German language course during my three-month stay.

While 'sustainability' is a buzzword in the U.S., it is a mindset and a way of life that pervades the German culture, as well as the cultures of the Scandinavian countries. In my research, I found that there are two important factors that contributed to maximum energy efficiency and affordability: (1) Standardization of construction including use of highly insulated thermal envelopes; and (2) Use of prefabricated panelized systems for walls and roof systems. These strategies yielded much higher quality, superior energy efficiency, and required less construction time, thereby reducing cost.

Another factor that contributes to affordability was the absence of a general contractor. For smaller residential projects, the architect assumes the responsibility of a general contractor. This decreases the construction cost by 10-15%, the typical contractor's fee for overhead and their profit.

Upon completing the research for the fellowship, I was eager to implement my newfound knowledge in the U.S. After returning to the states, I found employment at a small residential firm specializing in green building in Ventura, California. It was a productive time and I gained knowledge concerning green building. I felt this approach to building could make a positive difference. I also became interested in community volunteer work, and joined Habitat for Humanity to implement green building guidelines for budget-conscious projects.

With the recession of 2008 and after seven years at the firm in Ventura, I felt I was becoming stagnant in my career. I needed to re-assess my professional direction, so I took the opportunity to travel to South America for several months. Admittedly, the short sabbatical did not provide the answers I was looking for in my career path, but it did provide the resilience I needed to stay true to my values. I yearned to do work in sustainable architecture.

When I returned, I worked briefly for an architecture firm in Los Angeles, then returned to Ventura County to work with contractors on residential projects.

I learned how to work with builders and contractors as an important skillset to get projects built successfully.

Visioning Sol Haus Design

After more than twenty years of working for others, I realized that to have control of my own financial stability, especially during times of recession, I needed to be my own boss. I never intended to have my own business, but I felt there was a gap in the marketplace for architects that could produce well-designed housing for people with minimal financial means. I always believed architecture should cater to the masses, not only to those in the upper income levels.

After completing a course in small business entrepreneurship, I launched Sol Haus Design. The vision of Sol Haus Design is to provide quality, affordable and sustainable housing to everyone, regardless of income. My goal was to address critical issues such as affordable housing and social justice issues while reducing environmental impacts.

To tackle this goal, I developed a guesthouse prototype. I had seen many clients struggle with the cost of permitting and construction for a guesthouse, or second dwelling unit. Using prefabricated structural insulated panels (SIPs) and passive heating and cooling strategies, the structure would excel in energy efficiency and cost $100k, well under the typical market price.

For about a year, I worked diligently on the guesthouse prototype with builders and suppliers to market the concept to prospective clients. Unfortunately, the concept did not take off. But what I learned was that if at first you do not succeed, try and try again. By keeping faith that you can prevail, you will succeed. This holds true time and time again in achieving anything you want to accomplish in life.

Within a few years, my little company Sol Haus Design became an established business. I was a sole entrepreneur and remained profitable with some decent sized residential projects in the first year. However, what I really wanted was a project that would reflect my core values of sustainability and affordability. I wanted to design my own house or office to show others that it is possible to live well with minimal cost and to be kind to the environment at the same time.

I had grand visions of small compact spaces that could become my dwelling or place of work. I began collecting newspaper articles and images of compact efficient dwellings less than 300 square feet in size.

Introduction to the Tiny House Philosophy

I had seen Jay Shafer's tiny house a few times before. Jay Shafer's name is closely associated with tiny living and is credited with practically inventing what is now known as the tiny house. Tiny houses have become a minimalist design and lifestyle ideal. Their tiny size permits no extraneous stuff. They are often less than 300 square feet, and occupy a fraction of the spatial and carbon footprint of a normal home. They are usually owned outright, sidestepping expensive mortgages and financial institutions. And by virtue of the structures being built on a trailer, they can often avoid traditional building regulations. Jay Shafer has been building tiny houses since the late nineteen nineties. In 2009 he published a book about tiny houses, In 2010 he published the second edition of his book, *The Small House Book*.

I had not taken notice of these tiny houses until my friend and colleague Arne Steffen suggested I read more about them. I had worked with Arne in Germany during the fellowship in 2002. He was one of the architects whom I interviewed for my research..

Arne and I remained in contact after my fellowship in 2002. We both shared an interest in using architecture as a means to address issues in the world outside of architecture, such as sustainability. I had told Arne about my desire to design and build something of my own, something that would truly reflect my core values in sustainability.

My biggest challenge was finding property to purchase or a building that I could afford to remodel. With soaring real estate values in Ojai, CA and everywhere else in California, it was impossible to buy real estate without a large mortgage.

Understanding my conundrum, Arne suggested I look up Jay Shafer's tiny house. At first I was skeptical. The image of Jay's Gingerbread style house seemed unreal. I asked myself: "How can he create a fully functional house in less than 100 square feet?"

As I researched more, I realized that Jay's tiny house perfectly matched my values of living simply. It was not really about the house, but rather the philosophy behind it. I also realized I could design my house with my own aesthetics, like a modern reinterpretation of the traditional cabin. By building it myself, and without permitting fees, the cost would be greatly reduced and thus would fall within my budget.

Putting My Values into Practice

In spring of 2012, I decided to build a tiny house for myself. Luckily my partner Cliff Hultgren supported my idea from the beginning and agreed to help with the building. Later that year, I ordered the trailer which solidified my commitment to build the house. Like a proud parent of a newborn baby, Cliff and I picked up the trailer one month later.

Cliff and I worked on the trailer to build the floor foundation for the house in 2012. Working through months of rain and during the Christmas holidays, we completed the floor and wall framing. One of the most important parts of a tiny house is the structure and foundation. With the blood, sweat, and tears of my partner Cliff, the structure is ingrained with love and care from the bottom up. Without his unconditional help and support from the beginning, my tiny house would not exist.

After four months of building intensely with Cliff, I needed to get more help. I had a deadline to finish by October 2013 for Ojai's Annual Green Home Tour. I was honored and humbled with the opportunity, but with that came pressure to complete within an accelerated timeframe.

To expedite the schedule, I enlisted the help of local artisans and craftsmen. More importantly, I wanted to involve the community and highlight the work of talented local artists. I reached out to friends to design custom pieces such as art glass window, cabinetry, and textiles. As a result, there is undeniable positive energy that permeates the house. This collaboration is what makes my house truly unique. I discuss what the artists brought to my tiny house below.

Meaning-making with My Tiny House

The prime motivation for building my tiny house was to enable me to live a life that embodied my core values. I wanted to preserve our natural resources. I wanted to minimize my waste in landfills. I wanted to be self-sufficient with minimal dependence on fossil fuels. I wanted to live off-the-grid. In other words, I wanted to put my values into practice with the way I lived my life.

I have already touched on the importance of the structure and foundation, and how my partner Cliff has imbued our home with love and care from the bottom up. From the knowledge gained from the fellowship research study and from my experience working with firms, I felt equipped to apply energy efficient building systems that would also be affordable for my budget. I was excited to test my theory that green building does not have to be, and should not be, cost prohibitive.

I decided to use passive heating and cooling techniques with a well-insulated thermal envelope. For natural cooling without air conditioning, I employed natural cross ventilation with strategically placed windows throughout the house. I made sure that all the doors and windows were dual paned with low E glass. Even more important is the placement of the house relative to the trees on the property to provide shade on the south orientation of the house. Heating is achieved by a compact, gas propane stove, serving as the hearth of the house. With minimal electrical load, my tiny house requires a few solar panels to power LED lights, a small refrigerator, overhead fan, and a computer laptop.

To minimize environmental impact, I used reclaimed products as much as possible: windows and pocket doors from ReStore at Habitat for Humanity, French doors from Craigslist, and all the materials on the exterior deck were repurposed.

My favorite part of repurposing materials is giving new life to something old, such as the beautiful oak wood flooring. One of the local craftsman, Kris Mc-Courtney, specializes in using reclaimed wood and is an important contributor to my tiny house. Kris salvaged the oak flooring from an old house. To give it new life, we spent countless hours re-milling and re-finishing the wood to uncover the beauty of the oak floor.

Another talented local artist, Alicia Morris, uses a lot of repurposed materials in her work. With a shared mutual love of trees, we explored the idea of incorporating her sketches on large pillows for the sofa. Alicia took painstaking care in hand embroidering trees onto the pillows. Because the overall design of my house is simple and minimal, the artistry of the pillows became the focal point upon inside the great room.

For the window covering at the large window by the desk, Alicia used repurposed branches and old leather laces for an elegant window treatment. To minimize cost, Alicia used a painter's drop cloth for the pillows and curtains . These artistic touches are not only beautiful, they are functional, affordable, and good for the planet.

Another collaboration with a local artist was with Lynn Hegney - a talented glass artist who customized the glass for the pocket door into the bathroom. Following the theme of trees, Lynn embedded the leaf pattern of a sycamore tree with silver leaf. The result is stunning: a warm glow of sunlight streams into the kitchen and the quality of the light changes throughout the day. The pocket door which holds the glass is repurposed as well.

Still another artist who contributed was Maria Trimbell – an accomplished muralist. Maria continued the theme of trees on the wardrobe closet by creating stencils of leaves on the maple plywood doors. She took great care to place each leaf carefully, so they flowed naturally to the ground.

The collaboration with many local artists gives special meaning to my house. Everyone who enters my little home has recognized the positive energy in the artistic creations. By enlisting the help of local artist and craftsmen, my house embraces community spirit. I feel the presence of each person with his/her unique gifts, and I am grateful for their contribution.

CREATING COMMUNITY

Community has always been something I yearned for. It's a way to build connection in an otherwise disconnected world. During the construction of my house,
I tried to create community with the artisans and craftsmen who helped with the
build.

When I built the deck of my house, I never realized the implications it would
have in helping to create community. You may notice that most tiny homes have
some version of an outdoor deck or porch. But why such an emphasis on porches?
Why do so many tiny house on wheels seem to have some iteration of a porch? In a
recent online article, tiny houser Andrew Odom, explores this idea, and he believes
the reason is two-fold.

The obvious reason for a porch is that it brings the outdoors in and the in-
doors, out. It allows the world outside feel more like part of your home as you can
sit and warm in the sun or swing as the stars begin to illuminate. You can bring
the beauty of nature inside. The boundary between exterior and interior is blurred.

The large size of my exterior deck also provides additional square footage to
my living space. My deck is not only a transition space to the inside, it also functions as a dining room and gathering space when many friends visit.

Decks and porches are certainly a functional part of the house itself. But perhaps the real reason has a much deeper meaning?

As tiny housers we all seem to want to deepen our community ties in some
way or another. We want to be part of something bigger than us. And what better
way to do that than to strengthen our own home and hearth with a welcoming
porch?

In the US where the country is filled with political division, prejudice, and racial inequality, it really hits home how much we need a front porch in our homes.
Far too many homes built today have no transitional space. Our TVs and computers bound up inside. Social media and computer screens make us feel connected
but leave us empty still.

By building porches and decks on our tiny houses we are rekindling that flame
of community. It allows us to be part of each other's lives and we want to share
with each other. It allows for human connection with our neighbors, friends and
strangers. It allows us to break down barriers in an otherwise disconnected world.
Now I'm trying as best as I could to create tiny home communities by change zoning to allow for them.

Changing Public Policy for Tiny Houses

I believe tiny houses can address critical issues in the world today: affordable housing, environmental impact, and economic disparity. As many tiny house advocates would say: the tiny house movement is not about the house, rather it's the benefits that come with living tiny.

Yet there are legal obstacles to living full-time in tiny homes on wheels (THOW). Because THOWs are built on a trailer, they are mobile structures and permanent residency is prohibited. They are for temporary use only and do not fall neatly under any category. They can be considered RV's, mobile homes, or travel trailers. Because tiny homes on wheels are a hybrid of sorts, none of those categories fit exactly. THOWs is a new concept that require its own definition and category in the building and zoning codes.

Since November of 2015, I have been working with local public officials to propose THOWs as a means to provide affordable housing. Like many other municipalities, the City of Ojai has been challenged with meeting the need for affordable housing as required by the State of California. This is stipulated in the General Plan's Housing Element for each municipality.

Changing zoning and planning guidelines is a very lengthy and tedious process. Most ordinances have been in place for decades and are very difficult to change unless there is considerable financial resource to devote to making the changes.

It takes a dedicated team of people who have a bigger vision for the greater good for all. I have been fortunate to build a relationship with Planning Commission members, Chester Jagiello and Kathy Nolan, and with Dan Fitzpatrick, an expert consultant who are helping guide the City of Ojai to modify the existing ordinance.

Countless hours were spent for nine months behind the scenes, attending and strategizing at public meetings before the Planning Commission and City Council. Dan Fitzpatrick volunteered his time to propose amendments to the City's existing second dwelling unit to include THOWs.

While I was coordinating meetings with Dan, Chester, and Kathy, I was also in charge of gathering public support from the community. It was imperative that local residents attended the meetings and give speeches in support of tiny homes. Without this, public officials cannot adequately approve changes to existing public policy unless the public has voiced their desire for change. This was not easy.

How do you inspire others to take action and support your initiative? It takes perseverance, diligence, and also sacrifice in support of the cause. First, the cause has to be for the greater good for all. Second, it is necessary to get support from those who already believe in your cause. Trying to change others to support a cause they do not already believe in rarely works. Sometimes however, if there is overwhelming support from the masses, naysayers may be influenced to join in; because everyone wants to be part of a tribe.

Public meetings took place from November 2015 to May 2016 to support THOWs. We gained traction after each meeting and received positive feedback. The local paper in Ojai and social media sources created a buzz about the tiny house initiative. Even outlying areas like Los Angeles and Ventura County heard about the initiative, and people drove many miles to attend the meetings.

At the meeting on June 28th at Ojai's City Hall, victory prevailed! All three City Council members approved the inclusion of THOWs as part of the second dwelling unit ordinance. Bill Weirick, Randy Haney, and Severo Laro expressed enthusiastic support for THOWs and I was thrilled. Here is a quote from Ojai's City Council member Bill Weirick:

> "I think tiny homes are an important component [of the Housing Element and affordable housing]. I hope I can convince my colleagues to get more aggressive in looking at the possibility of a tiny home village as a demonstration project."

I am especially excited about the tiny house village as a demonstration project. I have always had a bigger vision for a tiny house community to address many critical issues we face today including homelessness, affordable housing, economic disparity, and environmental impact.

A tiny house community can employ the concept of the sharing resources. Imagine all the benefits of sharing vegetable gardens, work studios, libraries, washer/dryers, work tools, bicycles, and electric cars. With the shared economy, we can reduce the use of natural resources and minimize our impact on the environment. Even better, sharing resources puts money in our pocketbook.

The shared economy can also help support communities and invigorate local economy. A tiny house community can be self-sufficient by employing energy efficient systems and permaculture principles (a system of agricultural design principles which utilizes the patterns observed in natural ecosystems).

My greatest hope is to create a tiny house community that can serve as a model for other cities to follow. A tiny house community can embody sustainability and its connections to social justice, affordability, and environmental impact. My reflection has made me realize that I practice leadership for sustainability, consistent with the principles defined by the University of Cambridge Institute of Sustainability Leadership (2011). I highlighted these principles in my narrative and summarized these as tips for leadership for sustainability at the end of my chapter.

COMING FULL CIRCLE

I can still remember my father saying to me: "A rolling stone gathers no moss." I think he was concerned about me. I think he could not understand my propensity to travel to foreign countries, especially traveling to Europe for the first time on my own.

For most of my adult life, I moved from one apartment to another every six to twelve months. I changed jobs every several years and moved to different cities throughout the country. My way of being perplexed him, and perhaps the rest of my family.

Unlike traditional Filipino culture, I could not be tied down to a job that did not challenge me or keep my mind active, just for the sake of a stable paycheck. I preferred to be mobile and not be bound by large debts or a house mortgage. My family, and particularly my father, could not understand my desire to explore, to stay untethered, and to remain flexible.

Now that my father has passed, I realize that I am actually much like him when it comes to giving back on social justice issues. *Itay* [father] had a passion to give back to his community in the Philippines. He started a scholarship organization to help students with financial need. He gave a lot of attention on this effort. For years, I struggled with feeling unimportant and secondary to my father's philanthropic endeavors.

Now I see the same quality in me with a desire to give back, often times sacrificing my personal relationships with people closest to me, such as my husband Cliff and other family members. As I become more involved in legalizing tiny homes and providing alternative housing options, I realize I need to be more mindful of the people closest to me.

For many years, I did not understand the drive and motivation my father had in order to give back to his community. As I reflect upon the impact my father has made in his community, I would like to think he is smiling from above for the impact (I hope) I am making in my own community. I hope my father is proud of the efforts I have taken in the shadow of his footsteps.

LEADERSHIP FOR SUSTAINABILITY TIPS

1. Actively seek and apply new knowledge and divergent views.

2. Inquire about the connections between sustainability and affordability on economic issue; human rights to housing, a social justice issue; and home construction and its impact to the environment.

3. Have greater self-awareness about your motivations.

4. Keep faith that you can and will prevail, despite the difficulties and challenges.

5. Focus on creating a community culture that provides peer support and encouragement. Recognize how other's achievements are aligned to your vision.

6. Build and share an inspirational vision, help others understand how things will be different when the future vision is achieved.

❋

Across-Generations:
Mothers and Daughters

MARIA BEEBE, PH.D.

President, Global Networks
Filipina Women's Network Board Member (2014-2016)
FWN100™ GLOBAL 2013 & U.S. 2011

Developing an International
Leadership Repertoire

'The package has arrived safely' was the radio message for James my husband from the U.S. Marine on duty at the American Embassy in Khartoum, Sudan. The Marine was transmitting the contents of a "cable" from the State Department announcing the birth in California of Ligaya, our daughter on May 16, 1982.

As a U.S. foreign service officer with the United States Agency for International Development (USAID), James' first assignment in 1979 was to Khartoum, Sudan. I was the accompanying spouse. Our firstborn, David was 6 years old at the time and in Khartoum with James preparing to fly to the States for the anticipated birth. Although I had good prenatal care, the U.S. Embassy strongly recommended official American return to the U.S for childbirth. I had been medically evacuated to our home leave address which was my parents' home in Mountain View, California. My mother looked at my pregnant belly and exclaimed, "Your baby is doing the Filipino folk dance, the *Tinikling*." Ligaya was delivered by C-section to avoid a feet-first breach delivery. Maybe that explains why she hits the ground running.

Before we arrived in the Sudan, I had completed my masters in anthropology and my doctoral coursework for my Ph.D. from Stanford University but was a.b.d. (all but dissertation). My professional experience included working as an Assistant Director for Volunteers in Asia, the Stanford based organization that many believe was one of the models for the Peace Corps, teaching in the Philippines and in California, and serving as a U.S. Peace Corps Volunteer in the Philippines. These experiences qualified me for a personal services contract position as a Human Resources Development Specialist with USAID/Sudan. This started my trajectory as a consultant in international development and helped define my leadership. As evident in the narrative, leadership for me requires awareness of how I can make a difference in lives of the people and the world around me. The context informs my approach to leadership that has been influenced by my experiences over time.

Accompanying my husband in the Sudan, Philippines, Liberia, and South Africa, with an interlude in Corvallis, Oregon and Washington, DC, raising children with a global outlook, and working as a consultant allowed me to develop my leadership repertoire. This chapter reflects on the elements that enhanced this repertoire. A leadership repertoire can be thought of as a tool kit, a set of resources, abilities, skills, or competencies that provides options for specific leadership actions. A leadership repertoire affords individuals the flexibility to mix and match leadership skills in response to different situations, and manage the tension between individual agency and the constraints of working and leading in a globalized world. The socio-political context, zeitgeist [the spirit of the times], work responsibilities, and work-life challenges are key elements that have helped define my leadership identity overtime.

In this chapter I will explicitly examine the informed decisions my husband and I made about child-rearing and the implications of these decisions for raising children with global competence. Global competence, as defined by the National Education Association (2010), includes international awareness, appreciation of cultural diversity, proficiency in foreign languages, and knowledge of international economic, social, and technological changes. I will share a few vignettes that I believe have helped our children David and Ligaya engage with the world. Finally, the chapter ends with my daughter's reflections on aspects in her socialization that have made her a global citizen.

After my husband retired from USAID in 1996 to become a professor at Gonzaga University, I continued to work in international development. I was doing what Sarah Lawrence-Lightfoot (2009) identified as the third chapter of one's life, a time after one turns 50 that should be filled with passion, risk, and adventure. The focus of this chapter is on the early engagements with international development that prepared me for my third chapter, including work on telecommunication and the use of information and communication technologies (ICT) for development in Africa (see Beebe et al. 2003) and my work in Afghanistan discussed in "Harmonizing Global Teams in Afghanistan" in *DISRUPT* (Beebe and Escudero, 2015).

READINESS FOR GLOBAL ENGAGEMENT

My grandmother often reminded me that in addition to being smart, I had the blood of a *katipunero*! The *katipuneros* were Filipino nationalists who fought for independence from Spain and my grandfather was a *katipunero*, as a young boy during the late eighteen nineties. Thus, courage to fight for social justice became a guiding force in my leadership. Having grown up in the Philippines, I was thoroughly steeped in the Filipino social value of *pakikipagkapwa* [reciprocal interaction with a fellow human being] so building and maintaining relationships was a competency I brought to my work in international development. Marriage to an American was a cross-cultural affair. I consider my Peace Corps experience as my first foray into cross-cultural international development work. I grew up in lowland Philippines whereas my Peace Corps assignment was in Bontoc, Mountain Province in central Luzon. The Bontoc Igorots were never colonialized by the Spanish and were foreign to me. And to the Bontocs, I was a puzzle, because I looked like them but I seemed to be as foreign as my American husband. This experience and graduate work in anthropology sharpened my appreciation of cultural differences.

One of the often overlooked advantages Filipinas have is being multi-lingual. Growing up multi-lingual appears to "facilitate the development of perspective-taking tools that are critical for effective communication" (Fan and others, 2015, p. 1). Right after college, I taught high school where communicating information and ideas effectively was essential. As a teacher, I especially enjoyed teaching Philippine and English literature classes. I came to love Shakespeare whom I discovered while in 5th grade. I took to heart the lines from *As you Like it*, that "All the world's a stage, And all the men and women merely players; They have their exits and their entrances, And one man in his time plays many parts." Even before I fully understood the meaning of these lines, they resonated with me.

Public speaking was one aspect of showing presence called by Cuddy (2015) as "power posing" in her book Presence: Bringing Your Boldest Self to Your Biggest Challenges. Recognition that I was playing roles was useful during times when I really did not want to do yet another meeting with another governmental ministry official. I would tell myself, "Go to the meeting. Think about your purpose for being here." The ability to play a role while not feeling up to it can be authentic leadership when one maintains one's core values. I came to embrace that as individuals we have multiple identities and we tend to assert different aspects of ourselves in different socio-cultural contexts by drawing from our leadership repertoire.

SUDAN (1979-1982)

Intercultural Capability

While in the Sudan, I first learned to extend my cultural adaptability to a context outside the Philippines and the U.S. We lived in the capital, Khartoum which lies at the confluence of the Blue Nile and the White Nile. During our time in the Sudan it was relatively peaceful. In 1972 the Addis Ababa accord ended the First Sudanese Civil War. The South received representation in the national government and more regional autonomy. President Gaafar Muhammad Nimeiry talked about turning the Sudan into the industrial power-house of the Middle-East or North Africa and oil explorations looked promising. However, Nimeiry moved towards Islamism and imposed Sharia law throughout the country, precipitating the Second Sudanese Civil War in 1983. The two official languages, Sudanese Arabic and English, a legacy from the British colonial times, along with a variety of indigenous languages, such as Dinka, Nuer, Bari and Zande were spoken by the Sudanese. Sudan is home to the Meroe pyramids, named from the ancient city of Meroe, the capital of the Kingdom of Kush, an ancient African kingdom north of Khartoum. With archeologist friends and their children, we took our young son David to spend a long weekend at the excavation site in 1981. David who was in first grade won an award for the best essay for his report on our trip. "In the desert there is a place called Merowe. We drove vehicles that had 4-wheel drive. We camped there for 3 days. There was a big full moon. I saw lots of pyramids." In kindergarten David had learned Arabic greetings and to write Arabic script at the same time that he was learning his English alphabet. Even at an early age, David had shown an appreciation for other cultures and enjoyed learning other languages.

Managing the Work

I quickly learned to manage the work and the importance of finding common ground with my Sudanese colleague and my American supervisors. As the Human Resources Development Specialist, I managed the USAID funded long- and short-term participant training program that sent Sudanese to the U.S.; monitored a literacy project in the southern Sudan; coordinated the U.S. Private Voluntary Organizations (PVO) activities in-country; compiled a directory of U.S. and international PVOs working in the Sudan; and, coordinated in-country training in Sudanese Arabic language for both American and international USAID/Sudan personnel.

Work-life Challenges: Intersectionality

The intersections of identity of being a woman, a Filipina, and an American expatriate became problematic when I returned to the Sudan with a month-old baby. I negotiated half-time work for a total of four hours with time in-between to go home and breastfeed. The initial answer to the proposal to work half-time had been "No. It's never been done before." So I countered that I would stay at home with my new baby. The next day I received a "Please come back" message agreeing to my terms. The workplace needed me more than I needed them. Finding the balance among those aspects of my identity grew more awkward and controversial when I was asked to do a site visit to Juba, the capital of the South Region and received approval to travel with the baby. I did the site visit, discreetly nursing my baby in between meetings. I was thankful that my American male supervisor and Sudanese colleagues were able to accommodate my unusual request. The American resident manager in Juba, however, complained about the unprofessional conduct of breastfeeding a baby while on duty; calling attention once again to the challenges I faced in reconciling those facets of my identity as a woman, American, a Filipina, a mother, and a professional.

PHILIPPINES (1983-1987)

Adapting to Political Change

While travelling to James' next assignment with USAID, the Philippines, we heard the news that Benigno Aquino Jr., a Filipino political leader had been shot on August 21, 1983 as he stepped on the tarmac upon his return from a 3-year self-imposed exile in the US. We arrived several days later on the day of Aquino's funeral. The headlines of the local government controlled newspaper reported Manila had been gridlocked by traffic with only a passing reference that it was Aquino's funeral procession and the massive crowds lining the streets that had caused the traffic. Aquino's death was a turning point in Philippine history inspiring people to take to the streets to protest the government of President Ferdinand Marcos. Marcos called for a "snap" election on February 7, 1986. Cory Aquino, the widow of Benigno Aquino won the election. The incumbent President Marcos, at first, refused to concede leading to "people power" that began on February 22, 1986. Marcos fled the Philippines on February 25, 1986. Following the events before and after departure of Marcos was the best time to be in the Philippines working as an expatriate consultant for USAID.

Influencing Change

My job involved working with local Philippine PVOs on strategic planning, program development, budget formulation, and proposal writing to meet USAID registration and eligibility. I identified the need for specific operational and technical training for local Philippine PVOs and developed systems and procedures for working with local PVOs on proposal formats, monitoring, and evaluation. I worked with Philippine non-governmental organizations (NGOs) to form consortia based on geographic or sectoral criteria. On the USAID side, I was involved in recommending which PVOs and NGOS were ready for USAID funding and which projects to fund. The job called for travel which took me to contested tribal lands in Mindanao, Visayas, and Luzon for projects on primary health care, micro-enterprise development, human rights, and agro-forestry.

Building my Leadership Repertoire

While working with USAID in the Philippines I strengthened my problem-solving skills, ability to make timely and effective decisions, and ability to negotiate the use of time, roles, and resources with diverse individuals and groups. Large activities involving multiple sectors were especially subject to conflicts. Unintended consequences often involved environmental damages. For example, income generating projects based on gold-plating fruit, flowers, and other organic materials for sale as jewelry or home ornaments used acid copper and nickel solution that were "dumped in the ground." Income generating projects based on collecting aquarium fish used sodium cyanide to stun the fish. There appeared to be a lack of understanding or even a disregard of the long-term impact of this practice on the coral reef, the natural habitat of the fish. It was estimated that as much as 20 percent of the live fish traded on the Philippine market were caught using cyanide.

The time in the Philippines was critical for expanding my understanding of the need to consider the environment as well as social and economic objectives. This awareness of the need for balance among social, economic, and environmental objectives was consistent with the definition of sustainable development. I was becoming a leader in the sustainability movement.

Work-life challenge: Being Intentional with Raising Global Children

The work in the Philippines required travel about once a week. My husband and I coordinated our travel schedules so at least one of us would be home with the children to eat dinner with them, read books to them, and tuck them in bed.

As in the Sudan, we had full-time help with child care. One challenge was to help the child-care staff understand our child-rearing practices including the need to explain why things needed to be done, letting the children dress and feed themselves, limiting TV time to only one hour, and not tolerating whining. We reminded our children to share, be fair, and show respect and be polite to everyone, including the household help. Our aim was for our children to develop self-sufficiency with a sense of reciprocity balanced with the American value of being independent.

During this time in the Philippines, I tried to not mix work with home-life. The intersections of my identities as a Filipina woman working as an American expatriate in my home country were quite different from my situation in the Sudan. I wanted to be viewed as a competent professional; not a part-time professional. But sometimes, life got in the way of my best intentions. In the summer of 1984, I planned a work-related field trip to Baguio. When I found out that there was an Embassy owned cottage in Baguio, I asked our two maids to hop on a bus to Baguio with David and Ligaya and their four cousins who were visiting from California. After everyone was settled in Baguio, a major typhoon blew causing landslides along the Manila-Baguio road. The US Embassy requested an evacuation of personnel stranded in Baguio. Since I was there on travel orders, the US embassy officer on duty called and asked how many in my party needed to be evacuated. I sheepishly stated, "Me. My two kids and their four cousins. And two maids." To which the officer replied, "Confirmed. One van for Beebe. Party of 9." After that experience there was no more mixing business travel with pleasure.

While facilitating a workshop on monitoring and evaluation of USAID PVO Projects in Cebu, I received a frantic call from my supervisor who strongly advised me to take the next flight back to Manila as per my husband's request. When I asked, "Why? Is one of the kids sick?" The terse reply was "When your man tells you to come home, you come on home." Needless to say, I was annoyed with my supervisor and even more annoyed with my husband. I was still fuming when I got home and only calmed down when my husband said, "There was credible intelligence of a possible coup. We could not tell you over an unsecured line." And he and my supervisor agreed, it was best if I were home in the event of an evacuation of US personnel. That night there was no coup, but Marcos finally deciding to flee. For months afterwards, the PVO/NGO community thought we worked for an intelligence agency because how else would I have known to leave the workshop in a hurry. And just like that, some of my hard-earned trust evaporated!

We could have extended our stay in Manila. However, our 5-year-old daughter started receiving invitations to birthday parties at posh hotels. Feeling sure raising our children in an over-privileged environment was not the life my husband and I envisioned, we opted to go to the next assignment, Liberia, a very poor country in west Africa. I had a job offer prior to the move because of reviews of my performance at USAID/Manila.

LIBERIA (1987-1990)

Working in a Fragile Environment

The American Colonization Society founded the colony of Liberia in 1821 on the coast of West Africa. It was intended as a home for free-born blacks and freed slaves from the U.S.. The indigenous Liberians resisted the expansion of the Americo-Liberians. In 1980, Samuel Doe, an indigenous Liberian and a non-commissioned officer in the army, led a bloody coup d'état against President Tolbert, became President ending 133 years of Americo-Liberian political domination over Liberia. In December 1989, Charles Taylor, another indigenous Liberian, led a rebellion against President Doe.

When we arrived in 1987, Doe was the president, a constitution providing for a multiparty republic had been approved by referendum, and the outlook for Liberia's future seemed hopeful. USAID started to implement economic development activities and to support civil society development.

Balancing the Role of Non-Governmental Organizations and Government

I served as the Mission Private Voluntary Organization (PVO) Officer and was the liaison with the Government of Liberia Non-governmental Organizations (NGO) Coordinating Council. One of my initial tasks was to lead a sector assessment of the status, needs, and organizational, financial, and absorptive capacity of Liberian PVOs and NGOs. As a project manager, I established a system for selecting both US-based and local PVOs to participate in the technical assistance and training activities, and developed a multi-year budget. Another project funded a financially sustainable Micro to Small Enterprise Development Project that provided savings and credit services to very poor rural families and assisted a local health NGO consortium develop a private health care improvement project that focused on balancing preventive and curative services for a large percent of the population in Liberia. The organization running the Leprosy center requested a small grant for minimal infrastructure upgrade, including the toilet facilities. My son David was 12 years old by then and I took him along for the 270 plus kilometer drive when I did an assessment visit. His recommendation, "The need is obvious. Give them the grant." I concluded that my husband and I made the right decision to leave the privileged environment of the Philippines.

Balancing Policy with Grassroots Action

The work in Liberia built on leadership competencies I had strengthened in the Philippines. Unlike in the Philippines, I had to deal with stakeholders not only from the non-governmental organizations who were action oriented but also from the Government of Liberia who were policy oriented.

Work-life Challenges: Coping in a Fragile Environment

On the morning of December 26, 1989, my son, David joined his middle-school classmates, along with their teachers, on a field trip to Sapo National Park, a tropical rainforest with one of the highest mammal species diversity of any region in the world. The year before, my husband went as a chaperone and spent time with David while trying not to step on any green mamba snakes. Due to work commitments, including being the Embassy officer on duty, James did not go. The field trip party left early in the morning and planned to arrive in Sapo that afternoon. About noon the US Embassy received news the rebels fighting against Doe had cut off access to the main road to Sapo National Park on their bloody advance towards Monrovia. The U.S. Embassy assumed that the field trip group was already in the Sapo National Park. The challenge was to get a message to the teachers and chaperones to stay where they were until a way could be found to get them home without travelling on the main road. An emergency two-way radio system was activated. Luckily an American missionary was located near the entrance of the Park. He was able to send a runner to deliver the message and to arrange for a small plane from the neighboring country of the Ivory Coast to pick up the field-trip party. The students did not quite understand what the brouhaha was all about and reported that they discussed what could be done "if we get out of the forest and everyone we know is gone." The discussion was an offshoot of their middle school reading of William Golding's *Lord of the Flies* (1954).

In January 1990, the US ambassador asked who among the US embassy community would volunteer to go first for emergency evacuation. I was one of those who said, "No. I cannot abandon my Liberian colleagues." During Easter, we allowed David to go visit his friend whose parents were missionaries in a coastal community many miles from the conflict. Conditions changed very quickly and that weekend, the US Peace Corps Volunteers and US missionaries, along with David, were evacuated to Monrovia. Finally, in May the US ambassador ordered women and children-to be evacuated to Washington, DC. while the men, including my husband, who were considered essential personnel stayed on. The evacuees spent 2 days in London where Miss Saigon was playing. The hotel concierge found us tickets and we were entertained with a helicopter evacuation in the middle of our own evacuation. Life imitates art which imitates life. For his college entrance essay, David wrote about being evacuated from Sapo National Park, being evacuated from the coastal community, and being evacuated from Liberia and enjoying the helicopter evacuation in Miss Saigon. The essay demonstrated his evolving understanding of global economic, social, and security issues.

INTERLUDE:
OREGON (1990-1992) AND WASHINGTON, DC (1993-1994)

Adjusting to non-Expatriate Life

Before being evacuated from Liberia because of the civil war, my husband was already scheduled to spend at least one year at Oregon State University as part of a special program for exchanges between universities and USAID.

For the preceding 11 years the family had lived as expatriates in the Sudan, Philippines, and Liberia; and David and Ligaya had attended American/International Schools. Despite being called American school, these schools accepted students and attracted teachers from throughout the world, including from the host country. In 1990, David who was in high school and Ligaya who was in grade school attended a U.S. public school for the first time. Their adjustment was easy with only a minor issue of having for the first time in their lives to check a box for their ethnic identity.

Completing a Much Delayed Dissertation

My main goal during the time James was at Oregon State University was to finish my doctoral degree at Stanford. Stanford approved a new dissertation topic on the language of credit in a rural Philippine village. I conducted field research and gathered data by using semi-structured interviews, focus group interviews, video and tape recordings of natural speech during a training program, and responses to stimulus words. I examined the relationship between Tagalog language structure and other properties of discourse and Filipino social structure and processes in order to understand the social exchange and interaction involved in credit transactions. Finally, I discussed the implications of the research results for the design and implementation of development programs, including the need to train development workers on ways to increase participation that leads to shared ownership of activities and shared commitment to succeed. I agreed with my dissertation adviser that I would not let any other activities get in the way of my dissertation work. In response to an email from my adviser I confessed I was in Poland working on a proposal. His reply was "That is well and good but please send your chapters on time." Writing a dissertation required a vision of what can be. The finished dissertation was called innovative and creative in its use of qualitative research. The Poland project, discussed below, was also pronounced innovative and creative.

Seizing Opportunities

When a colleague at Oregon State University (OSU) asked if I would help write a proposal for the United States Information Agency, I agreed and developed a project to establish an enterprise development program in Krakow, Poland. In the early 1990s, Poland made great progress towards achieving a fully democratic government and a market economy so the timing for the proposed project was right. When the proposal got funded, I was asked to implement my vision. I agreed on the condition that I could only work part-time since I had a dissertation to complete. The program showcased my ability to forge alliances needed for achieving a common goal. It required coordination within OSU, with a local community college, and with local businesses. The project combined non-formal training in small business development with formal university training in business administration for our Polish counterparts. Technical assistance included strategic planning, needs assessment, and program planning.

Expanding my Functional Orientation

In the summer of 1992, we moved to Washington, D.C. when James was required to accept an assignment in the USAID headquarters. I secured a job as a Senior Program Manager with the Office of Environment and Natural Resources at the Global Bureau at USAID. My key responsibilities were to provide technical advice and field support guidance. I served as the principal advisor for the analysis, planning, budgeting, approval, justification, monitoring, implementation, and evaluation of the program activities of the office while ensuring that projects were consistent with US legislation. I participated in the development of a biodiversity framework, a multi-donor, multi-country program evaluation of the IUCN-Switzerland, including its field programs in Laos and Nepal, and an initial environmental analysis of 10 USAID-funded community development projects in the Philippines. Based on this analysis, my team developed written to enable Philippine organizations to conduct their own environmental analysis. I acted as interim project manager for the conservation of biodiversity project.

Appreciating Sustainable Development

I became more knowledgeable about sustainable development and discerning the importance of balancing economic, social and environmental issues. I learned the value of mentoring fellows and personnel who were proficient in their technical areas but more likely to think in silos and not the big picture and less knowledgeable about USAID development assistance. I was becoming more effective in developing other's strengths, motivating others, and managing teams and work groups to be more productive and successful. I learned to articulate and incorporate vision, purpose, and aspirations of sustainable development across our portfolio; broadening and deepening my leadership repertoire.

Work-Life Balance: Raising a Latchkey Daughter

Our son, David opted to finish his senior year at Corvallis High School and lived with a family friend in Corvallis, OR which meant that Ligaya was our only child while living and working in DC. We chose a neighborhood that was within walking distance of the Washington International School so she could continue learning French. This was also the first time that we had no full-time help with childcare and house chores. Ligaya at age 11 participated in several after-school activities and became a latchkey kid for about 2 hours on some days until my husband and I came home from work. I would like to believe that rather than a negative effect on her self-development, there were some positive effects, including development of self-reliance and adaptation to difficult situations.

I remember taking Ligaya to "bring your daughter to work day." She was unimpressed as I spent most of the time on the phone or on email following up with internal team members and with external partner organizations on implementation matters. This was a reminder that managing and organizing was not all about "bells and whistles" but also involved day to day routines that could get boring even while keeping the big picture in mind. The ability to move back and forth from looking at the big picture to looking at finer details has become an essential part of my leadership repertoire.

SOUTH AFRICA (1994-1996)

Learning from South Africans

Our arrival in South Africa in January 1994 for James' assignment would be quickly followed by the release from prison of Nelson Mandela in early February, all-race elections in April, and his inauguration on May 10. Mandela declared at his inauguration that "Never, never again will this beautiful land experience the oppression of one by another." Hillary Clinton who was part of the high level delegation to the inauguration was by herself in a secure area when I saw her. I had the audacity to motion to her so I can shake her hand and tell her how impressed I was with her speech.

Doing Social Soundness Analysis

As a social scientist, I participated in the strategic planning process of USAID/ South Africa as it moved towards a post-apartheid transition. As part of the strategic planning process, I drafted parts of the concept paper, the guidelines for the planning process, and the analysis of the country situation, including the Gender and Environment annexes. I coordinated the establishment of a performance monitoring and evaluation plan for gathering, analyzing, and reporting people-level results. As the social soundness analysis team leader, I participated in the design of new activities to ensure sustainability, consistency with the culture of the different groups in South Africa, and alignment with the goals of USAID that relate to social, gender, and race equity. I drafted the "Basic Information for Potential Partners in Sustainable Development" to help potential grantees. As the gender team leader, I organized the Mission's Gender working group, drafted a mission policy on gender, and coordinated work to ensure integration of gender in Mission's strategic objectives.

Ubuntu and Kapwa

What I learned about leadership from my South African experience can be summarized in the concept of *ubuntu* [I am what I am because of who we all are]. Ubuntu is closely related to kapwa with both concepts embodying the ideas of connection, community, and mutual caring for all. These concepts are the ideals I aspire to as a leader and that inform my leadership.

Work-life Challenges: Raising a Daughter Who Can Deal with Any Situation

"Mom, we have a situation here." My daughter, 12 at that time, called one afternoon after coming home. "There are people who say they are with the Embassy security company and they want me to let them in. And they want to know what I'm doing here." The heavily armed security personnel were responding to a silent emergency alarm which my daughter must have activated by accident. When my daughter answered through the security bars (all houses assigned to US embassy had security bars) without opening the door, they demanded to know who she was and what she was doing in our house to which she replied "I live here." What we did not know was that there were reports earlier that week of young girls in their school uniforms ringing doorbells in the upper class neighborhoods requesting for help as a way to get people to open doors that would be rushed by burglars. What my daughter had in common with the young girls who perpetrated the burglary incidents was, in addition to her age, her appearance as a mixed-race person. She was able to call on the self-reliance, confidence, and problem-solving skills she developed over time as an expatriate kid.

CODA

Beginning with simple projects in the Sudan and moving on to complicated programs in the Philippines, Liberia, and Oregon, and complex interventions in Washington, DC and South Africa, it is clear that a single way of leading would not have been sufficient. A leadership repertoire consisting of multiple competencies is more appropriate as different contexts require the use of different leadership tools. In addition to competence in one's area of specialization, other leadership competencies must come into play in order to face the complexity of global engagement. Early engagements with international development served as building blocks for the more complex work during the next chapter of my life, including work on ICT for development in Africa (See Beebe et al., 2003) and my work in Afghanistan discussed in "Harmonizing Global Teams in Afghanistan" in *DISRUPT* (Beebe and Escudero, 2015). To summarize, my leadership repertoire has built on individual leadership qualities that developed over time. The Filipino cultural value *Pakikipagkapwa* [reciprocal interaction with a fellow human being] is the foundation for my leadership.

Work-life challenges revolved around our children. I believe that being intentional about child-rearing practices while raising our kids overseas was instrumental in developing their global competence. Living and going to school overseas increased their international awareness, appreciation of cultural diversity, proficiency in learning foreign languages, and knowledge of international issues. Undoubtedly, David and Ligaya have learned to not only be curious but also to actively engage with their environment and this has put them on the path to being global citizens.

LIGAYA BEEBE: COMMENTS
BY THE DAUGHTER OF MARIA BEEBE

The path is an apt metaphor for global competence, and maybe too, for building a leadership repertoire. Building empathy, learning to be globally aware, and forming a leadership toolkit require ongoing work. It is a path. Unlike learning languages, there is no end-point like "true fluency." I am thankful for my parents' intentional guidance, be it through modeling the way, encouraging us through challenges and cheering us through victories, or curating the most effective environment for our development (i.e., no more birthday parties at posh hotels).

Growing up as an ethnically half-Filipino, one hundred percent citizen of the U.S., while living overseas (we had never actually lived in the U.S. for more than a summer until I was eight) helped me realize that identity is constructed and contested. I was baffled when we were evacuated from Liberia in 1990 and my new classmates in Washington, D.C. did not immediately recognize my "American-ness." That move was the first time I felt different from what an "American" was or encountered the idea that there was something an "American" was supposed to be. I asked my parents and my brother to call me Liann, a portmanteau of my Filipino first name and my American middle name. I kept my American name throughout our time in Corvallis and through the beginning of our time in South Africa. My parents were supportive, and this too speaks to their adaptability and effective leadership.

Thanks in large part to my upbringing, I have internalized a life-long love for languages, a passion for international travel, and an optimistic drive to work for a more just world. I studied Chinese history in college and graduate school. I taught as a special education teacher in a public school in Brooklyn, NY. I lived in China for eight years and learned Mandarin. As a volunteer with Volunteers in Asia (VIA), I worked at a small, local PVO run by Tibetan women; their main goal was to empower local women to design, raise funds for, implement, and monitor their own grass-roots development projects in their local communities. Later, I taught English to college students in western China and parlayed my teaching experience to become a Teacher Trainer. I provided a short, intensive teacher training course for VIA's incoming volunteers for five summers. During my last few years in China, I was a Project Manager at a small international non-profit that worked on access to education and job readiness skills for rural, Tibetan students.

Now, I am living in New York City again and working with the U.S. branch of the International Education and Resource Network (iEARN). iEARN is an international network that fosters global citizenship through online collaboration, international exchange through study abroad programs, and professional development for educators incorporating global competence into their curriculum. All of iEARN-USA's projects are guided by the mission to enable young people worldwide "to make a meaningful contribution to the health and welfare of the planet and its people."

At iEARN-USA, my main role is to coordinate immersive language programs for U.S. youth (ages 15-18) through the National Security Language Initiative for Youth (NSLI-Y). I am grateful for the opportunity to facilitate transformative, cross-cultural experiences for youth. I am also proud to be able to contribute to iEARN's important mission.

My brother and I are fortunate to have been born and raised on the path to being global citizens. Our mandate now is to continue on this path. If we are very fortunate we might help our own children, friends, colleagues, and students find their own paths to global citizenship.

ELENA MANGAHAS*

*Division Manager, San Joaquin Employment
and Economic Department
FWN Board Member (2005-Present)
FWN100™ U.S. 2007*

ELENA MANGAHAS
and
DAUGHTERS

Johanna Mangahas (Birthed 1978),
Elena's First Daughter

My mom likes to tell our origin stories.

We have our own baby photo albums, my sister and I: one blue and one red, padded plastic hardbound, our pink hospital bracelets nestled into a plastic sleeve, in each, above the photo of a smush-faced newborn cuddled in what looks like a toaster oven but was actually an incubator, in vogue at the time of our births and a fun new word for the small child browsing through her birth album.

Other words I learned fairly early include "Lamaze," "Apgar score," and "colonial mentality." These fit the central theme of my birthday story, that being my mom's fight for a natural child birth against the Manila hospital in thrall to Western technology. She succeeded both times (those Apgar** scores were 10, she always beams,) the second time distinguished by, in my sister's album, the smile-filled group shot of medical staff that my ever-energetic mom coordinated and photographed shortly after my delivery.

I also know she would bring me with her to work on University of the Philippines campus when I was a baby in the Philippines, planting me on her desk

---

* The views presented are those of the author and do not necessarily represent the views of the San Joaquin County Employment and Economic Development Department

** A score that quickly summarizes health of newborns with a 10 being the highest possible score.

and letting me interact with her *barkada* [peer group] in the Mass Communications department. Later, in the U.S., she made friends with other immigrant Filipino mothers, and they would rotate us kids around as a way to juggle childcare with other work. She also loved using the public library as a babysitter. Eventually we were joined in the U.S. by my grandmother and, later, her cook, who is also like a grandmother to me, to this day.

These facts have new importance to me now, as I have returned back to work with an infant of my own. Recently I found myself among a group of colleagues who were ribbing me for my sincere claim, "childbirth was wonderful!"

"It's my mom's influence," I deflected, "that woman is crazy. You know how you're supposed to get a colonoscopy after 50?" I went on to tell the true tale of how she flabbergasted her doctor by declining anesthesia. "Pssh!" she says, in a voice I invent for her, "I had kids. This is nothing."

We laughed—throw it onto the pile of crazy mom stories, everyone has those.

Birth stories, on the other hand, are intimate, or at least mine still feels that way. Although I did read an entire book of them in preparation for my own labor. In retrospect, I was seeking neither childbirth's romantic aura nor its dirty details. I just wanted to feel bonded to an experience so widely shared.

That is my point of reference for this book my mom wants me to contribute to. Something about women, Filipinas, leaders; I confess I never grasped the theme. It seems like the birth stories: unique voices within a common experience.

So, my two cents: if my mom tries to pass herself off as anything archetypical, do not buy it. She is unconventional, at the least. May well be crazy. She is also my superhero.

MARTHA MANGAHAS (BIRTHED 1980), ELENA'S SECOND DAUGHTER

"My work and community service are seamless." This has been my mom's leadership mantra since she began creating a new life for herself and for us in the United States.

My mom, whom I lovingly call *Nanay*, wryly brags that she brought me from the Philippines to America "in a shoebox," since I was only two months old at the time and could have fit in one. Meanwhile, my mom would have to try to fit into a new country, and thus she began her career in social services helping other new immigrant Asian families do the same. For my mother, however, this was not work; helping others in the community was a calling, as the many challenges facing new immigrants were challenges she had also undergone. By taking action to meet the needs of others, my mother impacted many lives, including mine. From her I learned to be empathetic and as the children of refugee families became my peers in school I copied her inclusiveness and natural way of mentoring others.

My mom's first job in America was for a non-profit organization called Maharlika, that helped Filipinos and other Southeast Asian families obtain various services, ranging from healthcare to housing, or simply social support. In return Filipino farmworkers would gift her fruits and vegetables from their day's harvest while Southeast Asians cooked for her their ethnic food (at a time when there were few local ethnic restaurants). That was our unpublishized privilege as she returned home with her gifts of bounty. My mother's oft-repeated humor was to throw the Scarlett O'Hara "we will never starve again" line to my sister and I. Coincidentally we became both English and Literature majors in college.

She also joined American Friends and Service Committee and Stockton Sister City Association, organizations that worked to build relationships between new refugee and immigrant groups who had settled in Stockton from the time of Japanese internment during the second World War to the present. With her background in mass communications from the University of the Philippines, my mom had the persuasive skills necessary for helping others navigate government assistance programs and find jobs. As a Filipino it also helped that her looks blended with the families she was serving. Eventually, my mom became a civil servant for San Joaquin County working as an employment specialist for its workforce development branch, where she continues to work today.

Once again, my mom was involved in more than just her job, and her involvement in the community was for me, the greatest educational advantage. As teenagers my sister and I joined the Asian American Repertory Theater where we performed plays about generational divisions, discrimination, and paving a new future as Americans. These plays, by celebrated Asian authors such as Jeannie Barroga and David Henry Hwang, became part of our literature world in college. While in college, I heard many Filipino student activists bemoan the lack of Filipino representation in the curriculum, and quietly I celebrate my exposure to Filipino American contributions following upon my mom's involvement in the Filipino American National Historical Society and the Little Manila Foundation, the only Asian historic preservation group in Stockton.

My mom can add numerous community organizations to her resume, many of which she has served in leadership roles. What I admire about my mom is not the many titles she has held, but her conviction to do what she feels is important, regardless of whether it is work-related or a volunteer opportunity. To my mom, the adage "follow your passion" does not simply mean do what you want to do, but make a difference wherever and whenever you can. Today, as a teacher, artist, and activist, I do not see my commitments as separate roles, but rather the natural outgrowths of my convictions, that ought to be, as my *Nanay* says, seamless.

ELENA MANGAHAS, THE MOTHER'S STORY

Motherhood came at the perfect age of 25 and my birthing my first child really became a reclaiming of my own mother's life. I was made to look back.

I am that child who lost her mother at age two-and-a-half.

From oral history I learned that my mother was harvesting corn in the backyard when her full-term womb took an uneasy turn. She climbed the stairs back to the house and quickly slipped me into this world, a moment jokingly referred to in the family as the alternative good news harvest since she left the corn bounty behind. I also learned that my oldest sister boiled corn from the corn harvest with the hope that my mother would regain her strength, postpartum. I find out years later that corn is a superfood for pregnancy and postpartum.

Although my mother was over 40 when she conceived one more child, she had already raised four pre-war children, two boys and two girls. How romance came between my father and mother when there was a lot of post war rebuilding in the province of Panay, in the city of Roxas ,escapes me. My brother joked that my Mama was the Visayan Scarlett O'Hara because she planted as much corn as our backyard would hold because she did not want her children to be hungry again. One fateful day, again while she was tending to her corn, her heart must have signaled trouble. She climbed the stairs back to the house and her hardy body fell on the floor. She left us the same way she gave birth to me, from the corn field, a climb, a crawl, a crowd of neighbors trying to resuscitate her. This time it was death that arrived.

My foundational nurturing came from a doting father and four siblings some twenty years older than me. From them my spirit of mothering was learned. I remember in my childhood that I uttered wishful prayers once I learned in catechism that one could ask: "Jesus, when will I meet my Mama?" By high school I learned a cover-up song taught in my Catholic school: "Jesus loves the little children, all the children of the world..." then follows the coloring book of skin color which I did not understand but by this time my maturing faith defied the theorists about growing up without a mother.

Coming of age I only needed to add natural childbirth to the legend of my mother who despite leaving too soon still lives in me had had such a strong influence. She put me in charge of myself and my accomplishments.

As I look back at my journey of leadership I dance around my mother's grave for she made possible who I have become.

1. Develop cooperative relationships among the people I work with.

I learned this early on because I grew up in a village always disciplined by five adults and my job was to please my family. As a family we were a tight organization. Our constantly articulated mission is to succeed in all we do. From this I learned to be a generalist, mimicking all skills and doing them for the approval of my caring adults. I learned that good work ethics yielded positive results and even afforded my siblings their promotional track.

When do those cooperative relationships come to play?

Let's take today's diverse workplace that I have inextricably become a part of being an immigrant and non-native born.

Work is valued in all cultures. I discovered that people's commonality power the engines of the workplace. While income and job satisfaction top the list of job motivators there are intangible benefits in inter-personal relations.

On my rise to supervisory positions I used my family dynamics of exciting my work team and took aim at one singular mission: that of shared success, attained in a well-supported and caring way. No resistance here. The getting-along part was effortless.

2. Actively listen to diverse points of view.

There were many, because everyone wanted to raise me; perhaps out of pity but that's a predictable Filipino sentiment to an orphaned child.

The trusted model by which I grew up in is one of encouragement, recognition and guiding feedback that builds confidence. While I am a product of diverse points of view I also received the assurance that they were intended for my own welfare.

In the workplace I re-enacted my siblings' motivational words and gestures. Hence I was primed for coaching others. And coaching I established as my own model. I stand behind coaching not because it is now found in the workplace parlance but because it is natural and born out of trust in oneself that affects the bottom line.

3. Seek out challenging opportunities that test my own skills and abilities.

I had to show that I was the girl they could be proud of. I thrived on my siblings' applause, the honor medals they pinned on my dress, the confidence

I built knowing I could do it, and even thrived on an invisible approving smile. Sometimes from heaven.

Accolades are natural supplements. I heard them as a child and I was told not to rest on them. In fact it was the presence of the adults that built confidence in me. They spoke openly about my strength and weaknesses and I took it as counsel.

I also realized that adults make a good audience. They taught me to always start on a high note and stay dynamic all throughout the presentation. Later it is all about topping the previous performance.

Leadership took shape when I became that same adult in my community of women. There are constant challenges of gender equity, opportunities and battlefields of empowerment. Enter mentoring and the honed lessons in coaching, always working on becoming the girl they could be proud of.

4. Challenge my circle to try out new and innovative ways to do their work.

This is how I earned the title promotora [promoter] in elementary school not knowing I was leading the pack. Even my high school friends would accord me the same title.

There are points along the path of leadership when growth spurts occur.

I call them bold steps. Bold steps are learned; then they are rehearsed. They are exercised, and delivered with grace and elan.

My peers always looked up to me because I was an initiator of new ideas and winning attitude, win or lose. Workplace teams turn relentless if it is suggested that bold steps are healthy risks. At this junction it can be said that everyone becomes a leader if everyone buys into the bold steps.

And there I stand on the wings applauding my team just like my siblings did to me.

5. Appeal to others to share an exciting dream of the future.

As I was my family's collective dream of success so have I become the collective dream for my own children. In this writing I unraveled my leadership pathway as I know it. Maybe it is a little bit of Jose Rizal "*ang hindi lumingon sa pinanggalingan ay hindi makakarating sa patutunguhan.*" [She who does not look back is not able to reach her destination.]

I am convinced that it is also from the voice of my mother.

Besides the fact that during my growing years, I boldly joined with others in the struggle for peace, for democracy, for justice, for cultural, and historic preservation and was motivated by the accolades I received; I also maintain that accolades are no longer needed in this day and age. The enduring spirit of mankind is that of unity and the spirit of my womankind is that of her voice and her legacy. I am on it.

Filipinas will find many uncanny ways to cultivate and power-up their leadership path. I offer my story because the over-all story is richer by increasing the number of witnesses.

MA. ALCESTIS "THETIS" ABRERA MANGAHAS

FOUNDING FELLOW, SOCIAL WEATHER STATIONS
FWN100™ GLOBAL 2014

A World Citizen

I t all started as a split moment decision. In September 1991, deep in protracted negotiation for a senior government career post in the Philippines, I got a call from the United Nations' (UN) International Labour Office's (ILO) Bangkok Office asking whether I would be interested in managing a relatively large project for returned migrant workers in Colombo, Sri Lanka. It was a compelling offer, simply because of the magnitude of the human story. Over 79,000 Sri Lankan women migrant workers, mainly household domestic workers had fled Kuwait during the 1991 Saddam Hussein invasion and after many months of desperate journey, were returning to their home country. The ILO was committed to provide the Sri Lankan government technical assistance for their reinsertion and resettlement back to their home communities.

Unbeknownst to me at that time, this initial yes started a 20-year career in international technical cooperation, a passion that has brought me all over the world to live and work. In over 15 years, I have lived in Colombo, Manila, Geneva, and Bangkok; and worked in seriously poor countries of Eastern Europe: Albania, Moldova, the Ukraine; South Asia: Nepal and Sri Lanka; and South-east Asia: Cambodia, Lao PDR and Yunnan in the People's Republic of China. I also had the privilege of working in the Philippines, as the ILO national coordinator of the national child labour program that brought me to the informal gold mines of Diwalwal, the child recruitment centers for fishing boats in Dumaguete, the wharf

Diwalwal, the child recruitment centers for fishing boats in Dumaguete, the wharf workers in Sasa, Davao, and participating in a multi-agency raids of brothels in Caloocan and Quezon City.

Over time, the nature of the assignment changed from direct services to beneficiaries to higher-level technical positions as a specialist on migration, forced labor specialist, and eventually into regional management. As I rose the management and leadership ladder, the responsibilities became more complex, not necessarily from the increasing demands of working with beneficiaries nor the technical requirements of different interventions but infuriatingly more often due to the political dimensions of international development cooperation.

In this chapter, I discuss the leadership required in international development cooperation. I became engaged with the world as a result of my college dissertation on Philippine poverty. The dissertation pushed me in the direction of services and programs for the poor that led to employment with the Department of Labour in 1974. Thus, the ILO mission of social justice is very consistent with my own vision of the world. My Sri Lanka experience proved pivotal to my leadership journey, leading to the development of global competence including global awareness, situational context, alignment to international agencies mission and vision, collaboration across cultures, and intercultural capability in dealing with diverse stakeholders. As a Filipina expatriate, I experienced the disadvantages and advantages of the intersections of being an expert; being a woman, wife, and mother; and, being a Filipino, as my national identity that guided my leadership.

Appreciating the Global Context of Leadership

Foreign employment is a natural phenomenon in many parts of the world. While the Filipino psyche is likely to attribute overseas jobs as a sorry reflection of the state of the Philippine economy, the truth is the country is only one of many countries that have its citizens working in foreign lands. At the time of the Iraqi invasion of Kuwait in 1991, over a million foreign workers were working in Kuwait, mostly coming from other Middle Eastern countries. Filipinos were a relatively small sized population of the 24,000 migrant workers, and similar to the Sri Lankans, consisted mainly of household domestic workers.

Women and Income Inequalities: the Case of Sri Lanka

Even in years prior to the 1991 Iraqi invasion, Sri Lankan migrant domestic workers were faced with very serious difficulties at work. As a domestic worker, the hired woman was often completely at the mercy of her "sponsor," the family that employed her. Workdays were long, often more than 12 hours a day, cleaning, cooking and looking after the children and elderly. Repaying their recruitment and travel costs, the women worked the first six months of the standard two-year contract for nothing. For the duration of the contract, the women surrender their passports to their employers. Under Kuwaiti law at that time, the only way the women could get out of the contracts was by reimbursing their employer for his full investment, at that time approximately $1,000.

The women persisted despite such difficulties. The seemingly low salaries often exceeded the wages they could have earned at home. Migrant women consistently asserted that their families could not survive on what their husbands earned, and argued that migration to the Middle East was their only available economic alternative. Family motives for migration usually include getting out of debt, buying land, and building a house. Women also supported their family's daily consumption needs, educated their children, and provided dowries for themselves or their daughters. Participants in the decision-making process, undergone repeatedly for migrants who returned several times to the Gulf, weighed financial necessity and household improvements against separation, incursion of loans, and alternate arrangements for childcare.

The Casualties of War: Women and Shame

In an environment of war and displacement, the return of the migrant workers to their home country is especially difficult. Many women migrants lose not only employment and life savings, but also the esteem in their home villages that comes with foreign employment. In particular, workers on their first contract are in very precarious situations. Typically, migrant workers start their foreign employment in deep debt having had to borrow the equivalent of 5 or 6 months of salary from extended family and local loan sharks to cover expenses related to recruitment.

For the Sri Lankan domestics, the Hussein invasion of Kuwait was a major shock that shattered their dreams and the hopes of their families. The traumatic return process further aggravated the loss. Having to depend on strangers for safety and the constant threat of harassment and abuse from the invaders and male co-workers inflicted damage on these women. Worse, their immediate futures at home were unclear. There were debts to pay without the possibilities of income. Rather than the high status the women received as foreign exchange earners, the women experienced considerable shame.

An emergency program funded by the UNDP, the Swiss Government, and

CIDA, was designed to immediately address the return workers' needs, with a traumatic counseling program, employment services and skills training projects, documentation of losses for compensation claims, and for the long-term, an investment in strengthening the Sri Lanka Bureau of Foreign Employment (SLBFE) in the management of a foreign employment program.

Understanding the leadership challenge required unpacking the interrelated factors that included a historical perspective and awareness of the global environment and its impact on Sri Lankan women workers returning from overseas employment because of war. While the causes were global, the solutions had to be appropriate to the local situation.

UNDERSTANDING MY ROLE

By the time I arrived in Colombo, the women had already been back in their home villages for over three months. Already there had been over 15 young migrant suicides, arising from hopelessness and feelings of shame. Unbeknown to their families, there were also over 40 unwanted pregnancies resulting from abuses by Iraqi soldiers or "sexual payments" to male co-workers who assisted their escape from Kuwait.

Each day as I went to work, I would see long lines of the migrant women, accompanied by anxious relatives at the SLBFE. There were also relatives and friends in the bureau to register names of missing unaccounted family members and to plead for any information. There was so much to be done; not only in organizing services for the migrant women but also, ensuring that the Sri Lankan authorities took responsibility for the processes and became better prepared to manage similarly difficult and challenging situations that unfortunately are part of an overseas employment program.

Listening to Diverse Stakeholders and Conflicting Messages

As is often the case in these types of chaotic situations, there were many competing interests: (a) from within government itself the then Minister of Labour would often ask the Director of the SLBFE why the ILO had hired counselors who spent all their time "whispering" to the migrant returnees; (b) among the UN agencies questioning "What! Why a center in that far-flung municipality?" and interestingly(c) between the needs of the migrant workers and those of their families.

In those early days in Colombo, I realized that my workplace for doing development work would hardly be a posh corporate office in a cosmopolitan city. My very first workday in Colombo made that very clear. After a short briefing session in a cramped ILO Office in Colombo, I visited my "permanent" field office at SLBFE. The main office was full of women of various ages, many pushing against doors, or standing at counters; all seeking help. There were a lot of angry voices, many tears, and screams of protest and complaint.

I seriously felt out of place and asked immediately for the project offices. My government counterpart, the Director of the Bureau, was clearly embarrassed. He pointed out that they have not had the time to prepare an office. He pointed the way to an old garage, full of non-functioning army vehicles. When I returned to the ILO office in Colombo, the Director kindly gave me a spare storage room, right next to the UNDP informal canteen. As I went on about the lack of system and order at the field office, Dr. Srivastava pointed out: "That's why you're here, Thetis, you are here to help manage."

My instinctive reaction then was "Only for a year." I thought, "This is an emergency program! Eighteen months was short; the difficulties of leaving the cushy comfort of a well-established senior government position and the comforts of home would be a temporary difficulty."

Listening to Myself: Moments of Self-doubt

There were many moments of self-questioning during the Sri Lankan assignment. Though I considered myself a veteran of overseas employment programs that addressed the needs of foreign workers, having been honed by years of experience in both the government and civil society organizations, the scale of displacement was large and the psychological stresses on the Sri Lankan seemed especially severe. The self-doubts would hound me over several days. "Are my skills, technical and managerial, sufficient enough to help these women and their families. Have I taken on more than I am capable of? Should I be focusing my services on returned Filipino workers back in Manila?"

Reaffirming my Commitment

Typically, in the midst of self-questioning, I would surround myself with many of the migrant returnees and visit the local level migrant support centers we had established to assist the returnees in different parts of Sri Lanka. Meeting with the migrant women, listening to their experiences, and helping understand the difficult choices they are confronted with, often led to reaffirmation of the project's value and reminded me of why I signed up for it.

Finding Shared Humanity

It was in one those visits that I had a true epiphany. As I was visiting Rat-napura, our local community counselor spoke to me about the case of a very depressed non-communicative returnee and she suggested a drop-in meeting. In her home, her parents shared the story of her traumatic return and the tremendous difficulties the family was experiencing in repaying the debts related to her employment abroad and forced return. Throughout the time, the returnee was absolutely quiet and hardly looked at me. As I was saying goodbye, our local counselor mentioned that I was a Filipino, and on hearing that, the returnee looked up, broke into a smile, and then anxiously asked: "You're Filipino? You know Emerita? She is my home-mate, my best friend. How is she? Did she reach her home safely?" I gently told her that I did not know Emerita but as I was taking leave in a few weeks, I would look for her and let her know her situation when I returned to Colombo. She smiled broadly, rushed to embrace me, and said that she was looking forward to my return.

In that short sweet epiphany moment, I realized that indeed, Filipinos are truly world citizens. Foreign travel and employment have strengthened not only our personal interactions with much of the world, but also reinforced our solidarity through our shared experiences and our human-ness.

Over a span of 18 months, this "emergency, crisis response" program served nearly 90 percent of all the Sri Lankan returned workers from Kuwait, assisting the women in documenting the compensation claims from the Iraqi and Kuwaiti governments, and referring them to direct services in employment, health, and entrepreneurship services. A special point of pride was that Sri Lanka was the first among the Asian countries to receive the full compensation from the UN Commission. And in the South Asian region, the Sri Lanka Bureau of Foreign Employment for many years represented a model government institution responding to needs of migrant workers and their families. In 1992, Sri Lanka sent its key foreign employment officials for a two- week training in Manila, with funding from the UNDP project. To many of these officials, the POEA experience helped define the design of their own market promotion and protection programs for migrant workers.

MY READINESS FOR LEADERSHIP IN
INTERNATIONAL DEVELOPMENT COOPERATION

My own expertise in overseas employment and international migration grew from being part of the government's foreign employment program. At the start of my own career at the Department of Labor and Employment (DOLE) in 1974, the new Philippine Labor Code articulated a renewed overseas employment policy. The national program envisioned the promotion of foreign employment through government-to-government arrangements, the phase out of private recruitment agencies, and the general protection of migrant workers. The timing of the overseas employment policy was fortuitous, with the oil boom and the expansion of Middle East job opportunities. As one of around ten new recruits to the DOLE from the UP School of Economics, I was both confident and fearful about the new assignment. I had originally intended to pursue an academic track and had the option to join the UP Los Banos economics faculty. But first hand exposure to Philippine poverty while writing my college research dissertation pushed me in the direction of employment services and programs for the poor.

Joining the Ranks of Overseas Filipino Workers

In 1975, in my first year in the Philippine overseas employment program 36,000 workers left for foreign jobs. By the time I was ready to leave the Philippine overseas employment program in 1990, annual job placements reached almost 600,000. In 2014, over 1.8 million Filipinos registered as contract workers with the Philippine Overseas Employment for foreign jobs. Twenty percent of these registrants were seafarers. Over the last decade, the overseas employment labor force appears to be aging, with veteran overseas workers dominating the outflows. About two thirds of the contracts registered at the POEA are on repeat contracts (rehires). New POEA destinations apparently are not widely opening for Filipinos, or perhaps, many more are confidently moving to foreign assignments on their own, especially in nearby destinations, such as Singapore and Hong Kong. And with entry-level jobs in the Philippines now increasing, along with higher entry-level salaries, the incentive for working overseas is no longer as attractive as it had been.

Working in foreign countries is not a uniquely Filipino phenomenon. With global employment opportunities opening for many nationalities, it is not uncommon to find Americans, British, and even Japanese and Koreans workers in countries not their own. Estimates of Americans living and working abroad range from 2.6 million to 6.5 million; approximately 5.6 million British nationals find employment elsewhere, and so with nearly a million Japanese living and working, often working with the many Japanese companies in foreign countries. Over 5 million Chinese citizens currently work abroad. All of these numbers are a small drop in the ocean of the nearly 240 million migrant workers worldwide.

But what is indeed striking about the Philippine diaspora is the breadth of foreign employment, in terms of destination and the range of occupations and skills. The Filipinos are perhaps the largest sized work force on foreign ships, as seafarers and also as performing artists. There are many Filipinos in the health industry in Europe and the Middle East. Filipinos are theater professionals in South East Asia, sales clerks in duty free stores in major Middle East airports, and domestic workers in many households all over the world.

While the Philippine overseas employment program has had its ups and downs, the institutional mechanisms implementing the programs have remained strong despite much criticism. The Philippines is largely seen as the model for many foreign employment programs of other countries in Asia such Indonesia, Pakistan, Sri Lanka, and Bangladesh.

Meeting Filipinos in International Development but Few at the Top

Shifting from a career in a national government to an international career in technical cooperation would seem like a natural, but in truth, it was quite different.

There are very few estimates of the numbers of Filipinos in the UN and in international development organizations. These numbers range from a few hundred to several thousand. These numbers fluctuate widely especially since many technical specialists are on time-bound technical assistance projects. But in the context of large flows of Filipinos in many occupations and different destinations, the numbers of Filipino UN and international non-government service organizations are really quite small.

There is no common stereotype for the Filipino UN staff member. This is because the Filipinos are employed at many different levels. While the more visible employees in the UN secretariat are those in the administrative and finance positions, there are also those who are in the "field", as teachers, nurses, and soldiers in peacekeeping.

In the course of my UN career, it was obvious that there were very few Filipinos in senior management. I was privileged to be one of the very few who made it to the highest possible rank for a career official in Asia Pacific. In addition to the having "reserved" positions for major donor countries, there is the difficulty of the quota system imposed on countries for the participation of their nationals, often based on the countries' financial contributions to the U.N. Filipinos are considered "over-represented," in the staff lists of UN organizations, as we dominate numbers in administrative secretariat jobs. For many of the Filipino professionals, the entry point for many are the short-term technical project positions, and many Filipino professionals stay in these "temporary" positions for their entire careers.

Vision and Commitment to Making a Difference

The single unifying factor of multi-national teams of professionals is the clear commitment to the organizational core values. "Social Justice at work" is the mantra of the International Labour Organization, and served as the beacon for service at its core. Establishing international labour standards is a primary emphasis. The goal is to have a global framework agreed upon by governments, employers, and workers that set the basic minimum social standards that have been agreed upon by all stakeholders in the global economy. While many would think that such standards live in too high a stratosphere and are almost impossible to implement in real life, this is not true. International labour standards are first and foremost about the development of people as human beings. Work is part of everyone's daily life and is crucial to a person's dignity, well-being, and development as a human being. Economic development should include the creation of jobs and working conditions in which people can work in freedom, safety, and dignity. In short, economic development is not undertaken for its own sake but to improve the lives of human beings; international labour standards are there to ensure that it remains focused on improving human life and dignity. It is this vision and commitment to making a difference that is my internal compass.

In various fields including anti-discrimination, social protection, occupational safety and health, skills training, the promotion of collective bargaining, and freedom of association; the commitment to make a difference in workers' lives is paramount. So, on issues of social security, or AIDS promotion at the workplace, or for that matter, discrimination against women or ethnicity on the workplace, there are international standards that define and shape the direction of the discourse. In technical cooperation projects, the broad aspiration goals take on a very specific focus. In Sri Lanka, we were concerned with Sri Lanka migrant women; many of whom were household domestic workers, and lived in various parts of Sri Lanka. An important first step in knowing about the women, was knowing the drivers that motivated their search for foreign employment, and understanding of their work experience and the circumstances of their return. Only then, would it be possible to design a custom made program that serves their needs.

In my own career, I gravitated to those issues of workers who are least prepared to fight for their rights, given environmental, political, and cultural constraints. These are migrant workers and their families, child laborers, victims of forced labour, and human trafficking. And typically, the most vulnerable are women and the very young.

Leadership at the Intersections

Leading diverse multi-cultural teams is the norm in international development cooperation. In 1991, being a female head of a technical assistance project was not usual. In the Sri Lankan setting, it could be quite frustrating. I worked with two international experts; a British Vocational Training specialist, and an Australian trauma counseling consultant as well as a large team of Sri Lankans counselors, trainers, and extension workers. Not many of them were used to having a female foreign expert, an Asian woman, direct a technical assistance program. In the first few months there were many uncomfortable moments. For meetings with government ministers I would walk in with our British expert and often, the ministers and senior officials, all men, would address their questions to the white male! It did not help that he was 6'2" and I was a 5'3". It was not unusual for many to think I was the project secretary! Our British expert was a real trouper, and he would go out of his way to acknowledge my role.

After Sri Lanka, the teams became even more diverse. Responsibility for a five-country regional project for the Greater Mekong Sub-region meant I managed a staff with over 10 nationalities including Swede, Japanese, Canadian and Thai in the main Bangkok office; and a project field team consisting of nationals of Thailand, China (Yunnan), Cambodia, Lao PDR, and Vietnam.

Preconceived stereotyping of nationalities can sometimes lead to difficult and sometimes humorous situations. On a training mission visiting the Yunnan province of the People's Republic of China, I went with my team members to register at a local hotel. The counter staff immediately gave the relatively larger hotel room to our Caucasian technical officer, thinking he was the team leader. Being blonde and blue eyed certainly reaffirmed his status! Other team members were offended, not at the counter staff for their misconceptions, but at our officer for accepting the larger room, without acknowledging the mistake and giving me the room. Up to this day, I am not sure he fully understood why our Japanese and Swedish managers were annoyed with him! He simply thought that he was extremely lucky to get a bigger room, without fully understanding the nuances of the situation.

There were also many examples while managing the Eastern European projects that demonstrate how preconceptions can stand in the way of better understanding. In a particular instance, I was sharing the Philippine (Caloocan) and Thai recovery experiences with policemen and NGO workers in Bosnia-Herzegovina. There was strong skepticism about the Asian experience, with many of the conference participants assuming that Asians and Europeans were very different in their action and response. But my own experience proved otherwise. There were more similarities between the two cultures than anticipated! Truth is, migrant workers, regardless of nationality, shared the same precarious conditions in the destination country and often experienced similar shocks in the new countries.

Compassion and Sensitivity: Unintended Consequences

For many of those working in development cooperation, compassion, and sensitivity to the needs of others would seem to be part of their DNA. This is very often the incentive of many professionals for embarking on a development cooperation career. While the characteristic may be seen as part of the core profile, it can sometimes be difficult to have compassion and sensitivity when the beneficiaries of your programs turn against the help that is given.

As part of the national child labor program, the multi-agency network campaigning against the employment of children and teenagers in the entertainment sector embarked on a child recovery program in the cities of Caloocan and Quezon City. Most of the participants in the recovery effort, such as raids, thought that they were engaging in a public good in bringing children out of these clearly unacceptable work situations.

Right as the young girls were being escorted from these clubs and bars, there was open resistance among them to being separated from their bar colleagues and opposition to the prospect of being housed in separate quarters for children and young people. In a number of follow-up visits, the young women would throw their personal hygiene kits at the supposed "saviors", in protest to what they saw as intrusive and invasive action against them.

Lessons are drawn from the experience, primarily that massive raids against bars and brothels do not yield the desired results, especially as the city had no adequate areas of safety for these young people. There were clearly strong bonds of loyalty between the younger and older women of the clubs and being separated resulted in deep feelings of anxiety.

In many situations in development cooperation projects, it is impossible not to have pre-judged conceptions of "right" and "wrong", but keeping an objective balance is essential to achieving success.

There is also a need to have sufficient emotional distance in situations of extreme vulnerability. There is a special strength and courage needed in dealing with young children recruited as soldiers in national liberation movements in many parts of the world, or when meeting with child victims of muro-ami or deep-sea fishing in the Philippines, Thailand, and Indonesia. Muro-ami fishing uses an encircling net together with pounding devices. These devices are often large stones fitted on ropes that are pounded into the coral reefs. The pounding devices are repeatedly and violently lowered into the area encircled by the net, literally smashing the coral in that area into small fragments in order to scare the fish out of their coral refuges. Muro-ami has been described as one of the cruelest, most cataclysmic forms of illegal fishing that destroys the coral reefs and exploits children who get caught in the big nets that are used. Women domestic workers, whether Sri Lankan, Nepali, Ethiopian, face similar vulnerabilities regardless of country of employment. The vulnerability is often due to the nature of work, and often is not covered under national legislation of the different countries.

LIFE AS AN EXPATRIATE

Part of an international development cooperation experience often involves residing in different countries. There is substantial cultural adjustment not only in work life but also in dealing with the local community councils, landlords, and neighbors; deciding on where children should go to school; and balancing personal life with work.

Adjusting to the Local Situation

Deciding on a place to stay is often quite important since work assignments do not allow for many different changes. In Geneva, finding a suitable apartment was a well-known challenge. After a long search, I finally found a possible apartment that would meet my family's needs. The apartment was easily available perhaps because of a recent robbery. The then current owner, trying to make me accept the apartment more easily, spoke about the value of the apartment's bright light, especially in the living room. Coming from a hot tropical country, I was somewhat aghast at the notion of bright light and its effects on my Filipino furniture. Only when I finally experienced the dark grim weather of a European winter did I finally appreciate the value of his statement.

Balance Between Personal Life and Work

Working in an international setting away from family takes its toll. Keeping the family together especially in the early years was an important consideration. In Sri Lanka, I brought my then two-year old daughter and household domestic with me, while my sons and husband stayed in Manila. The Colombo bomb blast of 1991 forced me to send my daughter home to the Philippines and I continued my assignment alone. Despite such a traumatic memory, my children have very happy memories of their multiple visits to Colombo.

In both Geneva and Bangkok, my daughter stayed with me, enrolling in the International Schools of these cities. At some point, she tired of moving with me and losing friendships along the way. For high school and college she opted to return to Manila. One of the perks of an international career is subsidized education up to the college level. Yet my sons and daughter finished both their secondary education and university studies in Manila. Their father and I always felt that keeping strong ties with the home country would be important and that the best time would be during those formative years. I do ask myself years hence, whether this was the best path for the children; I only hope that had they thought otherwise, they would have had the confidence and courage to let us know.

Family priorities were the main reason I moved back to Bangkok from Geneva, despite the obvious job mobility opportunities available in Geneva. Being in Bangkok allowed me to return to Manila very often (every month) and to be present for key milestones in their lives. During the over 15 years of overseas assignments, we have always spent Christmas holidays together. Perhaps only three times did we spend it out of Manila; once in Geneva and twice in Bangkok.

My husband Mahar was deeply committed and dedicated to academic freedom. He is recognized as a leader in research methodology, especially survey research, and knows the importance of understanding social causes. His academic interests helped ease the likely conflicts that could have emerged from having a head-strong partner. Thank goodness for truly helpful mothers and mothers-in-law who took on surrogacy mother roles during the times I was away.

CODA

Relocating to Manila in 2015 has meant undergoing the same experiences of many overseas migrant workers as they retire from a foreign-based career. Depending on their situation when they returned, there are diverse needs of the migrants, from economic concerns; particularly finding employment or a source of livelihood or capital to either start or expand a small business; to concerns about the cost of medical care and other health needs. Among the psychosocial issues of some single, ageing female returnees is the fear of being alone and the lack of companionship. Among the married returnees, the well being of their children was a concern that was articulated, especially concern about their children being able to complete their education.

As a UN professional, my return home has had only minor problems. But concerns remain. After more than ten years abroad, I had adapted to very independent living and was unsure whether I wanted to revert back to the traditions of a Filipino home. Six months later, I am convinced there is nothing like the joy and freedom of being home with family.

Angelica Mangahas: Comments by the Daughter of Thetis Mangahas

I could not tell you precisely when I lost my excitement for travel, but sometime between the ages of ten and thirteen I had had it. Try as she might, my mother rarely succeeded at convincing me to join her on weekend trips to towns and cities near Bangkok and Geneva. Tired of moving around, I cared more about spending time with friends or watching TV. One memorable Christmas, Mom gave twelve-year-old me the gift of a Lonely Planet guide to France. I think she hoped I'd read it and find places for us to explore. I never read it.

At 12, I may have been simply too young to appreciate trips to castles, cathedrals, and wats—my mother's preferred destinations. I admit that in those days I found them boring. Looking back, I should have been more grateful for the opportunity to learn about the heritage of my then-homes. I was clueless about how much more difficult it would be to do the same today as a young adult with some responsibilities.

Even at that age, however, I did pick up a few things that are indispensable to me today. The first was a deep appreciation for inter-cultural respect. At school, my teachers and fellow pupils came from different places, with unique cultural practices and personal ways of expressing themselves. Differences were celebrated, but they were also taken in stride. At first, I wanted to gawk at every Sikh wearing a turban. Not long after, I wanted only to beat them in math, which they happened to be great at. (I don't believe I succeeded.)

The second thing I picked up while living abroad is my love for languages. For the first time, I had options to study more than English and Filipino. I had a little bit of Thai and a little more Spanish and French. My Spanish teacher in Geneva didn't speak English! She was the single best contributor to my French abilities, as I had to learn a lot of French to learn even a little Spanish. Today, my French isn't too bad and my Spanish is nada, but the principles I learned then apply even to the languages, like Mandarin Chinese, that I make a little more time for now.

While in Geneva, I picked up a third attitude: independence. It was safe to walk to school or take the bus to the mall alone. I had a mobile phone, my own set of house keys, and free afternoons! I got used to a great deal of freedom of movement and very much enjoyed it. Needless to say, 'reverse culture shock' hit hard when I came back to Manila. No longer used to uniforms, leading the class in prayer, or even standing when called, my classmates must have thought me a rumpled little barbarian.

My Catholic high school smoothed out some of my rough edges and taught me discipline, which I now also value. Nevertheless, after a few years of this in high school and well into my time in college, I was chomping at the bit. Mom understood this, I think, and helped me look for places where I could be an intern while joining her for a summer. I spent a few weeks with Save the Children in Bangkok.

Bangkok had a tense summer in 2010. The famous "Red Shirt" movement had shut down some of the city's major arteries. The Save the Children office was situated along one of those main roads, requiring me to pass through picket lines and bamboo stakes to get to and from work. As in Geneva years prior, I could get around on my own again—just not in the way I had expected! Near the end of my short time with Save, I was allowed to join a field visit outside Bangkok, to a wonderful storytelling workshop held for refugee children from Myanmar. After making puppets together, the children presented their personal stories at the local market. The children and the protesters alike demonstrated the importance and power of free expression—as well as its light and dark sides. It was a good lesson for me.

Back in Manila, my stint in Bangkok had not eased my interest in getting more international experience. If anything, it only pushed me to travel more. I found out that I could spend a term abroad. I applied to, and was accepted at, the Institute of Political Science in Paris, better known as SciencesPo. Apart from getting to practice my French again, I finally made some of those trips that Mom tried very hard to interest me in eight years prior. It was a good thing that I was a little more mature this time around.

By the time that Mom had retired in 2015, she and Papa had helped see me through these experiences and a few years' more: another internship, my first job, and most recently my Masters' degree in Georgetown University in the U.S. There has been no shortage of both failures and successes.

✳

MARIE CLAIRE LIM MOORE

Development Director
The Women's Foundation
FWN100™ Global 2014

Positively Filipina

I f there is one thing I have learned as a Filipino-Canadian-American working mother it is that the right attitude, combined with an appreciation of one's own roots and values, is a winning formula in leading a successful and positive life. No doubt, this has been engrained in me by my positively Filipino parents and upbringing.

Three years ago, I wrote my first book to try to capture some of their story. *Don't Forget the Soap* is a collection of anecdotes from my family's global journey starting with my parents' migration from the Philippines to my current experiences living abroad with my husband and our children, two when we first moved abroad, now three. The book has been described as everything from a "happy family handbook" to a "great big hug in a book." However, I was not purposely going for that. There are a number of books like *The Happiness Project* (Rubin, 2011) or *Stumbling on Happiness* (Gilbert, 2006) that methodically try to measure and dissect happiness. I just wanted to share stories about my family while recounting lessons from my mother. I guess I could have anticipated the result. For as long as I can remember, someone was always commenting on the happy disposition of our family.

In general, Filipinos are a happy bunch. Survey after survey and year after year, the Philippines comes up on top of every happiness index from *The Economist* to Instagram. This is one of the reasons why the country's recent tourism tag-line, "It's more fun in the Philippines," could not be more perfect. Launched in 2012 to attract visitors to the country, this campaign has been incredibly successful in creating positive buzz. In fact, marketing intelligence service Warc released its annual Warc 100 list of the world's top marketing campaigns and ranked the campaign as third, behind only Vodafone's Fakka (Egypt) and Amer-ican Express' Small Business Saturday (USA). Using Filipinos themselves as the inspiration for the campaign and slogan was pure genius.

Beyond the seemingly inherent Filipino trait, however, I attribute our happi-ness to my parents from whom I learned nearly everything. My mother taught me how to stock a pantry to be always visitor ready, how to perfectly wrap a gift, and how to properly greet my elders. My father taught me how to drive a stick shift on the hills of Sao Paulo, how to talk to anyone about anything, and how to efficient-ly pack a *balikbayan* box. Both of them taught me how to be kind, thankful, and patient. But, the most important lesson I learned from them is this: the happiest people do not have the best of everything—they *make* the best of everything.

"Making the best of everything" encapsulates what I love most about my parents. It also summarizes their immigrant experience as well as our family exis-tence. It has been so engrained in me that I subconsciously apply it to all aspects of my own life. I often think about how my parents lived their life and the impact this has had on me personally and professionally with a particular focus on my leadership style. Whether managing teams, building relationships, developing and influencing others, or managing change, I have learned that a positive attitude combined with an appreciation of one's own roots and values goes a *long* way.

LIVING YOUR BEST LIFE: AT WORK

One area where people generally need help living their best life is at work. Bet-ween books like *Office Space*, *The Office*, and *Horrible Bosses*, there is no short-age of horror stories about the monotony of corporate life. While they are admit-tedly hilarious, nailing the multitude of acronyms and overused buzzwords, you definitely do not want your life to imitate this art.

The following section will likely resonate more with people who work in a corporate setting than with those who do not. Entrepreneurs, consultants, and work-at-home professionals have their own set of challenges (less structure, un-predictable days, not to mention irregular paychecks), but staying motivated is usually not one of them. Speaking from my past experience as well as discussions with friends who are independent professionals, it is easy to stay inspired because you have a vested interest in everything you do. Sure there are frustrating days, but independent professionals are building their own brand, their own business, their own relationships. In many cases, they are doing what they love.

Those who work in a corporate setting, on the other hand, have to find ways to stay inspired; by nature, they do not have as much skin in the game. They have to carve out time to do things for themselves, for their own development, and their own growth. They need to learn how to invest in themselves. It is easy to get lost and too comfortable in a big organization. It is easy to clock in, but also easy to lose motivation.

I read an interview with Richard Branson when he was asked what daily activities he finds motivating and inspiring. He responded, "On Monday, I went out to the Mojave Desert to watch Virgin Galactic, our space tourism company, complete its first rocket-powered flight; it was a truly awesome sight. I treasure such moments, when my team and I find ways to make the impossible possible, inspiring ourselves and others to attempt even greater feats."

Richard Branson is one of those iconic larger-than-life figures. His vision is disruptive, his management style is innovative, his execution is, usually, flawless. But not everyone is able to go out to the Mojave Desert to witness a rocket-powered flight of their team's own creation, and if you read his interview to try to get motivated, it may actually do the opposite. You might come away feeling a little uninspired about your daily life. Instead of looking forward to your team building outing this Thursday, bowling and karaoke may suddenly sound depressingly cliché.

Last year marked fourteen years for me at Citi and I have to admit that a part of me winced a little inside whenever someone congratulated me on this anniversary. "Thank you, LinkedIn." It is not that I did not take pride in working at Citi; far from it, as anyone who knows me will tell you; but nobody wants to be known as a "lifer." Okay, nobody born after the 1960s wants to be known as a "lifer." Sure, at one point, everyone might have aspired for that gold watch symbolizing loyalty and long service. Nowadays, however, job-hopping is the new normal, especially with millennials and it is often considered more exciting and advantageous to have various companies on your resumé. This has come to mean you are aggressive in your career, you are not afraid to take risks, and you are constantly pushing yourself.

Indeed, it holds true that the longer you are with an organization, the more comfortable you get and the more conscious you need to be about staying inspired. In 1999, one of my best friends, Sheldon Gilbert, convinced me to leave my cozy job at American Express to join former classmates from Yale who were starting an Internet company called MagicBeanStalk. The fact that it was Sheldon who convinced me to join an Internet startup was pretty ironic, because amongst our friends it was a running joke that Sheldon was light years behind on technology. He was the only one in college who never embraced email. He was the last person to get a cell phone. But there we were, two years after he graduated, and he was speaking passionately about the "dot com revolution" and "MBS" as he affectionately called MagicBeanStalk.

The idea of MBS was to connect startup companies to everything they would need to get off the ground, beginning with employees. My friend and MBS co-founder James Gutierrez had mastered the art of the job fair back in college where he had put on several successful recruiting events connecting banks and consulting firms to minority students at Yale. With the number of dot coms sprouting across the country, we were matching up-and-coming startups with college grads from fifty leading US universities. That was our elevator pitch.

When I came on board, there were six of us working out of a loft in Williamsburg across from a Mexican bakery. James' bedroom was to the right of my desk. Sheldon sat in front of me next to the kitchen. It was a big change from the American Express headquarters in the World Financial Center. So was everything about working for a startup. It took a little while to get used to taking the L train to a "gentrifying" neighborhood, using a 718 telephone number on my business card, and making cold calls without a big recognizable company name. Yet, there was an underlying cool factor in being part of what people were calling the "dot com revolution."

It was not long before I embraced the startup life. One of the great things about it was that I went from Business Analyst to Head of Marketing. In this role, I got to lead every aspect of the marketing function from picking our company logo, hiring our PR firm, securing sponsors for our events (I was so proud of myself for nailing Handspring, the only competitor out there to Palm Pilot), and planning our industry parties which were cleverly called BeanScene. I was going to "Convergence" conferences and exchanging business cards with the likes of Jeff Bezos from Amazon and Steve Case of AOL. These were the pre-Google days when most people were using AOL and CompuServe, and the sound of the dial-up 56k modem was pervasive and exciting.

In less than a year, we were able to raise $5 million in venture capital, recruit a legitimate senior management team, and grow to more than fifty employees with offices in New York and California. Eventually, the Internet bubble burst and we all needed to move on to our next gigs. Some continued down the entrepreneurial path and found even more success. James went on to become a leading social entrepreneur and innovator in lending and financial technology. *BusinessWeek* even selected James as one of America's most promising social entrepreneurs in

2010 after he started Progreso Financiero and helped pioneer new policies on financial empowerment for lower-income consumers. Sheldon ended up developing his own algorithm and became founder and CEO of Proclivity Systems, the leading provider of solutions that give marketers insight into online consumer behavior.

A number of us went back to banks, consulting groups, and law firms. People are often surprised to hear how I came to work at Citi. It was not through Yale Career Services or Citi's campus recruiting program or even a big headhunter. I got my first job at Citi through Monster.com, one of the largest employment websites in the United States and now the world. I did not think much of it at the time. After all, I was following all the latest startups and we had our eye on Monster.com, and HotJobs.com, as one of the biggest competitors in the job websites space. But whenever I am asked how I first joined Citi, people think I am telling a joke when I tell them the truth. "Get out of here!" is the typical response. "For all your high powered schools and contacts, you're telling me you got your job at Citi through a mass online jobs site?" "Yes."

And so I found myself back in the middle of skyscrapers, marble elevators, and office cubicles. Sure, I missed feeling like my own boss and running my own shop but there were advantages to working at a big company again. And I am not just talking about the unlimited stacks of bond paper by the industrial Xerox machine or the complimentary Swiss Miss packs in the pantry. The big household name on your business card was a powerful tool. So too was the company global directory. *I can send an email right now to Former Secretary of Treasury Bob Rubin if I want to. I don't have to share a hotel room. I can attend any one of these leadership courses. That fancy black car is taking me to the airport.* These were the thoughts constantly running through my mind.

I returned to corporate America with a kick in my step. There was a world of resources at my fingertips and I took nothing for granted. As my parents taught me, I would carve out time to reflect each day. I actually found myself asking the following questions:

- Did you have butterflies in your stomach at least once this week? This meant I was pushing myself and doing something outside my comfort zone. For me, it often happened before speaking up during a meeting with seniors, asking a question during a town hall meeting, or doing a presentation;

- Did you have lunch or coffee with someone new? Even for extroverts, it's easier to have a lunch at your desk, especially in a place like New York when this is the norm; in other countries people tend to go out and have a proper sit-down lunch. If you do not get into the habit of going out for lunch, you are missing out on opportunities to connect with other people;

- Did you do something to make someone else more successful this week? This could be an introductory email written for a mentee or volunteering to help out on a time-consuming project for a colleague.

If my answers were yes to these questions, then it was a good week. The hard work, high energy, and meaningful networking I learned from my parents paid off. I joined business task forces, I used my Filipino connections to help Citi promote our new online remittance service, and I volunteered to lead teams for Global Community Day. I connected with people in every part of the business and every part of the world. Soon, I was identified as "high potential" and selected for unique leadership opportunities.

Several years later, however, the excitement of a big new company had worn off and the "I'm going to run the world" high of a management program faded. Things started to become a little BAU (business as usual). A term commonly used in big organizations, "BAU" refers to the normal execution of standard functional operations. The minute you start catching yourself saying "BAU" on a regular basis, it is a wakeup call that you need to do something to spark up your work life. I do not know when it happened exactly but I started to notice that I was going to lunch and coffee with the same people every day, the awards and training photos and diplomas on my desk were starting to get dated, and my résumé had not been updated for a couple of years. I no longer felt like the high-energy person with the extra bounce in her step. It was then that I realized I had to start making a conscious effort to reinvigorate my work life.

Below are some tactical things I started to do, which to this day continue to keep me motivated. Whether you are working at a big company, building your own business, taking time off, or going through transition, some of these ideas may resonate with you.

1. Remind yourself of your goals: it is easier to stay motivated when you see where it is all going. My mother writes her goals down on a yellow legal pad she keeps with her at all times. Mine are on the Evernote app. Putting these goals in writing and reminding yourself about them provides clear direction in your day-to-day life and always makes you feel like you are working toward something meaningful.

2. Identify benchmarks: use the benchmark to regularly track your progress. I do a quick self-assessment to gauge if I am making progress toward my big goals. Did I grow my business at the rate I targeted? Did I get in front of

the right people to share this progress? Did I focus on the right projects that got me closer to my goals?

3. Reward yourself when you achieve a milestone: rewards for me these days can be a lunch by myself after a successful meeting. A guilt-free salted caramel chocolate cupcake from Sift, a bakery I have just discovered near my office in Hong Kong. It can also mean a new pair of Tory Burch shoes.

4. Keep up with leaders and others who inspire you: read what they're reading. Sheryl Sandberg recommends *A Short Guide to a Happy Life* by Quindlen (2000). Jeff Bezos asks all his senior managers to read *The Effective Executive* by Drucker (2004). Watch the TED talks they are watching. Do not be too cool for Town Halls. These things remind you to think about how you fit into the whole scheme of things.

5. Say your plans out loud to your family and friends: I know some people who never do this. I realize it is because they never want to disappoint or "fail" at something, but when you put your goals out there you are more likely to achieve them because you put some pressure on yourself. I knew the moment I said, "Yes, I'm writing a second book," that I would get it done.

6. Go to conferences and training. Get out there: the longer you are inside an organization, the more important it is for you to get outside. When I was at MagicBeanStalk, going to conferences was integral to my job. I have learned that this is critical whether you are in a startup or with a large multinational firm. Client conventions, industry trade shows, and external trainings are all good ways to get re-inspired while keeping up with trends and ideas.

7. Schedule a lunch or coffee at least once a week with inspired and inspiring people inside and outside of your organization: even though you are busy, make time to get a cup of coffee with the eager beaver fresh out of business school. You have a wealth of experience to share with them and they give you that fresh new perspective that you do not even realize you need. By the same token, take the initiative and schedule time with colleagues and mentors who think big and motivate you. My good friend Sandhya Devanathan is Head of Retail Products at Standard Chartered Singapore and she is one of the busiest people I know. Yet somehow she makes time once a week to meet and connect with mentees and mentors inside and outside of her firm.

8. Maintain a social media presence: even if you do not want to put your life on Facebook, make a point to connect with people on LinkedIn. In this day and age, with everyone moving among companies so often, it is the best

way to stay in touch with your professional network. There are also great connections to be made on Twitter. That is how I met Susie Orman Schnall, author of *On Grace* (2014) and *The Balance Project: A Novel* (2015). I was still relatively new to Twitter and I remember how excited I was to find a tweet from Susie inviting me to be part of The Balance Project, a popular interview series about the tragically glorified "doing it all" craze featuring inspiring and accomplished women including Reese Witherspoon and Molly Sims.

9. Keep your biography and résumé updated: I knew I was in a good place when people started asking for my bio and résumé that I could send to them instantly. This meant that others were asking for it as well. I was getting out there, and getting known. When someone asks for your résumé and it feels like a daunting project, it is a wakeup call.

10. Interview: people often ask me to interview potential candidates. Sometimes it can feel like a chore when I have a laundry list of to-dos. But then I remember that each interview is an opportunity to do market research. Or as my friend Christine Amour-Levar encouragingly puts it, "Every conversation is a chance to discover something new." Similarly, going on interviews is an opportunity to learn and understand your worth.

Part of the reason there are so many caricatures concerning corporate life is because the concept of "Do what you love" (DWYL) has become the unofficial work mantra of our time. It has been considered the opposite of the monotonous corporate job. Between Steve Jobs, Oprah, and every speaker who delivers a commencement speech, doing what you love is the only way to live.

Most people who DWYL have an integrated life. They do not consider work to be work because they love what they do. What they do professionally is what they care about personally. However, most people who DWYL also tend to have a little extra money. They are not necessarily multi-millionaires but their lifestyle may be partly subsidized by a trust fund, their spouse may earn enough so they can pursue their passion, or they may know that one day they will inherit a $3 million dollar apartment that their parents bought for a fraction of that amount decades ago.

"In the Name of Love" is a wonderfully provocative piece about DWYL written by Miya Tokumitsu for *Slate*. In the article, she submits the "Do what you love" mantra that elites embrace actually devalues work and hurts workers. In doing so, she underlines the idea that DWYL is for the privileged few with wealth, social status, education, and political clout. Tokumitsu writes, "DWYL is a secret handshake of the privileged and a worldview that disguises its elitism as noble self-betterment."

While DWYL is a lovely idea, it is just not something most people have the luxury to do. But alas, what I have learned from my positively Filipino parents is that instead of finding a job you love, you can learn to find meaning and success in the job you have. I want to share a few attitudinal tips that have helped me find my balance and DWYL in spite of, and sometimes even because of my corporate job.

Live a Life of Purpose

As new immigrants, my parents were not necessarily doing what they loved but they were doing great work and living a meaningful life. Their jobs supported our family, allowing us to spend time together and providing us with opportunities to give back to the community.

While my mother has always been incredibly passionate about her art, her full time job as we were growing up was in early childhood education. Being a teacher at the United Nations International School allowed her to have the same schedule as her kids, it paid the bills, and she was naturally great with children. That said, she found ways to continuously incorporate art into her life whether it was organizing exhibits for students or helping emerging Filipino artists present their work. She also pursued art in the evenings. She would spend all day with 18 five-year-olds, work on a church fundraiser while my brother and I did our homework, sit down for dinner with the family, and then she was off to the art studio for the remainder of the night to work on her pieces. Eventually her work was picked up and noticed by influential members of the United Nations community and soon she was exhibiting all across the globe. As long as she had a purpose, she could do her day job and figure out a way to do what she loved.

My husband, Alex, has a similar point of view. One of the first things that struck me about him was that he was the first person I knew, aside from my very practical parents who did not buy into DWYL. "No, you don't need to do what you love; you just need to have a purpose," I remember him arguing over *caipirinhas* [Brazil's national cocktail] at Posto Seis, one of our favorite restaurants in São Paulo.

Alex grew up in a small town in upstate New York. To paint the picture of just how tiny of a town, he often tells the story about how his zip code changed after their postman retired. He and his three siblings could run around acres of land, they recognized every car that passed them by, and they were on a first name basis with everyone at the grocery store. While it was a wonderful place to grow up, he was always looking forward to moving to the city when he got older. He aspired to work on Wall Street, build a successful career, and have a big family. No one he knew from back home had taken this path so he never had an example to follow.

When he visited the West Point Military Academy, however, he saw how much it had to offer by way of exposure and access. He made it a personal goal to get accepted to the prestigious academy and he achieved it. Anyone who knows my husband well knows that he would be an unlikely fit at West Point. He never liked being told what to do, he would often challenge authority, and he was not exactly clean cut. But my husband can do anything when he knows it is for a greater purpose.

Today, Alex is the regional treasurer of Citi's broker dealer business in Asia. He is great at his job but I do not know if he would classify it as doing what he loves. At least for him, equally important as loving your job is loving the impact your job has on others. This can mean the internal clients who benefit from the work his team is doing or it can refer to the family he is able to help support.

Do Something for Yourself Each Day

I bookmarked a great list I came across a few months back called, "How to Make Your Life Better by Sending Five Simple Emails" by Eric Barker. The five emails were as follows:

1. Happiness: Every morning, send a friend, family member, or co-worker an email to say thanks for something.

2. Job: At the end of the week, send your boss an email and sum up what you have accomplished.

3. Growth: Once a week, email a potential mentor.

4. Friendship: Email a good friend and make plans.

5. Career: Send an email to someone you know but do not know very well and check in.

The point is that you carve out time to do something for your own betterment. This is easy to overlook when you have mountains of tasks in front of you, but invest this little time in yourself and everything else actually gets easier.

Think Fulfillment and Integration Over Having it All

I learned this phrase from a panel session called "A New Vocabulary: Fulfillment and Integration over 'Having It All'" at Claudia Chan's 3rd Annual S.H.E. Summit: The Global Leadership & Lifestyle Event. Not everyone can quit their job to pursue their passion. Most of us have to find ways to integrate the two. For me, one definition of success is achieving an integrated life. Writing my books has allowed me to integrate my personal and professional life, essentially simulating DWYL. My books have added these other dimensions to my life:

- I have established my personal brand and platform to share what matters most to me;

- I picked up what often feels like another master's degree, this time in social media;

- I have broadened my everyday world outside of my industry. This has allowed me to be better at my job;

- The books have helped me to minimize the importance of corporate politics and hierarchy;

- They allowed me to connect with so many interesting people around the world about their families, their careers, and their dreams.

However, long before I had written a book, I was also pursuing this integration. I had a great job that I was enjoying but I still had other interests, so I looked for opportunities to get involved in different areas of the bank where I could pursue them. As my friend Claudia Chan says, "Even in a job you enjoy, you never fully utilize all your talents or fulfill all of your interests so it's important to have other outlets."

One advantage of working for a large company is that somewhere in the organization there is a group focused on something near to your heart. No matter what your passion is, some part of the firm is doing it. Diversity: there is a whole department for that. Non-profit work: there is a foundation dedicated to enriching communities. Education: you bet. Big organizations sponsor so many worthy causes, be it Habitat for Humanity, March of Dimes, or The Junior League. There is always a corporate table that needs to be filled. Ask anyone in Corporate Affairs. They are often scrambling to find people in the business who can attend.

My world opened up when I connected to Citi Community Relations. All it took was one email saying how I was interested in our Habitat for Humanity efforts and soon I was on the distribution list for all related events. I remember how thrilled I was to receive my first invite from Dana Deubert, Head of Corporate Communications. I still have her amusing response to my thank you email, "Here's to many more nights of rubber chicken!" Nothing could have made me happier.

Don't Let Perfection Hold You Back

As I was writing my first book, I thought my mother was crazy when she asked if I would be ready to publish it a few short months later. She was reading through my first draft and said, "This is it already. You just need to have it professionally edited." She proceeded to draft a timeline. Two weeks for copy editing, two weeks for book layout, two weeks for back and forth changes, two weeks for printing, and *voilà*.

"I won't be ready. I may still want to add a few more chapters about our move to Singapore. I was also considering a recipe section ..." I rationalized.

"Save it for the next one. If you don't stick to a deadline, you'll never be done. If you wait for it to be perfect, you'll never finish the book," she said matter-of-factly.

She was right. I have come across so many people who tell me that they once started a book and never finished it. I know I am no better than they are; but they did not have my mother. Around the same time, I was reading *Lean In* by Sheryl Sandberg (2013) where she poignantly stated, "Done is better than perfect." I could not agree more.

Succeed on Your Own Terms

When I was first considering a job in Singapore, many people warned me that I would not be able to see my kids during the week. "They work late in Asia," it is commonly known. This turned out to be true but I am glad it did not dissuade me from making the move. When I first got to Singapore, I followed what seemed to be the default schedule, which meant a later start than what I was used to in New York and a later end. Not only did I find myself staying late in the office but when I got home, because I was managing the Global Client business, I was also on evening calls with New York. After a few months I realized I needed to adjust my schedule to make time for family.

When you are a professional, you know what you need to do to get the job done. Being at the office when my kids were having dinner and going to bed was not required to get the job done. I made a schedule that worked for me and it had no negative impact on my boss or my team. I came to the office early and got home in time to have dinner with my kids, and then I went back online to answer emails and take calls after my kids went to bed. Had I listened to all the people telling me not to take this job while my kids were young, I would have missed out on an incredible opportunity to work in Asia.

To succeed on your own terms, you have to make your own rules and be confident in who you are. While I was working in New York, the general counsel for my business, Neil Barry, coined me the nickname Sunshine. "You're just always so upbeat and happy," he explained genuinely. So I have heard. Upbeat and happy were fine traits and all, but "Sunshine" was not the nickname I wanted as I was working my way up the corporate ladder. It does not exactly give off a "serious business woman" vibe.

Since then, I have come to realize, "So what?" I generally have a cheerful disposition but that does not stop me from being great at what I do. It may actually be part of what makes me effective at what I do. As cliché as it may sound, Judy Garland's advice has come to resonate with me now more than ever: "Always be a first-rate version of yourself, instead of a second-rate version of somebody else."

LENORE LIM: COMMENTS BY THE MOTHER OF MARIE CLAIRE LIM MOORE

My husband, Jose, and I are opposites in many ways but when it comes down to the things that matter most to both of us we could not be more similar: How we envision family. How we see ourselves raising children. How we define success. How we define happiness.

One of the things we were intent on doing was raising our children with a sense of a responsibility to give back. I shared this in the chapter "Full Circle" which I wrote for *DISRUPT 1*, as an FWN100™ U.S. 2009 awardee. The biggest reminders we continue to give Claire (Marie Claire Lim Moore) and her brother Justin are the following.

- You have been blessed with unique talents and abilities and you must use these in service of others.

- Your relationships are everything. It is important in a leader to be people-oriented. It is through social interaction that you will be able to gain the social skills to build a team for whatever common undertaking may be pursued. There is nothing I have accomplished without the help of others.

- The happiest people do not have the best of everything, they make the best of everything.

By way of background, I graduated from the University of the Philippines, College of Architecture and Fine Arts in 1967. After graduation, I taught art at the International School Manila and Assumption Convent in Manila in the late sixties and early seventies. My teaching career brought me and my husband, Jose, to Mobile, Alabama USA in 1975 as an Art Resource Teacher in the Mobile County Public School System. We then moved to Vancouver, British Columbia to start our family.

In Vancouver, Jose and I were regularly involved in various projects that international understanding. That took the form of sponsoring and hosting Philippine Nights at different Catholic church parishes, as well as presenting concerts, and shows featuring different Filipino performing artists from the Philippines.

In the late eighties, we moved the family to New York City. We had just entered our forties and we both felt strongly that we had another adventure to pursue. Jose looked for opportunities in real estate and I applied for an opening at the United Nations International School. There we continued to remain active in the Philippine Community. Since 2003, I have been a volunteer member of the Art Committee of the Philippine Center New York. The Philippine Center exhibits works of Filipino artists regularly and the Art Committee reviews the portfolios of the artists applying to have an exhibit at the Philippine Center. As an active member of the Philippine Association of Printmakers and a Board of Director since 2010, I have conducted workshops for the printmakers and have sponsored the two PAP exhibits at the Philippine Center New York.

One definition of success for me has always been living a balanced life. One where I can balance family, career, community, and spirituality. Being a teacher complemented my being an artist. Both fields require discipline, dedication, organization, setting timetables, and focusing on one's goals. Both involve hard work and a supportive family.

Since I was a full time teacher, I did my art after school hours and on the weekends. I set aside spring breaks and the summer vacation to do my exhibitions. I also had to think ahead. When I moved to New York, I wrote down my goals and made plans to achieve them. I wrote down the year when a specific goal had to be worked on. This has been my guide. I had to be flexible, too. I had to do some adjustments once in awhile like when I was ill for a couple of years. I used those years to do my studies and develop my concepts more.

Art and music were family activities; both my children were studying violin. So while I was at the studio, they would do their music lessons. We would make trips together collecting and buying my art materials. As a family, we coordinate our schedule to meet everyone's needs. My husband who is in real estate often times will have some showings and once in a while the family will assist him in presentation and staging property units.

Besides being an artist, I was also a full time teacher, mother, wife, and an active member of numerous organizations in the community. I have had to manage my time efficiently and computer technology, which I embraced at its infancy in the eighties, helped fulfill the different demanding roles I played. Jose, Claire, and Justin also learned how to use PageMaker and Photoshop with me.

Together we worked on newsletters and catalogues. With their help we would put my guest list in a database. To this day the family supports me whenever I have an art show. They help me with press releases, brochures, price lists, and title cards.

Since I left the Philippines in 1974, I have been involved in assisting Filipino artists in any way I can. In Vancouver, I co-founded a non-profit music foundation that regularly sponsored performances of world class Filipino performers. When I relocated to New York, I focused more on assisting Filipino visual artists both from the Philippines and abroad by encouraging them, giving them ideas based on my personal experiences, as well as helping them put up art shows. Claire and Justin have been a part of all of this too and I think it has helped inspire and motivate them to contribute to their communities in any way they can.

As I fly in and out of our established homes in the Philippines, Canada, and the US, ; the global Filipino diaspora, is no longer dispersion from one's homeland. Instead, it has become a coming together, a full circle; a state of opportunity to dialogue and to exchange thoughts and ideas in order to give back to our motherland and the global community for our greater good. One of my biggest accomplishments is seeing my children work towards this common goal.

GIZELLE COVARRUBIAS ROBINSON

Managing Director IT
(Software Application Development and Strategic Engineering)
Charles Schwab & Co
FWN100™ Keeper of the Flame 2014

Roots and Wings

The kind of leader I am today is in large part because of my mom. She was my inspiration, my confidante, and my rock. My mom passed away on November 13, 2015. On December 23, 2015, I wrote a eulogy for her that is at the end of this chapter and that provides a summary of what she meant to me. My mom was a beautiful petite woman. Some people say she bore a likeness to Barbara Perez and Hilda Koronel. They were two famous Filipina actresses in the 60s and 70s. To me, she looked like Ali McGraw, an American actress famous for her role in the 1970's movie "Love Story". My mom looked years younger than her real age; people were always astonished when she told them how old she was. Two years ago in St Scholastica's College, a little four-year-old boy who was with his mommy walked up to her just to say "hello." Delighted, she responded in kind to his cheery greeting, and told him that his mommy had been her student when his mother was a young girl. The little boy could not hide his surprise, so much so that he had to ask her, "Why, how old are you?" To which my mom shot back, "How old do you think I am?" His confident reply, "You are FIVE years old!" Such was my mom's spirit and youthful presence that a little boy would think she was just about his age albeit a year older.

My mom loved listening to speeches and enjoyed quotes. If she really liked the messages she got from them and felt that these were words to live by, she would write them down in her notebook. As I read through my mom's notebook of affirmations, I see how they helped her deal with life and ultimately form the type of person and leader she wanted to be. She always wanted to better herself for others and amongst all the things I learned from her, this is probably the one thing I aspire for most. She gave me roots. A foundation to establish the kind of person I could be. Throughout my life she planted seeds of knowledge to help me be the person I am. My mom gave me wings so I can seek opportunities, take risks, make a difference, and motivate others while my roots keep me grounded in my traditional Filipino values like respect for elders, my moral compass, and my purpose in life. I would like to share these affirmations by starting with the quotes from my Mom's notebook, highlight the relevance of these quotes to my Mom's life, and my reflections as to how those life lessons developed into my leadership competencies.

"WINNERS WIN BY PUSHING THEIR LIMITS TILL THEIR LIMITS BECOME THE NORM."

Growing up we lived in a row of townhomes that had a long narrow driveway fenced in by a gray concrete wall that stretched out across all five homes. We lived in the one at the end of the row so my mom's 1978 Classic Red and dad's Alpine White Volkswagen beetles were parked there. Every morning I would sit at the step of the front door of our townhome patiently watching my mom back her red VW beetle out of the driveway on her way to run errands. My dad would ask our helpers to stand guard between the concrete walls of the driveway and my mom's car as she backed out. My dad, just so you all know, was a precise kind of person. His VW beetle was always shiny, clean and in tip-top shape. He washed his car and changed the oil regularly. When he popped the hood at the back of the car where the engine sat, you would see an engine that looked like it was brand new. That was my dad. He loved his VW beetle. If he saw a scratch on his car or my mom's car it would not be a good thing. So during those mornings I would watch my dad wave hand signals at my mom to help her navigate slowly out the driveway till she got to the gate. He would scold her out loud whenever she got too close to the walls. I could tell by the look on her face that she did not like the reprimand. But then that look would soon be replaced by one of sheer determination. She would then square out her shoulders and start the car up and begin backing out again. It took a while but she mastered it. Days passed and soon I noticed I was no longer sitting on our front door step watching her back her car out. Years later my mom became quite the expert driver and boy did she love driving. She said it gave her a sense of independence.

Growing up my mom was our tutor. My siblings and I are close in age. I am the middle child. My sister is a year older and my brother, a year younger. When we came home from school, we would have an afternoon snack and then soon after eating, it was study period. When it was time for tests and examinations my mom would review our work and make sure we were prepared. I remember watching her review with my sister and my brother. When they got the answers wrong she would scold them and they would end up in tears. When my turn came, the same thing would happen. She would scold me when I did not get the answers right. I did not like being scolded, so I decided to study on my own and review by myself till I knew the answers perfectly. I did not tell her about studying on my own till I got my grades back and showed them to her. It took a while until I noticed my mom no longer felt the need to prepare me for tests.

When I was a freshman I promised my mom that I would graduate from high school with honors. I remember in my junior year that I faltered, as there were all these parties that I attended. She reminded me of my promise. So I decided to focus on my studies and cut down on the parties. In 1980, I graduated 6th in our batch with honors.

As a leader, be self-aware. Know your strengths and weaknesses and have a willingness to improve until what you have learned is now part of your norm.

"THE PERSON WHO SUCCEEDS
IS NOT THE ONE WHO HOLDS BACK FEARING FAILURE,
NOT THE ONE WHO NEVER FAILS....
BUT RATHER THE ONE WHO MOVES ON IN SPITE OF FAILURE."
Charles R. Swindoll

By the time we were old enough to be left on our own, my mom was ready to go to work and do something else with her life. Her older sister, Tita Rose, was a member of the alumnae board of St. Scholastica's College in Manila. She told my mom that there was a position open for a substitute teacher in the high school department. The subject she had to teach was Economics. Well, my mom had a degree in History. She did not know much about Economics but that did not stop her. She learned Economics together with her students. She was honest about what she knew and what she did not know and that is how she got her students to learn it with her. Needless to say they all did well on the final exams. My mom did so well with the class that the school offered her a permanent teaching position, this time teaching subjects that she did know something about: Philippine History, World History, and Spanish.

As a leader, it is important to take risks and to persevere. When you take on challenges you will learn what you are capable of. I remember when I had to develop a brand new replenishment retail system for a Switzerland based department store. I was only given a month to build it as our client was coming to visit at the end of the month to review it at that time. He needed to compare it with the retail system that was running that he had built. The system I built would eventually include 50 programs running both online and in batch mode. At this point in my career, I was primarily an online programmer so I had to learn how to build batch programs. I also ended up having to test this system myself because there was no one available to help me. Management warned me that our client was not a very easy man to please. They told me that we really needed this system to work for the client because it would mean other business for the company. So I worked day and night that whole month to have it ready in time to demo it to our client. I remember being exhausted and sick but I worked through all that because I wanted to succeed. When the client finally arrived to review and watch the demo of the system, he was very impressed. He told me that he had missed several details in the system that he built. He was very happy I caught all these and built a system that contained every feature and functionality the store needed to ensure they were continually stocked. I was awarded a trip to Zurich to personally install the system. Our client and his wife who both worked for the department store were so happy they invited me to their home for dinner to thank me. That was an unexpected surprise but worth all my hard work. So, this experience taught me several valuable lessons that have served me well during my career. Hard work, perseverance, and the ability to apply education and training can help you solve the most challenging problem. Apply your skills and abilities to all you do and it will take you on a wonderful and fulfilling career journey.

"TWENTY YEARS FROM NOW YOU WILL BE MORE DISAPPOINTED
BY THE THINGS THAT YOU DIDN'T DO THAN BY THE ONES YOU DID DO.
SO THROW OFF THE BOWLINES. SAIL AWAY FROM THE SAFE HARBOR.
CATCH THE TRADE WINDS IN YOUR SAILS.
EXPLORE. DREAM. DISCOVER."
Mark Twain

My mom found her true calling in education. From a classroom teacher my mom progressed to becoming an Assistant Principal of the high school department and then became the first lay principal. During that time, they only appointed nuns to be the high school principal. After years of success and lots of support from others, she met an advocate who believed in her. Sr. Bernardita encouraged her to work hard. After lots of hard work, determination, and drive she proved that a lay person could be a successful high school principal. When she was 46 years old, she was recognized by an appointment as the high school principal of St. Scholastica's College de Manila.

My mom loved being a principal of St. Scholastica's College. She enjoyed all that her teachers, the administration. and parents were able to accomplish under her leadership. Her passion for education was so great she decided to obtain her Masters and PhD in Education. We were all extremely proud of my mom's success since she was the first one in our family to achieve a doctorate degree and be worthy of the title "Doctor." The status of becoming a doctor at 56 years of age did not change my mom at all. She was the same person to her family, friends, and colleagues. What she did do however was remain true to what she believed was her calling which was to do things for others through education.

My mom's love for education took her beyond being the principal at the high school level to being the Dean of Liberal Arts and Sciences at the College Department of St. Scholastica's College.

My mom embodied the true meaning of the word education. She never stopped learning and growing her skills. She continued to teach herself new techniques to make learning exciting for her students. She used visual arts to teach Philippine History and even authored a book about the subject. The students who learned Philippine history through visual arts got higher grades than those who learned it through the traditional way. She proved that it was easier to remember what happened and who made things happen in the past with the use of visual aids.

My mom was well read. CNN and BBC were a constant source of information. And, when the Internet came along, it became an even greater source of information for her. She used these resources to help stay abreast of what was going on in the world. They helped shape her ideas for programs and tools to enable her students and teachers to be the best that they could be.

I learned that as a leader, you need courage to keep on keeping on even when the tasks are daunting. In order to better yourself you have to keep growing.

IT SHOULD BE SAID THAT A MARK OF A TRUE LEADER IS PERSEVERANCE
AND DETERMINATION—THEY STRIVE TO BE THE BEST THEY CAN.
Anonymous

As a young girl, I witnessed my mom strive to achieve and contribute in so many ways. She followed her passion and her dream. I am proud to say, I had a first-row seat at the dinner table, on the living room sofa, and even at the back of the VW beetle to observe as my mom did all these great things. She was a shining role model for me. I truly believe I was in the midst of a leader. And I guess it is true what they say when someone is surrounded by positive influence and passion to help others, a bit of it rubs off. From my Mom I learned to motivate those around me so that they can grow and be better at what they do and be better as a person. This is what leadership is about; making everyone around you better than when they first met you. This creates loyalty and followership.

By the time I graduated from De La Salle University with a degree in Industrial Management Engineering, I was ready to take more computer programming classes because what I learned in college was an outdated computer language. When I told my mom about what I wanted to do, she said go for it. So I enrolled at the Ateneo Business School located in Makati, which was close to where we lived. I took Flowcharting and COBOL programming classes and completed them with very high marks. I knew this was what I wanted to do. I landed my first job at Far East Bank as a computer programmer. The language I needed to code in though was not COBOL it was a totally different language called Dbase3. I learned it and delivered programs. After 3 months of probationary status, they offered me a permanent position and moved me to another group that wrote programs for the bank, but this time in COBOL.

Three years after I began my career as a programmer for Far East Bank in the Philippines, I was promoted to a software development manager position. I enjoyed having the ability to make things happen for my team and for the firm. Being responsible and accountable for what my team was supposed to deliver was energizing for me.

During my first year as a manager, I began to realize that it was time for me to spread my wings and see what I could do on my own outside of the Philippines. To achieve true independence, I needed to move away from my family's shadow. What did my mom say to this, you might ask? "Go and do what you were meant to do, and be who you were meant to be." So I applied for a job outside of the Philippines. I had to go back through the ranks and start as a programmer. I was offered a job in New Zealand and another in Australia. Since I had an aunt in Australia and wanted to truly be independent from my family, I decided to go to New Zealand to work for a large technology firm. Was I scared, "YES"!

When I arrived in New Zealand it was winter. I was cold and did not know anybody. I lived in a flat with five other Filipinos and had to learn to share in maintaining a home with them. I remember having to learn how to cook and go to the grocery store for six people. I learned to clean a whole house, do laundry, and iron my clothes for work. My first venture at cooking was a disaster. The chicken was cooked outside but quite raw in the middle. My left hand had burn marks from ironing. When I woke up late for work I would end up having to take a cold shower as my 'flatmates' used up all the hot water. I remember ironing only the sleeves and collar of my blouse, as the suit jacket would cover the rest of the crumpled blouse. I told myself, if I survive winter I could make it here. I did!

Within my first year at the technology firm I was promoted to a software development manager. A short time thereafter, I was offered an entry-level programmer position in the United States. This was difficult for a couple of reasons. First, moving to the U.S. meant being further away from my family, which was scary. Second, I had to return to a programming position after holding a managerial position for several years. As I thought about my decision, I weighed the pros and cons. I reflected on what my mom said to me, "Go and do what you were meant to do, and be who you were meant to be." So I left for the United States in search of new opportunities. Once again with determination, perseverance, and hard work; after three years working as a programmer for a Retail Software company I was promoted to a Software Development Manager.

Like my mom, I learned that being resilient is an important trait to have in one's life. Today, I am pleased to say that I am a managing director for a key organization at Charles Schwab and someday hope to lead an entire enterprise to help the individuals in the enterprise be the best that they can be. I like problem solving, fixing things, transforming organizations, building high performing teams, and helping my team be the best that they can be. I continue to read a lot on leadership, technology, building organizations, mentorship, and sponsorship; practically anything that can help me be a better leader for my organization. I continue to want to better myself so I can help my teams, my firm, and our customers. It is a good day when I know that I have helped a transformation occur.

"TRY NOT TO BECOME A MAN OF SUCCESS
BUT RATHER TRY TO BECOME A MAN OF VALUE."
ALBERT EINSTEIN

About 11 years ago I attended a Women's Leadership conference in Boston. I was the only one sent by the company but what I learned I felt had to be shared with other women. The stories from the keynote speakers about how they struggled to overcome prejudices, inappropriate behavior in the workplace, and to gain a seat at the table were inspirational. So I decided to petition the different officers of our firm to send their high-potential women to attend the conference the following year. I was able to get 33 women to attend that year and the following year 45. The attendance numbers continued to grow every year.

Since then I have joined several non-profit organizations for women and young women to help spread the word that there is a need for diversity in all levels and industries in our society. Diversity is important because it allows for different ideas, insights, and input. Everyone is raised in unique ways. Everyone's experience and exposures are varied. Because of this, diversity broadens and opens our minds to all kinds of perspectives. It allows us to grow and see things through a different lens. It allows us to consider things we never would have considered before. For example, as a Filipina who grew up in the Philippines, we listen to and respect our elders without question. Here in the United States, I learned not to be afraid to question those who are in higher levels than I am, not out of disrespect but out of desire to learn from them. As a leader, be purpose-driven. Make a difference, do what it takes to help achieve your goal. The values and principles instilled in you are part of your moral compass.

"FAILURES ARE ONLY TEMPORARY TESTS TO PREPARE US FOR PERMANENT TRIUMPHS."
Charles R Swindoll

In the year 2001, my mom was feeling pressure at St. Scholastica's College to retire. Employees in their 60's are encouraged to retire. My mom was worried that the school would not renew her contract. During her time there, the school was considered one of the top schools in Manila having won several competitions and for consistently having a record of 100% of their school population graduating, getting a college degree, and starting a professional life. At this point in her life she was consulting with a very good friend of hers who owned a school for special needs children and was offered a "forever" job with the school. So after 27 years at St Scholastica's College, she left but continued to fulfill her calling at St. Mary of the Woods and School of Mount St. Mary as VP of Academics. She created programs for special needs kids and underprivileged kids from the rural area of the Philippines with the ultimate goal of helping them be integrated into mainstream education and succeed in their chosen profession.

Her triumph at these schools is noted by the following dedication from the special education (SPED) family:

> "To laugh often and much, to win the respect of intelligent people and the affection of children...to leave the world a better place...to know even one life has breathed easier because you have lived. This is to have succeeded."

> "We are blessed to have you."

Privately the school president expressed gratitude about my mom in the following way. She communicated this to me in a note following the passing of my mom.

> *"I would like to share with you the things I wish I could have told your mom.....*
> *Maryann, I will never know if you knew how much everyone loved you. You were*
> *everyone's mentor, inspiration, and our mother here at St. Mary of the Woods*
> *School and School of Mount St. Mary. You had your way of making us realize our*
> *potentials and capabilities we never thought we had, and encouraged us to build*
> *up on it. Through your guidance, we... your administrators, faculty, staff and stu-*
> *dents, developed and learned to work as a team to help make our schools what they*
> *are now. You were able to bring out the best in us and truly exemplified your belief*
> *in everyone's "everyday genius". We are truly blessed to have experienced that kind*
> *of person in you in our lives. Maryann, there are no words to describe how grateful*
> *we are to you for being there with us through all the obstacles and victories that our*
> *schools went through. Thank you for your tireless and directed efforts in leading us*
> *to live the vision and mission of our schools. Thank you for the friendship and the*
> *many beautiful memories that we've shared, thank you for the love, dedication, and*
> *your many years of service which will serve as our inspiration. We still have a lot*
> *more to accomplish and more room for growth, but you left us with that spark of*
> *love and many years of guidance to help us get by. Rest assured we will continue*
> *the legacy you left behind, not only through the walls of the schools but also in*
> *the hearts of everyone you have touched. We love you so much and we will really*
> *miss you!*
>
> *Gizelle, it has been a great privilege for us to have known your mom and we will be*
> *forever grateful for that."*

The true measure of a leader is not what a few people say about them but it is what the many say. Clearly my mom's legacy lives on through the teachers and students that she has touched in her life.

> ## "The pessimist sees difficulty in every opportunity.
> ## The optimist sees the opportunity in every difficulty."
> *Winston Churchill*

Leadership is about addressing the easy as well as the difficult. Leadership is about how people respond to a stiff wind as compared to the prevailing wind. Nobody celebrates the people who have an easy path in life. We all experience difficulty in our lives. The real question is whether we see these challenges through an optimistic eye or a pessimistic eye. My mom was the eternal optimist. She always saw the glass as half full and she also saw the good in everyone and every situation.

My resilience was tested in 1999, when I was removed from a major project. I had been with the company for approximately two years and was considered a seasoned software development manager. My performance ratings had always been above average. It was clear that I was doing very well at the company and I could never imagine that this could happen to me. One day my supervisor informed me that her boss thought his views and mine were not in sync and so he moved me to another organization. I was confused as to why this was happening. Further, the organization I was to move to had an archaic system that was seldom used and not automated to support their operations. I was given a single staff member to help me make improvements. As I learned more, I found out that it was considered a dead end job with a limited future. The larger disappointment was that I later learned the reassignment decision was not supported by my former business partners. Despite these challenges I remained committed to my work. One day I remember working late and my previous superior stopped by. He told me that this reassignment was an opportunity for me which I knew was untrue. Despite this deceit, I told him, "I will turn this challenge into an opportunity, just wait and see." And so I did. Within 3 years, I automated their manual processes. I grew my staff to twelve high performing software engineers. Together we retired the archaic system and created one of the first web-based systems for corporate actions in the industry. As for the superior, he was laid off after a couple of years. As for the project that I was reassigned from, it faltered and took several years to get completed.

As a leader, seek opportunities and make them work. You learn, you grow, and you get better at what you do. This will only help those around you.

LIFE WITHOUT GOD IS LIKE AN UNSHARPENED PENCIL
—IT HAS NO POINT. SO GO AND TOUCH THE SKY AND BELIEVE.

My mom's faith in God was strong. I remember during mass she would sing so loud "YAHWEH I KNOW YOU ARE NEAR". And respond to the prayers even louder, "THANKS BE TO GOD!!!"

I had to ask her one time, "Mom why do you have to sing so loud and pray so loud?" She answered with her all-knowing smile, "I want to make sure God can hear me." Well, no argument there.

I remember having long discussions about religion with my mom. Some of them would go like this: "Mom if God is everywhere, why do I need to go to Church on Sundays to pray?" She would say, "It is God's house, it is special. You will receive Him there." At times rational thinking just did not help me make sense of some of her answers. Her faith never faded and through her last days her faith in God's plan for her was what got her through the pain.

FAITH TEACHES US TO BELIEVE NO MATTER WHAT THE SITUATION WE ARE HAVING RIGHT NOW. HOLD ON, BE STRONG, DON'T GIVE UP. GOD WORKS IN WAYS WE CANNOT SEE.

When I pray, I usually pray to give thanks. When I left for New Zealand one of the things my mom gave me for my trip was a prayer of thanks and a letter that I was supposed to read once I was on the plane. I pray the prayer of thanks every day and still have my mom's letter with me. When my mom became ill, I prayed for God to save her and to alleviate her pain and suffering. I prayed every day to the Virgin Mary to intercede for us. As I continued to pray I felt a sense of peace knowing that our worries and our troubles were in God's hands and that He would make everything all right. I felt closer to God because I know in times of trouble He is there. I am not alone. God did save my mom and took away her pain by taking her home to Him.

We all do not get to choose our parents, so when God decided to give me to my mom, it was one of life's greatest gifts. Every day I thank my mom for giving me roots and wings, for believing in me and for helping me turn into the person I am. I thank her for teaching me to live a life that matters.

When my mom transitioned to eternal life she did so the way she wanted to; it was in the early hours of the morning with a smile on her face. Days after she passed I found a poem from an unknown author that I know she left behind for us. Until the very end she was about others.

> Miss me, but let me go
> When I come to the end of the road
> And the sun has set for me,
> I want no rites in a gloom-filled room,
> Remember the love that we once shared
> It's all part of the Master's plan
> A step on the road to home.

My goal in life is to be about others like my Mom was. From her I learned to be strong, resilient, and purposeful. All these traits are needed to be a leader. She was true to herself, and this taught me to be authentic. She worked well with all her peers and students, this taught me to be collaborative and build relationships in order to succeed. She had a mission and vision for her school, that taught me to be a strategic and visionary leader. She was empathetic to all those she worked with and most especially her students, that taught me to have emotional intelligence. She made good decisions about what was best for the school, that taught me to have good judgment. She continually looked for improvements, that taught me to be a change-agent. She was someone who everyone could rely on to deliver, that taught me to be responsible and to be accountable. My mom's faith was strong and unwavering, that taught me to believe that anything is possible and to stay humble in the midst of God's glory. Most importantly my mom listened to the teachers, the parents, and the students, that taught me to be a learner. All these she did to help those around her, be the best that they can be. Because of this they trusted her and followed her lead. Leadership is about followership.

For those of you who have read our story and are blessed to have had a mother like mine, I wish for you what my mom wished for me. And that is to, "Go and do what you were meant to do, and be who you were meant to be." I share with you her words of wisdom: *"Grow in every way, cultivate yourselves holistically. Develop a desire for goodness, an eagerness to live life to the fullest, and a desire to reach out to others. Appreciate the beauty around you and most especially, develop your concern for others. As you grow, do not stop exploring new fields, new areas, and new ideas. Grow through all your years. Never let the years stop you from thinking you have learned enough—never think that way."* Finally, her parting words: *"One is never finished, One never arrives, One must continue to Grow."*

MY EULOGY FOR MY MOM

Today marks the 40th day since my mom's passing. These past weeks have been really difficult. The feeling of loss, the sense of regret, the emptiness in my heart, the physical ache and the finality of the situation has been hard to bear. My salvation was my family, friends and God. I know this was best for my mom. She is no longer in pain. Thank you to everyone, for your love, support, thoughts and prayers. They mean so much.

Since finding out about my mom's cancer in July of this year, I would call her every 6 am Philippine time to check in on her. She called me her morning caller. In the morning of the inurnment service, I woke up to talk to my mom at our usual chat-time. I walked over to her room and had my one-way conversation with her. Then I started looking through her things trying to feel connected to her. As I did this I found a notebook of hers where she wrote quotes, birthdays of friends and family and fun facts. As I read through some of the pages of her notebook, I felt this was a sign to say something during her inurnment service and share what my mom was about.

I found this one quote in my mom's notebook that personifies my mom and her purpose in life: "TO TEACH IS TO TOUCH LIVES FOREVER."

My mom was an educator and a learner. She created innovative programs to help her students. She helped us all be the best that we could be. She made each one of us feel special because of how she listened and how she championed us. When my mom found out she had stage 4 endometrial cancer she said, "75 years that's a bonus already." Then she asked me, "I think I did good already right?" Well, my mom knew how to turn negatives into positives. "This is a blessing. Our family is closer. During this challenging time we all got closer to God. So for me this is a blessing," she said.

My mom was a pillar of strength. She fought for us, stood up for us and taught us how to be strong. One of her entries in her notebook says: "BETTER TO BE A LION FOR A DAY THAN A SHEEP ALL YOUR LIFE.

She selflessly took care of my dad and her best friend forever (BFF), Tita Myles through their illness. She said: "AMOR CON AMOR SE PAGA." [LOVE IS REPAID WITH LOVE.]

So to your question mom, "I think, I did good already right?" the answer is "Yes mom you did more than good." I am so proud of you and all that you have done in your life for all your students from St. Scholastica and St. Mary of the Woods, batch 76 through the current year. To the teachers you worked with and mentored. To family members and friends you gave advice to and had fun with. And, to us your three children who you were there for always. Your capacity to love and give of yourself to so many is amazing and inspirational. Hearing all the stories of those whose lives you touched affirms that you have fulfilled God's plan for you here on earth.

I found another note that speaks to how my mom lived her life: "I SHALL PASS THROUGH THIS WORLD BUT ONCE. ANY GOOD THEREFORE THAT I CAN DO OR ANY KINDNESS THAT I CAN SHOW TO ANY HUMAN BEING, LET ME DO IT NOW. LET ME NOT DEFER OR NEGLECT IT FOR I SHALL NOT PASS THIS WAY AGAIN."

I dreamt of my mom on the 17th of December. The dream was about me heading out to work. Instead of going to work though, I grabbed my bag from the car because I wanted to stay home. When I arrived "home" I saw my mom sitting on a cable car full of people, facing outward. I said, "Mom where are you going?" frowning and feeling sad that she was leaving. "I want to spend time with you," I added. She did not say anything. Instead she smiled and waved. I woke up at this point but remember feeling really good about seeing my mom smiling. She looked beautiful, happy and healthy.

Mom I will miss you all the days of my life. I will continue to be your morning caller, this time, no need of wifi or phones. You taught us roots and wings—now you have your own set of real ones where you are, I know you will watch over us.

Lastly I wanted to share that while I was in the Philippines, I was using my mom's cell to respond to all her connections for her. That morning of the inurnment I saw an email with the subject line—Love Quote. When I opened it I saw an ad on a cure for bunions. For those of you who know my mom, you would know that she has this on her foot so I decided it was a message from her. Underneath the ad, the quote read, "ULTIMATELY WE WISH THE JOY OF PERFECT UNION WITH THE PERSON WE LOVE."

I love you mommy. I miss you so much. I know you do not want me to cry but sometimes I cannot help it. I wish I could have saved you, I wish we could talk some more but I know it was time for you to go home to God. I know you are in a better place and there is no more pain for you. So till our perfect union, I will live my life and hope I make you proud.

SYNTHESIS

Maria Africa Beebe

The stories in this collection continue to make the compelling case started in Disrupt I that there are many global Filipina women who are leaders and not victims of globalization. The Filipina Women's Network (FWN), a professional organization for women of Philippine ancestry with members worldwide, identified as one of its objectives changing the way Filipina women are viewed and in many cases the way they view themselves. The women are global Filipina Women Leaders (FWLs) where their global status is defined by a combination of life and work. As global FWLs some of them live in the Philippines and own or work with companies or public sector organizations that have global reach. Other global FWLs live and work in their adopted country, such as the U.S., Canada, U.K. but maintain strong ties back home to the Philippines. In their adopted countries, global FWLs own or work with companies or public sector organizations that have a global reach. For some of these women, their career is marked by extensive experience in many countries. For example, during her 15-year overseas career, Mangahas lived in Colombo, Manila, Geneva, and Bangkok; and worked in Albania, Moldova, the Ukraine, Nepal, Sri Lanka, Cambodia, Laos, and the People's Republic of China.

As global leaders they have been involved in the political processes in both the Philippines and their adopted homes, with some of them maintaining dual citizenship. They care about issues that have affected them, including racism, sexism, exchange rates, gender politics, and geo-political issues, such as control of the South China Sea. The FWLs who are based in the Philippines keep up with global issues that affect their organizational, community, and personal lives.

In *DISRUPT 1*, the Filipina women were shown to be guided in their leadership journeys by specific factors. These factors included the importance of relationships, in Filipino culture characterized as *kapwa*; character, values, and self-awareness. The women identified the reasons for their leadership as a combination of having a sense of purpose and responding to a call as well as their desire to give back. In Cain's review (2015), he marveled at how "the values and leadership styles expressed by the Filipina women also lead to advancements toward world peace, justice, generosity, and more equitability worldwide."

In *DISRUPT 2*, the global FWLs referenced competencies that were relevant to various global settings. These competencies can be organized by the competencies listed by the Center for Creative Leadership's [CCL] (2015) "Benchmarks by Design." The synthesis discussion will follow the key CCL categories of: (1) leading yourself, (2) leading others, and (3) leading the organization.

LEADING YOURSELF

Leadership of self is about being aware of one's strengths. These FWLs have shown the capacity to adapt, learn, and cope in both the Philippines and in international environments. Their commitment to making a difference is evident in the healthcare industry (San Agustin), in advocacy to bring about policy change (La Chica), the execution of policy (San Agustin), combining energy medicine with traditional western medicine (Lorica), and serving the disabled (Gamez). Some of the global FWLs have transformed others (Aranza, Florendo), promoted the full and equal participation of women and girls (Moore), and helped the local immigrant community through the arts (Nuyda), community development (Araullo), job creation (Yao), or political action (Caoile). In order to make a difference, these FWLs learned to quickly adapt and to embrace flexibility. They learned by observing (Abele) and through hands-on experience (Robinson). The FWLs sought opportunities to expand their knowledge whether in certificate courses in real estate (Edelman), study abroad programs (Lustado), professional degree training in law (Austriaco, Alado), masters degrees (Boac) or doctoral studies (Beebe, Bonifacio).

Some of these FWLs acknowledged experiencing disruptions in their lives through migration (Boac), nearly losing (Lorica) or losing a loved one (Nuyda, Robinson, San Agustin), an unexpected medical diagnosis (Se-Liban), or a traumatic head injury (Orquiza). While the disruptions caused disequilibrium, the FWLs showed composure in carrying on with their lives, discerning the bigger purpose, and not giving in to despair. They moved forward. They disrupted the status quo by being first and foremost. Sometimes they disrupted the disrupters.

To some extent, the FWLs explained their leader identity as a function of challenging environments and values developed over time. This is consistent with identity development theory that suggest that self-conceptualization can range from relatively simple and unsophisticated to complex and integrated (Day and Harrison, 2007, p. 365). Their experiences have made each global FWL unique.

LEADING OTHERS

Effectively leading others can be done as part of a team or as part of an organization. As team leaders, supervisors or employers, these FWLs delegate, empower, coach, mentor, manage, organize, prioritize, negotiate, listen, communicate, innovate, and enact leadership actions in diverse local and global settings. The FWLs show compassion and sensitivity, put people at ease, and build collaborative relationships in a competitive environment. The competence to maintain and sustain different levels of relationships by FWLs could be attributed to *kapwa*, the cultural norm embodying the ideas of connection, community, and mutual caring for all (Bonifacio, 2013; Beebe, 2016). A more nuanced meaning of *kapwa* includes the terms "being with others," "shared identity", and "equality" (Guevarra, 2009). These relational values are aligned to the definition of leadership as "a process whereby an individual influences a group of individuals to achieve a common goal" (Northouse, 2015, p. 6). *Kapwa* facilitates collaboration across cultures and contributes to intercultural competencies that are associated with global competence.

Global perspective is essential for Filipina women leaders regardless of whether they are expatriates working with corporations, the diplomatic corps, or international development organizations and regardless of whether they are immigrants, overseas workers, or based in the Philippines with a global reach and impact. The FWLs authors in this collection of stories have adapted to diverse cultures and cultural differences, know how to navigate the global environment, and understand the international context of their work. Closely linked to a global perspective is a spirit of mutual respect and open dialogue.

LEADING THE ORGANIZATION

The FWLs lead at various organizational levels and are responsible for setting vision and direction, building commitment, and creating alignment. Global FWLs have founded and successfully led companies such as, Austriaco & Associates (Austriaco), Imperial Homes Group of Companies (Imperial), Magpie.IM (Romero), Perfect Plus Professional Support (Specht), Richprime Global (Yao),

Sol Haus Design (Lustado), Surrey Hearing Care, Inc. (Santos-Greaves), U.S. Lumber (Abele); and consulting and networking firms including aranza.com (Aranza), What if You Could (Florendo), Arteche Global Group (Arteche-Carr), and networking women (Mondejar). Global FWLs have led organizations as partners (Se-Liban). Global FWLs have provided leadership of organizations as Presidents and CEOs of not-for-profits engaged in community development (Araullo, Edelman, Nuyda, San Agustin) or global connections (Beebe). Global FWLs have been effective organizational leaders in their role as civil servants (Alado, Bautista, Mangahas).

As heads of departments or organizations, they have defined vision and strategy, shown business acumen, set goals, led change, made decisions, taken risks, introduced innovation, and expanded their functional orientations. In addition to their main professions, almost all of the FWLs report pro-bono service to their communities. The FWLs found time to operate a not for profit foundation (Yao), offer pro bono services as board members (Dilsaver), or volunteer for medical (San Agustin) and hearing aid missions (Santos-Greaves).

DERAILMENT FACTORS

As leaders, these Filipina women kept their focus despite disruptions in their lives. The types of derailment identified by the CCL was not part of their narrative. There was no mention nor acknowledgment of difficulty building and leading a team; difficulty changing or adopting; failure to meet business objectives; problems with interpersonal relationships; or too narrow a functional orientation. If these factors troubled FWLs in their careers, they have chosen not to focus on it. One can only surmise that the FWLs may have instituted corrective actions that helped them reached their goals and succeed as leaders despite the presence of factors that might have been derailments.

LEADERSHIP AND SUSTAINABILITY

In many ways, these FWLs inspire and support action towards a better world consistent with the notion of a sustainability model of leadership (Visser, 2011). Several of the FWLs were explicit about their sustainability vision. For example, Imperial's leadership is focused on sustainable solar powered housing community, Lustado on tiny homes as a way of creating community, and Lao-Noche on sustainability for a world-class railway and property company based in Asia.

Similar to the CCL benchmarks, the sustainability model requires understanding the individual leader. The sustainability model is explicit about the leadership context and the leadership actions that interrelate with the individual leader competencies. The leadership actions include those that are internal to the organization such as informed decisions, strategic direction, management incentives, performance accountability, people empowerment, and learning and innovation and those that are external to the organization such as cross-sector partnerships, sustainable products and services, sustainability awareness, context transformation, and stakeholder transparency. The leadership context includes the external conditions under which the organization operates including ecological, economic, political, cultural, and community and the conditions internal to the organization including sector/industry, organizational reach, organizational culture, governance structure, and leadership role (Visser, 2011).

LEADERSHIP REPERTOIRE

Beebe (this edition) suggests that to lead in a complex environment requires having a leadership repertoire made up of a combination of competencies that provides options and that are relevant to the context. The CCL benchmarks are useful for identifying key competencies of individuals since knowledge about the self can guide leadership actions. Visser's (2011) articulation of the various external and internal conditions is a good reminder of the importance of context for leadership actions. The Filipina women leaders in this collection have explained how socialization, self-reflection, and feedback from mentors and others have developed their sense of self over time and how this has in turn influenced their leadership actions. The Filipina women leaders discussed both the role of context in their leadership and their own influence on the context.

✳

ACKNOWLEDGEMENTS

This book required a collaborative effort that was made possible by the following:

- Marily Mondejar, Founder and CEO of Filipina Women's Network provided executive oversight and recommended the use of the Center for Creative Leadership's (CCL) Benchmark for Design.

- Thirty–five contributing authors shared their leadership reflections, narratives, vignettes, and leadership competencies; whether en route to London, Manila, New York, San Francisco, getting ready for the U.S. national conventions, or caring for an ill parent.

- For book cover design, Lucille Lozada Tenazas, FWN100™ Global 2013 and Henry Wolf Professor of Communication Design & Associate Dean of Art, Media and Technology, Parsons The New School for Design.

- Our two associate editors gave comments on all the abstracts and suggested areas for improvement to the chapter authors.

  Glenda Bonifacio, Ph.D. an associate Professor at the University of Lethbridge in Alberta, Canada. Glenda who was on study leave and doing research in Tacloban, Leyte persevered in sending comments despite poor Internet access.

  Vangie Meneses, Ed. D. is Board President of the Council of Philippine American Organizations of San Diego County and is an adjunct instructor for Claremont Graduate University. Vangie fit in writing comments between her teaching schedule and later on, her long planned vacation.

- Edwin Lozada, President of the Philippine American Writers and Artists (PAWA), Inc. served as our layout designer as well as provided an extra set of critical eyes

- Our external readers read the whole book and gave us their invaluable advice:

  James Beebe, Ph.D. recently finished the second edition of his book on qualitative research, Rapid Qualitative Inquiry: A Field Guide to Team-Based Assessment. James was a professor in the Doctoral Program in Leadership Studies at Gonzaga University for 17 years and, prior to that he retired as a U.S. Foreign Service Officer with USAID who served in Sudan, Philippines, Liberia, and South Africa.

  Madanmohan Rao, Ph.D. an author and consultant from Bangalore, research advisor at the Asian Media Information and Communication Centre (AMIC), and editor of five book series: The Asia Pacific Internet Handbook, The *Knowledge Management Chronicles, AfricaDotEdu, World of Proverbs,* and *The Global Citizen.* He is the research director of YourStory, a leading platform for startups and investors.

- Our peer reviewers provided comments, recommendations for improvement, and suggestions for edits – Ligaya Beebe, Wennie Conedy, Kristine Custodio, Amelia Duran-Stanton, Penelope V. Flores, Maria Hizon, and Isabelita Manalastas-Watanabe. Although we publicly acknowledge our reviewers, the identity of the reviewers was not disclosed to the authors.

- The daughters who commented on their mother's narratives: Ligaya Beebe (Maria Beebe), Angelica Mangahas (Thetis Mangahas), Johanna Mangahas and Martha Mangahas (Elena Mangahas); and, the mother who commented on her daughter's narrative: Lenore Lim (Marie Claire Lim Moore).

- For giving us permission to quote her poem, Dreamweaver, Dr. Marjorie Evasco. As a writer, Marj commits her vision through her poetry, believing that the worthy warrior and healer is adept at giving voice to the vision so that others may sing it, too. She is currently a fellow at De La Salle University. Read her poems at http://marjorieevasco.jimdo.com/

- FWN's first Fellow, Leah Laxamana fact-checked references, made comments, and stepped up as necessary.

- Franklin M. Ricarte (Draft Orange), Social Media and Tech Guru updated the Filipina Leadership website http://www.filipinaleadership.org/ and Raissa Alvero, FWN Fellow provided various media communications support.

- The Columbia River Peace Corps Association Writers' Group provided moral support and encouragement.

- Colleagues from the Global Networks read the introduction and synthesis and gave comments and feedback; Jerri Shepard, Ed.D., Gonzaga University; Robert Bartlett, Ph.D. Eastern Washington University; and Mark Beattie, Ph.D., Washington State University.

- FWN Filipina Leadership Global Summit (21-24 August) 2015 Steering Committee and Committee Chair, Myrna T. Yao, President and CEO Richprime Global Inc.

- Media Committee for the 2 press conferences in Cebu and Manila: Chit Lijauco, Managing Editor, Philippine Tatler and Susan Bautista-Afan, Managing Director, ABS-CBN Lingkod Kapamilya Foundation, Inc.

- Cebu Book Launch Chair: Rosario Cajucom-Bradbury, Managing Director & CEO, SGS Philippines & SGS Gulf Ltd. ROHQ; Sponsor: Ace T. Itchon, President and CEO, Aspen Philippines Inc.

- Manila Book Launch Chair: Emma Imperial, President and Chief Executive Officer, Imperial Homes Corporation; Sponsors: Bizu, Olivia Limpe Aw, President & CEO, Disteleria Limtuaco & Co., Inc.

- For collaborating with FWN for a book launch in Cebu, the University of Cebu and Chancellor Candice Gotianuy and in Manila, the Asian Institute of Management and AIM President Dr. Jikyeong Kang.

Other *kapwa* global Filipinas too numerous to mention here who gave us support in spirit and cheered us on.

Maraming salamat!

Appendices

Appendix A

REFERENCES

Abele, I. M. & Eastman, E. L. (2010). *The self-architect: Breaking diversity obstacles with strength and structure.* Prospect, KY: Professional Woman Publishing.

Abele, I. M. (2012). Establishing a companywide vision for success: Leading executives on updating your company's long term strategy, setting and achieving goals and motivating employees. Inside the Minds Series; Eagan, MN: Aspatore Books-Exec Blueprints Press.

Barker, E. (2015). How to make your life better by sending five simple emails. Retrieved from http://www.bakadesuyo.com/2013/07/make-your-life-better/

Beal, V. What is agile software development. Retrieved from http://www.webopedia.com/TERM/A/agile_software_development.html

Beebe, M. (in press). The Leadership Repertoire of Select Filipina Women in the Diaspora and Implications for Theorizing Leadership. In J. Storberg Walker and P. Haber-Curran (Eds). *Theorizing Women & Leadership: New Insights & Contributions from Multiple Perspectives.* Info Age Publishing.

Beebe, M. A., & Escudero, M. O. (Eds.). (2015). *Disrupt. Filipina women: Proud. loud. leading without a doubt* (First ed.). Philippines: Filipina Women's Network.

Beebe, M., Magloire, K., Oyeyinka, B. & Rao, M. (Eds.). (2003). *AfricaDotEdu: IT Opportunities and Higher Education in Africa.* New Delhi: Tata McGraw-Hill.

Bennis, W. (1988). Foreword. In M. W. McCall, M.M. Lombardo, and A. M. Morrison. *Lessons of experience: How successful executives develop on the job.* New York, NY: The Free Press.

Bonifacio, G. T. (2005). Filipino women in Australia: Practising citizenship at work. *Asian and Pacific Migration Journal*, 14(3), 293-326.

Bonifacio, G. T. (2008). Doing democracy in the classroom: Challenging hegemonic practices. In D. E. Lund, & P. R. Carr (Eds.), Doing democracy: *Striving for political literacy and social justice* (pp. 195-211). New York: Peter Lang.

Bonifacio, G. T. (2008). I care for you, who cares for me? Transitional services of Filipino live-in caregivers in Canada. *Asian Women: Gender Issues in International Migration (Spring)*, 24(1), 25-50.

Bonifacio, G. T. (2009). Activism from the margins: Filipino marriage migrants in Australia. *Frontiers: A Journal of Women's Studies, 30*(3), 142-168.

Bonifacio, G. T. (2009). From temporary workers to permanent residents: Transitional services for Filipino live-in caregivers in southern Alberta. *Our Diverse Cities: Prairies Region, 6*(Spring), 136-149.

Bonifacio, G. T. (2009). Migration and maternalism: (Re) configuring Ruddick's maternal love. In A. O'Reilly (Ed.), *Maternal thinking: Philosophy, politics, practice.* Toronto: Demeter Press.

Bonifacio, G. T. (2010). Building communities through faith: Filipino Catholics in Philadelphia and Alberta. In G. T. Bonifacio, & V. S. Angeles (Eds.), *Gender, religion and migration: Pathways of integration* (pp. 257-273). Lanham, MD: Lexington Books.

Bonifacio, G. T. (2010). Five daughters and a PhD: Pinay and mothering in Canada. In S. Geissler, L. Loutzenhiser, J. Praud, & L. Streifler (Eds.), *Mothering Canada: Interdisciplinary voices.* Toronto: Demeter Press.

Bonifacio, G. T. (2013). *Pinay on the prairies: Filipino women and transnational identities.* Vancouver, Canada: University of British Columbia Press.

Bonifacio, G. T. (2015). Live-in caregivers in Canada: Servitude for promissory citizenship and family rights. In M. Kontos, & G. Bonifacio (Eds.), *Migrant domestic workers and family life: International perspectives* (pp. 145-161). New York: Palgrave Macmillan.

Bonifacio, G. T. Becoming an Australian citizen: A total buy-out for the Filipina? (2003). *Review of Women's Studies, (January-June) 13*(1), 126-156.

Bourdain, A. (2016). Unfinished business in the Philippines. Retrieved from http://www.cnn.com/2016/04/22/travel/anthony-bourdain-parts-unknown-manila-essay/

Buckingham, M. & Coffman, C. (1999). *First, break all the rules: What the world's greatest managers do differently.* New York, NY: Simon & Schuster.

Cabrera, A. (2012). What being global really means. Retrieved from https://hbr.org/2012/04/what-being-global-really-means

Caoile, G. (2015). Stepping Up. In Beebe, M. A., & Escudero, M. O. (Eds.). *Disrupt. Filipina women: Proud. loud. leading without a doubt.* (First ed.). Philippines: Filipina Women's Network.

Center for Creative Leadership. (2015). Benchmarks by design. Retrieved from http://www.ccl.org/Leadership/360bd

Chan, C. (2014). *A new vocabulary: Fulfillment and integration over "having it all."* 3rd Annual S.H.E. Summit: The Global Leadership & Lifestyle Event, New York, NY.

Clinton, William J. Public Papers of the Presidents of the United States. (1995) Book 1 – January 1 to June 30, 1995. National Archives and Records Administration. Washington, DC: Government Printing Office.

Coloma, R. S. (2008). Border crossing subjectivities and research: Through the prism of feminists of color. *Race Ethnicity and Education,* 11(1), 11-27.

Coloma, R. S., McElhinny, B., Tungohan, E., Catungal, J. P., & Davidson, L. M. (2012). *Filipinos in Canada: Disturbing invisibility.* Toronto: University of Toronto Press.

Cuddy, A. (2015). *Presence: Bringing Your Boldest Self to Your Biggest Challenges.* US: Little, Brown and Company.

Day, D. V. & Harrison, M. (2007). A multilevel, identity-based approach to leadership development. *Human Resource Management Review 17,* 360-373.

Davidson, A. W., Ray, M. A., & Turkel, M. C. (2011). *Nursing, caring, and complexity. Science.* New York, NY: Springer

Drucker, P. (2004). *The effective executive*. New York, NY: Harper Collins.

Ebron, G. (2002). Not just the maid: Negotiating Filipina identity in Italy. *Intersections: Gender, History and Culture in the Asian Context, 8*.

Excellence in Design for Greater Efficiencies (EDGE). Retrieved from http://www.buildup.eu/en/learn/tools/excellence-design-greater-efficiencies-edge-0

Fan, S., Liberman, Z., Keysar, B. & Kinzler, C. (2015) The exposure advantage: Early exposure to a multilingual environment promotes effective communication. *Psychological Science.* doi 0956797615574699

Frost, R. The Road Not Taken. Retrieved from https://www.poetryfoundation.org/resources/learning/core-poems/detail/44272

Gbowee, L. The Nobel Peace Prize 2011Ellen Johnson Sirleaf, Leymah Gbowee, Tawakkol Karman. Retrieved from http://www.nobelprize.org/nobel_prizes/peace/laureates/2011/gbowee-facts.html

Gentry, W. A., & Eckert, R. H. (2012). Integrating implicit leadership theories and fit into the development of global leaders: A 360-degree approach. *Industrial and Organizational Psychology, 15*, 224-227. doi:10.1111/j.1754-9434.2012.01434.x

Gilbert, D. (2005). *Stumbling on happiness*. New York, NY: Random House.

Goldfrank, L., San Agustin, M., Dash, S., & Samms, T. (1978). Linking emergency room and ambulatory services: North Central Bronx Hospital. *Urban Health. 7*(6), 12-4.

Golding, W. (1954). *Lord of the Flies*. NY: Penguin Group.

Gonzales, J. L. (1998). *Philippine labour migration: Critical dimensions of public policy*. Singapore: Institute of Southeast Asian Studies.

Guevarra, J. P. (2005). *Pakikipagkapwa [Sharing/Merging oneself with others]*. In R. M. Gripaldo (Ed.), *Filipino cultural traits* (Chapter 1). Washington, DC: The Council for Research in Values and Philosophy. Available at http://www.crvp.org/book/Series03/IIID-4/chapter-1.htm

Gupta, V., Surie, G., Javidan, M., & Chokker, J. (2002). Southern Asia cluster: The organizational and societal worldviews and their foundations. In B. Pattanayak , & V. Gupta (Eds.), *Creating performing organizations*. New Delhi, India: Sage.

Hernandez, M., Eberly, M. B., Avolio, B. J., & Johnson, M. D. (2011). The loci and mechanism of leadership: Exploring a more comprehensive view of leadership theory. *The Leadership Quarterly, 22*, 1165-1185.

Hill, Linda (May 5, 2010). Leading from behind. *Harvard Business Review*. Blog Post. https://hbr.org/2010/05/leading-from-behind/

Hooijeerg, R., Hunt, J. G., & Dodge, G. E. (1997). Leadership complexity and development of the leaderplex model. *Journal of Management, 23*(3), 375.

House, R., Javidan, M., Hanges, P., & Dorfman, P. (2002). *Journal of World Business, 37*, 3-10. Phong Van Đac Biet: BAO VE BIEN ĐÔNG. (About the Philippine-China Relations). Retrieved from https://www.youtube.com/watch?v=Yr-b9xN_g8A&app=desktop

Hunter, W. D. (2004). Knowledge, skills, attitudes, and experiences necessary to become globally competent. Doctoral dissertation, Lehigh University.

Ignacio, E. N. (2005). *Building diaspora: Filipino community formation on the internet.* New Brunswick, NJ: Rutgers University Press.

Imperial Housing Corporation. Retrieved from https://www.facebook.com/ImperialHomesCorp/

Lawrence-Lightfoot, S. (2009). *The third chapter: Passion, risk, and adventure in the 25 years after 50.* US: Sarah Crichton Books.

Liebelt, C. (2008). "We are the Jews of today": Filipino domestic workers in Israel and the language of diaspora. *HAGAR Studies in Culture, Polity, and Identities 8*(1): 105-128.

Lim, L. (2015). Full circle. In M. A. Beebe, & M. O. Escudero (Eds.), *Disrupt. Filipina women: Proud. loud. leading without a doubt* (1st ed.). Philippines: Filipina Women's Network.

Lorenz, D. E. (1925). *The round the world traveler: A complete summary of practical information* (4th ed.) New York: Fleming H. Revell.

Mactas, M. Leadership in turbulent times. Retrieved from http://www.leadersmag.com/issues/2009.1_jan/turbulent/mactas.html

Magpie.im softwaretools to accept payments over the Internet. Retrieved from https://magpie.im/

Mandela, Nelson (1995). *Long walk to freedom: The autobiography of Nelson Mandela.* New York, NY: Little, Brown and Company.

Manifesto for agile software. Retrieved from http://agilemanifesto.org/

McRaven Urges Graduates to Find Courage to Change the World. Retrieved from http://news.utexas.edu/2014/05/16/mcraven-urges-graduates-to-find-courage-to-change-the-world

Moore, M. C. (2013). *Don't forget the soap: And other reminders from my fabulous Filipina mother.* New York, NY: Canlink Press.

Morgan, K. (2007). Here comes the mail-order bride: Three methods of regulation in the United States, the Philippines, and Russia. *The George Washington International Law Review, 39*(2), 423.

National Education Association. (2010). Global competence is a 21st century imperative. Retrieved from http://www.nea.org/assets/docs/HE/PB28A_Global_Competence11.pdf.

netsuite.org. Retrieved from http://www.netsuite.org/

Northouse, P. (2015). *Leadership: Theory and practice* (7th ed.). Los Angeles, CA: Thousand Oaks: Sage.

Parreñas, R. S. (2001). *Servants of globalization: Women, migration and domestic work.* Stanford, CA: Stanford University Press.

Petrie, N. (2014). Future trends in leadership development. Retrieved from http://insights.ccl.org/wp-content/uploads/2015/04/futureTrends.pdf

Pyke, K. D., & Johnson, D. L. (2003). Asian American women and racialized femininities: "Doing" gender across cultural worlds.". *Gender & Society, 17*(1), 33-53.

Quinndlen, A. (2000). *A short guide to a happy life.* New York, NY: Random House.

Rafael, V. L. (1997). Your grief is our gossip: Overseas Filipinos and other spectral presences. *Public Culture, 9*(2), 267-291.

Remo, M. V. (2012). Stop illegal remittance agents, BSP urged: Informal forex channels a problem in the region. Philippine Daily Inquirer.

Rost, J. C. (1991. *Leadership for the Twentieth Century.* New York: Praeger.

Rubin, G. (2011). *The happiness project: Or, why I spent a year trying to sing in the morning, clean my closets, fight right, read Aristotle, and generally have more fun.* New York, NY: Harper.

San Agustin, M. (1970). The Montefiore-Morrisania comprehensive child care project. Testimony before the senate appropriations committee, Washington DC. *Postgraduate Medicine, 48*(10), 942.

San Agustin, M. (1978). Primary care in a tertiary care center. *Annals of the New York Academy of Sciences, 310,* 121-128.

San Agustin, M. (1992). Population based medicine: A case study from a traditional school. In K. L. White, & J. E. Connelly (Eds.), *The medical school's mission and the population's health* (pp. 132-163). New York: Springer-Verlag.

San Agustin, M., Goldfrank, L., Bloom, R., Grossman, S., Lloyd, W., Smith, D., & Kindig, D., et al. (1979). Primary care conference Part I : Delivery of services. *Journal of Ambulatory Care Management, 2*(2).

San Agustin, M., Goldfrank, L., Matz, R., Hamerman, D., & Bloom, R. (1976). Reorganization of ambulatory health care in an urban municipal hospital. *Archives of Internal Medicine, 136*(11), 1262.

San Agustin, M., Kuperman, A. S., Hammerman, D., Boufford, J., Alpert, J., Bloom, P., & Belmar, R. (1979). Primary care conference Part II: Education. *Journal of Ambulatory Care Management, 2*(2).

San Agustin, M., Sidel, V. W., Drosness, D. L., Kelman, H., Levine, H., & Stevens, E. (1981). Controlled clinical trial of family care compared with child only care in the comprehensive primary care of children. *Medical Care, 19.*

San Agustin, M., Starfield, B., Kindig, D., Bass, M., & Moorehead, M. A. (1979). Primary care conference III: Research. *Journal of Ambulatory Care Management, 2*(2).

San Agustin, M., Stevens, E., & Hicks, B. (1973). An evaluation of the effectiveness of a children and youth project. *Health Services Report, 88*(10), 942.

San Juan, E. J. (1998). *From exile to diaspora: Versions of the Filipino experience in the United States.* Boulder: Westview Press. xx

San Juan, E. J. (2007). *Balikbayang Mahal: Passages from exile.* Morrisville, NC: LuLu.com.

9 ptSandberg, S. (2013). *Lean in: Women, work, and the will to lead.* New York, NY: Knopf.

Saroca, C. (2006). Filipino women, migration, and violence in Australia: Lived reality and media image. *Kasarinlan: Philippine Journal of Third World Studies, 21*(1), 75-110.

Scalabrini Migration Center. (2013). *Country migration report: The Philippines 2013*. Philippines: International Organization for Migration (IOM).

Schnall, S. O. (2014). *On grace*. Tempe, AZ: Sparkpress.

Schnall, S. O. (2015). *The balance project: A novel*. Tempe, AZ: SparkPress.

Stevens, M.J., Bird, A., Mendenhall, M.E., & Oddou, G. (2014). Measuring global leader intercultural competency: Development and validation of the global competencies inventory (GCI). In J. Osland, M. Li & Y. Wang (Eds.), *Advances in global leadership* (8 ed., pp. 99-138). Bingley, UK: Emerald.

Swindoll, C. (1983). Starting over: Fresh hope for the road ahead. Portland, OR : Multnomah Press.

Szent-Gyorgyi, A. (1960). *Introduction to a submolecular biology*. New York: Academic Press.

Tadiar, N. X. M. (2004). *Fantasy-production: Sexual economies and other Philippine consequences for the new world order*. Manila: Ateneo de Manila University Press.

Taylor, S. E., Peplau, L.A., & Sears, D. O. (2006). Social Psychology. Pearson/Prentice Hall.

The center for creative leadership handbook of leadership development (2010). In Van Velsor E., McCauley C. D. & Ruderman M. N. (Eds.), (Third ed.). San Francisco, CA: Jossey-Bass.

Thoreau, H. D. (1854). *Walden, or, life in the woods*. Boston, MA: Ticknor and Fields.

Tokumitsu, M. (2014, January 16, 2014). In the name of love. *Slate,*

Tomeldan, R. (1988). In Oxford, Filipina means domestic help. *Manila Standard*, p. 3.

Verzuh, E. (2008). The fast forward MBA in project management. Hoboken, NJ: John Wiley & Sons.

Visser, W. (2011). *Sustainability leadership linking theory and practice.* Cambridge, UK: University of Cambridge Institute for Sustainability Leadership.

Werbner, P. (1999). Global pathways: Working class cosmopolitans and the creation of transnational ethnic worlds. *Social Anthropology, 7*(1), 17-35.

Williams, R. L., McDowell, J. B., & Kautz, D. D. (2011). A Caring leadership model for nursing's future. *International Journal for Human Caring* 15(1) 31-35.

World Economic Forum. (2015). *The global gender gap report*. (No. 10th Anniversary Edition). World Economic Forum.

Yao, M. (2015). *The gift of a dream – The GREAT Women Project*. Philippines: Vidal Publishing.

Appendix B

ADDITIONAL WEB-BASED RESOURCES

Center for Creative Leadership. 360 by design Facilitator's guide. Retrieved from
http://www.ccl.org/leadership/pdf/assessments/360BDfacguide.pdf
The guide provides information on conducting CCL's 360 By Design assessment and facilitating a
feedback workshop and one-one-one sessions with participants. 360 By Design is an assessment
tool that uses feedback to identify the highest valued competencies for an organization in order to
support the professional development and success of its participants.

Comprehensive Assessment of Leadership for Learning
<https://www.leadershipforlearning.org/>
CALL surveys all administrators, teachers, instructional support staff, and student support staff
concerning leadership practices throughout the school. Its purpose is improvement of student
learning to support practitioners in their work, not performance evaluation of employees.

Filipina Women's Network. 2007-2015. Interviews with FWN100 2007 awardees.
The Filipina Women's Network interviews its Top 100 Most Influential Filipina Women awardees
as part of its time capsule project with the objective of documenting the contributions of Filipina
women to society to inspire future generations.

Filipina Women's Network. 2007-2015. FWN Global 100: The 100 Most Influential Filipina
Women in the World. Filipina Women's Network has published the Filipina Leadership Summit
magazine from 2005-present. The magazine serves as a program and resource for attendees.
The 2013 issue showcases the first group of the FWN Global 100 Most Influential Women in the
World.

Global Competence Aptitude Assessment (GCAA)®. Retrieved from
http://www.globallycompetent.com/aboutGCAA/about.html
the only assessment that measures all the dimensions necessary for global competence - a 21st
century skill.

Institute for Intercultural Communication. 2014.
Retrieved from < http://intercultural.org/training-and-assessment-tools.html>
Provides a list of selected intercultural training and assessment tool.

Kozai Group. The global competencies inventory (GCI). Retrieved from http://www.kozaigroup.
com/global-competencies-inventory-gci/
Global Competencies Inventory measures three facets of intercultural adaptability in identifying
personal characteristics related to successful performance in contexts where cultural norms
and behaviors vary from one's own. This tool is generally used for purposes such as professional
development, team building and succession planning.

Leadership Assessment Tool Inventory - Assess Your Skills. Retrieved from
http://www.kellogg.northwestern.edu/faculty/uzzi/htm/teaching-leadership.htm
These exercises assess ability to apply critical management skills to identify and solve key organizational problems.

Leadership and Management Development Strategy. Retrieved from http://www.exec.gov.nl.ca/exec/hrs/forms/Peer_Assessment_Form2_Forms_and_Applications.pdf
Developed to endorse learning and development opportunities to strengthen the leadership and management capacity of the Newfoundland and Labrador Public Service.

Najafi Global Mindset Institute. Global mindset inventory's three capitals.
Retrieved from http://globalmindset.thunderbird.edu/home/global-mindset- inventory/three-capitals

The Global Mindset Inventory is an assessment tool for identifying one's capacity to lead and influence individuals and companies in a global context, particularly those who are from a different culture.

Northouse Authentic Leadership Self-Assessment Questionnaire. Retrieved from http://people.uncw.edu/nottinghamj/documents/slides6/Northouse6e%20Ch11%20Authentic%20Survey.pdf
This questionnaire contains items about different dimensions of authentic leadership.

Office of Personnel Management Assessment & Evaluation LEADERSHIP ASSESSMENTS
Retrieved from https://www.opm.gov/services-for-agencies/assessment-evaluation/leadership-assessments/
A suite of leadership tools that enhance self-awareness by measuring leadership effectiveness from multiple approaches.

Self Assessment Tools. Retrieved from http://www.swansea.ac.uk/dts/leadershipandmanagement/personaldevelopmentgrowth/selfassessmenttools/
Free self-assessment tools that can help identify where your leadership strengths and development needs lie, to assist with personal development.

Ronald E. Dolan, ed. 1991. Philippines: A Country Study. Washington: GPO for the Library of Congress, 1991. Retrieved from http://countrystudies.us/philippines/

Via Institute on Character. Do you know your 24 character strengths? Retrieved from http://www.viacharacter.org/www/the-survey
The VIA survey was created to help individuals identify the make-up of their character strengths that are classified under six virtue categories. The survey can be taken online and is free of charge.

Appendix C

FWN Award Categories

Behind the Scenes Leaders

This award category recognizes Filipina women who may not have the big title or corner office, but is a driving force behind the success of a social cause or life issue, a community organization's project or initiative; or her employer's organizational business unit or department. Someone who has gone beyond the call of duty to devote time, energy, and resources to advocate for those who need a voice, or support the organization she represents or works for.

Builders

Builders have demonstrated exceptional business impact at a large workplace environment; displaying deep passion for a cause through collaborative initiatives or alliances with nonprofit organizations on behalf of her own organization; demonstrates high potential and skill with measurable results at a government agency, or organization in the public and private sectors. "Buildership" is about building better organizations, leading broken organizations to adjust, repair, and re-align.

Emerging Leaders

This award category recognizes Filipina women below age 35 who are making their mark in a leadership role, are on the pathway to principalship and building capacity across a system. Emerging Leaders have powerful mindsets and skill sets that drive achievement for their organizations.

Founders and Pioneers

This award honors Filipina women in their capacities as the chief executive, president, executive director or founder of a company, community organization, non-profit, or business venture that they helped start, build or significantly grow. This award category is for the trailblazers who have marshaled resources and applied innovative practices, processes and/or technologies in a new and groundbreaking way to address a significant business or organizational opportunity.

Innovators and Thought Leaders

This award recognizes women who have broken new ground in the global workplace, have delivered new and unique applications of emerging technology transforming the way people think, in the fields of sports, literature, the arts and pop culture, or have improved the lives of others by helping develop a product or service in the fields of science, technology, engineering, arts, or mathematics. This award category is also for someone who have either launched a new enterprise, a learning function, or completely overhauled an existing development or community initiative that has sparked a following.

KEEPERS OF THE FLAME

Sustaining Pinay Power. As the excitement dies down and reality sets in, many will drop out and others will pick up the torch. The Keepers of the Flame are the caretakers, ensuring that the Pinay Power Vision is kept alive.

NICOLE

This award honors Filipina women whose words, actions, and activism, inspire others to act and revolutionize society's way of understanding traditional beliefs and customs thus leaving behind a Filipino global imprint. "Nicole," who sparked an international dialogue about women's rights, national sovereignty, and international law, as she steadfastly pursued justice against her rapists, inspires this category.

POLICYMAKERS AND VISIONARIES

This award recognizes Filipina women leaders who have demonstrated exceptional acumen combined with a forward-looking vision in the development or influencing of policies, campaigns or laws that impact business, industry, and society. Leaders who enrich the lives, careers and businesses of others; someone who shares the benefits of their wealth, experience, and knowledge; actions that significantly change how we think and live.

Appendix D

List of FWN Awardees

(2007-2016)

100 Most Influential Filipina Women in the U.S.
(US FWN100 ™)

BEHIND THE SCENES LEADERS

2007

Asia Yulo-Blume
Aurora Cavosora Daly
Cheely Ann Sy
Cora Basa Cortez Tomalinas
Denielle Palomares
Edna Austria Rodis
Evangeline   -Buell
Flor Alcantara-Reyes
Kai Delen-Briones
Laarni San Juan
Lolita Kintanar
Lorna Lardizabal Dietz
Maria Jocelyn Bernal
Perla Gange Ibarrientos
Rosalinda Medina Rupel
Susie Quesada

2009

Aileen Suzara
Belle Santos
Cherie Querol Moreno
Daisy Magalit Rodriguez
Dolly Pangan-Specht
Elsie Rose
Helen Marte Bautista
Jian Zapata
Kathleen Davenport
Lorrie V. Reynoso
Lottie T. Buhain
Lovette Rosales Llantos
Lydia Castillo Fontan
Lyna Larcia-Calvario
Mady Rivera
Maria Concepcion Banatao

2009 *(cont.)*

Naomi Tacuyan Underwood
Nerissa M. Fernandez
Nida L. Recabo
Priscilla Magante Quinn
Roselyn Estepa Ibañez
Shirley Orille Brazis
Sunny Dykwel
Tess Ricafort Alarcon

2011

Bennie Lou Quevedo
Cherina Viloria Tinio
Evelyn Javier-Centeno
Evelyn Luluquisen
Francine Villarmia-Kahawai
Gloria Ramil Omania
Gretheline Bolandrina
Henni Espinosa
Julieta Zarate Hudson

2011 *(cont.)*

Mary Ann C. Ubaldo
Pearl Parmelee
Rosario "Puchi" Carrion
   Di Ricco

2012

Angie Louie
Edcelyn Pujol
JoAnn Fields
Marian Catedral-King
Maritessa Bravo Ares
Pureza Belza
Theresa Noriega-Lum
Yong Chavez

Builders and Emerging Leaders

2007

Arlene Marie A. "Bambi" Lorica
Bettina Santos Yap
Claire Oliveros
Edna M.Casteel
Genevieve Jopanda
Jennifer Briones Tjiong
Laura Izon Powell
Laureen Dumadag Laglagaron
Lorna Mae DeVera
Lyna Larcia-Calvario
May Nazareno
Melinda Poliarco
Milagros "Mitos" G. Santisteban
Nieves Cortez
Paz Gomez
Polly Cortez
Rachel Buenviaje
Rebecca Samson
Regina "Ging" E. Reyes
Rose-Ann K. Ubarra
Shirley Raguindin
Sonia T. Delen Fitzsimmons
Susan Afan
Sylvia Lichauco
Thelma Boac
Theresa Tantay Wilson
Zenei T. Cortez

2009

Ana Julaton
Cielo Martinez
Cynthia Aloot
Denise Castañeda Miles
Gel Santos Relos
Isabelita M. Abele
Jannah Arivan Manansala
Jennifer Ong
Katherine Abriam-Yago
Katrina R. Abarcar
Maria (Mimi) Amutan
Mivic Hirose
Raquel Cruz Bono
Raquel R. Redondiez
Rebecca Delgado Rottman
Rowena Verdau-Beduya
Stephanie Ong-Stillman
Valerie Pozon-de Leon

2011

Cynthia Rapaido
Diana Reyes
Estela Matriano
Esther Misa Chavez
Genevieve Herreria
Gloria B. Gil

2011 (cont.)

Kathleen Quinn DuBois
Keesa Ocampo
Leah Beth O. Naholowaa
Leia Lorica
Maria Africa Beebe
Melanie A. Caoile
Mila M. Josue
Odette Alcazaren Keeley
Selenna Franco-Cefre

2012

Belinda Muñoz
Cora Aragon Soriano
Cynthia A. Bonta
Eleanore Fernandez
Esther Lee
Jacqueline Dumlao Yu
Lili Tarachand
Nadia Catarata Jurani
Natalie C. Aliga
Olivia Finina De Jesus
Prosy Abarquez-Delacruz
Rita Dela Cruz
Rocio Nuyda
Sheryll Casuga
Stefanie Medious
Theresa Chua

Founders & Pioneers

2007

Celia Ruiz-Tomlinson
Connie S. Uy
Cora Alisuag
Ellen M. Abellera
Erlinda Sayson Limcaco
Gina Lopez Alexander
Gloria T. Caoile
Joy Bruce
Linda Maria Nietes-Little
Loida Nicolas Lewis
Ludy Payumo Corrales
Luzviminda Sapin Micabalo
Marietta Aster Nagrampa Almazan
Mary Carmen Madrid-Crost
Nimfa Yamsuan Gamez
Patricia Aldaba Lim-Yusah

2007 (cont.)

Rozita Villanueva Lee
Sony Robles Florendo
Tessie Guillermo
Virna S. Tintiangco

2009

Alice Bulos
Adelamar Alcantara
Analisa Balares
Carina Castañeda
Cora Oriel
Delle Sering Fojas
Ethel Luzario
Evelyn Silangcruz Bunoan
Fe Martinez

2009 (cont.)

Fe Punzalan
Fely Guzman
Imelda Ortega Anderson
Judy Arteche-Carr
Maria Maryles Casto
Mivic Hirose
Mona Lisa Yuchengco
Nanette D. Alcaro
Nelsie Parrado
Nini RB Bautista de Garcia
Norma Calderon-Panahon
Patricia Espiritu Halagao
Rosie Abriam
Ruthe Catolico Ashley
Sherri Burke
Zenaida Cunanan

Founders & Pioneers

2011

Alma Onrubia
Chateau Gardecki
Christina Rodriguez
  Laskowski
Dellie Punla
Geri Ferrer-Chan
Herna Cruz-Louie
Janelle So
Josefina R. Enriquez
Jossie Alegre

2011

Joy Dalauidao-Hermsen
Lillian Pardo
Maria Benel Se-Liban
Marjan Philhour
Perla Paredes Daly
Rhoda Yabes Alvarez
Soledad Manaay
Tess Mauricio
Vellie Sandalo Dietrich-Hall

2012

Betty O. Buccat
Conchita Bathan
Constance Valencia
  Santos
Elaine R. Serina
Josie Jones
Kristine Custodio
Victoria J. Santos

Innovators & Thought Leaders

2007

Angelita Castro-Kelly
Carissa Villacorta
Charmaine Clamor
Connie Mariano
Diana J. Galindo
Edith Mijares Ardiente
Elena Mangahas
Elenita Fe Mendoza Strobel
Gemma Nemenzo
Jane Hofileña
Leila Benitez-McCollum
Lilia Villanueva
Malu Rivera-Peoples
Marisa Marquez
Mutya San Agustin

2009

Brenda Buenviaje
Cora Manese Tellez
Esminia "Mia" Luluquisen
Hazel Sanchez
Jei Africa
Lenore RS Lim
Marlina Feleo Gonzales
Marissa Aroy
Nana Luz Khilnani
Norma P. Edar
Ma Rowena Verdan-Beduya
Robyn Rodriguez Canham
Sokie Paulin

2011

Angel Velasco Shaw
Celia Pangilinan-Donahue
Christina Dunham
Evelyn Dilsaver
France Viana
Gemma Bulos
Minerva Malabrigo
  Tantoco

2012

A. Fajilan
Cris Comerford
Janet Nepales
Maricel Quiroz
Penélope V. Flores
Vivian Zalvidea Araullo

Nicole

2007	2009	2012	2013
M. Evelina Galang	Jessica Cox	Nilda Guanzon Valmores	Annalisa Enrile
		Paulita Lasola Malay	

Policymakers and Visionaries

2007

Christina Arvin Baal
Eleonor G. Castillo
Grace Walker
Gwen de Vera
Irene Bueno
Kris Valderrama
Kymberly Marcos Pine

2007 *(cont.)*

Lillian Galedo
Lourdes Tancinco
Marissa Castro-Salvati
Miriam B. Redmiller
Mona Pasquil
Norma Doctor Sparks
Rida T. R. Cabanilla

2007 *(cont.)*

Ruth Asmundson Uy
Sonia Aranza
Tani Gorre Can-
  til-Sakauye
Vanessa Barcelona
Velma Veloria
Vida Benavides

POLICYMAKERS AND VISIONARIES

2009

Carmelyn Malalis
Carmen Lagdameo Stull
Faith Bautista
Hydra B. Mendoza
Gertrude Quiroz Gregorio
Joanne F. del Rosario
Joselyn Geaga-Rosenthal
Lorraine Roder0-Inouye
Lynn Finnegan
Marissa Garcia Bailey
Myrna L. De Vera

2009

Noella Tabladillo
Rose Zimmerman
Dr. Rozzana Verder-Aliga
Stephanie Ong Stillman

2011

Agnes Briones Ubalde
Amy Agbayani
Arlie Ricasa
Cheryl Nora Moss
Katherine M. Eldemar

2011 *(cont.)*

Mae Cendana Torlakson
Melissa Roxas
Monique Lhuillier
Pat Gacoscos
Rosa Mena Moran

2012

Alicia Fortaleza
Rosita Galang
Zenda Garcia-Lat

KEEPERS OF THE FLAME

2007

Al Perez
Arlene Marie "Bambi" Lorica
Elena Mangahas
Franklin M. Ricarte
Genevieve Herreria
Maria Roseni "Nini" M. Alvero
Marily Mondejar
Maya Ong Escudero
Nida Recabo
Rowena Mendoza Sanchez
Sonia T. Delen Fitzsimmons
Thelma Boac

2009

Al Perez
Arlene Marie "Bambi" Lorica
Elena Mangahas
Ellen Abellera
Franklin M. Ricarte
Gloria T. Caoile
Jocelyn Bernal
Josephine "Jopin" Romero
Lilia V. Villanueva
Marily Mondejar
Mutya San Agustin Shaw
Shirley S. Raguindin
Sonia T. Delen Fitzsimmons
Thelma Boac

2011

Al Perez
Arlene Marie "Bambi" Lorica
Franklin M. Ricarte

2011 *(cont.)*

Gloria T. Caoile
Josephine "Jopin" Romero
Lilia V. Villanueva
Mutya San Agustin Shaw
Shirley S. Raguindin
Susie Quesada
Thelma Boac

2012

Al Perez
Arlene Marie "Bambi" Lorica
Cherina Tinio
Cynthia Rapaido
Elena Mangahas
Esther Chavez
Franklin M. Ricarte
Gloria T. Caoile
Josephine "Jopin" T. Romero
Judy Arteche-Carr
Lilia V. Villanueva
Mutya San Agustin Shaw
Shirley S. Raguindin
Sonia T. Delen Fitzsimmons
Susie Quesada
Thelma Boac

2013

Al Perez
Arlene Marie "Bambi" Lorica
Alicia Fortaleza
Cynthia Rapaido
Edcelyn Pujol
Elena Mangahas

2013 *(cont.)*

Franklin M. Ricarte
Gloria T. Caoile
Marily Mondejar
Maria Roseni "Nini"
   M. Alvero
Maya Ong Escudero
Mutya San Agustin Shaw
Shirley S. Raguindin
Sonia T. Delen
   Fitzsimmons
Susie Quesada
Thelma Boac

2014

Arlene Marie "Bambi"
   Lorica
Alicia Fortaleza
Delle Sering Fojas
Edcelyn Pujol
Elena Mangahas
Franklin M. Ricarte
Gizelle Covarrubias
   Robinson
Gloria T. Caoile
Marily Mondejar
Maria Roseni "Nini"
   M. Alvero
Maria A. Beebe, Ph.D.
Maya Ong Escudero
Mutya San Agustin Shaw
Shirley S. Raguindin
Sonia T. Delen Fitzsimmons
Susie Quesada
Thelma Boac

2013 Awards – 100 Most Influential Filipina Women in the World (Global FWN100™)

Behind the Scenes Leaders

Bessie Badilla
Elizabeth Ann Quirino
Emma Cuenca

Genevieve Jopanda
Loisa Cabuhat

Maria Beebe
Regina Manzana-Sawhney

Builders

Carmela Clendening
Imelda M. Nicolas

Jocelyn Ding
Nina D. Aguas

Rebecca Delgado Rottman

Emerging Leaders

Ariel Batungbacal
Christina Luna

Meriam Reynosa
Michele Bumgarner

Patricia Gallardo-Dwyer

Founders & Pioneers

Allyson Tintiangco-Cubales
Bella Aurora Padua-Belmonte
Dawn Bohulano Mabalon
Delle Sering-Fojas
Ernestina de los Santos-Mac
Evelia V. Religioso
Isabelita Manalastas-Watanabe

Joselyn Geaga-Rosenthal
Julieta Gabiola
Librada C. Yamat
Loida Nicolas Lewis
Lydia Cruz
Maria Almia de los Santos

Mariedel Leviste
Marife Zamora
Norma Fulinara Placido
Patricia Zamora Riingen
Rosemer Enverga
Tess Mauricio

Innovators and Thought Leaders

Amelia Duran-Stanton
Annette M. David
Carmencita David-Padilla
Janet C. Mendoza Stickmon

Janet Susan R. Nepales
Lirio Sobreviñas Covey
Lucille Lozada Tenazas
Mary Ann Lucille L. Sering

Mary Jane Alvero-Al Mahdi
Mira Soriano Gillet
Rozita Villanueva Lee
Suzie Moya Benitez

Policymakers & Visionaries

Astrid S. Tuminez
Cora Manese Tellez
Eleanor Valentin

Hydra Mendoza-McDonnell
Imelda Cuyugan
Gloria T. Caoile

Kris Valderrama
Margaret Lapiz
Patricia V. Paez

2014 Awards –100 Most Influential Filipina Women in the World (Global FWN100™)

BEHIND THE SCENES LEADERS

Consuelo "Chit" Lijauco
Elvie Abordo

Fritzie Igno
M. Evelina Galang

BUILDERS

Aida Garcia, Esq.
Carmen Lamagna Ph.D.
Filomenita Mongaya-Hoegsholm
Ivic Mueco
Judy Arteche-Carr
Ma. Rhodora "Ayhee" L. Campos
Marianne Hontiveros
Marie Claire Lim Moore

Marilyn "Wafa" Roscales-Kasimieh
Mary Ann Covarrubias Ph.D.
Milagros Sering
Myrna Obligacion Carreon
Nora Kakilala-Terrado
Olivia Valera Palala
Sarah Songalia
Zenei Triunfo-Cortez RN

EMERGING LEADERS

Janice Lao-Noche

Melissa Ramoso

FOUNDERS & PIONEERS

Analisa Balares
Angelica Berrie
Catherine Feliciano-Chon
Conchita "Chit" Bathan
Darlene Marie Berberabe

Delia Domingo-Albert
Edith Villanueva
Karen Batungbacal
Ma. Victoria Añonuevo

INNOVATORS AND THOUGHT LEADERS

Boots Anson Roa-Rodrigo
Cris Comerford
Grace Princesa
Ida Ramos-Henares
Jennifer Lopez Fernan

Josefina "Chef Jessie" Sincioco
Maria Lourdes (Marides) Fernando, MPS
Maria Ressa
Patricia Espiritu-Halagao
Teresita Pullin

NICOLE

Monique Wilson

POLICYMAKERS & VISIONARIES

Delia Rodriguez-Amaya, Ph.D.
Maria Castañeda
Maria Teresa Bonifacio Cenzon

Rida Cabanilla
Ruth Uy Asmundson, Ph.D.
Thetis Mangahas

2015 Awards –100 Most Influential Filipina Women in the World (Global FWN100™)

BEHIND THE SCENES LEADERS

Agnes Joyce Garlit Bailen
Angelica Ligas
Cheryl Sevegan
Em Angeles
Hazel Dolio Tag'at
Leonor S. Vintervoll
Leslie Y. Tabor
Lisa Suguitan Melnick
Maria Cecilia "Cecile" Gregorio Ascalon
Susan Bautista Afan

BUILDERS

Aimee Alado
Anny Misa Hefti
Aurora Abella Austriaco
Catherine Campbell
Catherine Salceda Ileto
Elizabeth J. Bautista
Grace Trinidad Vergara
Imelda "Emmie" Collado Ortega Anderson
Leticia "Letty" Quizon
Pet Hartman
Salve Vargas Edelman
Sonia Lugmao Aranza,
Stephanie Lomibao
Tess Martillano-Manjares
Tiffany Bohee
Trina Villanueva

EMERGING LEADERS

Francine Maigue
Juslyn Cabrera Manalo
Kharissa Fernando
Michelle Joyce Florendo
Noelani Sallings
Patricia Quema La Chica

FOUNDERS & PIONEERS

Ace T. Itchon
Hedy Marie Leuterio Thomas, PE
Irene Sun-Kaneko
Juanita Nimfa Yamsuan Gamez
Maria Nieves Santos-Greaves
Myrna Tang Yao
Tessa Yutadco

INNOVATORS AND THOUGHT LEADERS

Glenda Tibe Bonifacio
Melissa Orquiza
Ramona Diaz
Vina Lustado

POLICYMAKERS & VISIONARIES

Lorna G. Schofield
Luisa Vicerra-Blue

KEEPERS OF THE FLAME

Amar Bornkamp
Alicia Fortaleza
Bambi Lorica, MD, FAAP
Edcelyn Pujol, CFP
Elena Mangahas
Gloria T. Caoile
Maria Beebe, Ph.D.
Maria Roseni "Nini" M. Alvero
Marily Mondejar
Colonel Shirley S. Raguindin
Sonia T. Delen
Susie Quesada
Thelma Boac

Biographies

MARIA AFRICA BEEBE

EDITOR

DEVELOPING AN INTERNATIONAL
LEADERSHIP REPERTOIRE

Global ❧ Scholar Educator ❧ Katipunera

Maria Beebe, Ph.D. is an applied sociolinguist whose research interests include critical discourse analysis, women's leadership, and information communication technologies (ICT) for development. She has a Masters of Arts in Anthropology and Ph.D. in Education from Stanford University. Dr. Beebe co-edited *DISRUPT. Filipina Women: Loud. Proud. Leading without a Doubt* based on the leadership journeys of 35 Filipinas who shared their stories in 2015. She is the author of the chapter on Harmonizing Global Teams in Afghanistan, the book introduction, and synthesis. She is the author of The Leadership Repertoire of Select Filipina Women in the Diaspora and Implications for Theorizing Leadership in the 2016 book volume *Theorizing Women & Leadership: New Insights & Contributions from Multiple Perspectives*. She is working on a book on *Afghan Women and Leadership*. Dr. Beebe co-edited *AfricaDotEdu* to share lessons learned from the use of ICT to create networks among higher education institutions in Africa. Dr. Beebe has over 20 years of experience in international development, higher education, and the use of the Internet for teaching and learning in Afghanistan, Ethiopia, Liberia, South Africa, Sudan, Tanzania, Uganda, Poland, and Philippines. Dr. Beebe created Global Networks to continue collaborations by global citizens or organizations for a sustainable world.

AMBASSADOR DELIA DOMINGO ALBERT

PREFACE WRITER

Dedicated ❧ Dynamic ❧ Devoted

Ambassador Delia Domingo Albert, the first career woman diplomat to become Secretary of Foreign Affairs (Minister) of the Philippines and in Asia, has served in Switzerland, Romania, Hungary, the former German Democratic Republic, the Federal Republic of Germany, and the Commonwealth of Australia. She chaired the United Nations Security Council in 2004 and introduced "The Role of Civil Society in Post-Conflict Peacebuilding." She attended the University of the Philippines, the Institute of International Studies in Geneva, the Diplomatic Institute in Salzburg, Boston University Overseas in Bonn, the J.F. Kennedy School of Government at Harvard University, among others. The Philippine Women's University conferred on her Doctor of Humanities, honoris causa for building a gender-fair society. Her awards include: Most Distinguished Alumna of the University of the Philippines in 2012, Order of Sikatuna rank of Datu for her meritorious service to the country, *Bai-A-Rawatun sa Filipinas* for assisting Muslim women in their search for peace and development. The Federal Republic of Germany awarded her the Knight's Commander's Cross of the Order of Merit with Star for promoting bilateral and ASEAN-EU relations. The Australian government awarded her for exceptional performance as former Ambassador in 2016. She is married to Hans Albert, a German television journalist and mother to Joy and Arne Jerochewski and grandmother to Oskar.

About the Assistant Editors

GLENDA TIBE BONIFACIO, PH.D.

LEGACY IN THE ACADEME:
INTEGRATED ACTIVISM FOR SOCIAL JUSTICE

Scholar ❦ Mother
Activist

Glenda Tibe Bonifacio, Ph.D. is an associate Professor at the University of Lethbridge in Alberta, Canada. Dr. Bonifacio holds a BA in the Social Sciences major in Political Science (magna cum laude, University of the Philippines); MA in Asian Studies (University of the Philippines); and a Ph.D. from the School of History and Politics, University of Wollongong, Australia in 2004. Dr. Bonifacio's research interests include: gender, migration, citizenship, development, globalization, religion, activism, and feminist spirituality. Dr. Bonifacio edited *Gender and Rural Migration* (2014) and *Feminism and Migration* (2012); co-edited *Migrant Domestic Workers and Family Life* (2015), and *Gender, Religion and Migration: Pathways of Integration* (2010). She is the author of *Pinay on the Prairies: Filipino Women and Transnational Identities* (2013). *Pinay on the Prairies* uses "Pinay feminisms" as a theoretical frame for analyzing the transnational lives of Filipino Women in Canada.

VANGIE MENESES

ASSOCIATE EDITOR

Educator ❦ Counselor
Empowerment

Vangie Meneses, Ed.D. has been involved in higher education for over 40 years having served in various capacities as a counselor, instructor, and administrator. She has served as the Vice President of Student Services of Economic Development and the Chief Academic Officer. Her educational background includes a Bachelor's Degree in Social Welfare, a Master's in Social Work, and a Doctorate in Educational Leadership and Change. Currently she serves as Board President of the Council of Philippine American Organizations of San Diego County and is an adjunct instructor for Claremont Graduate University. She has taught numerous classes and facilitated workshops in Personal Development, Human Development, Cultural Diversity, Organizational Leadership, and Leadership Development. As a first generation high school and college graduate, she has a deep appreciation and understanding of education and its equalizing effect on the quality of life for individuals. She firmly believes in the empowerment of the individual; to find voice and use voice. She has dedicated her professional life to seeking out and advocating for educational opportunities for students. Her goal is to serve her community.

About the Contributing Authors

ISABELITA "LITA" MARCELO ABELE

GOING AGAINST THE GRAIN

Award Winner ❧ *Philanthropist* ❧ *Entrepreneur*

As President and CEO of the South Jersey-based, family-owned lumber supplier, U.S. Lumber, Isabelita Abele has successfully "gone against the grain" and positioned her certified 'woman' and 'minority-owned' lumber and building materials company as leader in sales throughout New Jersey, Delaware, Maryland, and Pennsylvania. She represents the best of success in American Diversity as she breaks the barriers of the glass ceiling and opens opportunities for Filipino women and men in America. Lita's outstanding leadership in a non-traditional woman-owned corporation has been recognized for over twenty years with national, regional, and local business awards. The corporation has repeatedly been ranked as one of the fastest growing firms from 1999 to 2014. Under the leadership of Lita and her partner and husband Merrill Abele, U.S. Lumber is expected to continue the climb in the years to come. As an involved community leader, Lita contributes her expertise and experience with various entities including business groups, local and statewide government, university students and administration, women's advocacy associations, and Chambers of Commerce on both a state and national level. Lita is a member of the Board of Trustees at Rowan University. She is a published author. Her awards include, but are not limited to: The International Alliance for Women's (TIAW) World of Difference 100, NJBIZ 50 Best Women in Business, 100 Most Influential Filipina Women in the United States, Top 100 Women in Business as identified by the Philadelphia Business Journal, and The Alice Paul Institute's Equality Award.

AMELIA ALADO

AN ILONGGA'S GLOBAL JOURNEY

Hardworking ❧ *Tenacious* ❧ *Driven*

Amelia Alado has more than fifteen years of professional experience since qualifying as an attorney-at-law in the Philippines in 1999. She successfully completed a Graduate Diploma in Law and Legal Practice in 2008 at BPP Law School in London. She has worked in private, government, and third sectors in various jurisdictions. Amelia has worked at the Department of Trade and Industry and the Court of Appeals in the Philippines. While in the UK she worked at the Ministry of Justice and the Government Legal Department. Amelia was a recipient of Intellectual Property Fellowship under the auspices of the Japan Patent Office (JPO) and the World Intellectual Property Office. She did her training and research at the Asia Pacific Intellectual Property Centre and the Japan Institute for Promoting Invention and Innovation. Her thesis, "A Comparative Study of the Philippines and Japan Intellectual Property Laws," was published by the JPO. Amelia spoke on the "Strategic Forum on Women, Business and Economic Development" at the 5th Southeast Asian (SEA) Studies Symposium in April, 2016 organized by Project Southeast Asia at the University of Oxford. Amelia currently lives in London.

SONIA LUGMAO ARANZA

TRANSFORMATIONAL LEADERSHIP BEGINS WITHIN

Dynamic ❧ *Innovative* ❧ *Tenacious*

Fortune 500 corporations recognize Ms. Aranza as a high impact global speaker, master facilitator, and executive consultant. Her clients include Boeing, Chevron, Coca-Cola, IBM, McDonald's, NASA, Sandals Resorts, Toyota, Wal-Mart, and many more. She is a seasoned professional with 20 years of experience specializing in global leadership development, cross-cultural communications, and diversity & inclusion strategies.

     The U.S. Department of Labor describes her work as "Outstanding!" The Society for Human Resource Management (SHRM) consistently ranks her among the top speakers at conferences based on audience evaluations. Respected by her colleagues, she is Past Chairperson of the Diversity Professional Experts Group of the National Speakers Association. She earned a B.A. in Communications from University of Hawaii while she was an International Exchange Student to Russia. She earned an M.A. in Cross-Cultural Communications from University of Hawaii and an M.A. in Public Communications from American University in Washington, DC. She actively mentors students and received the "Outstanding Woman of the Year" award from National Association of Professional Asian American Women. She was honored as one of the "100 Most Influential Filipina Women in the United States" (2007) and one of the "100 Most Influential Filipina Women in the World" (2015). Read her story at www.SoniaAranza.com

VIVIAN ZALVIDEA ARAULLO

ROCK THE BOAT BUT STAY ON COURSE

Progress Not Perfection

Vivian Zalvidea Araullo is a commissioner for Recreation, Parks and Libraries of the City of Daly City, California and the executive director of West Bay Pilipino Multi Service Center. The Center helps underserved Filipino immigrant families in San Francisco and other parts of the Bay Area. Vivian was named by the Filipina Women's Network as one of the most influential Filipina women in America in 2012 for her innovation and thought leadership. She has spearheaded a series of public service fairs that has helped thousands of Filipino Americans across California gain access to free legal and medical aid and advice on housing issues and credit. Vivian, a multi-awarded broadcast and print journalist, comes from the corporate world. She headed the news department at The Filipino Channel that has bureaus across the United States and Canada. She worked at CBS news, ABC news, Japanese broadcaster NHK, and collaborated with CNN. As a journalist, Vivian's reporting spurred Philippine legislation that continues to protect migrant Filipinos around the world, the Overseas Filipino Act of 1995. After winning television's highest honor, the Emmy award, Vivian changed course and joined the non-profit sector, and subsequently appointed to public office. She continues to write for publications such as ABS-CBN.com, Inquirer.net and New America Media. Vivian was an international fellow of the United Nations and is a lifelong student and teacher with great respect for education. She has taught university-level Spanish, French, and yoga, and has mentored many new and aspiring journalists. Vivian speaks four languages, and is a graduate of the University of the Philippines.

JUDY ARTECHE-CARR

LEADING BY EXAMPLE

Pillar ✛ Bridge ✛ Warm

Judy Arteche-Carr is the CEO of Arteche Global Group, management consulting company specializing in strategy and global sourcing with a select clientele of international companies and higher education institutions. She has worked with management teams in transformation strategies; aligning information technology to business and risk and financial management in various institutions such as Salomon Brothers (Citigroup), JP Morgan (JPM Chase), EDS (HP) and Unisys. Prior to this, Judy worked at Children's Television Workshop (Sesame Street) as a Treasury Analyst, managing risk and the investment portfolio. Before she moved to New York, Judy started out in market research with Consumer Pulse then joined Minds Marketing, a female run advertising agency, as Head of Account Management. Currently, she gives back to the information technology business community by being an active Board member of the Society for Information Management. She has been an adjunct professor of Fordham University Business School. Judy has participated and spoken at conferences in the US, Europe and Asia. As President of the HIC Alumni International, she tirelessly helps raise funds for deserving students and women in need in Tacloban City, Philippines. She lives in New York and is married to Michael D. Carr.

AURORA ABELLA-AUSTRIACO

BEING A FILIPINA LITIGATOR IN A SEA OF DARK BLUE SUITS

Professional ✛ Result Driven ✛ Effective

Aurora Abella-Austriaco, Principal and Owner of Austriaco & Associates, focuses her practice on business and real estate litigation, mechanic's liens, defense of mortgage foreclosure, title insurance claims, and other special chancery remedy cases. She worked for Harold I. Levine and Attorney's Title Guaranty Fund (ATGF). Aurora graduated from De Paul University with a B.S. in Finance and a Juris Doctor (J.D.) degree, a professional degree earned by completing law school. Aurora served as the past President and first Asian President of the Chicago Bar Association, was elected as the first female and first Asian President of the Illinois Real Estate Lawyers' Association, and was a founding board member of the Filipino American Bar Association. She currently serves on the Board of Director for ATGF and is Chairman of the Board for a subsidiary of the ATG Legal Serve Corp. Aurora is currently serving her 11th term as Chair of the Cook County States Attorney Asian Advisory Council. She served 10 years as Commissioner for the Cook County Human Rights Commission, 8 years as Commissioner for the Park Ridge Planning and Zoning Commission, President of the Asian American Institute, board member of Hubbard Street Dance of Chicago, and Commissioner to the Illinois Courts Commission. Aurora received the Asian American Coalition of Chicago (2015) *"Ping Tom Memorial Award," Today's Chicago Woman* (2013), *"100 Women of Influence in Chicago,"* Philippine Chamber of Commerce *"Ten Most Outstanding Filipino American Businessmen," "Leading Lawyer"* in Real Estate Law (2011-2015), *"Top 100 Women Consumer Lawyers," "2011 Top 100 Under 50 Diverse Executive Leaders"* and *"Super Lawyer in Real Estate"* from 2012-2015. Aurora is fluent in Tagalog. She is married to Dr. Jerome Austriaco and they have two girls, Danielle and Isabelle.

ELIZABETH BAUTISTA
Synergistic Change

Driver of Change

Elizabeth Bautista is the Operations Technology Group Leader (OTG) at Lawrence Berkeley National Lab's National Energy Research Scientific Computing (NERSC) Center, the primary scientific computing facility for the Office of Science in the U.S. Department of Energy (DOE). Elizabeth manages a staff that ensures 24x7 management and operation of NERSC in order to ensure continuous resource availability to users. OTG's Operations Bridge is the central location for monitoring, problem reporting, triage and resolution, data collection, and emergency response for the high performance operations and data storage system. OTG also functions as the Network Operations Center (NOC) of the Energy Sciences Network (ESnet), a high-performance, unclassified wide area network that supports scientific research and collaborations globally. Elizabeth is active with the Lab's Computing Science Diversity and Outreach Programs that involves women and girls in Science, Technology, Engineering and Mathematics (STEM) activities. A former delegate for the Council of University of California Staff Assemblies, she champions issues of retention and diversity. Elizabeth manages the NERSC student internship program, creating a pipeline for workforce development and staff recruitment. She has a B.S. in Computer Information Systems and an M.B.A. in Technical Management from Golden Gate University. Elizabeth is a big Disney fan and her favorite character is Stitch, an alien originally associated with causing chaos and who is known for his mischief but also for his love of his adoptive family. She is also a fan of Hayao Miyazaki, a storyteller known for his strong female leaders.

THELMA B. BOAC

FROM MY TWO MOTHERS: A LEGACY BORNE

*Educator, Professional Coach/Mentor
Community Leader*

Thelma was born in the province of Bohol, Philippines. She came to America at the age of ten and lived with her adopted parents in Grover Beach, California. Her adopted father, a World War II veteran, was one of the original "manongs" who immigrated to America in the 1920s. Thelma's adopted mother, her own biological aunt, came to America as a young war widow. Both parents were active in community affairs. Thelma received her Bachelor's degree from San Francisco State University and attained a Master's degree in Educational Leadership at San Jose State University. Thelma retired after a 37 year-career in education. She continued her dedication to education at San Jose State University, and The National Hispanic University, where she supervised and trained graduate students entering the teaching profession. She currently coaches newly appointed principals and administrators for the Santa Clara County Office of Education. Thelma was re-elected to the San Jose Berryessa Union School District Board of Trustees for another term, thus continuing her commitment to youth and the community.

Thelma is a sought after educator and mentor and has been the recipient of many awards and has been recognized by many organizations for her dedication to community service.

GLORIA T. CAOILE

BEYOND OUR DREAMS

Trailblazer 🎗 *Advocate* 🎗 *Cancer survivor*

Gloria Caoile is a recognized civic leader, as co-founder of the Asian Pacific American Women Leadership Institute and the Asian Pacific American Labor Alliance. She has served on the boards of the Filipino American Civil Rights Advocates and the National Federation of Filipino-American Associations. She was appointed by President Clinton to the White House Advisory Commission of Asian Americans and Pacific Islanders to advise on how best to respond to their health needs. Philippine President Fidel Ramos presented Gloria with one of the Philippines' highest civic award in 1997. In 2001, Filipinas Magazine presented Gloria its Achievement Award for Community Service. She is the recipient of the 1999 "Filipina First" award by the Philippine American Foundation to honor Filipino-American women and their unique achievements. Gloria's experience includes more than 30 years of service with the American Federation of State, County and Municipal Employees (AFSCME), a 1.3 million-member union. At the time of her retirement, she was the assistant to the AFSCME President. Even after retirement, Gloria heads special assignment teams. She led a team to help 3,000 AFSCME survivors of hurricane Katrina. She managed the AFSCME September 11 Fallen Heroes Fund to assist members affected by that tragedy. Gloria encourages the immigrant community to vote, to volunteer in civic organizations, and to do their part in maintainin a healthy democracy in America. Civic involvement continues to be her lifelong passion and commitment. Gloria is married to Benjamin Caoile. They have a daughter and granddaughter

EVELYN DILSAVER

LEADERSHIP. POWER. INFLUENCE

Business Leader 🎗 *Award Winner* 🎗 *Philanthropist*

With a Certified Public Accountant background, Evelyn Dilsaver transitioned to general management as an executive in financial services moving from finance to sales, business development, product development to being president and CEO of a large investment management firm. Recently, Evelyn moved to her next great adventure of serving on corporate and non-profit boards. Her specialties are mergers and acquisitions integration work, product development, general management, non-profit, growing a business, financial controls. Evelyn currently serves on 6 corporate boards: Aeropostale (ARO), Tempur Sealy (TPX), Health Equity (HQY), Blue Shield of California, Protiviti (Advisory Board) Global Consulting and Internal Audit firm, and Bailard REIT- Private Real Estate Investment Trust. Evelyn also serves on 5 non-profit boards: The Commonwealth Club, Women Corporate Directors National Advisory Board, National Association of Corporate Directors (Nor-Cal Chapter), Blue Shield Foundation, and Cal State East Bay Foundation. Her awards include: Filipinas Magazine Corporate Award 2003, San Francisco Business Times "100 Most Influential Woman" awarded 2004-2009, San Francisco Business Times "Forever Influential Award" 2010, California Women's Leadership Alliance Award 2006, Legal Momentum's Women of Achievement 2007, California State University East Bay Alumnae of the year 2008, FWN100™ U.S. 2011, and San Francisco Business Times "Outstanding Director" 2014. She received an Honorary Doctorate of Humanity from California State East Bay in 2016.

Salve Vargas Edelman

To Dream the Impossible
Begin to Make it Possible

Performing Artist 🏃 Entrepreneur
Community Leader

Salve is the Founder and President of the Rising Asian Pacific Americans Coalition for Diversity (RAPACD); Executive Director of the RAPACD Cultural Center; Creator, Executive Producer, Director, Host of the Isla Vegas, the Ninth Island TV Show. Salve is Chapter President of the Las Vegas Twin Lakes Community Clinic; Founder and President, CEO, and Chairman of the Board of the Twin Lakes Community Clinic; and, the National President of the Filipino American Heritage and Arts Museum. Salve is a Topnotch Licensed Real Estate Professional in Nevada and was the Top Sales Agent for 2012 and 2014. Her community service awards include: One of 200 Distinguished Women in Nevada, RUMI 2016 Award as an Outstanding Business and Community Leader, FWN100™ Global 2015, Outstanding Community Partner by the Youth Advocacy Program, Filipino American Heritage and Arts Museum's Protector of Legacy Hall of Fame, and Jefferson Award for Excellence in Public Service in 2016. Salve has traveled to Asia and Europe as an International Performing Artist and sang in various languages since 1975. She was the Lead Singer of Roy Leano and His Orchestra in the Bay Area for over 16 years. Salve's philosophy in life is to share her God-given talents wholeheartedly and unconditionally and to live life to the fullest with love, passion, and purpose. Salve has lived in Las Vegas for over 20 years, with her husband, Paul and their dog, Angel!

Michelle Florendo

The Old Rules No Longer Apply

Passionate 🏃 Illuminating
Sage

Michelle Florendo is an engineer by trade, a Type-A management consultant, and a Fortune 500 brand marketer turned career coach. After a decade working alongside corporate professionals, she saw too many peers get stuck in soul-sucking jobs and golden handcuffs. As someone who understood the frustration of high-achieving professionals, Michelle decided to follow her heart and start her own career consulting firm, What If You Could. She is known for her analytical approach to career consulting - with a BS in Management Science and Engineering from Stanford University, and an MBA from UC Berkeley's Haas School of Business, Michelle uses analytical expertise, careful questioning, and personal experience to help her clients craft fulfilling careers. Over the years Michelle has led workshops both domestically and internationally, and has shown hundreds of driven professionals how to find jobs that satisfy them. In 2015, she was honored to serve on the inaugural coaching team for Seth Godin's altMBA, a five-week intensive workshop for change-makers around the world. She now maintains a portfolio of work that includes personalized 1:1 coaching, group programs, curriculum development, and speaking engagements.

JUANITA NIMFA Y. GAMEZ

FROM TRAVAILS TO SUCCESS:
CARING LEADERSHIP

Entrepreneur ✵ Philanthropist
Community Leader

Juanita Nimfa Y. Gamez is the President and CEO of Caring Hearts Foundation and Mission-Hope Developmental Services. Her family business and philanthropic efforts are focused on serving and advocating for the developmentally disabled community, as well as providing micro-finance and other forms of assistance to underprivileged families in the Philippines. She moved to the United States in 1995, where she went from being a housewife to a successful business owner in the health care services field. Ms. Gamez is motivated to provide employment to hundreds of people, especially Filipinos, to assist others on starting their own business, and to inspire single-mothers worldwide with her story. Her commitment to social impact and civic engagement has been recognized by a resolution of the California State Assembly, being honored and awarded by the Filipina Women's Network (FWN) as one of the 100 Most Influential Filipina in the US (2007) and in the World (2015). She was born and raised in Quezon City and attended the Philippine Science High School and the University of the Philippines. She is a mother to eight children.

EMMA MARCHA IMPERIAL

LEADING FOR SUSTAINABLE SOLAR POWERED
HOUSING COMMUNITY

Trailblazer ✵ Passionate

Inspiring

Emma Marcha Imperial is President and CEO of Imperial Homes Group of Companies, one of the Philippines largest developers of socialized and affordable housing with over 16,000 homes built since 1983. Her company was recently awarded the following: (1) Shortlisted in the Financial Times/ IFC Transformational Business Awards 2016 for Achievement in Low-Carbon Urban Transformation. (2) IFC- World Bank Excellence in Design for Greater Efficiencies (EDGE) Certificate for Green Building. (3) Poster Child of IFC-World Bank for its residential case study, the development of the nation's first affordable housing fitted with solar panels, with water-conserving toilets, and energy reducing construction materials. 4) Social Enterprise grantee of Netsuite.Org, who is committed to supporting capacity building efforts for non-profits and social enterprises around the world. She is also a Go Negosyo Awardee for Woman Entrepreneur in 2015 and awarded as one of the 100 Most Influential Filipina in 2015 by Filipina Women Network. Ms. Imperial has a BS Economics from the University of the Philippines and is an Alumna of Harvard Business School's Owner Management Program. She ranked 3rd in the Philippine Broker Board Examination, in 2000. She was also the Corporate Broker Officer of the Financial American Exchange in California, from 1982-1995.

TRISH QUEMA LA CHICA

SURVIVING SAN FRANCISCO:
HOW I LANDED MY DREAM JOB AT 28

Go-getter. 🦎 *Curious*
Peripatetic

Trish is the Policy and Advocacy Director at the Hawai'i Public Health Institute, where she works with the state government and community advocates to enact legislation to promote healthy eating and active living, promote smoke-free policies, and discourage the use of tobacco products and electronic smoking devices. Her career has included previous roles with the Office of the Governor in Hawai'i, the Asian and Pacific Islander American Health Forum, the United Nations Development Programme, and ABS-CBN, the Philippines' largest television network. Trish is passionate about creating meaningful partnerships and collaborating across sectors to achieve healthier communities. She earned her Masters in Public Administration from the University of San Francisco and her B.A. from the Ateneo de Manila University. Trish is interested in using data and storytelling for social change and is currently pursuing her certification in Healthcare Analytics from the University of California, Davis. She lives in Hawai'i with her husband, Cricket, and their dog, Lucy. She spends most of her free time reading on the beach, taking scenic hikes, and baking cookies. They are expecting their first child in October 2016. You can follow Trish on Twitter and Instagram: @trishquema and #lachicalife.

JANICE LAO-NOCHE

DISRUPTING STEREOTYPES: BEING YOU

Mother 🦎 *Scientist*
Servant-Leader

With more than a decade experience on sustainability; environmental, and social development issues, Janice leads the sustainability team at a world-class railway and property company based in Asia with interests in Hong Kong, China, Australia, London, and Sweden. Previously, she worked on sustainability issues for the Swire Group a 400-strong multinational conglomerate and Cathay Pacific Airways, a 5-star international airline. Under her leadership, both companies received international recognitions for their sustainability practices. She is a recipient of several international sustainability awards for her leadership in this area and has been one of the youngest recipients. Prior to her corporate work, she worked at international environmental think tanks and consulting firms. She has worked across the Asia Pacific region; Europe, the Americas, Africa, and the Middle East. She graduated from the Ateneo de Manila University, Environmental Science (ES) program and was the first ES student to graduate with honours. She is the first Filipino to graduate from the University of Oxford, Environmental Change Institute where she was the recipient of the prestigious Shell Chevening-British Foreign and Commonwealth Scholarship. She is a board member of the Renew Foundation that actively supports issues such as anti-sex trafficking in the Philippines and the Green Tray Project with its focus on environmental education in Hong Kong. She is also a mother of two young children. Janice likes to call herself a "storytelling scientist" who enjoys communicating complex science matters to a broader audience.

ARLENE MARIE "BAMBI" A. LORICA, M.D.

LEADING FROM BEHIND:
SHE-PHERDING AND ENERGY MEDICINE

Creative 🐾 Courageous
Compassionate

Arlene Marie "Bambi" A. Lorica, MD is an environmentalist, holistic pediatrician, community advocate, and lyric soprano. Sub-specializing in energy medicine, she is currently doing a fellowship in Regenerative Medicine. She is a member of the American Academy of Anti-Aging Medicine, Institute of Functional Medicine, and the International Society for the Study of Subtle Energies and Energy Medicine. She co-produced the critically and internationally acclaimed film "Busong" that was chosen for presentation by more than 35 Film Festivals, and won awards in Asia, Europe and North America, including the most prestigious award given by National Geographic for indigenous films. She is recognized for medical diplomacy, and is an active advocate both in the US and in the Philippines for numerous causes and supports humanitarian and artistic endeavors. A mother of four, her passion includes singing, ballroom dancing, gourmet cooking, and painting. Her other interests include organic farming, sustainability, and renewable energy development. A board member of FWN since 2007, she is committed to improving the Filipina image globally and helping end domestic violence everywhere.

VINA LUSTADO

DREAM BIG; LIVE TINY

Determined 🐾 Passionate
Collaborative

Vina Lustado is the founder of Sol Haus Design, a boutique design firm that specializes in sustainable building. After receiving a professional degree in architecture and more than twenty years on the high-end corporate path, Vina decided to focus her career on smaller-scale projects that could make a positive difference. Staying true to her values, Vina has completed the design and construction of her off-the-grid tiny house. Equipped with simple luxuries, Vina has manifested her dream home in 140 square feet. It reflects her philosophy about simplicity, sustainability, and living within her means. Since its completion, Lustado's tiny house has inspired others all over the world to live tiny while minimizing their impact on the earth. Her house has been featured in countless online media articles, television shows and architectural book publications. Vina Lustado lives in her tiny house in Ojai, California. She is married and finds balance and joy living on the same property with her husband in two separate tiny cabins. In her free time, Lustado enjoys being out in nature climbing, camping, or practicing yoga.

Francine Maigue

Becoming A Global Pinay Powerhouse

Global 🦎 Pinay 🦎 Power

Francine Maigue graduated with her Master's degree from Harvard University, where she received the prestigious Harvard Commencement Speaker Prize, hosted the Philippine Presidential Debate at the Harvard Law School, served as Diversity Ambassador for Women Entrepreneurs for the Harvard's Business Society, and founded the Women's Empowerment Convention and Network (WECAN). Francine graduated with her B.A. from UCLA, where she was a leader and member of eight honor societies, Commencement Speaker, Homecoming Queen: and honored with the Distinguished Bruin, Outstanding Senior, Chancellor's Service, Woman for Change, and Young Humanitarian Awards. Francine was crowned Miss Philippines of San Diego 1999 and, in 2012, was selected by His Excellency Ambassador Cuisia as an inaugural delegate to the Filipino American Young Leaders Program and honored with the Filipino American History Achievement Award in the areas of Humanitarianism, Arts, and Community Service. Francine received the 2015 BAYANI Award and was named "One of the 100 Most Influential Filipina Women in the World" and the "Global Face of Pinay Power." Francine is the District Director for California State Assemblywoman Lorena Gonzalez, International Friendship Commissioner for the City of Chula Vista, President and CEO of the Filipino-American Chamber of Commerce, and writes The Filipino Press's popular column "Francine & Friends."

Ma. Alcestis "Thetis" Abrera Mangahas

A World Citizen

Global 🦎 Development 🦎 Expert

Ma. Alcestis (Thetis) Abrera Mangahas is a senior labor expert, with over forty years of professional experience in international technical cooperation concerning labor migration, forced labor and human trafficking, child labor, and workers in informal and precarious employment including domestic workers. A magna cum laude under-graduate from the University of the Philippines School of Economics, Thetis completed her graduate degree (1978) from the London School of Economics and Political Science. She rose through the ranks of the Overseas Employment Development Board and its successor organization, the Philippine Overseas Employment Administration. She is credited with the design and development of important initiatives for the protection of migrant workers. After she moved from a Philippines national government career to international development work with the UN's International Labour Organization (ILO), Thetis oversaw multi-country programs on child labor, labor migration, and human trafficking. Towards the end of her international development work, Thetis was appointed Deputy Regional Director for Policy and Programmes of the ILO's Regional Office for Asia and the Pacific. After retiring from the ILO in 2015, she was given active Fellow status with the Social Weather Stations, the Philippines' primary survey research institute on quality of life, public opinion, and governance. Thetis' current research interests center on the impact of overseas (foreign) employment on the well-being of migrant family households in the Philippines. She is married to Mahar Mangahas, and mother of four children; Kelley, Fabian, Mahar and Angelica.

ELENA MANGAHAS

ELENA MANGAHAS AND DAUGHTERS

Youth ❧ Community ❧ Empowerment

Elena and her husband Fred have two grown daughters, the oldest a Professor in Math in upstate New York and the youngest an English and Literature high school teacher in Stockton. Fred is retired from the State of California. Elena has been a 28-year civil servant in workforce development. She is currently a Division Manager at San Joaquin County Employment and Economic Development Department and oversees an annual $3 million budget for youth jobs programs in the county. She supervises a staff level that ranges from 12-40 on a year-round basis with temporary staff for the summer programs. Elena's workforce development includes farmworkers' transition program, refugee entry level jobs program, welfare-to-work-program, non-traditional career pathways for women, and youth community leadership and empowerment. She calls the youth programs as her own thousand-points of light. As a community leader Elena has represented both marginalized communities of color and communities that have not been historically disadvantaged. She has advocated for greater attention to the Filipino community for their tremendous contributions to Stockton, CA, beginning in the 1920's. Elena has been with the Filipina Women's Network since 2004 with an active role in its anti-violence against women and girls' campaigns. She was instrumental in the productions of The Vagina Monologues and PINAY POWER Futures Search that led to the publication of the leadership books DISRUPT I. Elena holds an AB in Journalism and Communication from the University of the Philippines

MARILY MONDEJAR

OWNING YOUR INFLUENTIAL POWER AS A LEADER

Fearless Leader ❧ Grassroots Organizer
❧ Community Advocate

Marily Mondejar, the Founder and CEO of the Filipina Women's Network (FWN), has dedicated the last decade transforming how global Filipina women view themselves and how others view them. The transformed image is of women exerting influence. Her initiatives to bring about this transformation have included producing more positive search results on the Internet for the term "Filipina," embracing Ensler's "The Vagina Monologues" and the campaign to end domestic violence and human trafficking, and facilitating the creation of a pipeline of Filipina leaders with the skills to compete at all levels in all economic sectors. As the sixth of 13 children, Marily learned early how to get her voice heard in her family and carried this skill into her career in roles such as a senior business leader, board member for organizations working on the Status of Women, and former Commissioner on the San Francisco Redistricting Task Force. Marily also draws from her experience as a survivor of an abusive relationship, a single mother, and a U.S. immigrant who started her professional life from scratch to a successful organizational consultant in mergers and acquisitions, corporate image, preparation of witnesses for court appearances and depositions, implementation of culture due diligence, as well as promoting networks for advancing the status of Filipina women globally. Her impact can be measured by the countless number of women she has brought along with her to positions of leadership. San Francisco Mayor Ed Lee appointed Marily as Commissioner of the Office for Community Investment and Infrastructure which is responsible for $20 billion in assets used to create jobs, affordable housing, commercial space, and parks and open space areas.

MARIE CLAIRE LIM MOORE

POSITIVELY FILIPINA

Banker ❧ Author ❧ Speaker

Marie Claire Lim Moore is currently the Development Director at The Women's Foundation in Hong Kong, a leading non-profit organization dedicated to improving the lives of women and girls. Claire has over 15 years of international business experience managing global consumer banking and payment products across the US, Asia, Latin America, and Europe. Most recently, Claire was Asia Pacific Regional Director at Citi where she was responsible for the retail bank's global services across 12 countries. She started her career at American Express in New York City where she managed strategic relationships with the company's largest travel partners. She joined Citi in 2001 to grow the Citi Cards American Airlines portfolio and lead the shift from traditional to digital marketing. In 2005 she was selected for the Global Consumer Management Associate program and since then she has held various senior level positions throughout the Global Retail Bank. Claire is also the author of Amazon.com best sellers *Don't Forget the Soap (And Other Reminders from My Fabulous Filipina Mother)* and *Don't Forget the Parsley (And More from My Positively Filipino Family)*. She is passionate about promoting career-family balance and uses her talks as well as her writing to promote this balance. She is regularly ranked among the top female leaders and her experiences have been documented by *CNN*, *The New York Times*, *USA Today*, *Smart Parenting*, and *People Asia*. In 2014, she received the FWN100™ Global 2014. Claire received a BA from Yale University and an Executive MBA from Fordham University. She currently lives in Hong Kong with her husband and their three children.

ROCIO NUYDA

ROCIO, A MORNING DEW

Perfectionist ❧ Artistic ❧ Compassionate

Rocio Nuyda is a retired Management Executive (Executive Vice President) in credit card processing, having worked for the largest processor in the U.S. In her retirement, she owns and runs an event planning business. She is a staunch advocate for women's rights. She keeps busy with social, political, and civic services in the U.S. and the Philippines. She promotes Filipino arts and culture as Chairman of FilAm Arts (2014-2015); and concurrently is a member of the Board of Directors of the Filipino American Symphony Orchestra (FASO), the only symphony orchestra of its kind and ethnicity in the nation. She is a member of the US Pinoys for Good Governance, ASEAN Women Circle of Los Angeles, Consultant to Feed2Succeed, Team Leader of Filipino Americans for Hillary Clinton-Asian American and Pacific Islander, and member of the Filipina Women's Network. She was an Outstanding Alumna of St. Agnes' Academy, Legazpi City 2012, a Benedictine school of St. Scholastica's College, Manila. Rocio graduated from the Philippine Women's University with a Bachelor degree in Liberal Arts, major in Communication Arts. She is a mother of five children; Hermel (Assistant Chairman, College of Nursing, Los Angeles Valley College), Robert Jr. (Purchasing Director, Toshiba), Carlyn Calloway (owner, fashion designer Thumbelina Atelier), and Clinton (Executive Chef, Roy Yamaguchi Chain of Restaurants). She is grandmother of seven grandchildren.

JOHANNA MELISSA DISINI ORQUIZA

THE BIG BANG

*Thoughtfully silly ✺ Full of dreams
Hardworking*

Melissa has worked in film music for the last 17 years. She has worked on *Moana, Frozen: Live at the Hyperion, Suicide Squad, McFarland, USA, Minions, Jurassic World, Inside Out, Straight Out of Compton,* and *Batman versus Superman.* Her past credits include the *Pirates of the Caribbean* franchise, *Transformers: Age of Extinction,* the *Dark Knight Rises, Up* and others. Melissa works for Booker White, head of Music Preparation at Disney, whose credits list over 300 movies. Melissa is comfortable with classical music, hip hop, and pop. Melissa started playing piano at age three and composed her first piece at age six. She was awarded a Deans Scholarship to the University of Southern California and studied Music Composition with an emphasis in Film Scoring. She was awarded the Elaine Krown Klein Scholarship and earned a Masters in Arts in Music Composition from UCLA. She is working on symphonic transcriptions of native Filipino music for orchestra in the hopes that when symphonies program "Asian" or "Spanish" music, the Philippines will be included. Melissa firmly believes that music and mathematics are key components to the future. Music provides an emotional outlet, discipline, and the power of self-worth; all building blocks for the components to understanding science and math, and both music and mathematics are vital for our youth's future.

GIZELLE COVARRUBIAS ROBINSON

ROOTS AND WINGS

*Passionate ✺ Determined
Loyal*

Gizelle is an award-winning transformative information technology leader with broad based global experience across multiple industries and over 31 years of experience in this field. A strategic, visionary, driven, results oriented leader with a consistent record of successfully leading multiple initiatives across various platforms and several enterprises at Charles Schwab & Co. Gizelle delivers solutions and innovative services that enable firms and the business to improve their clients ability to achieve their financial goals. She implements process improvements and creates a culture of efficiency. She is recognized for her motivational leadership style. Gizelle is a strong advocate for women and believes the best way to achieve gender partnership is to generate sustained awareness early and often. She majored in Industrial Management Engineering and minored in Chemical Engineering. She was recently named as one of the 10, 2013 Professional Business Women of California Industry Leader Awardees.

She currently serves as Board of Director at Large and Treasurer for Professional Business Women in California. She is a member of the Executive Committee, Programming Committee and the Audit Committee. She focuses on current and anticipated issues and challenges facing women of all ages in professional settings.

Josephine Romero
15 to 51
Intuitive ❧ Depth ❧ Fun

Josephine Romero is a strategist who likes to develop business ideas. With over 20 years of experience in private, corporate, diplomatic, and public sectors, she has shown professionalism, creativity, and entrepreneurship. She is CEO of a fintech start-up in the Philippines. She was the Senior Managing Director of the biggest Filipino American information technology outsourcing company in the U.S. As Commercial Counselor of the Philippine Embassy in Brasilia, she setup the first Philippine commercial office in Sao Paulo. She initiated discussions for Brazilian and Filipino food companies to trade goods and facilitated the expansion of the biggest South American foreign direct investment to the Philippines. Her other overseas posts include Silicon Valley, New York, and Washington, DC where she encouraged public-private cooperation through the Philippine Business Process Outsourcing Council, the Global Sourcing Council, the World BPO Forum, the Silicon Valley Science and Technology Advisory Council, and the 100 Most Influential Filipinas Project of FWN. She initiated the first government-hosted Filipino Business Plan Pitch Competition at the 2010 e-Services Philippines Conference, which spurred the entry of Silicon Valley and Asian venture capitalists and the establishment of Philippine angels and venture capital funds in support of startups and technopreneurs in the Philippines. She obtained her Economics degree from the University of the Philippines in 1991 and attended the Regis Executive MBA program at the Ateneo de Manila University in 2000. She completed the Leadership California's California Issues and Trends Program in 2010 and the Society for Information Management Regional Leadership Forum US Northwest Program in 2011. Josephine is an avid tourist destination reviewer, consistently rated in the top 3% of Trip Advisor contributors from the Philippines.

Mutya San Agustin, M.D. FAAP
Revolutionizing the Health Care Delivery System
Leader ❧ Innovator ❧ Visionary

Mutya San Agustin, MD FAAP is a Retired Professor, Pediatrics, Clinical Epidemiology, Social Medicine, Albert Einstein College of Medicine, Bronx, NY and Founding President, Philippine Ambulatory Pediatric Association, Inc. Recognized internationally, she was key to the integration of medical education and training of physicians in the primary health care delivery system in the U.S.. She established the Departments of Ambulatory Medicine, North Central Bronx Hospital and Primary Care Medicine at Montefiore Medical Center, University Hospital of Albert Einstein College of Medicine. She established the Primary Care Residency Program in Pediatrics and Internal Medicine at Montefiore Medical Center and North Central Bronx Hospital. She helped establish the International Pediatric Fellowship Program at Albert Einstein College of Medicine. As founding president of the Philippine Ambulatory Pediatric Association, Inc. she continues to provide guidance in programs focused on advocacy and coalition building. Dr. San Agustin received the following awards: Outstanding Alumnus for Medical Education, UPMASA; Bela Schick Award, Albert Einstein College of Medicine; Maternal and Child Health Services Award, Department of Health, Education and Welfare, Washington DC; Altran Foundation Scholarship Award, Albert Einstein College of Medicine; Community Leadership Award, Bronx Community Health Network, Inc.; and, Centennial Award as "Builder in Medicine," UP College of Medicine. Mutya's four children are all in the arts: Emmanuel, Ariel, Angela, and Joanna.

MARIA SANTOS-GREAVES

*LEARNING MANAGEMENT
FROM THE MOST UNLIKELY*

*Entrepreneur ❧ Leader
Motivator*

Maria Santos-Greaves decided to start her own hearing clinic in Canada, in order to provide compassionate and quality care to those needing to hear better. A major motivation: she had become hearing-impaired due to a side-effect of a medication. With a strong determination to succeed, Maria Santos-Greaves built and nurtured Surrey Hearing Care Inc. Because of her efforts, many people of various age and ethnic groups can now hear better in Greater Vancouver. Through the years, Maria has used the company mobile hearing van to provide free hearing tests to the members of the public who need these services. Maria is active with the Canadian Medical Mission Society and contributes her time, expertise, and resources in helping those with no access to health care in the Philippines. For her tireless efforts to help and give back to the community, she was voted across Canada as one of the Top 25 Immigrants in 2015.

"I grew up a Filipina in the Philippines. My heart and soul will never forget my roots, my beloved home country that molded me to become the woman I am today; an entrepreneur in my adopted and appreciated new homeland of Canada."

BENEL SE-LIBAN, CPA

A LIFE THAT MATTERS

*Spiritual ❧ Selfless
Leader*

Benel Se-Liban, CPA, is the first Filipina partner of Vasquez and Company, one of California's most venerable accounting firms. She is the non-profit Practice Leader of the firm and oversees all aspects of assurance, accounting, and consulting services to nonprofit clients. Her area of expertise includes all aspects of financial and compliance audits. She has extensive experience in nonprofit community healthcare organization, financial audit and compliance, corporate best practices, and governance. Benel is the Founding President of the International Society of Filipinos in Finance and Accounting (ISFFA). She is also the Audit Committee Chair/ Board of Directors, St. John's Well Child and Family Center; Finance Committee Chair/Board of Directors of Life Steps Foundation, Kalayaan of Southern California; and Board of Directors and Member, Profitable Solutions Editorial Board. In 2011, Benel was honored as one of the 100 Most Influential Filipina in the U.S. by the Filipina Women's Network (FWN). Benel was also the 2011 Awardee, Centennial Award for Outstanding Agnesians, St. Agnes' Academy Alumni Association; and 2012 Nominee, Los Angeles Business Journal's Women Making a Difference Award. Benel holds a Bachelor of Science degree in Accountancy from De La Salle University.

JOSEFINA "CHEF JESSIE" SINCIOCO

SAYING "YES" TO GOD'S WILL

Innovative ❧*Culinarian*
Foodie

Josefina "Chef Jessie" Sincioco, started her career in the kitchen when she won the grand prize in the baking category of the Great Maya Cookfest in 1983. Chef Jessie is known for her innovative and sumptuous culinary masterpieces served in her upscale fine dining restaurants: Chef Jessie Rockwell Club, Top Of The Citi By Chef Jessie, and 100 Revolving Restaurant. Chef Jessie has been promoting Philippine cuisine by doing Filipino food promotions and judging culinary competitions here and abroad. She co-authored a book entitled Kulinarya, a Guidebook to Philippine Cuisine, with five other top chefs of our country. Chef Jessie earned the title "PAPAL CHEF" when she was appointed to prepare the food of the Holy Father during his entire Philippine visit in January 2015. Chef Jessie was one of the eight BRAVO Empowered Women awardees given by Zonta Club and Security Bank in 2015 and one of the five Club Bulakeño's *Huwarang Anak ng Bulakan* 2015 awardees. Chef Jessie won L' Assite D' Or for the Best in Market Basket Chefs on Parade (1986), Gold with Distinction on Cold Desserts Display Chefs on Parade (1987), L' Assite D' Or for the Best in Market Basket Chefs on Parade (1992), and 2nd Place, Silver Medalist, Member of the 5-Man National Team, Salon Culinaire in Singapore (1992).

DOLLY PANGAN SPECHT

SERVANT LEADERSHIP

Funny ❧*Dynamic*
Confident

Dolly Pangan Specht is one feisty lady who lives her life by laughter. She likes to say she was born with a decent pedigree and a love of history. She proudly owns up to being among the great-granddaughters of Epifanio delos Santos, the Philippine national hero whose name was made more famous by the 1986 EDSA People Power Revolution. Her more pop-culture association is that of being the youngest sister of the Philippine beloved comedian, now deceased, Chiquito. An Assumption girl at heart, this convent-bred woman once desired to be a nun, but was advised by her Mother Superior that there are other ways that she could serve the Lord. And so with that option gone, Dolly did manage to find ways and means to serve in her everyday life, ranging from being a professional to a servant-leadership life as a volunteer. She is the owner of a homebased business Perfect Plus Professional Support, Dolly simply serves.

LUCILLE LOZADA TENAZAS

GRAPHIC DESIGNER

The Designer as Cultural Nomad

Lucille Tenazas is the founder and principal of Tenazas Design, a communication graphics and design firm with projects in the cultural, educational, and non-profit sector. She was awarded the National Design Award in Communication Design by the Smithsonian Cooper-Hewitt National Design Museum in 2002 and is considered one of America's leading design innovators. Active in the AIGA, the professional association for design, she served as the national organization's President from 1996 to 1998. Additionally, Lucille is a design educator and is the Henry Wolf Professor of Communication Design at Parsons School of Design in New York where she is the Associate Dean in the School of Art, Media and Technology (AMT). She was the Founding Chair of the MFA Design Program at California College of the Arts (CCA) in San Francisco with an emphasis on form-giving, teaching, and leadership. She is working on an autobiographically-inflected publication of her design work that spans 30 years.
Contact: lucille@tenazasdesign.com

MYRNA TANG YAO

LEADING ONE TO MANY

Visionary ✗ Strategist ✗ Action Oriented

Myrna Tang Yao is a highly successful and multi-awarded woman in the Philippine business. She is President and CEO of Richwell Trading Corporation and Richprime Global Inc., an exclusive distributor and Licensing Agent of Mattel toys and other leading brands of toys, shoes, and baby products. A staunch advocate of women's economic empowerment, Myrna is the founding Chairperson of the Philippine Federation of Local Councils of Women, founding President of the Filipino-Chinese Federation of Business and Professional Women of the Philippines, and Chair Emeritus of Pearl S. Buck Foundation Philippines. She has held leadership positions in the ASEAN Confederation of Women's Organizations, the International Alliance of Women, the Philippine Movement for Good Governance, and Women for Women Foundation. In 2004, she was appointed by President Gloria Macapagal Arroyo as Chairperson of the National Commission on the Role of a Filipino Women now called the Philippine Commission on Women to promote women's rights and women's economic empowerment. During Myrna's term as Chairperson, the Magna Carta Law for Women and the National Action Plan on Women's Peace and Security were signed. During this time, Myrna designed and then led the implementation of the Great Women Project. Her numerous local and international awards include the 2013 International Women Entrepreneurial Challenge Awards held in Lima, Peru; Global Summit of Women's International Entrepreneur Award, and Gold Prize Award for Women's World Excellence Award in Beijing. She received the Presidential Merit Award from President Gloria Macapagal Arroyo for her success in the field of entrepreneurship at the local and international level.

Significant
FWN MOMENTS
2014-2016

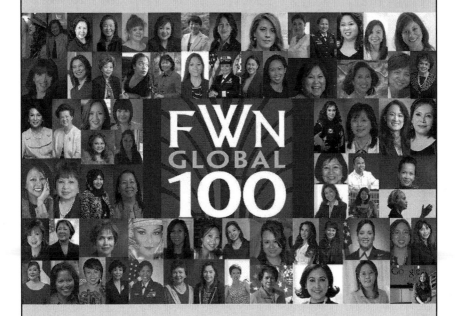

11th Filipina Leadership Global Summit 2014
in Manila at the Makati Shangri-La

Photo Collage: Global FWN100, 2013

464

Cris Comerford Cooking Demo at Black Sheep Restaurant during the Filipina Summit 2014

(L to R: Adam Reed Collick, Gloria T. Caoile, Cris Comerford)

Cris Comerford Cooking Demo at Black Sheep Restaurant during the Filipina Summit 2014

(L to R:: Adam Reed Collick, Gloria T. Caoile, Cris Comerford, Ruth Selby)

FWN2.0 LEGACY

MOTHERS

&

29–31 OCT 2015

FILIPINA LEADERSHIP GLOBAL SUMMIT

SAN FRANCISCO

DAUGHTERS

NEXT GENERATION LEADERS

12th Filipina Leadership Global Summit 2015
in San Francisco
at the Marines Memorial Club

Global FWN100™ 2015 Awardees in San Francisco

468

Global Pinay Power Search at the Filipina Summit 2015

(L to R: Myrna Yao, Sonia Delen, Belle Zatlin, Judge Lorna G. Schofield, Tess Martillano-Manjares, Pet Hartman, guest, Helen Marte, Delle Sering, Susan Afan, Agnes Bailen, Elena Mangahas. Front row, Gloria T. Caoile, Kristie Gan)

Global Pinay Power Search at the Filipina Summit 2015

(L to R: Thelma Boac, Edcelyn Pujol, Teddy DeRivera (Wells Fargo), Sonia Delen, Marily Mondejar, Amar Bornkamp, Susie Quesada, Gloria T. Caoile, Elena Mangahas, Raissa Alvero, Juslyn Mamalo)

470

13th Filipina Leadership Global Summit 2016 in Cebu

DISRUPT 2.0 book cover and book launch flyer
(University of Cebu and Asian Institute of Management 2016)

DISRUPTing Hollywood chaired by Rocio Nuyda (2nd from left)

DISRUPTing Hollywood Hosts Edwin and Lani Raquel with
Marily Mondejar at their Mary Pickford Estate

474

DISRUPTing Japan chaired by Lita Watanabe

DISRUPTing Manila 1 (*L to R: Marilmy Mondejar, Gloria Caoile, Delle Sering, Sonia Delen, Ruth Asmundson, Delia Rodriguez-Amaya, Lenore RS Lim*)

476

DISRUPTing Manila 2 (L to R: Maria Beebe, Maya Escudero, Lenore RS Lim, Mely Nicolas, Cris Comerford, Loida Nicolas Lewis, Carmen David-Padilla)

DISRUPTing Manila 3 *(L to R: Cris Comerford, Marife Zamora, Susie Quesada, Patty Paez)*

DISRUPTing Portland chaired by Maria Beebe

DISRUPTing Portland livestreaming
Marily Mondejar and Maria Beebe

DISRUPTing San Francisco Panel
(L to R: Theresa Noriega-Lum, Sonia Delen, Susie Quesada,
Gizelle Covarrubias Robinson)

DISRUPTing San Francisco
hosted by
Charles Schwab

DISRUPTing Singapore chaired by Astrid Tuminez

DISRUPTing Washington DC
June 26, 2015
A Historic Day

DISRUPTing Washington DC chaired by Nini Alvero (L to R: Edcelyn Pujol, Hank Hendrickson of US-Philippines Society, Nini Alvero, Marilu Mondejar, Susie Quesada, Maria Beebe, Shirley Ragutindin, Cris Connerford, Patrick Chuasoto of the Philippine Embassy, Bambi Lorica)

FWN Magazine
2014:
Maria Beebe on the cover

FWN Magazine
2015:
Shirley Raguindin
on the cover

FWN V-Day San Francisco 2016 – FWN's 11th year raising awareness to stop violence against women

FWN V-Day San Francisco 2016 Cast and Crew

V-Diaries 2016 Cover Fiona Ma
Chair of the California Board of Equalization

Global Pinay Power Launch with FWN Board

(L to R: Maria Beebe, Marily Mondejar, Amar Bornkamp, Susie Quesada, Francine Maigue, Jessica Caloza)

Face of Global Pinay Power:
Francine Maigue

Face of Global Pinay Power: Francine Maigue in Rosie the Riveter pose

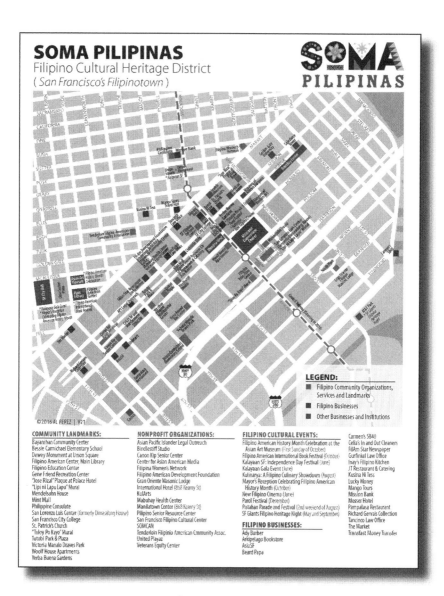

Soma Pilipinas "Filipino Town"
in San Francisco

DISRUPTing Washington DC at the White House

*(L to R, back row: Shirley Raguindin, Susie Quesada, Nini Alvero;
L to R, front row: Maria Beebe, Edcelyn Pujol,
Marily Mondejar, Bambi Lorica)*

The FWN Board was at the White House
lit up in rainbow colors in commemoration
of the Supreme Court's ruling to legalize
same-sex marriage on Friday, June 26.
The court ruled that states
cannot ban same-sex marriage,
handing gay rights advocates
their biggest victory.

Women's History Month San Francisco 2016 Speaker Panel
(L to R: Marily Mondejar, Trina Villanueva, Vivian Araullo, April Veneracion Ang, Myrna de Vera, Denise Miles, Dory Cantinong, Tiffany Bohee, Cecile Ascalon.)

Women's History Month 2016:
Denise Miles
Senior Vice President, Wells Fargo
and
Genevieve Jopanda
Chief of Staff,
Chairwoman Fiona Ma,
California Board of Equalization

Raissa Alvero
Awesome FWN Fellow 2015-2016

Franklin M. Ricarte
FWN's Forever Tech Guru

[Photo credit: Gani Ricarte Photography]

Filipina Women's Network
Board of Directors

About the Filipina Women Leadership Book Series

The Filipina Women Leadership Book Series project aims to fill the gap in the leadership literature that highlights the unique qualities of Filipina women whose culture, values, and faith make them effective leaders and managers. The leadership book series chronicles Filipina women's leadership skill sets, capabilities and expertise and how we contribute as active participants in the global workplace. The DISRUPT leadership series is a key component of our game plan to elevate the presence and participation of Filipina women in the public and private sectors.

DISRUPT Book Orders:

Cebu Launch: August 22, 2016 at
University of Cebu

Manila Launch: August 26, 2016 at
Asian Institute of Management

Book orders: http://ffwn.org/event-2289844

- 1.415.935.4396
- www.filipinaleadership.org
- filipina@ffwn.org

Cover Design by **Lucille Tenazas, Tenazas Design/NY**